DEATH
BENEFIT

DEATH
BENEFIT

▼

A LAWYER UNCOVERS A
TWENTY-YEAR PATTERN OF
SEDUCTION, ARSON, AND MURDER

▲

DAVID HEILBRONER

HARMONY BOOKS

NEW YORK

Published by Harmony Books, a division of Crown Publishers, Inc.,
201 East 50th Street, New York, New York 10022.
Member of the Crown Publishing Group.

Random House, Inc. New York, Toronto, London, Sydney, Auckland.

HARMONY and colophon are trademarks of Crown Publishers, Inc.

Manufactured in the United States of America

Library of Congress Cataloging-in-Publication Data

Heilbroner, David.
Death benefit : a lawyer uncovers a twenty-year pattern of
seduction, arson, and murder / David Heilbroner
—1st ed.
1. McGinnis, Virginia. 2. Criminals—United States—Biography.
3. Murderers—United States—Biography. 4. Women murderers—United
States—Biography. 5. Serial murders—United States—Case studies.
6. Insurance crimes—United States—Case studies. I. Title.
HV6248.M4653H45   1993
364.1'523'0973—dc20   92-28728
CIP

ISBN 0-517-58284-8

10 9 8 7 6 5 4 3 2

To Deana, Cynthia, Bud, and Dick

CONTENTS

▼

PREFACE AND ACKNOWLEDGMENTS

▼

The research for this book took me to a box seat at the Kentucky Derby, a down-and-out trailer home in upstate New York, and the cornfields of Normal, Illinois. At other times, I found myself on a witness stand in San Diego—the object of a defense subpoena directed at my interview notes—or driving into the Pennsylvania countryside. Everywhere I went, I was greeted by a cooperative, willing spirit, without which *Death Benefit* never could have been completed.

Throughout the text, I have tried to present the truth as best I could ascertain it. I attended all the legal proceedings, and later conformed quotations to the official transcript. (The one exception being my own court appearance, which I deleted as being simply a distraction.) With few exceptions, I personally interviewed the individuals quoted, often over a period of days or even weeks. Certain scenes from the remote past are the result of composite interviews, but otherwise I have related the story just as I found it. A handful of names of people and locations have been changed where privacy might be violated.

I owe special thanks to Sergeant R. D. Jones of the Jefferson County Police Department, Detective Jack Haeussinger of the San Diego Police Department, Deputy District Attorney Luis Aragon and Investigator Scott Lawrence of the San Diego District Attorney's Office, Ken Goodnight, Dr. Emanuel Tanay, Spike Lampros, Butch Rearden, and Bobbie Jo Roberts. I thank Rick Rosenberg, Tim Knowlton, and Irene Skolnick for bringing this story to my attention. Above all, I owe a debt of gratitude to Steven and Wynn Keeney and their children Christian, Mark, and Kelly. Steven Keeney, in particular, provided indefatigable support, reams of background information, and an incisive editorial eye. And although Mr. Keeney read this work in manuscript form and offered many valuable suggestions, he bravely resisted commenting on the portrayal of his own character.

Lastly, I wish to thank my two editors. Peter Guzzardi at Harmony Books lived up to the glowing reputation that preceded him. My wife, Kate Davis, filled her customary role of unofficial, and indispensable, editor in chief.

▼

PART ONE

A
ROUTINE
DEATH

CHAPTER 1

SEAL BEACH

▼

APRIL 2, 1987

The dawn is still a good hour away. Deana, B.J., and Virginia leave Chula Vista, a quiet, dusty suburb of San Diego, and head north. Virginia sits in the passenger seat of their Ford LTD. Her husband, B.J., drives. Deana lounges in the back, pressing her wide-eyed face against the window.

After passing Los Angeles, with its snarl of traffic, they veer off the freeway onto Highway 1, the coastal route. Virginia reminds Deana they're taking Highway 1 for her sake. The route adds at least two hours to the drive from San Diego to Monterey—five hundred miles in all—but it is the only way she will get to see the ocean and the famous Big Sur cliffs.

"Look, Deana, dear, I bought a camera just for the trip," Virginia says, her thin lips forming a smile in her large, motherly face.

Deana leans across the seat and gives Virginia a hug.

At three o'clock that afternoon, B.J. pulls the car into a roadside diner outside the college town of San Luis Obispo. Virginia buys Deana a late lunch: a cheeseburger, fries, and a Coke. Then they press on.

The dry grassland of the Southern California coast quickly becomes undulating hills. And soon, Highway 1 narrows to two lanes as it climbs up the craggy cliffs of Big Sur, skirting precipices like a deer trail. Deana—twenty years old, and just six months in from Louisville—bubbles her excitement from the backseat, pointing out the sights.

The steep, brown-grassed picachos and cool redwood forests of Los Padres National Park rise to the east. Westward, the ground falls away, hundreds of feet in places, down to rock formations jutting out of an immense plain of ocean that careers toward the rim of the world. Out past the breakers, sea otters loll amid the kelp forests. Pelicans skim the water, hunting for prey. A few houses nestle high among the hills and the canyons. But these stand far enough inland and far enough from one another that long stretches of Highway 1 still feel lonely and wild.

They pull over once, maybe twice, to enjoy the view from turnouts that punctuate the coast. Virginia takes out her Kodak disc camera and snaps a few photos: an expanse of ocean; a rubble-strewn cliff descending to the surf; Deana perched on a rock. In the photos, Deana's face is a smile masked by dark glasses. Her feet, in blue high-heeled shoes, dangle over the edge.

By 4:10 P.M., a quilt of gray clouds has rolled in and fog creeps up the ravines. The LTD makes a sharp left-hand turn onto the Seal Beach overlook, one of the last turnouts before the road steers inland toward Carmel and Monterey.

The overlook is a small gravel-surfaced semicircle no more than twenty yards in diameter, with boulders set about the cliff edge to form a gap-toothed barrier. The northern rim of the turnout looks down four hundred feet onto a small cove populated by sea lions known as Seal Beach.

Everyone piles out of the car. With the fog settling in and the sky darkening, the Pacific turns from blue lapis to a sheet of stained and pitted pewter. Virginia picks up her camera. Deana and B.J. put on windbreakers and walk to the edge. The barking of the seals echoes up the canyon walls.

B.J. takes Deana by the shoulder and walks her between the boulders. They lean over to hear the seals. Emptiness spreads out at Deana's feet, the ravines, the ocean, a few ice plants clinging to the ground. It is one of the most beautiful sights she has ever seen. . . .

▼

At 5:15, a Monterey Sheriff's Search and Rescue van driven by Deputy John Burke rumbles onto the Seal Beach turnout. Burke groans as he assesses the scene. Between the ambulance crew, the sheriff's green and white cruiser, three or four families standing by their campers and station wagons, and a television news van just coming into view, the place is already pandemonium. Search-and-rescue operations are difficult enough without lines of lookie-loos staring over your shoulder and reporters jabbing microphones into your face.

Burke pulls the tan rescue vehicle over to the center of the turnout. He and his team of deputies snap to work arranging orange traffic cones, roping off the cliff edge, radioing for helicopter support, and setting up the rescue equipment. They hustle, gruff and intent, like a company of fire fighters.

Burke knows they have no time to waste. The radio run came in more than half an hour ago. With the winds picking up, the sun sinking, and the temperature falling, the girl's chances of survival slip a few notches every minute. The ocean basin in Monterey is among the deepest in the world, three thousand feet in places. It stays bitter cold yearround and chills the surface air ten degrees. If the impact didn't kill the girl, Burke fears, exposure will. First shock, then hypothermia, and, finally, death.

They scout the area, but from the turnout it is impossible to see where the girl landed. Big Sur is full of such spots, and Burke, a lanky, weather-beaten forty-year-old, has been down most of them. About once a month, the rescue team gets called in for a rescue somewhere along the fifty miles of Big Sur's coastline. Deana's is the kind of accident Search and Rescue members consider routine.

Burke clips a nylon body bag to a Stoke's litter, a cradle used for hoisting incapacitated victims out of inaccessible spots. He and his partner, Richard Niemi, strap on shin guards and safety helmets and fasten their utility belts to a steel cable run off the truck's payout spool. The two men start down, leaning back into the cable.

The ground slopes down gently to a ledge where a single blue high-heeled shoe, scuffed and dirty, lies on its side. Burke tosses the shoe up to one of the deputies topside. Then, after a few backward paces, he and Niemi reach the point where the police lines recede from view and the cliff falls away below.

The victim most probably tumbled along the contour of the cliff face, Burke thinks, which means southward. He notes a few scrubby bushes bent over, and places in the soil where someone or something had skidded. Still, there is no guarantee they are in the right place.

A military rescue helicopter moves in overhead, buzzing furiously and sending down showers of pebbles. Burke and Niemi squeeze their eyes shut and keep their heads down. Burke tries raising the pilot over the radio, to find out if they can see the victim, but the signal is virtually inaudible. Finally, the helicopter pulls back behind the cliff edge and Burke squints up again at an empty sky. He and Niemi will have to do the job on their own, slowly zigzagging down in search of the body.

About twenty-five yards below the top, Burke spots a second blue shoe: They are in the right area. A few yards farther down, he finds a more certain indicator: fresh blood on the rocks. Both deputies look around hopefully for the girl. Nothing. They continue down, following dabs of blood like a set of grim trail markers.

Four hundred feet below the rim, the ground levels off. Due south, Burke spots a lump of dark blue clothing. He unhitches himself from the cable and jogs over.

Deana's body lies facedown. She is a tall young woman, about five foot nine, Burke estimates. She has on jeans and a navy blue windbreaker. Her feet appear badly bruised. One stocking is torn at the heel. The left leg twists at an unnatural angle. A sheet of blood, now partially dried, covers her head and neck and soaks her dark brown hair.

In spite of the blood and the injuries, Burke is surprised at how peaceful she looks. He has seen lots of dead bodies and each one is different—angry, shocked, mangled. This girl looks placid, almost like a sleeping child. He touches her, first at the wrist, then the side of the neck. Her skin feels cool to the touch. He presses his fingertips into her flesh, but there is no pulse. "I've located the victim," he radios to the surface. "Call in the chopper. It's a body-bagger."

Together, Burke and Niemi zip the corpse into the dark green nylon bag and secure it to the Stoke's litter. The helicopter moves in. Minutes later, Deana Hubbard Wild's twenty-year-old body is airlifted out, turning at the end of a cable, silhouetted against the steel sky.

CHAPTER 2

BURIAL INSURANCE

▼

Steven Keeney rose, as usual for a Sunday, at 7:00 A.M. He washed and shaved in the upstairs bathroom of his Louisville, Kentucky, home, where a needlepoint sampler on the wall reminded him daily: "Trust in God." Keeney lived by this advice and, with the exception of a recent divorce, the good fortune he enjoyed left him little reason to doubt it.

Six feet two, he still cut a handsome and trim figure in his custom-tailored suits and Hermès ties. His thick head of hair, worn in a jaunty JFK cut, hadn't thinned in the least, although its original black was modulating to salt-and-pepper. Underneath the suit, he bore the scars of a childhood bout with rickets: a pair of bowlegs and a bulbous sternum that his physician father called a "rickety rosary." All of which made him look, perhaps, a few years older than he was. But his smooth forehead, bright coins of eyes, and easy smile bespoke a playful spirit, one unaccustomed to frustration or failure.

At thirty-nine years old, Keeney already had amassed most of the accoutrements of success due an ambitious corporate tax attorney:

an elegant home in Castlewood, a bedroom community known as Louisville's "socialite showcase"; a white Jaguar sedan in the garage; private school for his son, Christian—now spending the week with his mother. In all, it was the kind of prosperity and serenity Keeney had hoped for.

While putting on his white Sunday suit, starched shirt, and cuff links that morning, Keeney glanced out the upstairs window. A summer haze, warm and humid, hovered over the neighborhood. "Tolerable shooting weather," he said to himself, and recalled somewhat wistfully that it had been weeks since he last shot at the range.

Ever since grade school, he had practiced regularly—targets, hard clay, picking off matchsticks—albeit against the wishes of his father, Dr. Arthur Keeney, now Dean Emeritus of the University of Louisville Medical School. Over the years, Dean Keeney had seen too much human wreckage from gunshots dragged through hospital emergency rooms to allow his son that kind of play. But having his wishes denied was not something young Steven took in stride. He pursued his interest in the sport with such tenacity that Dr. Keeney finally caved in. One Christmas, he presented his son with a match-grade Anschutz .22-caliber "tack driver," a rifle so named because it could drive a tack at five hundred yards or clip the wings off a bee.

Firearms, with their precision-tooled machinery, remained a life-long passion for Steven Keeney. Even entering middle age, he continued to think of certain weapons in his collection as "exquisitely exact" or "a masterpiece of precision." Firing five shots at a bull's eye one hundred yards off and finding a single hole, or punching out the letters in a newsprint target, those were transcendent moments, times when the world ticked along according to predictable rules. And Keeney believed in rules—from the letter of the law to the lessons of the Bible. He could be seen on the weekends, like clockwork, working on the tulip bed outside his house, in the vest and trousers from a three-piece suit. And few friends could remember having sat down to dinner with the man without his wearing a jacket and tie.

But this morning, other responsibilities called. He was due at Sunday school within the hour, introducing his students to the Pentateuch in a course he called "The Bible in 'Five Easy Pieces.'" Putting thoughts of the rifle range aside with a sigh, he went downstairs, filled a tall-boy Styrofoam coffee cup, and set off for church.

A low Kentucky sunlight slanted through the boughs of Castlewood's hundred-year-old oaks and lit the lawns with an almost hallucinatory intensity. A splendid morning, Keeney thought as he drove through the quiet streets, the kind that lies at your doorstep like an unexpected gift. Years later, he would look back on that perfect morning with an altogether different feeling. On that day, he picked up the first threads, threads that led him into a labyrinth of deception, treachery, and what he came to know as "pure evil."

By 9:00 A.M., cars crowded the parking lot and side streets outside the Second Presbyterian Church, a massive neo-Colonial brick building with a stately white belltower. Friends and business associates, PTA acquaintances and singles—a few hundred worshippers all at their perfume-and-shirt-starch best—shook hands and exchanged smiles as they climbed the church steps. Keeney brought his Sunday school class through the day's lessons and then returned to mingle with the congregation, a white suit in a sea of white suits and extravagant southern-belle hats.

At 9:15, a bespectacled minister ascended the pulpit in the greater sanctuary with its white walls and immense blue stained-glass window. A rustle of clothes and the scent of soap rose from the pews as people settled in for the day's brush with the Eternal.

"It is good to give thanks to the Lord, and to sing praises to our God, who does wonders," the minister's flat "Kentuckiana" tones boomed from speakers recessed in corners of the sanctuary.

Several hundred voices responded in unison: "It is good to show forth God's loving kindness every morning and his faithfulness every night."

As Keeney canted along with the group and scanned the sea of faces, his eyes passed over a dark-haired woman sitting by herself near the center aisle at the rear, a few rows away. She had a white, oval face, and long, finely formed fingers, all highlighted against the folds of a plain black dress. She clutched a handkerchief in one hand. Keeney looked away.

Bobbie Roberts didn't notice Keeney's glance; she was focusing all her energy on not becoming a weepy embarrassment.

Months had passed since her tragedy and only recently had she begun to feel in control of her life. Right after learning the news, she had taken a leave of absence from teaching at Louisville's Mann High School. For weeks, she had gone to bed at six-thirty and slept until morning. Sleep, long, dark, dreamless nights, were her one solace. "A gift," she said to herself. Now, feeling somewhat recovered, she thought she might sell the house and leave behind the memories that lingered in its familiar corners.

The minister continued: "This is the Lord's doing; it is marvelous in our eyes." Once more, the communal voice murmured its response: "This is the day which the Lord has made; let us rejoice and be glad in it."

As the responsive readings droned on, Bobbie's thoughts drifted back to April 2: *What on earth could be so important?*

That had been her first thought. It was midnight, an hour when telephones in the quiet community of Fincastle, Kentucky, rarely have occasion to ring.

"Mrs. Bobbie Jo Roberts?" an unfamiliar voice inquired. "Deputy David Dungan from Monterey, California. I hope I didn't wake you, ma'am."

"That's all right, Deputy," Bobbie answered. She spoke with just a trace of Kentucky twang, an accent largely refined away during fifteen years of teaching school.

"Ma'am, are you the mother of a twenty-year-old female by the name of Deana Hubbard Wild?"

"Yes, sir, I am. She's my daughter." Bobbie sat up and turned on her bedside lamp. Light would help focus her thoughts. Deana had been the last thing on her mind. That evening, she had gone to bed thinking of Afghanistan, its peoples, bordering countries, primary exports—her lessons for the remainder of the semester.

"Deana's all right, isn't she?" Bobbie asked tentatively.

"I'm afraid she's not, ma'am," Deputy Dungan answered. "Your daughter died this afternoon at about four-thirty P.M. I'm calling from the Monterey Coroner's Office."

The congregation's voice rose up: "Wait on the Lord; be of good courage. . . ."

The coroner? What could he mean, "died"? That was impossible. Bobbie had seen Deana less than two months ago and she had been brimming with life. The girl couldn't wait to go back and stay with that couple in California. She had even talked about patching things up with her husband.

"That can't be right," Bobbie protested. "Is this some kind of April Fool's joke?"

"I'm sorry, ma'am. She was wearing high heels at a turnout overlooking Seal Beach in Big Sur, and it seems she slipped and fell. To be honest, it's not the first time this sort of thing has happened out here."

Bobbie's stomach clenched as if her body felt the truth even before her mind could grasp it. Then her thoughts tumbled: "It's just—are you *certain* it's Deana? Has anyone identified the body? It can't be. . . ."

"I'm very sorry, Ms. Roberts. She was positively identified by her travel companions."

"Where—where is she now?"

"Her body's at the morgue."

Bobbie wanted to ask another question, a thousand more questions, anything to keep the voice on the telephone talking. But she knew talk would only postpone the inevitable. Moments later, she would be sitting alone on the edge of her bed, her bedside lamp glowing yellow through the shades of a two-story clapboard home with its small, shuttered windows—a house that looked remarkably like every other house in Fincastle.

With the sermon over, the congregation headed for Fellowship Hall, a room the size of an ocean-liner ballroom, and festooned with bright banners like medieval escutcheons. Fellowship Hall was the only place Keeney considered livable after a sermon, the one room under the "Second Pres" roof with a perpetually fresh-brewed pot of coffee. "Some things are basic," he liked to joke, but he had to admit it: He was a late-night workaholic with a caffeine habit.

Promptly after services, he stationed himself near the silver urn, holding the tall-boy cup he had brought from his kitchen and would carry around for the rest of the day. A boisterous crowd flowed in, their voices rising and filling the room.

Ordinarily, Bobbie Roberts avoided the social scene of Fellowship Hall, the sympathetic looks and ever-so-kind remarks. But today, she steeled herself and headed toward a white-suited figure at the center of a busy circle near the coffee urn, a man laughing and balancing a large Styrofoam cup.

"Excuse me?" she asked shyly. "Mr. Keeney?"

Steve Keeney turned. She smiled at him, but the firm set of her mouth betrayed her cheeriness.

"My name's Bobbie Roberts. I was wondering if I could talk with you, just for a moment."

"Pleased to meet you, ma'am," Keeney answered. "Now you'll have to excuse me for asking an awkward question. But, have we met?"

"I—I'm awfully sorry to bother you." Bobbie's voice stumbled. She lowered her eyes. "I need some help and I understand you're a lawyer. A friend of mine knows you from your law firm, and he says you're very competent."

"Well, I *am* a lawyer," Keeney joked in a voice that was an easy blend of Kentucky bourbon and New England prep school. "Now what seems to be the problem, Mrs. Roberts?"

"That's *Ms.* Roberts. I'm divorced." Bobbie glanced around to see whether anyone could hear. "It's about my daughter. She died last April in an accident in California."

"Oh, I'm terribly sorry."

Bobbie returned a quick thank-you, then the conversation stalled.

"Pardon me for sounding businesslike," Keeney pressed after a moment, "but why do you think you need a lawyer?"

"Well, it's my insurance company. They owe me some money, and I'm having trouble getting paid."

Keeney looked at this stranger anew. Her black hair sat parted in a wavy inverted V around a graceful, dark-eyed face that belonged on a Victorian cameo. Her ruler-straight posture showed that she still held on tightly to her pride. It obviously wasn't easy for Bobbie Roberts to ask for favors.

All the more of a shame, Keeney thought, since she's come to the wrong lawyer. *Ma'am,* he could say in all honesty, *I'm a corporate attorney. I represent businesses and consortiums. I haven't had a human client in years. And I'm probably much too expensive.*

Then he hesitated. He wasn't sure whether was it the echoes of Sunday school, or the subject of the day's sermon, or simply because Roberts seemed a nice, decent woman, but he heard himself agreeing to listen.

"It's a bit outside my area," he said. "But why don't you tell me the basics? Then we'll see."

As Bobbie explained the situation, Keeney put down his coffee cup and pulled a panatela out of a leather case. Kentucky is tobacco country and smoking, even in church, is like waving Old Glory. Through clouds of smoke, he took in the woman's story.

It was simple, really. Bobbie's daughter had fallen from a cliff during a sight-seeing trip to Big Sur in April. The funeral had cost $3,500. Her high school teacher's insurance policy covered burial costs, but the insurers wouldn't pay until the coroner issued a final death certificate. The Monterey Coroner's Office, meanwhile, said a final certificate still hadn't been filed. Bobbie insisted that the coroner's explanation didn't make sense. After all, three and a half months had gone by without a single phone call from the police.

Keeney mused: A daughter lost in a tragic accident? Well, it happened. People die, every one. When you wiped away the tears, Bobbie's was just a simple case of bureaucratic bottleneck.

"You know, Ms. Roberts," he said, working his way around to an exit line, "from what you've told me, I can't see much to be overly concerned about. The Coroner's Office is bound to get around to—"

"Mr. Keeney," she interrupted. "Couldn't you help me? Thirty-five hundred dollars may not seem like much money to you, but, on a schoolteacher's salary and with one daughter to raise, it means a lot."

Am I really going to stand here in Fellowship Hall and brush off this nice lady? Steve thought. *Besides, we're looking at four, five hours' work tops.*

"I tell you what," he said, pulling out a business card. "If you want to give me a holler at the office, I'll see what I can do. Sometimes just a lawyer's letterhead speeds things along. Until then, try to put your mind at rest."

Bobbie thanked him with a quick handshake. Then she blended back into the crowd of hats and suits. Keeney thought, half-hoped, Bobbie Roberts just might forget the whole thing. Lots of would-be clients approached lawyers at parties, even in elevators, and most of the time they were just sniffing out a free legal opinion. He strolled back to his friends.

CHAPTER 3

CAUSE OF DEATH: PENDING

▼

JULY 19, 1987

Monday. Steve Keeney and Pete Lazar, a silver-haired partner of Keeney's at the law firm of Barnett & Alagia, rode down in the elevator on their way to lunch at the Pendennis Club.

Keeney didn't belong to the blue-blooded Pendennis; it was one of the few old-boy institutions whose membership invitations he had declined. But its steaks, blanketed in Henry Bain's sauce, a murky, bluegrass version of sweet-and-sour sauce served throughout the city with the same pride as a mint julep on Derby Day, ranked high among Louisville traditions. Keeney figured there wasn't much harm in going as a guest.

The moment the office elevator doors opened, he headed off through the lobby at his usual lunchtime clip.

"Whoa, Secretariat!" Lazar jogged to catch up. "That's lunch hour New York–style."

"Just a defect I picked up from going to a New England college," he said, looking over his shoulder. "Besides, a good table is worth a little rush." He whisked through the ground-floor double doors and directly into a woman standing just outside the entrance.

"Excuse *me*, ma'am," Keeney said, pulling up short. "I didn't notice you standing there."

"Why, good afternoon, Mr. Keeney. I was just coming to see you." She squinted up at him in the July sunlight.

It took Keeney a moment to recognize Bobbie Roberts, even though they had spoken just yesterday in church. She dressed more formally today: a beige suit and a burgundy blouse closed with a brooch. She could have passed for an attorney on the way back from court, except for the distracted look in her eyes.

"This *is* a surprise," he smiled and sighed inwardly: A Henry Bain's steak would have to wait. "Pete, you go on ahead," he said. "Ms. Roberts is here on business."

"Afternoon, ma'am." Lazar excused himself with a nod and left Keeney to tend to his client.

Bobbie Roberts may have dressed like an attorney that day, but when she stepped out of the elevator into the reception hall of Barnett & Alagia—a foyer crowned by skylights and carpeted with an immense Oriental rug—Keeney sensed she felt like turning on her heels and forgetting the whole thing. Bobbie glanced around uneasily at the plush hallways, and stood a few seconds too long before taking a seat in Keeney's office. It was an L-shaped partner's suite with leather-upholstered chairs, a mahogany door that hissed as it closed over the pile, and a pair of large windows overlooking the downtown skyline.

Keeney watched Bobbie Roberts shifting in her chair. He had to admit the situation was a little absurd. Barnett & Alagia was a thoroughbred law firm, its attorneys trained in hotel partnerships, LBOs, and reverse triangular mergers out of bankruptcy. B & A members didn't even like to think of themselves as Kentucky lawyers. Opening in 1974, the firm had grown quickly, rolling across the country like a high-powered Kentucky wagon wheel. Every few months, a new office opened: Washington, D.C., Atlanta, Nashville, Palm Beach, even Bangkok. Their partner roster swelled with a list of former U.S. senators, a UN ambassador, even the heir apparent to the presidency of the American Bar Association, Louisville local Stan Chauvin. By 1987, their 140 lawyers represented clients ranging from the State of Israel to the Shah of Iran. Young, upstart Barnett & Alagia saw itself as a piece of the New York City skyline grafted onto a small town.

And Bobbie didn't need Oval Office connections or the firm's private plane to settle up some plain-vanilla paperwork. But he had offered to help, and he was not about to go back on his word.

"All right, Ms. Roberts." He picked up his Styrofoam cup and sipped some lukewarm coffee. "As I recall, you were interested in getting reimbursed for your daughter's burial expenses? Isn't that right?"

Bobbie nodded.

Within minutes, Keeney collected what he needed to know: names, addresses, Deana's date of birth, Deana's husband's name— Jay Wild.

"I think that about sums it up," Keeney said, stealing a glance at his desk clock.

"Well . . . how do we proceed from here?" Bobbie asked. Keeney caught the signal.

"There's no need to sign a contract or pay a retainer, Ms. Roberts. This one's on the house."

Bobbie thanked him with one of her hard-edged smiles but remained seated. "You know," she started up again, "I just can't help feeling anxious. Shouldn't the police have closed the case by now?"

"Honestly, Ms. Roberts, I can't see a thing to worry about. This sounds like business as usual—for a state agency," Keeney quickly added. "You know how many lunches it takes with a zoning-board member just to get him to *consider* granting a variance for a shopping mall? Here you're looking at a major California law-enforcement office where everybody's got too much to do and too little time to do it. My guess is, half of the papers that are supposed to get filed never do. That's no three-alarm fire."

"I understand that, Mr. Keeney. But that couple in San Diego, Mr. and Mrs. McGinnis, the people who were with Deana when she fell. Deana was staying with them while her husband, Jay, was at sea. Do you know, they never sent back any of her belongings? In fact, they only called me *once*, the day after she died. Just that one time." She shook her head disapprovingly. "Isn't there something wrong with that?"

It seemed a strange question, a little out of the blue. But then, so was Bobbie Roberts. She hadn't called to make an appointment or brought along any paperwork. Keeney managed a second glance at the clock. He imagined the last of the Pendennis steaks being served up and devoured. He and Bobbie could go on like this all day. People who have been through tragedy often look for something or someone to blame, he reminded himself. But the police hadn't found any reason to follow up with her even once in the past months. That seemed to say it all.

"Don't think I'm cross-examining, but have *you* tried to reach them and ask for her belongings?"

"I haven't really wanted to speak to them," Bobbie said defensively. "But they could—they *should* have called and told me my own daughter had died."

"Well, Ms. Roberts, if you take my advice, this kind of fuss and feathers is only going to cause you more worry. I'm sure the McGinnises were mighty upset themselves. They probably even felt responsible. I'll do what I can to get your insurance money, but maybe the biggest favor I can do is take this whole problem off your mind."

"I'm sure having you on the case will help." Bobbie offered one more injured smile before leaving.

The moment she disappeared between the brass elevator doors in the foyer, Keeney rang for another car. There was still time to catch up with Lazar at the Pendennis. That afternoon, between billable hours, he would knock off Bobbie's case. A two- or three-letter fix.

The AmEx insurance company servicing Louisville's Mann High School confirmed Bobbie Roberts's account. Before AmEx could start processing the claim, they needed a final copy of the California death certificate, and the certificate currently on file listed Deana's cause of death as "pending." That might do for a cat with three more lives to go, Keeney thought, but Deana was a human being, months in the ground.

"Sarah"—Keeney called his secretary over his desk intercom— "could you get the Monterey, California, Coroner's Office on the line?"

Sarah West, a sturdy four feet and eleven inches of midwestern unflappability and fierce loyalty, raised to five foot three by an elaborate beehive hairdo, had traveled with Keeney from his small associate's office in the middle of a B & A hallway all the way to his partner's suite. Like many talented secretaries, she was the invisible engine that made the corporate machine run. Keeney called her "the brains."

She rang the coroner's office and put the call through. Sgt. Glen Brown came on the line, and Keeney explained the problem.

"Oh, sure, I know the case," Brown said. "But I can't discuss an ongoing investigation with every lawyer who happens to call up."

This was, more or less, the answer Keeney expected.

"I'm aware that technically the file is still open, Sergeant. But isn't it just a question of filing an amended certificate that states an actual cause of death—cliff fall, heart attack, that sort of thing? Heck, my own cause of death is still pending, and this lady needs her insurance."

"That's not quite so easy," Brown said.

"Well, did you investigate the death?"

"Sure."

"And?"

"A deputy coroner found it was an accidental cliff fall."

"Doesn't that wrap things up?"

"Counselor, as far as I'm concerned, the case is still open. Call it technical if you want—you're the lawyer. Meantime, send me a letter and a check for seven-fifty. I'll get you your certificate and a copy of our report."

Keeney put down the phone. So far, so good, he thought. Brown's just got a cop's protective instincts; that's why he's touchy about a lawyer meddling with his business. Besides, a government file could remain open for all kinds of wooly reasons: a late-filed memo, or a signature that never got where it was supposed to go. The final certificate might be sitting in some sergeant's desk between a pastrami sandwich and the sports section.

He dictated a one-paragraph letter to Sergeant Brown and turned back to work on a case that had stymied him for weeks: a railroad bankruptcy. It was a deliciously complex piece of litigation that generated enough work to keep two partners and half a dozen associates busy for months.

As far as Deana Wild went, he assumed that, sooner or later, her death certificate would arrive, "pending" or not. The insurance company would pay up—he would see to that—and Bobbie Roberts could get on with her life.

But as Sarah West typed out the request for a death certificate on a twenty-year-old girl, she wondered, *A letter to the Monterey Coroner? What was Steven Keeney doing with a case like this?*

CHAPTER 4

CLIFF FALLS
ARE CLIFF FALLS

▼

A humid midwestern ninety degrees penetrated even B & A's air-conditioned offices. Outside, the sun was turning cars into double boilers and softening asphalt. Inside, everyone just sweated through the day and prayed for a cool evening.

From his office window, Keeney surveyed the Louisville cityscape, shimmering in the afternoon heat waves. His eye traveled from the skeletons of redbrick factories baking in the sun at the west end of town to the silver and black First National Bank Tower and up to the green horizon. An evolving portrait, he thought: City in Motion. Over the past seven years, he had helped assemble some of the packages that made the downtown skyline possible, including the new I. M. Pei–inspired Arts Center just below his window. This was his domain, and he took a gardener's satisfaction in watching its steady growth.

A call from Sgt. Glen Brown interrupted his meditation.

"Got a minute, Mr. Keeney?" Brown's voice crackled from a speaker phone.

"Sure thing, Sergeant." Keeney strolled back to his desk and clipped a cigar. "How goes the death certificate business? Still pending?"

"Afraid so. But I thought you'd want to know your insurance company's been calling me—State Farm."

"Did I hear that right?" Keeney cued in. "You sure you're not talking about AmEx, the Kentucky outfit? They're my client's company, not State Farm."

"No way. A guy named Mike Hatch at State Farm called just yesterday, one of their head honchos. Chief of Life Claims. Hatch said there's a thirty-five-thousand-dollar life-insurance policy on Deana and the primary beneficiary is James Coates, Deana's 'fiancé-to-be'—whatever that is."

"You're not telling me the kid's a bigamist, are you?" Keeney laughed. "Deana was already married. If she was planning to get divorced and remarried, my client would've known."

"Well, Hatch over at State Farm says the girl came in and filled out a life insurance application naming Coates beneficiary. Once it was approved, Virginia McGinnis came back and paid for the policy—one day before the girl died."

"Excuse me, Sergeant." Keeney sat up at his desk, laid down the cigar, and reached for a pen. "Maybe *I'm* the one who's a little out of step here. Did you say, *one day before she died?*"

"It came as a surprise to us, too, I can tell you that. At the scene, the McGinnises were asked point-blank whether they knew of any wills or insurance policies connected with Deana. They said, 'Absolutely no, no way.'"

"Now hold still. The McGinnises were the ones at the scene, and they also paid for the insurance on Deana?"

"Affirmative. Mike Hatch tells us that Virginia McGinnis went to an insurance office down in Chula Vista. Paid for the policy on April first. Next day, Deana's dead. Doesn't sound too good, does it?"

"Sergeant," Keeney said as he scratched a few notes, "that was months ago. Surely State Farm's looked into the matter since then."

"Hard to tell. Their investigators called us the other day. I figured you had something going with 'em, too. That's the reason I called."

"Has anyone talked to Bobbie Roberts about this?" Keeney asked.

"Not that I know of," Brown answered.

▼

Half an hour later, Keeney leaned back in his chair and ran over his notes. The police, it seemed, had gathered only a handful of facts, and Brown insisted that "As far as foul play goes, it all boils down to speculation and raw suspicion."

Keeney stared out into the hallway, quiet with late-afternoon doldrums. He rolled the details over in his mind, examining them the way he would a good cigar.

Accidents happen, he reminded himself, even bizarre ones. What seasoned lawyer hasn't run into a left fielder? And nothing in God's universe can stop someone from buying insurance at just the right moment. On April Fool's Day, no less. It could happen.

Besides, Keeney decided, putting away the yellow notepad, it's none of my business. My job is to get Bobbie's burial insurance. Period. If something turns out to be seriously wrong, then Deana's case will wind up where it belongs: in the Monterey District Attorney's Office, not Barnett & Alagia.

Early that evening, Keeney was still at his desk, nursing the tail end of a cup of coffee. Briefs stood in piles in various corners of his office, along with newspaper clippings, Xeroxes, memos, and dog-eared copies of the Federal Bankruptcy and Income Tax Codes. He had spent the remainder of the day bushwacking through the provisions on railroads and had finally cleared a path through the technicalities.

He looked at his watch: 6:45. Already. This week, he had custody of his son, Christian, now five years old. He had promised himself he would get out of the office by seven every evening and send the maid home early. Time with Christian, now five years old, always flew by: tee-ball, Chutes and Ladders, reading Tom Swift adventure stories. Then back he went to his mother, and the big Castlewood house emptied out.

But during the last few hours, details from Sergeant Brown's telephone call had rankled, and those concerns intruded on his work. It all put Keeney in a sour mood. His practice was to move deliberately, get things right the first time around, and not look back. Rethinking problems just wasted time. But the unanswered questions in Deana's case were like stray threads in a sweater: Pull one and either it came out or the whole thing unraveled. That was just unacceptable. He took a stroll down to the firm's kitchen and let himself mull over the story one more time before heading home.

Evening had begun to settle over Louisville, but B & A's associates remained bent over carrels in the library and partners clung to telephones. These were the firm's quiet hours, times when clients and secretaries were gone and the hallways became peaceful and empty.

What are the odds of someone from my church being pushed off a cliff for insurance money? he wondered as he poured a cup of coffee. There are over 250 million people living in the United States of America and less than 25,000 murders per year. Already it was an extreme longshot. About 10,000 to one. On top of that, $35,000 is just too little incentive. Why not at least make it a few hundred thousand and then slip over the border into Mexico? And who would be so incredibly obvious as to push a person off a cliff the day after buying insurance on her? That was laughable. No, plotting murder was too far-out—even if the McGinnises hadn't told the cops about the insurance. Maybe in the horror of the moment, they just forgot . . .

As Keeney left his office, he caught a last glimpse of the city going through its nightly transformation. Street lamps and steeple lights came on. White and red car lights ran in streams along the avenues, and offices in nearby skyscrapers glowed in Mondrian strips and squares against a sunset that modulated from orange embers at the horizon to a magenta velvet sky.

"Night, Pete," he said as he walked by Lazar's office. Lazar was on the phone, but he shot back a friendly salute.

It was 7:30 by the time Keeney pulled into his driveway. Christian ran to the door, clutching an unplugged Nintendo joystick.

Working in the kitchen helped Keeney sort out bothersome thoughts. He loved to cook: He talked to the food while Christian wrestled with video warriors in the living room. Then, when supper was over, the dishes washed, and Christian tucked in bed, Keeney climbed the stairs to work in his study. That was the routine.

As he sat in his skylit study that night, amid rows of walnut bookcases, Deana's story came back to bother him yet again. He wanted to think about his paying clients, but Sergeant Brown's words continued to distract him. They were like the notes of an annoyingly out-of-tune melody played over and over in the background. For one thing, what was a "fiancé-to-be"? Either you were engaged or you weren't. It reminded Keeney of the old line about being a little bit pregnant. How thoroughly did State Farm check things out? And since when could you buy life insurance on the basis of so flimsy a relationship, anyway?

It was worth one more call.

Of course, he needed to give the powers at State Farm a damn good reason to divulge whatever facts they might have uncovered. Keeney had represented plenty of insurance companies at Barnett & Alagia, and he knew that talking with Mike Hatch, their Chief of Life Claims, would quickly become a bureaucratic minuet. Hatch no doubt wielded immense power and bore responsibility for steering State Farm away from troublesome situations. The moment he sensed that State Farm might get dragged into a messy lawsuit, he would close off communication permanently.

Making matters worse, California numbered among the toughest states in the country when it came to paying life-insurance benefits. In recent years, their courts had carved out a new legal claim called "wrongful denial" of life insurance, and some of the watershed cases came right out of San Diego. Unscrupulous insurers, it seemed, had delayed paying legitimate claims and in the interim pocketed a few extra months' interest. The money didn't amount to much in each particular case, but all together it added up to millions. California judges and juries slammed down hard. In one infamous case, they awarded $5 million in punitive damages against an insurer who balked at paying a $45,000 death benefit!

And State Farm, the granddaddy of insurance companies, was the archetypal deep pocket. With $17 billion a year in proceeds—equal to the GNP of many a small nation—they might well prefer handing over a mere $35,000 on Deana's policy, rather than fight the issues in a California court. It wouldn't be out of heartlessness, just sound economics.

On the other hand, Hatch himself was still calling the police—four months after Deana's death. Keeney imagined Hatch couldn't be in a great hurry to close the file. He might even welcome a new reason to delay paying. Either way, it was worth a try.

Given the one-hour time difference between Louisville and State Farm headquarters in Normal, Illinois, Keeney hoped he might still catch the man at work. As he dialed, Keeney cooked up an argument on behalf of Bobbie Roberts.

Mike Hatch, miraculously, was still at his desk and answering his own phone. Hatch immediately recalled the case, almost too quickly for someone in his position, Keeney thought.

"What I'm looking at here is a bit worrisome, Mr. Hatch," Keeney started out. "Your company issued a life-insurance contract on Deana one day, and the next day she's dead. But that's about all I know. That and the fact you're still investigating."

"Like to help you out, Mr. Keeney. But detective work is handled by the folks over in the SRU, our Senior Referral Unit." Hatch's easygoing midwestern accent belied an underlying intransigence. Keeney sensed, as well, a battle-weary air.

"Fair enough," Keeney answered. "But maybe we could save each other some work, pool a few facts from time to time. You see, my client may have a right to those proceeds."

Keeney explained his theory of the case: If Deana had still been married when she died, then she couldn't legally have been engaged to James Coates. State Farm, however, would still have to pay *someone* the money. After all, it was Deana's policy, issued and paid for. That someone was probably Deana's husband, Jay Wild. Only, what if Jay died before the case was settled, or he out and out declined the money, or he was otherwise ruled ineligible? Then Bobbie Roberts might stand to collect under California's Trusts and Estates laws.

"Right now, I'm not really worried about who's owed what," Hatch said, sounding only marginally interested. "The case is still being evaluated by our field investigators. We might even deny coverage altogether if the girl lied about her health on the application. But, if it makes you feel any better, I can tell you that State Farm isn't close to paying a nickel to anybody."

"I suppose that rates as good news for the moment." Keeney forged ahead. "Meanwhile, maybe you can tell me *why* you're still looking into it."

"Well, since you represent a potential claimant, I can tell you the basics," Hatch replied, cautiously. "After Virginia McGinnis tried to collect on behalf of James Coates, we interviewed all the beneficiaries. They all gave us more or less the same story they'd told the sheriff."

"Maybe I'm missing something here," Keeney said. "If they gave you the same story, why aren't you close to paying?"

Hatch paused. Keeney pictured the man sitting in his office, surrounded by actuarial tables and calculating the risk of leaking a few facts. A bureaucrat in his element.

"Mr. Keeney," he said at last, "I can tell you that Virginia's husband Billie Joe McGinnis came in the same day as Deana, and he filled out an application, too."

"Well?"

"Truth is, Billie Joe never stood a chance of getting insured."

"Why not?" Keeney asked.

"Medical reasons. Very poor health. And James Coates, the primary beneficiary on Deana's policy, is Virginia McGinnis's son. Virginia and B.J. were named as successor beneficiaries."

"Mr. Hatch, this whole thing isn't exactly putting me at ease. Has anybody checked out Coates? He's first in line for the money."

"Sure. He's got a rock-solid alibi. Coates was in state prison for parole violation at the time of Deana's death. Virginia made the claim for him using a power of attorney."

"The primary beneficiary was in *jail*?" Keeney coughed out the words.

"That's right, counselor. Of course, that doesn't mean a whole lot. I tell you what. If you want to help, why don't you send us a photo of Deana? That at least might help rule out the possibility of body substitution."

"Body substitution?" Keeney asked incredulously. "Excuse me, Mr. Hatch, but the last time I was offered a long shot like that was at the Derby. I took it and lost, and I don't like to make the same mistake twice."

"I'm sorry, Mr. Keeney," Hatch signaled the end of the call. "I feel for your client, not knowing about Coates, the insurance, and all. But thirty-five thousand dollars is one of the smallest life claims our company has this year. Sure the facts are worrisome, and I know what you're thinking: that the McGinnises might have pushed her off that cliff. But you've got to remember that the girl came in and signed the application herself. Nobody had a gun to her head. On top of that, the Sheriff's Office investigated and ruled her death an accident. Best you get one thing straight right now. Cliff falls are cliff falls and it's very hard to prove otherwise."

Keeney paused a moment to digest the thought. Then he answered: "Sure enough, Mr. Hatch. But I'd like to see a copy of Deana's policy. And until we know a little more, any objection to my sending you a notice letter about Bobbie Roberts?"

"Tell the truth, you'd be doing us a favor."

Keeney thanked Hatch and went downstairs to his kitchen for another cup of coffee. *Cliff falls are cliff falls.* Hatch certainly seemed a far cry from the insurance-claims investigator in *Double Indemnity*, nagged by "a little man inside him" every time a suspicious case crossed his desk. Hatch sounded as if he were delivering an apology. *One of the smallest life claims that year.* Still, they had managed to meet halfway. Keeney had handed Hatch a legitimate reason to stall paying the McGinnises. In return, Hatch managed to pass along some disturbing, and probably confidential, facts—and all without compromising State Farm in the least.

The next step was to have a long talk with Bobbie Roberts and stake her claim to the insurance proceeds—assuming she wanted to go forward.

He went to put Christian to bed, then spent the rest of the night hacking at his computer on behalf of paying clients.

Keeney left Christian with the family maid the following evening, and rode out through the widening semicircles of Louisville suburbia to Bobbie Roberts's house in The City of Fincastle, a "city" with no stores, no post office, no school system, no public transportation, no gas station, just a convocation of a few hundred houses encircled, like a miniature medieval village, by an eight-foot-high brick wall.

As he motored along the freeway, Keeney wondered where he could even begin. Deana's death had to have been an accident, he kept telling himself. The life insurance policy, standing alone, didn't mean a thing, nor did the business about a "fiancé-to-be"—even if Coates was doing prison time and Virginia had a power of attorney that let her act as his agent. No, nothing at all *disproved* the accident theory. But he still had a duty to tell his client the facts.

He tried to imagine how his grandfather would have handled the situation.

For two generations, Presbyterians in Indiana and Kentucky had considered the Reverend Arthur Hail Keeney an orator and minister of the highest order. On occasion, the reverend would assume the pulpit with a handful of peppermints hidden in his pocket and invite the children in the congregation to sit on the chancel steps. When the youngest ones began to squirm, he would lean over and slip them a few candies. Folks knew he had "the touch." But corporate law hadn't given his grandson much practice in hand-holding.

Bobbie greeted Keeney at the door with an expression that looked patched together: hope, worry, and pain all vying for prominence. He forced a smile and glanced around as they went inside. The small kitchen, the stucco walls, the narrow rooms all enforced an impression of loneliness. The living room looked immaculate, almost over-scrubbed, the kitchen sink wiped dry with a cloth. The home of a woman who's holding on tight, Keeney thought.

Seated across a dining room table from Bobbie, Keeney stuck to the script he had prepared on the ride over.

"Ms. Roberts, I wanted to talk with you about the direction this insurance claim of yours should take. As far as the burial money goes, that all looks routine. Meantime, I've come across certain facts about Deana's death that might want some looking into."

"What 'facts' are you talking about?" she asked.

Keeney avoided a direct answer. "Deana wasn't planning to get remarried, was she?"

"Not that she ever said." Roberts answered with the hesitation of someone wondering if they'd been asked a trick question. "The last time I saw her, she said she and Jay were patching things up. Now what are you trying to tell me? I'm Deana's mother, and if something's wrong I think I can take whatever it is."

"I don't want to alarm you, but I recently spoke with Sgt. Glen Brown from Monterey. You were right. The police say they're still investigating Deana's death. There's no way to know where their investigation will ultimately lead, but—"

"Mr. Keeney," Bobbie cut him off, "what are you trying to tell me?"

Keeney thought of lighting a cigar, asking for a cup of coffee, anything to buy a few minutes. At last, he forced out the words in a single shot: "Ms. Roberts—Bobbie—there's a possibility that Deana's death was not an accident. Another insurance company has been in touch with the police over the death."

Bobbie looked at him, her expression suddenly gone blank. *"Another* insurance company?" she repeated.

Slowly, Keeney laid out the facts.

After he finished, Keeney could practically hear his words reverberate off the plasterboard walls. They sat for a moment, the silence broken only by the hum of the refrigerator and the whir of an occasional passing car out on the highway. Bobbie gazed out a window into the darkness.

"No, Deana wouldn't buy insurance," she said, eventually. "And it just never made sense about the high heels and all. But I suppose I wanted to believe it was an accident. And the police sounded so sure." She turned to Keeney. "Could anyone really do such a thing?"

The thought sent a brief shiver through them both.

"I don't know, Bobbie," Keeney said at last. "I don't even know what all this means."

"Well, what should we do?"

"How about a cup of coffee?"

While Bobbie filled the kettle, Keeney stood up and strolled into the living room. A floral sofa-and-chair set and a pair of Oriental chests stood facing a panel of sliding glass doors that opened out onto a green yard and a communal parking lot. An oil painting of elongated Kentucky Derby racehorses hung on one wall opposite a pair of Monet and Renoir art posters in metal frames.

More than once, he imagined, Bobbie must have felt she had it made—husband, children, good job—only to watch her happiness slip away like the brass ring at a carousel. First by divorce, and now by death. The wear and tear had begun to show in small lines at the edges of that cameo-perfect face.

He picked up a framed photograph from a collection of bric-a-brac on a side table. There was Bobbie, groomed and posed beside two teenage girls.

"Deana?" Keeney asked.

"That's Deana on the right," Bobbie called from the kitchen. "Janie's my other daughter. She lives part of the month with her father Tom."

Keeney looked closer. Deana had a softly rounded face, straight brown hair, and a flawless, roses-in-bloom complexion. But something was wrong with her smile. Though open and friendly and silvered with braces, it was a vague smile, and it lent her whole expression an out-of-focus quality.

A few minutes later, he and Bobbie were back at the dining table, coffee cups steaming. Bobbie picked up the thread of conversation.

"You know, Mr. Keeney, at first I was so happy Deana had found some older people to live with in San Diego. Virginia had even lived in Louisville, which made me feel better. Now, I just don't know what to think."

Keeney searched his soul for the right thing to say. The tax code, blue-sky laws, and boardroom politics were his areas of expertise. The most serious criminal case he had ever handled involved a drunk driving charge. He thought about referring Bobbie Roberts to a good criminal lawyer. But criminal lawyers required cash up front, or the prospect of money down the line, and neither were in the offing in a case like this. Somehow, the job had fallen into his hands.

"Bobbie," he finally spoke up, "we can't jump to any conclusions about what happened in Monterey. But I did speak with State Farm yesterday. I told them you may want to make a claim for Deana's life insurance."

"I don't want a dime of that money," she cut in vehemently. "The whole idea makes me sick. I just want to know how my daughter died."

"That's going to take time. But if we tie up the claim, the McGinnises and James Coates will wait around to see what happens. That will buy the time we need to find out some hard facts. It's entirely possible this is all one terrible misunderstanding."

Bobbie lapsed into silence again and peered into her coffee cup. "I guess I'm willing to do whatever it takes to find out, Mr. Keeney. But as far as I'm concerned, I don't want anything to do with those people or the money."

"I tell you what. Take a few days to think all this over. If you can find peace with God and with yourself, so be it. Remember, we may never know much more than we do right now. And in the end, I'll be just another lawyer on another case. You're the one who's going to have to live with this." It occurred to Keeney that his grandfather would have approved of his impromptu little speech.

As they walked outside into the muggy evening air, Bobbie agreed to sleep on the decision. In the blue-white streetlamp light, it seemed to Keeney that she looked tired. He wondered whether she might not be better off just getting on with her life. But that was her decision.

"Call me in a day or two." He picked up the thread of conversation. "I'll help find out the truth if that's what you want. That's a promise. Meantime, try to remember what you can, anything Virginia or Deana said that might explain things. That's the best starting place."

"I really don't think there's all that much," Bobbie said. "When Virginia called me the day after Deana died, she seemed so nice, saying what a beautiful person Deana was and such. Why, Virginia even told me she knew just how I felt. She said that when she lived in Louisville, she lost a daughter in an accident, too."

▼

As he drove off, Keeney tried to reign in his suspicions. Virginia's daughter? *Another* accidental death? The very idea of Virginia being present at two fatal accidents seemed mighty improbable. It also raised a distinctly unpalatable possibility. But the police were on the case, he reminded himself, as was Mike Hatch over at State Farm. Everything would surely turn out to be one ghastly misunderstanding.

CHAPTER 5

SLOTH

▼

Keeney woke after his usual five hours' sleep. Most evenings he was up well past midnight hammering out deals on the phone or crafting meticulous memos for clients. At seven in the morning he rushed back to the office. Among the lawyers at B & A he had won a reputation for workaholism after he had the firm's legal research system wired directly into his study. Even for the few vacations he took, he prepared itineraries that ran to twenty pages. Everything had to be planned, right down to the quarter hour.

Recently, however, the smooth pace of events was interrupted when his ex-wife brought *criminal* charges against him for nonpayment of child support. Here was his son, going to private school, playing with expensive computer toys, and getting pampered by the day maid. Yet Keeney now faced the humiliation of going before a grand jury to show that Christian wasn't the victim of criminal neglect. It was—he smiled darkly—a lot harder to be sitting on the client's side of the table.

But this morning, he woke in a lighter mood. After leaving Bobbie

Roberts's condo the night before, he had gone on another date with Wynn Bukholder. He had known Wynn in passing for years as a member of his church and part of the tight Louisville social circle. She was divorced, too, and the mother of two children, Kelly, ten, and Mark, eight. She was an auburn-haired powerhouse in her swooping white hat, stoplight-red blazer, and black pumps. Everything about her, from her throaty alto to her broad-shouldered figure, declared that she was happier being with the boys than gossiping at the Louisville Ladies' Club, and that she could drive a golf ball, or a business deal, as hard as any man.

A few months after his divorce went through, he considered asking Wynn out. But when it came to the dating scene, Keeney found himself reduced to a finger-wringing schoolboy. He could take on CEOs blustering about inflated bills and irate judges threatening contempt. That was all in the service of a client. Getting turned down for a date, however, was personal.

The only way, he decided, was a carefully orchestrated plan of attack: opening statement, cross-examination, summation. One Sunday, he spotted Wynn across Fellowship Hall. She looked unapproachable, smiling and laughing at the center of a circle of admirers, some of them mutual friends. Keeney encouraged himself: Other women saw him as a good catch, why wouldn't Wynn?

Ten minutes later, he was pacing the hall, clutching his Styrofoam cup and wondering what had gone wrong.

"It's not you, Steve," she had said in a confident voice that instantly unnerved him. "But you know how small Louisville is. People would talk. I'd just be too embarrassed."

That was one response that had never occurred to him. And worse still, she was right. Neither of them had been divorced more than a year, and they both knew how sweet southern talk quickly became nasty gossip when you broke the rules.

After a second cup of coffee, Keeney devised a new plan and circled back.

"Wynn, I tell you what," he said, touching her elbow with his fingertips. "You meet me next week at Diamond's restaurant. Take your own car, so we won't show up together, and I promise no one will see us. If you feel the least bit uncomfortable, you can just leave without even saying a word to me."

"Steve, I couldn't do that," she protested. Diamond's sat just down the road from church, and the chances were overwhelming that they would indeed be spotted together.

"Seriously, Wynn. It's the only way you'll feel right. If anything bothers you, you're outta there, no questions asked. How can you say no to that?"

"All right." She smiled cautiously. "It's a date."

Wynn arrived at Diamond's and the maître d' showed her to a table for two. The plush Art Deco restaurant seemed unusually quiet for eight o'clock on a Friday. In fact, Wynn noticed with a start, it was empty.

Seconds later, Keeney, wearing a green silk and linen suit, walked up to the table. Wynn thought she noticed just the trace of a swagger. "See anybody you recognize?" He smiled.

"Of course not, Steve," she said. "There's nobody here."

"There won't be, either," he answered as he took a seat. "I don't like surprises, so I rented the restaurant. I promised you we could get off by ourselves." Wynn couldn't stop laughing. Maybe Steve Keeney wasn't such a straitlaced corporate lawyer, after all.

Over dessert, he invited Wynn and her two children to join him for the Louisville's Children's Theater performance of *Pinocchio,* with a private reception to follow—he was, after all, a member of their board of directors.

"That's not exactly a very private place, Steve," she said. "But how can I say no after all this?"

Lying in bed that morning, Keeney smiled at his own awkwardness when he had reached across the table to kiss Wynn for the first time. It was weeks ago, but he still recalled how his Armani suit seemed to cinch up like a straitjacket.

He rolled over and looked out at the August dew rising from the trim lawns and topiary around the colonnaded houses. For the first time in months, his life seemed peaceful and orderly again.

Then, getting dressed, he remembered Deana's cliff fall and the strange mention of Virginia's daughter's death. In the midst of these bright new hopes was he really about to take on a full-scale death investigation? And all based on what? An insurance policy and some peculiar timing? The very word *homicide* stuck in his throat like a bone. If he had wanted to practice criminal law, he would have taken a job with the U.S. Attorney and gone after white-collar criminals. Maybe he had gone too far with his promise to Bobbie.

"Call from Ms. Roberts," Sarah West announced as he arrived at the office.

"Put it through, Sarah."

Bobbie came on the line, her voice sounding more determined than ever. "Mr. Keeney, I thought about what you said and I'm willing to do whatever it takes to learn the truth about Deana's death. Where do we start?"

Keeney took his time before answering. If he wanted to beg off, this was the moment. Then he remembered the sight of Bobbie Roberts outside her Fincastle condo. If he didn't help her, it looked like nobody would.

"Okay," he said, "here are a couple of things we can do right off. First, I'll send a letter to Mike Hatch and try to hold up the State Farm money. Second, we need to build a team with State Farm's and Monterey's investigators. If those efforts don't pan out, then I want to find out a little more about Virginia and B. J. McGinnis. Kind of what I call the 'Mother Teresa test.' If Virginia turns out to be Mother Teresa, I'd be willing to take her word about Deana's death being an accident. Saints don't sin.

"Until we hear back from Mike Hatch at State Farm, the most important thing for you to do is to pull together any facts you have—pictures, letters, anything. I'll handle the folks in suits."

"Well, I've got one thing I can show you right away," Bobbie said. "Just after Deana died, Virginia sent me some photos she said were taken on that trip up the coast. Should I bring them in?"

Keeney stifled a "now you tell me" reaction. "That's a starting place," he said.

In the interim, Deana's death certificate, the pathologist's report, and the Coroner's Register arrived by mail. Keeney hoped that the documents, the first official reports to come across his desk, would explain everything.

The pathology report consisted of a physical examination of the body and a toxicology test of Deana's blood and urine. Blood samples tested negative for alcohol or narcotics. There was nicotine, but then, Deana's smoking cigarettes didn't come as news. She was a Kentucky girl, after all.

Two unfamiliar-sounding drugs, however, turned up in Deana's urine: amitriptyline and nortriptyline. The report didn't describe their pharmacological effects; it just listed them as "present." Before going any further, Keeney decided to make a quick call to a local neuropharmacologist, a former student of his father's. The young doctor said he'd be delighted to do a favor for old Dean Keeney.

"Nortriptyline and amitriptyline are components of a prescription drug sold under the brand name Elavil," he explained. "It's used in treating depression, what you call a mood elevator. It comes in a pill form, usually."

"Would a person take it to get high?" Keeney asked.

"I can't see why. Until you get stabilized on it, Elavil just makes you feel queasy and dizzy. Most first-time takers complain about the side effects. And there's no black market in the drug, if that's what you're asking."

"What kind of side effects are we talking about here? A person wouldn't be stumbling around, would they?" That could easily account for a slip and fall, Keeney thought.

"They might be," the doctor answered. "Patients are warned not to drive when they're getting stabilized. How much was in this girl's system?"

Keeney checked the report. "It doesn't say."

"Too bad. If we knew, then we could really nail down the effects. I hate to sound critical," he added, "but that's pretty sloppy work, not quantifying the amount."

"Well, I'm just trying to do my best with the tools at hand," Keeney said.

"Send regards to your father."

"Sure thing. And thanks."

The rest of the pathologist's report cataloged Deana's physical injuries. Her left shin, left kneecap, two left-hand fingers, left femur, and skull were fractured. Both legs and arms suffered minor abrasions and contusions. The one fatal injury seemed to have been to Deana's head: the base of her cerebellum suffered what the Monterey pathologist termed a "shredding laceration." His report concluded: CAUSE OF DEATH: BASAL BRAIN LACERATION, MINUTES, DUE TO BASAL SKULL FRACTURE, MINUTES.

Keeney searched his medical dictionary, then called his father. Nobody seemed to know what *minutes* meant.

Nevertheless, the report made clear that Deana's fall was not the headlong plummet Keeney originally envisioned. Apparently, while she was dizzy from Elavil, she tumbled down a slope, breaking a few bones along the way. At one point, she must have smacked her head on a large rock and that one blow split her skull. It all seemed to fit together nicely enough.

Then Keeney turned to the last document, a fill-in-the-blanks form with a space for a summary of the incident, called the Coroner's Register. Written by Deputy Coroner Dave Dungan, it read:

On April 2, 1987 at about 16:21 hours, Deana Wild aka Hubbard, 20 years old, died when she reportedly fell from a cliff just south of Big Sur.

Wild was visiting the area of Big Sur with friends, Billie and Virginia McGinnis from San Diego. Wild had been staying with the McGinnis' for only a couple of months when she was dating their son. She stopped seeing their son and moved in with the McGinnis'. Mr. and Mrs. McGinnis knew that Wild had never see [sic] much of California and offered to take a trip which would include San Francisco and the Monterey coast line.

The McGinnis' left San Diego early on the 2nd of April and travelled up State Route 1. Periodically, they would stop and take photographs and ate lunch in San Luis Obispo. They stopped along Highway 1 near the Coast Gallery to take photos of the sunset and the ocean. . . .

Mr. McGinnis explained that he was standing along side of Wild and that his wife was taking their picture. They were standing with their backs to the ocean about two feet from the edge of the steep cliff. The area is very beautiful and would make a great photo. Mrs. McGinnis had just completed taking their photo and Mr. McGinnis walked away from Wild, towards the parked car. He and his wife were walking when they turned around in the direction from where Wild and Mr. McGinnis were standing and Wild was nowhere to be seen. Both looked around and then walked back to the site. Neither could see her but looked slightly over the edge and saw a high heeled shoe over the edge about twenty feet below. They looked further and saw Wild lying on the rocks at the bottom of the cliff. The McGinnis' immediately went to the Coast Gallery to call for help. The Monterey Search and Rescue team was dispatched to the scene. They were able to recover the deceased who fell to the bottom. The cliff is conservatively estimated to be 390 feet.

In the initial and subsequent interview with the McGinnis [sic] I found nothing to even slightly indicate foul play.

At the time of the accident, Wild was wearing a pair of high heeled shoes. One shoe was recovered by the Monterey County Sheriff's Rescue Team. . . . The recovered shoe had several gouge marks on the left side of the right shoe. A minor scrape on the right heel side. I saw several pronounced scrape marks on the sole of the shoe. Though this event was not witnessed it must be considered that Wild may have lost her balance in the loose soil combined with the type of shoes she was wearing causing her to fall over the cliff.

A Certificate of Death has been filed with the Vital Records Division, with cause of death pending and an amendment shall be filed upon completion of the investigation.

In spite of Dungan's reassuring conclusion—"nothing to even slightly indicate foul play"—the report as a whole seemed so much like a quick shuffle, it made Keeney sweat. He flipped on his computer and started a file of errors, inconsistencies, and oddities:

1. On line 19 of the fill-in-the-blanks section, Inspector Dungan listed Deana's cause of death as "massive head *and chest* trauma," yet no chest injury appeared anywhere in the pathologist's report.

2. The 5th line listed Deana's marital status as "single," yet the 26th line read, "nearest relative—James Wild; Relationship—Husband."

3. Under cause of death, Dungan had written "pending," yet elsewhere he stated "accident."

4. Dungan never mentioned getting signed statements from the McGinnises—the only witnesses to the fall.

5. The McGinnises apparently claimed they had pulled off the road to "take photos of the sunset and the ocean." But even in Northern California, the sun doesn't set at four o'clock in April.

6. The McGinnises also said they were walking back to their car when Deana disappeared, yet they never mentioned hearing screams or calls for help. Dungan had let that remarkable detail slide by without comment.

7. There was no list of people at the scene; no reference to accident-scene photos.

8. Later in the report, Dungan said Deana had been "staying with the McGinnis' for only a couple of months when she was dating their son." Then he said Deana "stopped seeing" the McGinnis' son, yet she "moved in with" his parents. Those lines folded back on themselves like some odd creatures in an M. C. Escher drawing.

Overall, the Coroner's Register read more like a travel guide: "The area is very beautiful and would make a great photo." Dungan's analysis reminded him of Oliver Wendell Holmes's quip about fellow Supreme Court Justice, Kentuckian John Harlan: Harlan had a "mind like a vise, the jaws of which did not meet; it held only larger objects."

How exactly did Deana fall? Keeney again tried to envision the scene. Did she walk backward off the cliff after posing for a snapshot, or stumble in her high heels while in a drugged stupor? Either way, nobody bothered explaining those "details." This was not how serious cases were treated at B & A, and it was probably not how they were treated in Monterey. It sure would be nice if somebody would get this story to hang together, he thought.

When Keeney next called Sergeant Brown, he decided to press a little harder.

"What do the accident-scene photos show?" he started in.

"We don't have any."

"I don't mean to be fussing with you. But isn't it customary to take accident-scene photos?"

"Mrs. McGinnis promised Dave Dungan she'd send in the photos she took at the scene. Under the circumstances, Dungan decided not to take any of his own. You know, we don't have a set policy about taking them in every case. Out here, people are falling off cliffs like logs. It happens all the time—like snowflakes in a snowstorm. Half of the time, we wouldn't even know what we'd be looking for."

"Well, did Mrs. McGinnis ever send in the photos?"

"As far as I know, she never did."

"And you never called Bobbie Roberts to see what she knew?"

"I suppose that's correct."

When Keeney put down the phone, he added one more item to his list of errors in the Coroner's Register:

9. Deputy Dave Dungan had checked off the box labeled "photographs—at scene." Yet now it turned out that the only photos taken were the McGinnises' own snapshots—promised but not delivered.

Dungan's report seemed to amount to: "Easy come, easy go. File it." Keeney wanted to pick up the phone again and tell Brown to get himself in gear. This was a death, not a traffic ticket. But he knew he suffered from terminal impatience, and there were limits to the kind of "help" Monterey would accept.

Ever since he first saw it on the cover of *The New Yorker,* he carried in mind Saul Steinberg's map of the United States: New York and Brooklyn looming in the foreground, the Midwest consisting of Chicago and unbroken rolling cornfields, and L.A. being the only feature visible on the horizon. The indication was clear: As far as the coastal states were concerned, the entire Commonwealth of Kentucky was good mainly for bourbon, tobacco, Derbys, and bluegrass. Louisville wasn't even so much as a blip on that screen.

The Monterey Sheriff's Office surely didn't want to hear from a would-be prosecutor from the sticks yammering on with a slew of complaints. Sergeant Brown was no doubt correct that people in Monterey "are falling off cliffs like logs." And they presumably did know a slip-and-fall from a homicide when they found one.

But Keeney was not, as he liked to say, "the last pumpkin off the truck." He would not settle for slothful work on behalf of a client. Not, at least, until he learned the whole story.

CHAPTER 6

FIFTEEN WITNESSES

▼

The first week in August, Bobbie Roberts came to Barnett & Alagia with photographs Virginia had sent her back in April. The photos were still in their little paper packet, along with the original Kodak disc negative. Bobbie apologized for not bringing them by sooner; she had left them with her sister in Lexington and, well, life got in the way.

Keeney immediately sent the disc negative out to be developed, just to be sure Virginia hadn't deleted any telling shots. Then he asked Bobbie if she could stay to answer a few questions.

"You remember I told you to recollect everything you could about Deana," Keeney said once they were settled back in his office. "Well, now's the time. Her habits, her boyfriends, her schooling—the good and the bad. If we ever end up in court, Deana won't be there to defend herself."

"I'm not proud of everything I did," Bobbie answered. "But I think I was a good mother and Deana was a good child. No worse than a lot of families." She forced a laugh.

"That's all anyone can ask," Keeney said.

Deana's upbringing turned out to be far from the "piano and Girl-Scouts" good time Keeney had imagined. She was the product of Bobbie's first marriage, an unhappy union with an unhappy man who worked for the telephone company. Deana was three years old when Bobbie walked out. Less than a year later, she married a soft-spoken law student named Tom Marshall.

Bobbie said that she had first asked Tom—a former prosecutor in town—to look into Deana's death, but he hadn't wanted to get involved. Keeney let that detail slide, family politics always being more complicated than they appear.

When Deana was born, Bobbie said, she dreamed of her daughter becoming a lawyer or a college professor. Then her fantasy came crashing down. School-board authorities administered an IQ test on which Deana scored an 85: a borderline learning impairment. By the tenth grade, she was performing only at a second-grade level. Socializing was Deana's strong suit, Bobbie said proudly. She even played peacemaker and mother hen to her gang of rowdy girlfriends.

After divorcing Tom, Bobbie kept custody of the children, but her relationship with Deana soured. "We had some rough moments," Bobbie confessed, "but Deana always had a home."

Then, suddenly—on Friday, September 5, 1986—Deana was gone. She hadn't even left a note. Bobbie figured Deana probably had stormed out and was staying with a girlfriend. But the next day, Deana called to announce that she had married her high-school sweetheart, a young navy man named Jay Wild, and they were moving to San Diego, where Jay was stationed. Bobbie heard from Deana every few weeks after that. She wrote the young bride letters whenever she could, but Deana's address in San Diego kept changing.

In January, Deana called home to say that she and Jay had argued over money and were going to live apart. She said she planned to move in temporarily with an older couple named Virginia and B. J. McGinnis, the parents of a new friend, Jimmy Coates. Then she would decide what to do next. Maybe she would find a job.

Once at the McGinnis house, Deana dropped out of touch again. "Mom," Deana warned one day, "if you keep calling, I'm going to have the people I'm staying with change their number. You're driving us all crazy."

"Call it mother's intuition," Bobbie said, "but I started to get terribly worried about my daughter. I was just determined to get Deana back home. So I sent her a round-trip ticket to Louisville, care of Virginia McGinnis."

On February 9, 1987, suitcase in hand, purse slung over her shoulder, Deana came home for the first time since she had eloped. Keeney made a note and underlined it. If Virginia shipped Deana home at Bobbie's request, how seriously could she have been contemplating an insurance scam? One more strike in favor of an accident.

Within days, Bobbie said, she and Deana fell back into their old pattern of angry fights. At the height of their last argument, she snatched away Deana's purse—which still had the return portion of her ticket inside. Deana stormed out and somehow got herself back to the West Coast. The next news of her daughter came from the Monterey Coroner.

After the funeral, Virginia had sent a condolence letter in the form of a rambling poem. Bobbie pulled out a folded square of paper and read:

"DEANA"

Deana was like a friendly puppy who gave a lot of love & needed a lot of love! Deana enjoyed taking the dog out for a walk in the park & Fields, I guess She stopped to look at Flowers, and nature in general.

Their. We left San Diego To drive North. She was so excited about seeing San Francisco, China Town & Fisherman's Warf. Also meeting our Family & Friends! Dean was just Bubbly all day— Look, at the water—Mist & Rainbow! Not to mention the Sun Shine.

Deana wanted to go back to Collage here. And we (B.J. and myself) wanted to help her.

Deana was a sweet girl—gentle and full of love.—

With our Deepest Sympathy.

B. J. and Virginia McGinnis

Keeney leaned back in his partner's chair, sipped coffee from his tall white cup, and let the words wash over him.

Like everything else in the case, Bobbie's narrative simply raised more questions. Could James Coates really have been engaged to Deana? But then why hadn't Virginia McGinnis told Bobbie or the police about the engagement? And sure, it was *possible* that someone could buy insurance and have the beneficiary die the next day. But the odds were dead against it happening to a "fiancé-to-be" alone at a cliff edge with the people who stood to profit from her death. The whole thing just didn't screw together all that tightly.

The developed photos, fifteen in all, arrived the next day. Keeney took them home and examined them over a cup of coffee and a Macanudo cigar. Daytime hours of meeting with clients hoping to build empires or wriggle through the tax code left no time for *pro bono* work. But at home in his wood-paneled study after Christian was asleep, he could give himself over to Bobbie's case.

He spread out the photos using the disc numbers for sequence and went over each shot as if it were captioned "What's wrong with this picture?" Each one of the fifteen shots, he sensed, was a mute witness. Properly understood, the entire sequence might add up to a "script" or storyline, one that began with the McGinnises' drive up the coast and ended with Deana's death.

At first glance, their very blandness seemed to corroborate Virginia's story about a sight-seeing trip that ended in tragedy.

Photos 1 and 2 were purely scenic: the view down a jagged precipice to a pebble-strewn beach, a road-cut winding around brown-grassed hills. Shots 3 and 4 were both full-length portraits of Deana looking happy and relaxed in jeans, blue pumps, and sunglasses. Was it merely by chance that the photos included Deana's high heels? Keeney wondered. Probably. And there was the same vague, eager smile he had seen in the family photo at Bobbie's.

Something about Photo 5 gave Keeney pause. He couldn't say precisely why, but it bothered him. Shot through a car windshield, it showed a heavyset man and woman—presumably the McGinnises—trudging toward a line of evenly spaced boulders at a cliff edge. Virginia, stringy-haired and overweight, wore a dark-colored pair of polyester stretch pants, a loose-fitting windbreaker, and a yellow scarf tied around her head. B.J., seen from the rear, had a paunchy, squarish stature, but given the camera angle it was hard to make out much else.

The McGinnises looked like perfectly ordinary working-class folk. They could have hailed from any trailer park or little one-family home in the country. They certainly didn't fit Keeney's idea of a pair of crooks. Still, the sloppily framed picture bothered him.

He slid Photo 5 off to one side of his desk.

Photo 6 was a close-up of Deana and B.J., who looked a little like Wayne Newton, with a trim silver-brown mustache and square, metal-rimmed glasses. They smiled for the camera, the Pacific Ocean and cliffs of Big Sur spreading across the background. Deana leaned her head against B.J.'s shoulder. Affectionately? Sleepily? It was hard to tell. B.J.'s arm curled around her shoulders. Keeney slid Photo 6 over to join number 5 on the corner of his desk.

The next group of pictures, 7 through 10, were all long shots of B.J. and Deana standing in various poses in front of still more cliffs and rocks. Out-of-focus and too-distant, none of them seemed particularly revealing.

Then came Photo 11.

Shot from behind, it showed B.J. standing beside Deana at a cliff edge, the bluffs of Big Sur falling away to the sea. B.J.'s right arm hovered at Deana's back and the square shape of his shoulder obscured the bulk of her body. But Deana seemed to be looking down at the precipice.

Photo 11 went to one side, with 5 and 6.

The last four photos, once more, were scenic: grassy knolls, wind-worn hillsides, and the broad, gray Pacific. In the final frame, the view angled down over a ledge, showing a pebbled beach hundreds of feet below.

Superficially, it all supported the gist of Dave Dungan's report and the McGinnises' story. Deana probably had gotten engaged to Coates without telling Bobbie. That was hardly surprising, given their testy relationship. Then, while Coates was in jail, Virginia bought her future daughter-in-law a life-insurance policy. The next day, they took a trip to visit relatives. Along the way, Deana took some Elavil—maybe she was a pill-popper and raided the McGinnises' medicine chest. Woozy and unsteady, she tripped and fell. It all makes sense, he repeated to himself.

The next day, Keeney sent Photos 5, 6, and 11 back to the lab for enlargement. He had the scene of B.J. and Deana at the cliff edge blown up to poster size.

Enlarged, the shot of the McGinnises in Photo 5 trudging toward the cliff became so grainy that the couple dissolved into a field of random colored dots. It was just a badly framed, badly lit photo, now rendered even less readable by enlargement. The only unusual thing, Keeney realized, was that it must have been taken from inside the car *by Deana.*

But why would she take a photo of two people's backsides, walking away? Perhaps Deana suddenly came to suspect the McGinnises. They're driving up the coast, and she starts to feel that things aren't right. Had she tried to leave some sort of message—her fingerprint—and caught her killers the one moment their backs were turned?

That was possible, he decided, but a little farfetched. Deana might also have been playing with the camera and it just went off.

Photo 6 also remained ambiguous, even when blown up. Deana leaned her head against B.J.'s shoulder. B.J., with his pale Wayne Newton face smiling from behind a pair of square glasses, looked more vacant and complacent than sinister. Deana's face, on the other hand, seemed puffy and her posture slumped. The eager expression in the full-length shots taken earlier in the day had changed. At some time between the first portrait and this shot, Keeney decided, the Elavil had kicked in.

The moment he looked at Photo 11, Keeney sensed he had come across some important evidence. In poster size, the scene became frighteningly alive. It was as if a missing witness had stepped forward. When he eventually showed it to Bobbie, he could see the blood drain from her face as she took in its meaning.

Deana and B.J. stood at the edge of the turnout under a gray sky, their figures almost blurred into the background of brown-gray cliffs to the north. Deana appeared anything but relaxed. The toes of her blue high-heeled shoes pointed straight between B.J.'s heels, her feet twisted parallel to her shoulders. Her knees were locked. And her head no longer seemed to be simply looking downward. It was slightly blurred, as if it was moving, or, more precisely, *turning* to look at the precipice that yawned at her feet.

B.J. seemed to be glancing over his right shoulder toward a section of Highway 1 to the north. His right arm pressed against Deana's back, while the other was pulling out of his pants pocket. Both his legs, in contrast to Deana's, unmistakably bent forward. The left knee was cocked at about fifteen degrees, the right at about thirty. He was moving toward the edge.

Keeney imagined a caption: *"Deana knows."*

But when he showed the photos to Bobbie Roberts at B & A, he urged caution. Over the weeks since the morning they met at church, Keeney had come to recognize his client's mood swings. Some days she complained about depressions that sent her retreating into nights of dreamless sleep. The moment her dinner ended, she said, she lay down and fell unconscious until morning. Other days, especially when she talked with her relatives in Lexington and Frankfort, anger boiled up inside her until her hands shook. The insurance policy, they said, was more than enough proof. They wanted to settle the whole thing "Kentucky-style"—with a posse and a gun.

Keeney did his best to comfort Bobbie. He was still getting used to the notion of counseling a flesh-and-blood client. And all he had against the McGinnises, really, were suspicions.

"Remember, Bobbie, Virginia told the sheriff's deputy that she would send him the disc of film taken at the cliff. We don't know for sure that *this* disc was taken where Deana fell. The pictures prove only that Deana and B.J. stood near a cliff edge. That much, the McGinnises themselves reported to the police on day one."

Bobbie nodded her agreement. They mustn't jump to conclusions. But as they walked to the elevators and Keeney said he'd be back in touch, they both sensed the pieces of the puzzle quietly falling into place.

That evening, Keeney headed back to Hill Road, the elegant street in his Castlewood neighborhood, to be with Christian. For once, he had made it out of the office before 6:30. Tonight, father and son would change into sweat suits, play ball, maybe dig some holes for tulip bulbs in the lawn, then fix supper. And he would send the maid home early. Keeney wanted to see Wynn, but he needed time alone with Christian.

As he turned off the highway onto Hill Road, he watched the tall, square shape of his house drawing near. Humid August weather had coaxed out every leaf to its lushest late-summer fullness. The Japanese thread-leaf maples cast a red-green shade across the swath of lawn fronting the street, a canopy of darkness broken by the yellow glow of dining room lights through the front windows. He imagined where the tulips might go. He looked closer. A white ghostly form seemed to be dancing there, twirling in and out of the light. It floated, then dove. Light. Dark. Lonely and hollow.

As Keeney eased his car into the driveway, the ghost swept toward him. Christian ran out of the shadows, his arms flapping in an oversized white T-shirt that billowed like a sail. He was a serious boy, dark-eyed, slim, and given to moodiness. He reminded his father of himself. Watching Christian's shape passing through the shadows, Keeney felt a flutter of fear. For an instant again, the leaping figure seemed a hallucination. How easily it could dissolve into the shade and be gone forever, a life withdrawn as swiftly and mysteriously as it had been given.

Then Christian was banging on the car window and yelling, "Daddy, you're home! Can we play tee-ball?" My God, Keeney thought, what if they actually killed her? He pushed the thought from his mind, swung out of the car, and lifted his son over his head with a flourish.

CHAPTER 7

BE STRONG,
BE BEAUTIFUL

▼

That night, after Christian went to bed, Keeney was sorting through his mail. Among bills and envelopes that read, "Steven H. Keeney, you may have already won $10,000,000," was a Trinity College bulletin recruiting alumnae to help organize a twentieth reunion—still two years away. After an obligatory groan—*twenty years!*—he spotted his name in the first paragraph: "Steven Keeney came back as a corporate lawyer." His personal metamorphosis, apparently, was peculiar enough to merit top billing. A memory flashed across his mental screen, something he hadn't thought of in years.

August 1968. A sophomore at Trinity College—more importantly, a member of Students for a Democratic Society—Steven Keeney hitchhikes into downtown Chicago. Tanks and jeeps enmeshed in barbed wire patrol the streets while thousands of police and National Guardsmen, armed in full riot gear, hover at street corners, waiting for an excuse to spring into action. Later that day, Hubert Humphrey, the Democratic presidential candidate, would weep on national television as battalions of police clubbed crowds and spread clouds of tear gas through the Loop.

Like many people drawn to Chicago to be part of history in the making, Keeney came with little idea of what to do once he arrived, or even where to go. At college, he staged a sit-in to force the creation of a minority scholarship fund, and he wrote heated editorials for the college newspaper, one headlined SCREW THE PEPSI GENERATION. Hair down over his shoulders, and toting an oversized military greatcoat, he hit the pavement and fell into a march.

Within minutes, a squadron of police officers scooped him up along with a group of other "obvious" radicals. "You're busted, turkey," were the first and last words he heard on the Chicago streets.

At the precinct station house, one officer sprayed Mace in Keeney's eyes. "That's terrible," another smirked, "let me help you wash it off." He jammed Keeney's face into a toilet and started flushing.

The next thing Keeney knew, he was slammed into a crowded holding tank. He looked up and, in place of the hookers and junkies he expected, saw two familiar faces. In fact, they were more than familiar: Abbie Hoffmann and Tom Hayden, luminaries of the New Left.

The first light of dawn angled between the bars of the Cook County Jail windows as an all-night political discussion trailed off into preparation for arraignment. Criminal court proved to be the usual overcrowded assembly line, and an ACLU attorney handily disposed of the charges of Inciting to Riot, Resisting Arrest, and Disorderly Conduct lodged against the college boy. Keeney walked out of court a few hours later, exonerated and wondering when the next bus left for Connecticut.

Back in college, he fired off an article in the Abbie Hoffmann tradition, entitled "hot town. pigs in the streets." It closed with the rallying cry "Police lines cannot hold us much longer. Be strong. Be beautiful."

A few months later, the telephone rang in "Cabaret Voltaire," his Hartford dormitory. It was 7:00 A.M.

"Steven Keeney?" a male voice asked accusingly. "This is the FBI."

"Yeah, sure it is," he said, and promptly hung up.

Now president of SDS, Keeney was accustomed to getting calls at all times of the day or night, usually from students involved in some sort of civil disobedience. The last thing he needed was a crank on the line, first thing in the morning.

Five minutes later, the phone rang again. The same voice, now considerably less imposing and half an octave higher, said, "This is the FBI—really."

Keeney's next call was to the ACLU.

Inside the Hartford federal building, Keeney and his civil-rights attorney listened while an investigator in a G-man suit informed the student radical that he was being eyed for possible violations of a federal law prohibiting interstate travel for the purpose of inciting to riot.

Mafia dons are running drug rings and extortion rackets, Keeney remembered thinking, yet this agent has nothing better to do than to roust a pipe-smoking preppie out of bed. What is this, the McCarthy era?

It had been a circuitous route from the FBI's interrogation room (no formal charges were ever filed) to Barnett & Alagia's carpeted hallways. After college, Keeney earned a master's degree in theology in seminary, then worked as an investigative reporter before turning to law school. Armed with his law degree, he left behind his seditious politics and promptly began representing some of the country's most powerful corporations, swinging deals that he might have slandered in his college column. Yet even though he had changed from blue jeans to business suits, he clung privately to vestiges of his youthful idealism: He voted Democratic, served on the boards of charities, and rose early Sunday mornings to teach "The Bible in 'Five Easy Pieces.' "

At the time that Bobbie Roberts approached him in Fellowship Hall, Steven Keeney had been running the B & A fast track for seven years. In many ways, he was just carrying on the family tradition. His parents, Arthur and Virginia Keeney, were both examplars of professional accomplishment.

Arthur, a handsome man with the gaunt, silvered features of a southern aristocrat, was dean of the Medical School. Virginia, a woman many compared in beauty to Katharine Hepburn, practiced medicine while raising her family. After their three children were all safely embarked on careers, she went on to earn a second M.D. in psychiatry. She eventually became an associate professor at the University of Louisville Medical School. Together, she and her husband served on the boards of charitable, cultural, and professional organizations, participated in church functions, and each year garnered a professional award or two.

The same effortless rise to success was expected of their children, especially of their eldest, Steven Harris, the young marksman. In October 1966, he wrote in a column for the paper of his Philadelphia prep school, Chestnut Hill Academy, "The path has been marked and seems to have been cleared. All that remains is to run."

It was a world where murder for $35,000 in life insurance was all but unimaginable.

Keeney woke out of his reverie and looked at a growing stack of papers in the farthest corner of his study. Bobbie Roberts's case—notes of interviews, the photos, police files, correspondence—was beginning to look like a full-fledged piece of litigation. Who was going to pay for all the work that lay ahead?

His partners at B & A would not take kindly to an expensive boondoggle. They gave no points for volunteer work unless it might attract new business. Keeney knew all too well that B & A's founders took a positive pride in their full-time devotion to paying clients. He had scrupulously avoided mentioning the case at partners' meetings. He had even managed to squeeze in his *pro bono* private-eye work after five, when offices in Chicago and the West Coast were still open and B & A was quieting down. But as the odds of an accident at Big Sur diminished, the pressure to begin a major effort grew.

Especially since no one else seemed to be looking out for Bobbie Roberts. In the eyes of a Monterey cop, Deana was just an estranged navy wife ostensibly engaged to an ex-con. They surely had higher priority deaths to investigate. Mike Hatch, too, sent a clear signal when he had said that this was one of the smallest life-insurance claims of the year. Keeney sensed that everyone would do their job, but in lockstep.

The McGinnises might not even be guilty, he figured. But finding the truth would be worth every effort. It was an elemental question of right and wrong. Of accident or murder.

CHAPTER 8

OCCAM'S RAZOR

▼

Dr. Barbara Weakley-Jones sat in her ceramic and stainless-steel office at the Louisville Medical Examiner's. A chilly odor of alcohol and formaldehyde permeated the room. Framed photos of Dr. Weakley-Jones's children grinned up at her from the corner of her desktop. Alongside the family pictures lay a set of reports and glossy eight-by-ten photographs documenting each step of Deana Wild's autopsy. The materials had come via Steve Keeney, who now sat facing Weakley-Jones, waiting for her analysis.

Dr. Weakley-Jones herself didn't look the part of an assistant ME. With her frosted blond hair and clear blue eyes, the forty-three-year-old doctor came across more like a TV mom-around-the-corner: friendly, cheerful, even a little self-effacing. Yet at the time she met with Keeney to discuss Deana Wild's death, the neighborhood mother of two had cut open, examined, and opined upon the cause of death of more than three thousand "patients."

It had taken Keeney several weeks and half a dozen phone calls to wrest the autopsy photos from the coroner's vault. Sergeant Glen

Brown had regretfully stated that he could not release autopsy photos to anyone but law-enforcement personnel. Private attorneys and family members didn't qualify. But Keeney was not about to bow out that easily.

He called back and offered personally to deliver the photos to Assistant Medical Examiner Dr. Weakley-Jones, an official member of the Kentucky law-enforcement team. Sergeant Brown balked for a moment, then he agreed.

"Of course," Brown said cannily, "if the photos fall out of the envelope, you better count 'em to be sure none are missing."

"An attorney's got a duty to be thorough, Sergeant."

"Remind me to call you if I ever get arrested in Kentucky."

The pathologist at the Monterey Coroner's Office had used an entire roll of film to document Deana's autopsy: twenty-four color shots, one for each step of the process. They showed the body clothed, naked, then in various states of dissection. That and a few pages of police reports piled on Dr. Weakley-Jones' desk were all that remained of Deana Hubbard Wild.

Keeney apologized that he couldn't afford to pay the doctor for her time. Dr. Weakley-Jones laughed: "One more medical opinion won't kill *me.*" Macabre humor seemed to come with the territory.

She spread the photos across her blotter and went through them seriatim.

The photos showed Deana's body, dressed in blue, lying on the coroner's dark autopsy table. A few scrapes and bruises were visible on her hands and feet. Blood matted her hair and stained her face. A stocking had torn around one of her heels.

"What I've tried to do," Weakley-Jones explained as she leaned forward and tapped a finger on the stack of photos, "is map out the injuries across the body and see if any patterns suggest themselves. The first thing that jumped out at me was that most of the abrasions and contusions she suffered are on her *right* side. In fact, if you look closely at the photos, you can see linear scrape marks. It looks to me like she slid down the cliff, almost like she was limp. She certainly didn't do a swan dive."

"But it was a four-hundred-foot cliff," Keeney interjected. "Even if she had taken a drug, she had to be grabbing at anything to hold on to, struggling for her life."

"Sure, she fell, all right. But remember, the *only* fatal injury out of the sixteen or so she suffered is that blow to the head. She might have hit her head on a rock just as she went over the edge. But she might just as easily have *been hit,* maybe with a blunt object, then thrown. After that, she could have slid down. That would account for both the single head injury and the linear lacerations.

"If you really want to get your imagination working," she said, looking as if she had just noticed a mistake in a grocery bill, "take a close look at these."

Keeney picked up two photos showing black-and-blue marks covering each of Deana's swollen hands.

"Those hematomas are all over the *backs* of her hands, yet as far as I can tell there's nothing on the palms," Weakley-Jones went on. "Nobody bothered to photo the palmar injuries, so they're either not present or unremarkable. But if you were trying to catch hold of a rock, a tree, anything to stop your fall, wouldn't you grab with an open palm?"

Keeney nodded. Sure, I would. It was one more fact that didn't jibe with the accident scenario.

"The *lack* of injuries suggests she probably slid the whole way down," Weakley-Jones said. "But it's just the beginning. Her fingernails—false nails, by the way—are all broken off. How? you might ask."

Keeney waited for an answer.

"Okay." The doctor leaned back, pulled up the sleeves of her lab coat, and started boxing the air with her fists. "Imagine a girl fighting for her life at a cliffside. She's hitting the people who want to push her over. That doesn't work—they're too strong. So she starts clawing. The black-and-blue marks and the broken nails are classic defensive wounds. Or to get truly grisly"—her housewife's grin returned—"maybe the McGinnises stepped on the top of her hands as she clung to the cliff edge. Maybe her nails broke while she was clawing at the edge." She paused to let the image sink in. "Either way, they're not the sorts of injuries I'd expect in a simple slip off the edge."

"So overall, what's your opinion? Is this an accident? I keep trying to convince myself it is."

"Given the timing of the insurance policy, and these injuries, I'd be seriously thinking about homicide. But based on the physical evidence alone—the path reports and the police reports—it's just not possible to reach a definite conclusion one way or the other. There's too much missing: scene photos, fall path, fingernail shreds and scrapings. There's not even a good clean picture of the fatal injury. And if you're asking me would I go out and arrest these people, that's not my area. You might want to get the clothes the McGinnises wore that day. Look for rips and tears, even blood if they clocked her over the head. It's been a long time, but sometimes criminals can be a combination of incredibly canny and incredibly dumb.

"By the way," she added, shaking her head, "it's a shame the pathologist didn't quantify the Elavil."

"That's unanimous." Keeney started to gather up the report and the photos.

"One more thing," she said. "I spoke to our chief medical examiner, George Nichols, about this case. He suggests you consult a forensic psychiatric expert, and I've gotta agree with him. If this is a murder, then Virginia McGinnis and her husband are seriously off the meter. Imagine actually doing something like that."

Keeney took Weakley-Jones's advice home with him. He tried to imagine the crime. Reconstructing Deana's last hours—writing death scripts—was late-night work, to be done after Christian fell asleep and the lights in the Castlewood neighborhood blinked out like so many fireflies. Keeney sat at his desk, surrounded by computer equipment and shelves of hardbound volumes, and tried out the various scenarios of Deana's death, testing each one against the law of Occam's razor. The law was paramount among the principles of scientific analysis his father had drummed into him. The rule of Occam's razor states that the most likely theory is the simplest one that encompasses, or explains, the greatest number of facts. Occam's razor, Dr. Keeney said, cuts away everything superfluous.

Steve kept juggling the facts to make the accident scenario work, but there were too many anomalies, and the number kept growing. After his meeting with Dr. Weakley-Jones, he now realized he could no longer avoid writing the murder script. He lined up the data on the screen, cutting and pasting all the available facts:

Deana arrives in San Diego in September. That fall she breaks up with her husband and meets James Coates, out on parole. Coates brings her home. Then he violates parole and is hauled back to prison. The McGinnises realize that Deana is an ideal victim: a naïve girl estranged from husband and family, alone in the world, unemployed and dependent. They keep her on as a guest. On April 1, they buy life insurance on her using a bogus engagement to Coates as a pretext. The cover story is buying insurance for B.J. "We're going to the insurance agent anyway. Come on along." Deana, with her 85 IQ, gets talked into signing. The next day, the McGinnises take her up the coast, looking for a remote turnoff. They probably know the road from past visits to the same San Francisco relatives. Virginia takes care to include Deana's high heels in two snapshots of the girl in case the shoes get lost in the fall. At some point they slip Deana some Elavil, perhaps in a Coke or a milk shake, or they tell her it's good for motion sickness. Once the drug kicks in hard, Virginia suggests another stop to take pictures. They pull over. Deana feels something is wrong. She snaps Photo 5 the moment their backs are turned. Virginia comes back for the camera and uses it to lure Deana to the cliff edge, after they're sure its steep enough. The Elavil keeps Deana in a fog. Dizzy, unsteady on her feet, she leans on B.J. and smiles sleepily at the camera, hoping everything will be all right. Photo 6. Then, they wander up to the edge. Virginia keeps shooting. B.J. checks the road for traffic, Virginia looks through the lens to make sure no one is watching. She snaps Photo 11. Then B.J. gives Deana one quick shove. Even in her drugged state, Deana recovers her balance. Adrenaline kicks in. Her hands become bruised from punching; her nails snap. One shoe slips off, her stocking heel tears. B.J. yells to Virginia for help: The girl is too much for him. Virginia picks up a rock or a flashlight and smacks Deana over the head. The girl's body slides limply down the cliffside. Injuries from being pushed off a cliff and falling accidentally are nearly impossible to tell apart. The police investigate briefly and move on. Virginia moves to cash in on the policy.

Keeney leaned back from the glowing computer screen. The script fit. It didn't really answer why Deana, a married woman, agreed to name Coates as her fiancé. Nor did it show precisely how Virginia's name ended up on the policy or how Deana came to take the Elavil. But it explained every other known fact.

Among Detective Donald Herbert Smythe's first calls was one to Steven Keeney. It seemed to presage good news. The man sounded tough, his voice a good octave lower than the average cop's. Better still, he sounded concerned. Smythe, a sixteen-year member of the force who had been hiking up and down the Big Sur cliffs for years, had just finished reading the file on Deana's death.

"Right away," Smythe said, "the McGinnises' story sounded hinky. Sure, people fall from Big Sur lookouts, but only when they try some stunt like climbing partway down and posing on one leg like a hood ornament. Nobody falls from the top without making a sound—even if only the sound of their bodies hitting the rocks."

Smythe said that before he could pitch the case to the local DA, however, he needed as many incriminating details as he could pull together.

Keeney jumped at the chance to pitch in.

On August 25, he sent Smythe a five-page single-spaced letter, copies of the cliffside photographs, and a summary of Dr. Weakley-Jones's opinions, all intended to spur the Monterey Sheriff's and District Attorney's offices into action. Keeney knew that any prosecutor would need a good deal more evidence before filing charges, but this was just the beginning.

He already had the next step mapped out.

CHAPTER 9

WORD FOR WORD

▼

"Bobbie, there's something you can do to help push the case forward. Of course, it may be more than you're up to at the moment."
Keeney's voice trailed off and the line went quiet.

He knew it was a bad time to call. Recently, Bobbie told him, she
had dreamed of her daughter plummeting off a cliff, the sea lions
braying up at two silhouettes at the ledge. Just three days earlier, he
had sent off his letter to Detective Donald Smythe. Bobbie must
surely have received her copy by now. Reading the facts all laid out
in coldly antiseptic terms surely could not have soothed her.

"I don't know." Her answer came hesitantly. "It's not a real good
time for me right now. My daughter Jane and I are doing the best
we can, but—it's just hard, that's all." At times, Keeney thought,
suffering could become a disfiguring scar, something easy to sympa-
thize with but no less painful to behold. He worried that this next
"assignment" would push Bobbie too far.

"You know, Bobbie, I wouldn't be troubling you if I didn't honestly think this could answer a lot of questions. I want you to call
Virginia and tape the conversation."

She sighed. A sound of gathering resolve. Keeney went on. "This case is going to come down to details. A tape will allow us to go back over what was said and do a cross-check, inch by inch. If Virginia's telling the truth, then nobody's harmed. If she's lying, we'll have the start of a body of evidence. Either way, you'll learn her story first-hand. And this might give Detective Smythe the evidence he needs."

"Isn't that illegal?" Bobbie asked.

"Not in Kentucky," Keeney said. "We'll worry about California later."

"If you think it'll help, Mr. Keeney, I'll do it. I can generally talk," she laughed. "That's my profession."

September 1, 1987. Evening. Keeney and Bobbie Roberts sat in the living room of Bobbie's new home. She had unloaded the Fincastle house in a quick sale, a thousand dollars cash down, the balance due over the next twenty-four months. Even at the time, Bobbie knew she might have negotiated a better deal, but she had to get out. Nightmares were bad enough without waking to a home haunted with memories.

Her new condo occupied the first floor in a sprawling complex of brick buildings, close to her school and downtown Louisville. It was usually busy: a place where she saw people every time she came and went. The condo itself, two bedrooms, hospital-white throughout, and with a large living room that looked out on a stand of pine trees, was the kind of comfortable home a schoolteacher could afford in the inexpensive Kentucky housing market.

Keeney sat across from Bobbie in a large wing-backed chair, and sipped coffee from his tall-boy cup. His pastel-striped shirt and three-piece Tasmanian wool suit had, as usual, made it through the day unwrinkled. Bobbie sat perched on the middle cushion of the same floral sofa he recalled from her Fincastle living room.

Keeney looked closely at her face. He was pretty sure he sensed a steel core beneath that gentle feminine exterior. She would do all right, he thought.

Bobbie Roberts dialed the McGinnis residence in Chula Vista, California. Keeney listened on the phone extension, a yellow note-pad balanced on one creased trouser leg.

"Hello?" a woman's voice answered.

"Virginia?"

"Yes."

Bobbie put her hand over the mouthpiece, whispered, "It's her."
Keeney signaled her to start talking.

"Hi, this is Bobbie, in Louisville, Kentucky. How are you doing? You said I could call you anytime."

"Oh, yes. Well, pretty good. How are you?"

"Well, sometimes good, sometimes bad. You know how that is after you lose a daughter." Bobbie leaned on the last phrase. The connection between Deana's death and the strange death of Virginia's own child had been gnawing at her.

"Yeah, I've been there, so . . . I can't say the hurt will ever go away."

Keeney was surprised at Virginia's voice. It was lighter and more feminine than he had expected, and it lilted at the end of sentences.

"No, I don't think it will. I think as time goes on, I miss her more. I think the thing I miss about her is that I want her to come home so I can yell at her a little bit," Bobbie joked nervously. "I'm just taking you up on your invitation."

"Oh, great," Virginia chimed back.

"You had told me I could call you, you know, anytime, and we could talk about it. I think when we talked initially, I was so numb that I just wanted to hear you tell me again maybe something she said about me or her sister and . . ."

Bobbie looked over at Keeney—Virginia wasn't talking. He put down his pen and circled his hand in the air: Keep going.

Questions started to spill out at random. "Ummm . . . tell me something she said about me or her sister. Start with whatever you can think about really, that, you know, can help me. The day of the fall, did she spend the night with you before she fell? Or . . . do you remember?"

"Yes, she was staying here," Virginia replied cheerily.

"Do you know how long she'd been staying with you?"

"She was here, I can't even remember now really. She had been here for several days, anyway."

Another dead-end answer. Bobbie began worrying whether the woman suspected she was being taped.

"Did she talk about me or her sister or do you remember anything she might have said about us?" Bobbie thought the question sounded absurd; she felt she was losing her grip—maybe she wasn't up to undercover work, after all.

"Well, basically, she said she wanted her sister to come out after school was over, and she thought you might come out, too."

That afternoon, Keeney had coached Bobbie. "Just get her talking, ask open-ended questions."

"What will I say if she asks, 'Are you taping this call?'"

"She won't ask if you don't give her cause," Keeney had said. "If it was an accident, it will all come out naturally. Just start out general and leave the details for last, the Elavil and especially the insurance. A tip-off that you're suspicious and know facts she didn't tell the police could shut down Virginia in a heartbeat. Just assume she's telling the truth, and this is the talk with her you've always wanted."

Bobbie remembered the advice but continued to worry. If she kept asking questions one after another like a police detective, wouldn't Virginia slam down the receiver?

"Well, I had planned on coming out," she pressed on. "Is there anything else that you can tell me? How did she meet Jimmy, for example?"

"She met him through some other people that he knew. I did not know them. He brought her home a couple of different times. As I said before, she literally did not have anyplace to stay. He didn't want to see her turned out on the street."

Bobbie asked whether Virginia still had any boxes of Deana's things. The blithe voice volunteered that she still had "everything," even "the little black bikini" she bought Deana. Bobbie said she'd mail twenty dollars to cover the costs, if Virginia would ship the things home. Virginia said she'd be happy to. Then Bobbie abruptly shifted the subject.

"Well, I'm trying to get in my mind exactly, you know, when she fell and everything. Did you hear anything as she turned around? I mean, you know—" Bobbie cut herself off self-consciously.

"We never heard a sound," Virginia lilted. "We were up a little bit from where the car was parked. The car was parked at a pull-over and we had walked up a ways to take some pictures of the old original brickwork along the road."

"Deana—was she that anxious to stop along the way? I mean, how many times did you stop?"

"I—I'll say that we stopped probably three or four different times. . . . An hour to an hour and a half previously, we had stopped and she had eaten."

That would be about 3:00 P.M., Keeney calculated. Why so late? That's a long drive from San Diego on an empty stomach. Of course, an empty stomach ingests drugs faster.

The conversation threatened to stall again. Bobbie searched for a way to draw things out. Keeney drew more circles in the air: Keep Virginia talking.

"What did she eat? Do you remember?"

"Yeah," Virginia said. "She had a hamburger and french fries . . ."

"Did she drive?" Bobbie blurted out. "Did Deana drive, or . . . ?"

"No, she wanted to gawk and look. She would go, 'Oh, look! Look! Look!' And then periodically, the sun would break through and make small rainbows and that would fascinate her." Virginia carefully drew out the syllables of *periodically* and *fascinate*. She sounded proud of her vocabulary.

"Oh. Sure." Bobbie choked on the words.

"But she was excited about going up to San Francisco and going up to Joanie, my husband's sister, and brother-in-law. They live just north of San Francisco. That was her first time to meet them."

"It must have been a shock to them when you guys didn't show up."

Keeney nodded his approval. Bobbie began to recover her composure.

"Well, we called them and explained initially what had happened. I did not want to stay in Monterey that night, but the, uh, everyone insisted that we stay because of everything that had happened. Then we turned around and went home."

The next thing Bobbie knew, Virginia began describing Deana's plans for the future. At one point, they had gone to get a brochure on nursing school, Virginia said. Keeney thought the idea of a high school dropout with an 85 IQ working as a nurse sounded absurd. But, he supposed, it was possible.

"I always thought Deana would have made a terrific nurse because she was such a caring person," Bobbie sighed.

"Yeah."

"Did you think that, too?"

"Absolutely. And one thing we both stressed to her was that if that was the field she was going to get into, she should not become emotionally involved. She could have lots of empathy for the patients, but not become totally overwhelmed with sympathy. I said it could be very rewarding and at times extremely discouraging. I said it's easier said than done, not becoming emotionally involved. I said you almost have to put up that shield for your own self-preservation."

Bobbie saw an opening, and her questions spilled out. "Is that kind of what you did when your daughter died? Can you tell me anything about that, and how you got over it and what did you do, what did you do with her things, and what were the circumstances? Is there anything that's similar here? I mean, history does repeat itself."

Keeney checked the tape recorder, took a swig of coffee, and went back to scrawling notes.

"Well, Cynthia was three, she would have been four, except she died in December."

"Why?"

"She wanted a ride on her pony. And when we were in Louisville, we had a couple of riding horses on a little horse farm. And the boys essentially took care of the horses. And it was a cold, windy day and I normally had just a sweater on when I went out to catch Sugar. And I couldn't get a hold of him and I don't know if it was because the wind was blowing and making the coat move or what. And he kept dancing away from me and finally she said, 'Mommy, I'm cold.' And I said, 'Well, honey, go on in the barn and get out of the wind.' And there was a small garden tractor there.

"Well, to make a long story short, she climbed up on top of the tractor, and the kids had taken gardener twine and pitched it up over the rafters, and she got tangled up in it and hung herself."

Keeney wrote a phrase and underlined it: *"Daughter hanged."*

"Oh my God!" Bobbie said. The line went quiet again.

Keeney mimed a question: "When?"

"When did that happen, what year was it?" Bobbie picked up. "In '72."

"And is that why you more or less ran away to California? To get away from the memories?"

"Initially, I lived in California. And my husband died in '74."

"This was Cynthia's father?"

"Yes. He had inoperable cancer, and . . ."

"Life sure does kick us around, doesn't it?"

"There was a lot of blaming myself when Cynthia died."

"Well, how could you blame yourself for that?"

"Well, what if I, well . . . well . . . what if I'd said, 'We'll get a ride on the pony after the boys come home'? Or if I hadn't told her to go in the barn, I mean . . .'" Virginia stumbled over her words, groping for an answer. "It's very easy, very natural to sit back and say, 'Well, what I could have done, what I would have done, what I should have done differently.' And essentially, you can beat yourself to death with a guilty conscience."

"That's true."

"And what we finally ended up doing with her things was, we called the church, and I wanted everything to be cordial and friendly, because she was the only granddaughter. And she had lots of material things, most of which we turned over to her grandfather and the children. And, um, it was something very hard to get over."

"Well, have you heard from Deana's husband? You never heard from Jay?"

"Nope."

"Well, I was just wondering when she came to live with you, did she bring her things with her like maybe a TV?"

"Oh, no, she brought only the clothes she had on her back. In fact, she said that they were never legally married. I don't know."

"Oh that's not true. They were indeed," Bobbie protested, then quickly recovered her temper. "Are there, do you have any other photos of when Deana fell? Is there anything else?"

"No, only what was in the camera, the film I sent."

"Okay, what about, you know, the photos that you did send? Where were those? Did you say . . . what did you say when those were taken and how were they taken?" Bobbie twined the phone cord around her fingers. "I mean, was that where she fell? Tell me."

Virginia paused. Bobbie and Keeney looked at one another nervously. Were they being too insistent, too obviously probing? They waited to see if she would hang up.

"Some of them were," she said, breaking the long-distance static.

"Oh, some of them were where she fell?"

"Yes."

One more scene in the murder script fell into place. Until now, Keeney had left open the possibility that Virginia's photos were not shot at Seal Beach. But in one word, Virginia formed the necessary tie between Photo 11 and the site of Deana's death.

"I think I took the last one—I'm trying to remember, anyway—in that roll of film. And, because the wind had picked up and it started to get cloudy again, and, ah, we had initially been looking at the seals, listening to the sea lions roar, on that dismal day. I think, if I'm not mistaken, it's called, the place was Seal Rock or Seal Point Lookout. I think it was Seal Rock. . . ."

Virginia veered off into safer territory. She claimed they had taken Deana to Mexico, then launched into how she and B.J. wanted to build a house down there by the beach, except Americans couldn't buy land. They were even thinking of going to Lake Tahoe after San Francisco. "Deana was excited in general about going different places," Virginia said. "They had magical, mystical qualities."

Bobbie asked how Virginia learned Deana had returned to California in February.

"She called when she was down there by Eighth Street. I think she took the trolley down from the airport. I went and picked her up."

"What did you say?"

"Initially, I said, 'What the hell are you doing back here?' She said, 'I couldn't take Louisville . . . there's nothing for me there.' "

"Is that what she said?"

"Her exact words." Virginia's voice turned suddenly gushy, yet tinged with blame. "She said she didn't have anything in common with any of the kids, and she said, I love my mother and I love my dad, but they have their own life, and California was home now."

"Did she mention Catherine, the housekeeper?"

"Oh, yes. How did Deana put it? 'She doesn't think I have any common sense.' And I started laughing. I said, 'Well, darling, it is very, very common.' I said, 'I know that at that time when my mother passed away, she didn't think I was capable at times of crossing the street by myself. But on the next breath, I was on the same plane as Einstein and then after that I was the village idiot.' I said that people, as they get older, I said they look upon you as the little kid and that you never outgrow it. I said it is really and truly a final blow. I said that sometimes you feel like you've been smothered by it. She said, 'Yeah, I guess so.' But she could see the pros and cons of it." Virginia laughed lightly.

"She could, you think?"

"Yes, she could—or at least she humored me enough to let me think that she could. Take your choice there," she trilled.

Keeney couldn't say why, but that insistent friendliness, and that string of *I saids,* bothered him. It had a practiced quality, flat and distant—like a condolence card from a mortician.

Bobbie's presence of mind began to give way as her feelings welled up. She burst out: "But . . . I miss her softness, ah God, I thought I would die the other—"

"She would walk by . . . she would walk by and give you a hug . . ." Virginia joined in.

"Wasn't she loving?" Bobbie asked.

Keeney hurriedly jotted a note, tore it off the pad, and slipped it in front of her eyes: "WHY DIDN'T SHE CALL?"

". . . or give you a kiss, say 'I love you,' " Virginia continued. "Just because—she was very, very affectionate."

"Yes, she was. I think she picked up one of my best qualities in that regard. The other morning, Janie spent the night—I s'pose it was Saturday night. And I walked in Sunday morning before going to church. And, Virginia, I saw her lying there and it looked so much like Deana, I could have just died, and I walked over and kissed her. It was just so emotional . . . it really was." Bobbie's voice fell and melted into tears.

Then, coming to, she straightened herself on the sofa. "Can you tell what happened next? When you called—you didn't call me that night. Why didn't you call me and say, 'Hey, Bobbie—'?"

"I did not have your number."

"Oh, you didn't? Because I thought . . . I always wondered why you didn't call me. I might have—could have taken it a little better from you than a damn stranger."

"I asked the coroner if I could have your number, and he said, 'No.' . . . I looked at him and I must have looked like a fool, and I said, 'I've got to try and call her mother.' "

"Sure."

"I said, 'That's my responsibility.' And he said that after he contacted you he would call me the next day and give me the phone number. But that's why I didn't call. I had no way of calling."

Keeney made a note. That was the kind of fact that could be pinned down.

"Well, what happened when the police came? What did they say to you?"

"I walked down to make the phone call. There was a small art shop there, a small art gallery, and they called. And the young lady went back up with me and it was maybe a half of a mile, if that far. And

B.J. had walked up the road a ways and went down as far as he dared to go. And he couldn't see anything, and the police came. They said for us to get in the car, they would handle it from there. And they finally went down with a block and tackle."

"What is that?"

"Off a winch off a truck. They recovered the body. Because we had no way of knowing how far she had fallen . . . because where we were located, we could not see. After that, everything's kind of blurry. I know that a TV reporter came and wanted an interview and I told them to go take a hike. I told them to show some consideration. We had no comment. And I think someone from UPI was there, and they wanted to know how it felt to have a friend meet a sudden end in a fall."

Keeney added the note "Find Reporter" to his list.

"What did you say?" Bobbie asked.

"I just looked at him, and B.J. said, 'Well, how do you *think* I feel?' Of course, they had no reply," she laughed. "Then we waited until they recovered the body, and they drove us to Monterey and gave the name to the coroner, and he didn't want anything basically other than our name, identification, phone number, and so on. And I asked for her purse so I could try to contact you, and he said I couldn't have it. And I said, 'But why?' And, of course, he told me that if only I had been thinking, I would have realized it was part of her personal property. But I wasn't functioning very well. I tried calling you when I got home, but there was no answer."

"Well, you're right, that's exactly right. This coroner called at twelve o'clock at night." Bobbie's voice turned plaintive. "It's the phone call no one ever wants if you live to be a thousand. Of course, my family came to Louisville and picked me up and took me back to Lexington. I was—well, anyway—"

"I can imagine. I know it's been a long, hard summer for you. . . ." Virginia described how she had taken Deana in and insisted the girl follow what she termed "the rules and regulations."

"I said that I'm a lot older than you are, and if I'm delayed some-place, I have the courtesy to call my husband and he does the same thing."

"Yeah," Bobbie replied. "Deana would agree to anything. Do you agree with that? She was so easy to get along with; she really was."

"Basically, she was very eager to please. All I could think of was a friendly puppy."

"Yes, thank you." Bobbie's voice stiffened; she forced a laugh.

"It's a poor analogy for someone," Virginia apologized.

Keeney's ears perked. The woman clearly sounded educated. And with her talk about building a house in Mexico, she even came off as well-to-do. A schooled, well-set lady didn't fit his imagined profile of someone who would kill a stranger for $35,000. That sort of behavior belonged to some sweaty-faced fugitive or a leering maniac. And then there was that unnerving syrupy voice.

The conversation drifted again. Bobbie explained that she was thinking of teaching abroad for a year. Virginia asked if there were support groups in Louisville; Bobbie said she hadn't attended any yet.

They had talked for close to forty minutes and were clearly winding down. "AUTOPSY/ELAVIL" Keeney wrote in block letters, and held up the pad.

"The autopsy said that Deana had Elavil in her body," Bobbie said, breaking the flow of conversation.

Keeney shook his head vigorously: too blunt, too dangerously leading a question. Bobbie ignored him.

"I just, I mean, it was something that rang out at me. What is Elavil, and did B.J. take that or did you take that? Where did she get that?"

A pause. Then Virginia prattled on.

"It was a prescription that was given to B.J. a long time ago for sleeping. It was a mood elevator, is what it was."

"Did he need that?"

"The doctor felt he needed it, but he had had surgery. This is some time ago, and the only thing I can think of is that they're extremely similar to Advil, if you know what they are."

Bobbie let her ramble.

"Well, it's on the order of aspirin, but they are a coated type of medication. And they're approximately the same color and I know that they were in the medicine cabinet. I don't know if she took one by mistake, but all it would do was make you more excited or hyper or more—it didn't make you sleepy; it just made you feel happier. I don't have a medical book right here at my fingertips to give you the side effects. But basically, they are a non-habit-forming drug used most generally on a short-term basis. There was a lot of it used when they were starting to take people off Valium and lithium. And as I say, it was not a depressant and it wasn't anything that would make you sleepy or drowsy. But some time ago, when the prescription was given, we had just put his mother in a nursing home and my own mother had just died. And he was going in for major surgery. I think it was a little bit much."

Keeney noticed Virginia repeating that Elavil didn't make you sleepy. Yet moments earlier she had said that B.J. took Elavil for a sleeping problem.

Virginia started describing Deana's daily routine in San Diego, but Bobbie broke in accusingly: "Did you worry at all about her having those fucking high heels on when she was near the cliff?"

"I didn't, um, because those were almost like a security blanket— there were those damn blue high heels. I mean, I did everything in the world to get her to get rid of those damn things. Number one, I didn't like them. Number two, one of the rubber taps had come off them. And she kept saying, 'But I love them. They're so comfortable.' I'd say, 'They're inappropriate.' To her, they were just part of her. . . . I had on a pair of boots that had a heel, and they had a broad base. . . . I'm sure you know the shoes I'm referring to. I think in one of those pictures I sent back, there is one with her sitting on a large rock where you can see them."

Keeney made another note. Virginia seemed to be confirming his suspicion that she took the photos of Deana to provide an explanation in case her shoes were somehow lost.

"Yes, yes, there is," Bobbie said, then stalled. She couldn't think of another question. She wasn't even sure she could go on at all. But now Virginia kept going, the lilt in her voice almost relentless.

"As I say, we never heard a sound. Period. We didn't hear any gasp; we didn't hear any—nothing. If it makes you feel any better or makes you feel worse—"

"Just talk, it doesn't matter." Bobbie sighed.

Keeney smiled. She had more stamina than he had ever imagined.

"The young lady that came up from the art gallery said that there was a lot of filling that had been put in there and it was considered unstable."

"How would she have known that? How would this girl have known that?" Bobbie repeated indignantly.

"Because she lived in the area."

"Oh, okay."

Keeney held up his yellow pad: "INSURANCE." Bobbie nodded.

"So, I've been working for the Board of Education for seventeen years, and I've filled out a lot of papers, you know, insurance papers. I really didn't understand that I had insurance on Deana, because it was a long time ago. And so, I got a letter from the board saying that I should fill out some papers for—and that I needed Deana's death certificate. And I called the Coroner's Office and they wouldn't let me have it. And they said that it was still under investigation."

A long pause followed. The static crackled. Bobbie waited. Keeney wondered if Virginia had quietly hung up the phone. Then she spoke up.

"Oh, really? Strange. Because, of course, we never heard anything. How strange." Another empty pause. "Uh, how long ago was this?"

"I don't know; haven't checked it out, you know. As a matter of fact, I got another letter just yesterday wanting me to apply for the insurance. And the Coroner's Office said no, that they wouldn't release the death certificate so I could get the insurance. And it was really strange because they said that, you know, Deana had taken out a life-insurance policy, which really threw me, you know. And, I don't know if you know about this or not. I just—help me out if you can. They said she had taken out one and—I don't know, can you help me out with that at all?"

In a different voice, metered and cautious, Virginia answered, "Yeah, she had taken out a life-insurance policy."

"She had?" Bobbie feigned surprise.

"At the time my husband had taken one out. Oh, I couldn't tell you how much it was, but it was a nominal sum."

"Well, okay."

"Uh, I think it was one of those things that matured at age something or other and it was, uh—I know B.J. had wanted to increase his insurance, uh, because he had quit the Veterans Administration; he'd taken out one. And she said, 'Well what about me, am I chopped liver?' And we laughed and said, 'Well, an insurance policy, what would you want with one at your age?' And the insurance agent agreed and said that, you know, at her age, that he wished someone had urged him to take one out. That it would have matured and made a nice tidy income. I think it was one of those things where you pay twenty years or something like that."

"Sure, okay," Bobbie said.

Keeney looked up and saw Bobbie's face flush. Virginia had never once mentioned the insurance on her own; now she tosses off a quick explanation. But the idea of Deana *wanting* life insurance made about as much sense as Deana wanting to study ancient Greek.

"Well, I know that I've imposed on you and I've taken up a lot of your time and so I'll let you go," Bobbie said.

Keeney signaled her to keep talking, but she shook her head.

"Have you sent the coroner a certified letter asking for the death certificate?"

"Have I done that? No, I haven't done that. It just makes me kind of sick to my stomach to even think about it."

"Well, why don't you have your brother do it? I don't know what else to suggest."

"I know. Would it be okay for me call you again if I need to?"

"Bobbie, you're more than welcome to call. It does help to talk to someone a lot of times. And, uh, I wish I had something positive to say except I guess time is a healer. It takes away the hurt."

"Oh, maybe I'll become involved with something. . . . Anyway, thank you for taking the time to talk to me."

"Okay, you take care now," Virginia cooed.

"Thanks."

"Bye-bye."

After Bobbie said a last "Good night," she fell back on the sofa. Keeney put down the extension line, looked up from his notepad, and smiled. "Bobbie, you did a great job. Nobody could ask for more." The words of praise floated past her.

"What could bring anyone to murder my beautiful child?" she said, half to herself. "I just can't understand how anyone could do such a thing."

"I wish I could tell you, Bobbie." Keeney turned to rewind the tape.

Driving home along the freeway that stretched from Bobbie's condo to his Castlewood neighborhood, Keeney replayed the conversation on the car tape deck. Virginia had certainly committed herself to some unlikely stories: The coroner telling her not to call Bobbie Roberts the night Deana died; nineteen-year-old Deana *wanting* life insurance; B.J. *increasing* insurance he had never owned. And there was the horrific story of how Virginia's own daughter died—an *accidental* hanging. Then came the remark about the Elavil and not having a "medical book" at her fingertips.

Her voice echoed in the car, that syrupy, lilting voice, all girlish sweetness, yet articulate and intelligent. At the same time, she sounded weirdly undisturbed by reliving the details of Deana's death with Bobbie Roberts, the girl's own mother.

Virginia did it, Keeney started thinking. *She did it.* The thought pulsed in his mind. Accident was no longer a possibility. This friendly, helpful woman in her fifties, who spoke about support groups and Lake Tahoe vacations and brochures for nursing school, had sent Deana screaming to her death. Did she smile as the girl went down, probably begging for her life, her fingernails tearing on the rock, wondering why her "friends" had betrayed her? Did she watch and laugh at the sight or turn her back—ever the lady—as B.J. did the dirty work? *She's gloating,* Keeney thought. *She knows we can't prove a thing. If we could, she and B.J. would already be in handcuffs. No, Virginia didn't miss a trick.*

But what chilled him more than any single fact or detail was how bloody *normal* she sounded. He'd probably think nothing of having her as a neighbor:

Hello, Mrs. McGinnis. Lovely day, isn't it?

Oh, yes. It's glorious. We're taking a houseguest up the coast for a scenic drive. She's never seen some of our most beautiful sights.

That sounds like a fine plan. Have a good day.

Was this the voice of evil? Did it really lie so close to home?

He pulled into his driveway and stayed in the car as the tape played through to the end. Tomorrow, he would start running down some hard facts.

CHAPTER 10

SIGNING HER OWN DEATH WARRANT

▼

Twelve-forty-five P.M. September 5, 1987. The crisp white table-cloth, mahogany wainscoting, and a four-course lunch catered by a black-tie staff were meant to create an atmosphere of ease for B & A's partners, an hour's respite from the pressures that loomed just outside the door. But Keeney was in no mood to relax.

"Our computers are late," he said without any pretense of the Kentucky gentility with which he treated clients. The comment was directed across the table to partner Jon Davis. A sandy-haired man in his forties, Davis appeared to be all but hiding behind a large silver candelabra.

Keeney kept up his complaint. "Every lawyer in this firm needs to have a desktop terminal with access to LEXIS and NEXIS, and that's just getting us out of the starting gate. We need on-line pleadings, interrogatories, motions, the latest O.A.G.'s tax opinions and E Mail. Jon, if we don't we're going to be left in the dust."

Davis helped himself to a glass of Montrachet. Between sips, he asked, "And who's going to foot the bill for these IBM racehorses?"

That was the final insult. The computers had been voted at the last general partners' meeting, and, in Keeney's estimation, if the firm was going to be able to compete with the big guns in New York City and Chicago they were a necessity. Let the partners think what they wanted, B & A had to prepare itself for twenty-first-century legal practice.

"Jon"—he tried to hold his colleague's eye as best he could through the candelabra bars—"you know as well as I do they'll pay for themselves. Besides, the whole deal was a lock."

"The figures aren't public yet, Steve." Davis kept his voice low and glanced furtively around the table. "Even among the senior partners. Let's just say this may not be the best year for new capital investments. As it is, we're reevaluating the Beechcraft. It's not like those flights out to farmer co-ops in East Pitchfork pay for themselves. And you know we're considering a new office."

Keeney wanted to smile and smooth this over, but his face reddened and his voice rose. "Jon, what in Sam Hill are you hinting at? Sell the plane, forget the new office deal. But for Pete's sake, we don't need to be moving bodies. We need to be moving information."

"Listen." Davis's face remained placid. "This just isn't the best time for the firm, cashwise."

"And what is that supposed to mean? We're talking fifty, maybe seventy grand, max."

"Not to worry, Steve. We haven't struck any reefs. Not yet, anyway. Just trimming the sails, that's all."

"Spare me," Keeney broke in, still talking too loudly but no longer caring. "Exactly who is 'trimming the sails,' anyhow? And what do you mean, 'Not yet'?"

"Easy does it. Just a short-term cash squeeze. You know that Stan Chauvin's a shoo-in for ABA prez. After the coronation, he's going to travel the world, make news, and money'll flow into the coffers like the Monongahela River. Those computers will be on our desks within a year, two tops. Meanwhile, just keep those time sheets coming. Full steam ahead." He raised his glass.

"Not with empty gas tanks," Keeney parried. "If we want to be rewarded, let's invest in our clients. Investing in 'traveling the world' is bull, and you know it." He stubbed out his cigar and went for the door.

"What's the rush?" Davis called after him.

"No rush. I just lost my appetite."

All the way back to his office, Keeney stewed. Each year at B & A had been more profitable than the one before. Bonuses and salaries swelled; the satellite offices doubled in size. He thought of the firm's most recent annual partners' meeting at the Breakers Hotel in Palm Beach. It had been wall-to-wall Dom Pérignon, mahimahi, and putting greens. Now they were balking at a few lousy PCs! This was the first he'd ever heard of cash being in short supply around the firm. Something was up and B & A's financial base was no doubt at the root of the problem. Keeney consoled himself with a favorite aphorism: "Every problem is an opportunity." But his brow creased as he muttered to himself, "I know what the problem is. Now, where's the opportunity?"

A quick look at his desk showed no shortage of starting places. Dozens of paying cases needed attention that afternoon, even that moment. Bobbie's phone call to Virginia McGinnis, too, had generated a long list of facts to run down and see if they jibed with reality.

Keeney had already called Don Smythe at the Sheriff's Office and learned that Virginia and B.J. stayed at the Day's Inn the night after the "accident." He asked Smythe to pull the telephone records for their room. If the McGinnises had really planned to visit relatives up north, then they would have at least called to explain why they weren't coming. He also ordered photos of all the available Elavil tablets from a pharmaceutical house to see whether they looked like Advil; and he placed a call to the local Monterey television station and UPI to track down any news footage from the death scene. The newsmen, however, told him that most of their film footage had been destroyed. He and Bobbie mailed off a letter to Virginia, asking her to please return Deana's belongings. They included twenty dollars to cover shipping. Sarah West, meanwhile, was assigned the task of investigating the "accidental hanging."

But that afternoon, after the partners' luncheon, a packet from Mike Hatch at the Life Claims Division of State Farm Insurance stared up at Keeney from atop the day's mail. It's about time, he thought. He glanced at a draft prospectus that needed to be vetted for Securities Act issues. But the envelope from State Farm was irresistible. "Giving Deana's insurance forms a quick once-over won't take more than half an hour," he rationalized. "And it'll help take my mind off firm politics."

He opened it and pulled out a sheaf of microfilmed papers:

Deana's insurance application and the policy. In all, it was a simple contract between Deana and State Farm, signed and paid for in full.

The face page of the policy bore the number 8,751,862. The number seemed more than just a means of identification. To State Farm, Deana's case was merely one of millions issued that year, no more than a flea on the back of a grizzly bear.

Below the number, in one sentence, the policy spelled out the basics of Whole Life Insurance: "State Farm Life Insurance Company will pay the policy proceeds to the beneficiary when due proof of the insured's death is received." The sole limitation concerned whether "the Insured dies by suicide while sane or by self-destruction while insane within 2 years from the issue date of the policy. . . ." Otherwise, death benefits were to be paid immediately.

Could Deana have killed herself? Keeney dismissed the idea as quickly as it arose: not without a note, probably not in the company of other people, and almost certainly not off a cliff. More than one expert in psychology had written that people, women in particular, dislike the idea of being disfigured in death. Besides, that kind of planning and forethought—buying insurance before flinging herself off a cliff—didn't fit the profile of a feckless young woman on the run from a troubled marriage. And the woozy smile in the photos at the cliff edge absolutely could not belong to a person preparing to plunge off a cliff in an act of "self-destruction." No, suicide was out.

One thing, however, seemed to be missing from the policy. The words *murder* and *homicide* were conspicuously absent. Murder, apparently, didn't cut off the death benefit.

A two-page Application for Life Insurance form, dated February 27, 1987, bore Deana's signature. She had signed the form in large rounded letters, typical high-school-girl penmanship: Deana Hubbard. Keeney wondered why she hadn't used her married name. It made the story about an engagement to James Coates all the more plausible.

The names of the beneficiaries, by contrast, were written in a crabbed, adult script: Primary: *James Coates—30—Fiancé;* Successor: *Virginia McGinnis—50—Mother-to-be;* Final: *Billie McGinnis—47—Father-to-be.* At least the agent hadn't actually used the term *fiancé-to-be,* Keeney noted. Of course, *Mother-to-be* did not look like business as usual on a life-insurance policy, either.

The rest of the document consisted of yes/no questions about medical history. She had checked the box that stated she had not "taken prescribed medication" in the last five years for any reason. Otherwise, Keeney read through each answer but found nothing remarkable. Deana seemed to be a perfectly healthy young woman.

A photocopy of Virginia's check for $68.10 payable to State Farm Insurance was appended to the last page. The check represented the first quarterly premium on the policy. It was drawn on the account of Virginia A. Rearden.

Why had Virginia used two last names? The fact was bothersome. Was she trying to avoid suspicion? But who would fail to realize that Virginia McGinnis and Virginia Rearden were the same person? Except, perhaps, a computer program or a drone in the Life Claims section. Still, someone who goes by two names just makes you wonder, Keeney thought.

Keeney held the check under his desk lamp. It was numbered 276, a low number, signaling a fairly new account. The signature was large and showy. The two *t*'s in State were crossed with a single bold slash, and the capital letters *V* and *R* towered above the lowercase ones. The writing looked entirely different from the squirrelly *Virginia McGinnis* penned in on the application.

He leaned back and tapped the check on his blotter. All the oddities in the application, the policy, and the check only spiraled out to more speculation. Really, he had to admit, it all looked terribly ordinary—except that the policy didn't list any of Deana's blood relatives and was paid for by a woman who used two last names, described herself as the "Mother-to-be," and lied to the cops.

Then he noticed the date in the upper-right-hand corner of the check, written in Virginia's flamboyant hand: *4-2 1987.* Thinking he had misread, he leaned forward and held the blurry microfilm copy under his desk lamp. The numbers stared back at him just the same: *4-2 1987.*

Virginia purchased the policy on April 1, April Fool's Day. That was strange enough. But April 2 was the day Deana stood at Seal Beach. The day she died. Could that date have been on Virginia's mind as she wrote out the check, in some revealing Freudian slip?

Keeney went to get some more coffee—the notion of the McGinnises insuring Deana made him ill. But still he knew that the evidence at hand didn't pass muster. Proving Deana's murder was turning out to be tantalizingly, frustratingly elusive, like chasing a silvery drop of mercury.

As he stalked down the hall, Pete Lazar, Keeney's Pendennis lunch connection, came up from behind and put a spidery hand on his shoulder.

"Hey, cowboy! What were you doing ducking out of lunch like that? You looked ready to kill. Not that you look a whole lot better now." He eyed Keeney. "You're still looking a little steamed, buddy. What's up?"

"Nothing to worry about, Pete." Keeney ignored the hand on his shoulder and kept walking. "Just a personal matter."

"Divorce got you running?" Lazar stopped and called after him. "Man, I know that can be real murder."

Keeney turned on his heel to answer, "You got that one right, Pete."

A few weeks later, Keeney sat in his office, listening to Detective Smythe's bass voice calling in from Monterey. "Your letter impressed everyone," he said, referring to Keeney's five-page point-by-point analysis of the case. "Impressed them enough to send me and my sergeant down to the McGinnises' home in Chula Vista for an interview."

"Well, Detective, what's the headline?" Keeney asked, sitting up at attention. "CRUEL COUPLE NABBED IN SAN DIEGO HIDEAWAY"?

"Not exactly, Steve." Smythe hedged. "In fact, kind of the opposite. They both said they were walking back to their car and, suddenly, Deana was gone. Neither one said they heard a thing. Same old story. And they both flat out *admitted* going to buy the insurance. They said they went in strictly for B.J., but the salesman had been able to sell Deana a policy. Also gave us the same line about Deana saying, 'What am I, chopped liver?' that they told your client on the tape. B.J. said that he never got his own policy, that he was turned down for health reasons, but Deana did get hers. I've gotta say, it all fits."

"Not as well as my scenario, Detective. I hear from State Farm that B.J. would've known he'd be turned down for health reasons. Now why would a man waste his time like that unless he had something else in mind?"

"You can't blame a guy for trying. Applying for life insurance isn't a criminal offense in California."

"Did you ask about the Elavil?" Keeney pressed, even as his hopes fell.

"Sure did," Smythe said smartly. He was obviously ready for that question. "There's news on two fronts there. First off, B.J. volunteered he had been taking the stuff. He showed me a prescription bottle in his name with maybe a dozen tabs left inside. It was refilled on February 20, 1987, for one hundred fifty-milligram tabs. B.J. says they were prescribed to help him sleep after his mother went to a nursing home." Keeney jotted down the date. One week before the insurance application.

"I offered them a lie-detector test. They said yes, then said they wanted to check with their attorney. That doesn't really prove a whole lot. Maybe more interesting is the report we just got from the Institute of Forensic Sciences. It's dated 8/31/87. We sent 'em a vial of Deana's urine from the coroner's refrigerator so they could quantify the Elavil in her system—just like you suggested."

"And?"

"Zippo. They didn't find any."

Keeney paused, puzzling out what could have gone wrong. The odds of Deana's urine *falsely* testing positive for a drug that B.J. had in his possession were astronomical.

"Don, that second test has got to be incorrect. Can't you send it back for a re-retest?"

Smythe let out a short whistle. "That's a tall order. Like I said, their story's fishy, but it hangs together better than some I've heard. Virginia told me she got cold and headed back to the car. B.J. followed. Next thing they knew, Deana was gone."

"I'd like to think they're telling the truth about this being an accident," Keeney said. "But I don't believe in coincidences; I believe in facts."

"The fact that they lied to Dave Dungan about the insurance policy is pretty damning," Smythe admitted. His sincerity came across even long distance, but Keeney also heard the voice of a cop juggling probably two dozen investigations. "But that's still not proof beyond a reasonable doubt they actually killed Deana. You know better than I do what a court of law is, Steve. I'll take it over to our DA, but I wouldn't expect them to jump all over it."

"How about the Day's Inn phone records?"

"I checked, and there's nothing. They didn't place any calls that night."

"You mean they just sat there in the room without calling their relatives?" Keeney asked.

"Maybe. Or they could've used a pay phone."

Keeney paused for a moment. "Let's keep at it," he said eventually. "Right now, I can't counsel my client that we know all we should."

Keeney put down the phone wondering, What am I missing here? I'm an amateur and I think the story stinks. Smythe's a pro and he's halfway to believing every word Virginia says.

Mac McCain's insurance agency in Chula Vista, California, is not much to look at. Set in a single-story, stucco storefront, the red letters stenciled on its floor-to-ceiling glass pane window read, MCCAIN INSURANCE. In Tijuana, it could pass for a bar or a pawnbroker's.

Inside, a secretary's reception desk greets visitors up front, a second desk occupies the middle of the room, and imitation-wood panels separate a small office at the rear. Mac McCain's insurance agency is, in its way, typical Chula Vista, a thin-walled, no-frills place, one that seems ready to blow away with the next dust storm or spontaneously combust in the southern heat.

Cleo "Mac" McCain had spent more than thirty years of his life in that office, and ten more than that as an insurance investigator. In 1958, Mac had struck out on his own in the then–frontier town of Chula Vista, California, a suburb within commuting distance of San Diego to the north and shooting distance of the Mexican border to the south. As San Diego grew from a rowdy prostitution-ridden naval base into the seventh-largest city in the United States, so did Chula Vista and, with it, Mac's business. Nineteen years later, Mac's son Art joined the trade and gradually assumed control of the small but stable family outfit. At the time Steven Keeney called, Mac McCain was wandering the office in a state of semi-retirement.

Art and Mac both got on the phone. The father-and-son team spoke with the upbeat Southern California patter of folks who have come south for the good life of sun, beautiful views, and endless freeways. For an instant, Keeney imagined this pair handing out life-insurance policies on fiancés like lollipops. Then again, he thought, they could be slick salesmen with one thing on their minds. But as it turned out, the transaction was not a simple matter of walk in, pay, leave with the policy. And the McCains were anything but happy about it.

Art was the first one from his office to deal with Virginia in person over Deana's insurance policy.

"She came in one day in February, around the eighteenth, along with Deana," Art said. "Mrs. McGinnis said she wanted to buy a life-insurance policy on Deana so the girl could get a visa to go down to Mexico."

"Mexico?" Keeney asked. "Are you sure?" Mexico would have been an ideal place to kill Deana, he thought. Crowded police stations and courtrooms all operating in Spanish. It seemed such an ideal place, in fact, it made murder at Big Sur *less* likely.

"I know it makes no sense," Art continued, "but that's what Mrs. McGinnis said. She said that to get the visa for Deana, they needed a Social Security number, and to get the Social Security number they needed a life-insurance policy. She even called a day or two later asking the same weird question. The idea was so far out there, I couldn't forget it. But we didn't bother making a note of it at the time."

"What exactly happened when Virginia and Deana came in?" Keeney asked.

"Nothing besides the Mexico story. After that, I told Virginia that we wouldn't even write a life policy without the insured herself showing us a Social Security number. Virginia said, 'Thank you,' and left. Just like that."

"Did Deana do any talking?"

"I don't think she said a word," Art said.

Mac dipped into the narrative: "A few days later, Virginia called back to ask more questions about getting life insurance, since the girl was going to marry her son James. I got on the phone and told her to bring them both in so each one could get a policy, but she said James already had plenty of insurance. I just happened to take the call. In fact, I didn't know until recently that she already had spoken with Art."

"Anyway," Art said, "on February 27, Virginia, Deana, and Billie Joe all came in together. Dad was away, so I asked what I could do for them. Virginia said that both Deana and Billie Joe wanted to take out life-insurance policies. I explained again that we still needed a Social Security number for Deana.

"This time, Virginia hands me a piece of paper with a Social Security number written on it. I agreed to write up an application for the girl, but decided right we were going to go nonbinding—basically send the application to State Farm for approval rather than seal the deal then and there. Dad and I had already agreed we wouldn't bind any more coverage on the McGinnises without approval from the top."

"Are you sure it was Virginia who asked for insurance and not Deana?" Keeney asked. There wasn't room for misinterpreting a few stray remarks.

"Sure I'm sure," Art said. "The girl didn't seem to pay much attention at all. But Virginia was quite the spokesman. She said right off the bat that Deana wanted a thirty-five-thousand-dollar policy. Deana just sat there until it came time to answer the questions about medical history. Afterward, I asked her who she wanted as beneficiaries.

"Virginia spoke up again and said her son James would be primary beneficiary, and she and B.J. would be the successors. Deana didn't say a word. To tell the truth, I even thought the girl might be a little slow upstairs. Right then I told Virginia we wouldn't take any money on the policy until our underwriter's office approved it, and so it wouldn't be in force until then. She said, okay. Next, we went through the same process with Billie Joe. We went nonbinding with him, too, even though she only wanted twenty-five thousand dollars on him. I told them we'd be back in touch as soon as we heard from our underwriters, but Dad and I hoped they'd never issue the policy."

"Why not?" Keeney asked.

"There were red flags all over. You usually have to go out and sell people life insurance," the veteran broker explained. "Almost nobody comes in off the street looking for it. And, of course, Deana was nineteen years old. Let's face it—nineteen-year-olds don't normally buy life insurance. And the fiancé, James Coates, didn't even come to the office.

"You know, in forty years I've never seen a situation where there was no reciprocal policy, where each fiancé didn't insure the other. Here, the insurance went in only one direction. We sent the applications off, but I drew a red flag on a memo to our regional manager. It said, 'Stan, please give me a call on this, it's important.' "

"And?"

"Stan called back and we discussed the situation. He said he'd pass the word to our underwriters."

"What was State Farm's reaction?" Keeney asked. "Did they send down an investigator?"

"They just went ahead and issued Deana's policy," Mac said.

Keeney thought he detected a note of bitterness. "Of course, B.J.'s was denied on medical grounds. That guy had so many problems, I'm surprised he's still alive. On top of everything else, he's impotent.

"Anyway, Deana's policy came in on March 31 and Art called the McGinnises. The very next day, Mrs. McGinnis and Deana showed up. I met them at the door and we went back to my office. I explained that they had the option of paying quarterly, semiannually, or annually. Virginia said she wanted to pay quarterly—the cheapest way to go—and then she wrote me a check. I started to hand the policy to Deana, but Mrs. McGinnis reached over and snatched it right out of my hand."

"Are you sure Deana didn't try to take it?" Keeney asked.

"Virginia just grabbed it, Mr. Keeney. But that's not the half of it. As she put it in her purse and stood up to leave, she asked, 'Now this is in force, right?' I said, 'Yes, ma'am. You've paid the premium and the policy is in force.' Then they left.

"But just a few seconds later, Mrs. McGinnis pokes her head back through the door. 'Does it cover accidental death?' she asked. I said it did, but not double indemnity. She said, 'Okay.' After that, she left."

Mac's words hit Keeney with a rush. Just keep asking questions, he coached himself.

"Mike Hatch tells me Virginia came back to your office to collect?"

"Maybe a week later, I had stepped out to do an errand," Mac said. "When I came back, there was Virginia, talking to my secretary. Her arm was in a cloth sling type of thing, like a baby diaper."

"You're positive?" Keeney pressed. That detail perfectly fit Dr. Weakley-Jones's scenario of Deana struggling for her life at the cliff edge.

"Heck, yes," Mac answered firmly. "A case like that doesn't come in every day. I remember asking how she got hurt. She said it was nothing. Just an old injury that flares up now and then.

"We went back to my office and she laid the policy on my desk and said, 'She's dead.' I said, 'You've gotta be kidding.'

"Then I asked how it happened.

"She told me they went to Big Sur. She and Mr. McGinnis walked on ahead; Deana was behind them. They missed her and went back to look for her. Mrs. McGinnis said, 'Next thing, we saw her down among the seals. She fell off a cliff.' I asked her to give me the names of the coroner and so forth, so we could go through the normal procedures. Then she said, 'I didn't realize police officers could be so cruel. They put us through the third degree.' Next thing, she asks, 'When do we get the check?' I told her we'd be sending her a claim form. She thanked me and left. Not a single tear. Just businesslike."

Keeney kept up with Mac's words, jotting down the vital details. "What did you think about Deana's death?" he finally asked.

"Well, this wasn't Virginia's first visit or her first claim," Mac said. "I first met her in December of '85 when she purchased a home-owner's policy on a house she owned with her mother at 1306 Calle Santiago. I've been her insurance man ever since, kind of kept up with her, her mother, and her husband. Around about October of '86, I removed her mother's name from the home insurance. Seems she'd passed away."

"Tell him about the past claims, Dad," Art piped in.

"I'm getting to it," Mac said. "You see, Mr. Keeney, Mike Hatch asked me to pull the dates together. On March 10, 1986, the McGin-nises claimed a one-thousand-one-hundred-and-sixty-nine-dollar windstorm loss under the home policy. On October 19, 1986, they claimed a nine-thousand-seventy-nine-dollar burglary loss. Two days later, they called in an eight-hundred-eighty-five-dollar water-damage loss. That October burglary was the really suspicious claim.

"She insured an eight-year-old Datsun pickup on October 13. Six days later, she came back and claimed her house had been burglar-ized and the truck stolen. The police eventually found the truck abandoned in a San Diego vacant lot. The odd thing was, the Datsun hadn't been stripped. Usually, when a car is stolen, a thief'll strip it and sell the parts. But the Datsun was just burned. The radio was still in and the car was sitting on all four tires, like someone had lit a can of gas in the front seat."

"It was weird," Art added, "but we still paid out on the truck, as well as the jewelry and stuff she said was taken from the home. Looking back, maybe we could've challenged the claim, but no one ever did. We just paid out."

"She had other claims, too, even before she came to see us," Mac went on.

"*Other* claims?" Keeney repeated, with an air of calm, covering disbelief.

"Right when she came to us in '85, State Farm's homeowner-policy computer turned up an address in the Palo Alto area. The house was insured both in Virginia's and her mother's names. It burned, too. Don't ask me why, but we paid up on that one, as well. To the tune of a hundred and twenty-five thousand dollars."

That evening at home, Keeney reviewed his notes of the McCains' interview. The story raised hairs on the back of his razor-trimmed neck. But there were problems. If the McGinnises always claimed on every policy, what did the McCains think would happen here? If they suspected murder, why didn't they just decline to write the policy? They must have seen it coming and passed the buck to State Farm. Small wonder Mike Hatch was keeping a low profile.

As he punched the new details into his computer file, building his "murder script," Keeney felt the McCains' story had cinched the legal issues. He couldn't remember a case where every detail pointed so unequivocally toward the same conclusion. Maybe the cops would find something exonerating Virginia, if they ever got around to executing a search warrant, but he doubted it. A rough chronology told the story in compelling terms:

> 2/11 (approx.)/87—Virginia calls the McCains asking about insurance for Deana
> 2/18/87—Virginia and Deana ask about insurance in person
> 2/20/87—B.J. refills Elavil prescription; Virginia calls the McCains again
> 2/27/87—Virginia bulldozes her way through Deana's insurance application
> 3/31/87—McCain calls, saying Deana's policy is in
> 4/1/87—Virginia pays for the policy
> 4/2/87—Deana dies
> 4/9 (approx.)/87—Virginia makes her claim

As Keeney read down the list of dates, he felt as if someone had finally loosened a belt from around his gut. He hadn't been suffering from delusions. These were the actions of a guilty party efficiently executing a well-planned murder.

CHAPTER 11

A LOUSY FREEZING DAY

▼

To Keeney's generally unflappable secretary, Sarah West, the odds of finding out anything about Virginia's daughter, Cynthia, seemed hopelessly stacked against her, but Keeney insisted she try. A week later, Sarah trooped into Keeney's office.

"It's no good, Mr. Keeney," she said, dropping a stack of notes on his desk. "Every place I could think of—the Coroner's Office, County Sheriff, Board of Health, even Child Protective Services— assured me that, as far as they knew, a little girl named Cynthia Elaine Rearden or McGinnis never lived in the Louisville area. I'm beginning to think Virginia just made her up."

"Virginia had the moxie to send Bobbie photos of Deana's last moments alive," Keeney agreed, ruminating aloud. "She certainly could be capable of concocting another lie just to divert suspicion from herself."

"Wait a minute," Sarah West said, her face brightening. "How about Coates, the same last name as Virginia's son James?"

"It's worth a shot," Keeney said, then reached for the phone.

Dora Kalprowski at the Jefferson County Coroner's Office answered the call in her wobbly voice. She put down the receiver for what seemed enough time to take lunch. When she returned, she said she had found a card on the case: "It reads, 'Cynthia Elaine Coates, 10105 Jefferson Hill Road, date of death 12-6-72.'" Keeney said he would be right over.

Heading out the door, he waved at Sarah and called, "Thanks for the tip, Brains."

He found Kalprowski in her warren of a cubicle, lost among other nearly identical government cubicles. When Keeney appeared, carrying his Styrofoam coffee cup, the white-haired woman looked up from her narrow desk covered with artificial flowers and fuzzy-bunny paperweights, and handed him a gray, dog-eared three-by-five card. Its handwritten words read:

> *Cynthia Elaine Coates, FWS age 3*
> *Died from accidental strangulation in barn*
> *Detective R. D. Jones*

Keeney copied the words onto a notepad and handed the card back. "You know, ma'am, you may just have helped to catch a killer."

"I don't know what I did, Mr. Keeney," the elderly clerk said as her face creased into a smile. "But you know, my retirement's coming up a few months from now. It'd be nice to go out in a ball of flames."

Jefferson County Police Department headquarters occupies the basement of Louisville's Hall of Justice, a squat modern building that sits in the heart of downtown, amidst skyscrapers, vacant lots and parking tarmacs. The PD's offices, in particular, are short on charm, although the windowless setting lends the operation a certain intensity, as if Louisville were a city perpetually under siege.

Keeney called the Police Department immediately after leaving the coroner's office and found that Detective R. D. Jones, whose name appeared on the fifteen-year-old filing card, still worked with the department. Now a sergeant in the evidence unit, Robert David Jones, or "R.D." as he was universally known, could be found at his desk.

R.D. had joined the police department only as something of a last resort. Fresh out of college, he made a stab at professional baseball, trying out for the Kansas City Royals. "Good glove, rotten hitter," he still joked. After twenty years, he now occupied his own office: a white, windowless cube, its main furnishings being a couple of metal filing cabinets, an imitation-wood desk, a reclining chair for himself and a straight-backed model for visitors. It was small and spartan, but at least he could close the door.

By the time Keeney arrived, R.D. was primed. Dora Kalprowski had telephoned the captain of detectives on the homicide squad, who, in turn, called the evidence unit.

"R.D., there's some hotshot attorney fella on his way over to your office to ask about a death you investigated sometime last century," the captain said. "A little girl named Cynthia Elaine Coates. Remember the case, by any chance?"

"Oh brother, it figures," R.D. groaned. "That's one of the few cases I wish I could forget."

"Well, you got about two minutes until he shows up. Try to show the gentleman what a tight outfit we run here."

R.D. returned Keeney's easy greeting with a firm handshake and the poker-faced offer of a seat. The instant he sat down, Keeney started explaining the story of Deana's death and its connection to Cynthia Elaine. It was a *pro bono* case, he added, a matter he was handling for a woman in his church.

As R.D. listened, he appraised Keeney with a practiced eye. What he saw made him worry. Lawyers in expensive suits usually meant trouble for police officers. Nine times out of ten, they were after money or publicity at someone's expense. Cynthia Elaine Coates's case, the first death he had ever investigated, had never sat well with him. He didn't relish the prospect of rehashing his rookie decisions at a deposition, or of being the fall guy for the department.

"I imagine this is what you're looking for," R.D. said. He pulled a yellowed file folder from his desk drawer and laid it on his blotter. Keeney spotted the name CYNTHIA ELAINE COATES typed on the tab. R.D. then casually spread his hand across the file. It was a large hand, Keeney noticed, and ornamented with a college ring.

"Your client related to the deceased?" R.D. asked.

"No, Sergeant," Keeney answered.

"You know, our files aren't open to anyone who wants to poke around in them."

"I understand. And chances are good I'm barking up the wrong tree. But I can't ignore something that's potentially this serious."

"You're not thinking of a lawsuit against the PD by any chance?" R.D.'s fingers started to drum on the file cover.

"Sergeant," Keeney said, "that's about the last thing on my mind right now."

"Because this file's been closed for fifteen years. Otherwise, it's kinda hard to figure your interest in something just this plain *old.*"

"Let's blow the foam off the beer right now." Keeney pulled a cigar out of his pocket, cut the end, and lit it, all without taking his eyes off R.D. The man looked as blue-eyed and mild-mannered as a cop in "Mister Rogers' Neighborhood." Traces of gray dusted his mustache, a small paunch edged out over his belt, and his blue eyes somehow managed to take in the entire room, even while looking you straight in the face.

When his cigar was properly aglow, Keeney started up again. "Sergeant, it just seems mighty odd that this woman found herself around two accidental deaths, one of which already looks a whole lot like a murder. And since you handled the investigation, I thought you might be willing to help us out. That's all I want, and all Bobbie Roberts wants. Just a little help."

"That's fine, Mr. Keeney," R.D. said. "But why aren't the California police out here doing this?"

"Beats me. You're welcome to call out there and find out."

"I tell you what," R.D. said, slipping the file back into his desk. "Give me a day or two. I'm not saying yes, and I'm not saying no. First off, I want to talk this over with my captain."

R.D. knew he had good reason to be defensive about his police work back in 1972. He had done the best he could at the time. But even after fifteen years, the image of the lifeless three-year-old in the rear seat of his cruiser had never completely left him. And any modern-day detective looking at Kentucky law enforcement fifteen years ago would have cringed.

In the early 1970s, all of Jefferson County still belonged more to the hollows and hills of the outback country than urban civilization. Fairdale, where Cynthia Elaine Coates died, had only recently ceased being a mosquito- and water moccasin–infested swamp. Kentucky's "boy governor" and later Commissioner of Baseball A. B. "Happy" Chandler had just pushed Interstate 65 out into the sticks. The Governor's $100 million project required the construction of a series of enormous drainage ditches and led to the reclamation of thousands of acres of land. Once the waters receded and the snakes and mosquitoes died off or took refuge elsewhere, folks started moving into the fertile plain that began at Fairdale and extended for miles.

Members of the present-day Louisville Medical Examiner's Office, now an exemplary outfit with a national reputation, still remember the old death investigations with unconcealed disdain.

"Folks used to say that if you wanted to kill your wife, do it in Kentucky," one assistant ME joked. "It's good ol' Joe, and if he wants to run for coroner, everybody elects him. Some were plumbers or carpenters, but the majority used to be funeral-home directors. That's how they got their business. They'd come on up to the scene of a death and slip their card to the next of kin and say, 'What funeral home would you like? If you bring your business to us, I'm sure we can avoid an autopsy.' Hell, if you killed your wife, what better way to get away with it?

"Even when they did perform an autopsy, the necessary medical expertise simply wasn't available. Bodies were carted down to the University of Louisville Medical School, where inexperienced residents did autopsies on a rotating basis. It was more like anatomy class. Some really complex homicides fell into the hands of D students just because they happened to be on the next rotation. Who knows how many solvable cases got lost that way?"

Two days after their meeting in the Jefferson County Police headquarters, Keeney greeted R.D. in the grand foyer of Barnett & Alagia. Keeney saw the sergeant's eyes dart around as they went back to his office.

For his part, R.D. still thought Keeney's "white knight" routine sounded dubious. Sarah West bringing a cup of coffee in the firm's china service only increased his discomfort. But settling his personal score outweighed the risk of getting sued.

The moment Sarah West left the room, closing the door behind her, R.D. opened his briefcase and took out the Cynthia Elaine Coates file.

"I guess this is the moment you've been waiting for," he grinned.

Keeney sat quietly as R.D. reached into a small manila envelope stapled to the folder and pulled out a loop of rough brown cord.

"This is the baling twine she hung from," he said. "I was supposed to throw it out five years ago, that's SOP around the evidence unit. Ten years and that's it. But I held on to the evidence just in case."

"Sergeant, you think the girl's death might have been a homicide?" Keeney asked.

R.D. answered as if he were thinking out loud: "It just never sat right with me, a three-year-old girl getting accidentally hanged from a seven-foot rafter. It was the only case that ever stayed with me like that. Back then I was ninety-five percent sure it was accidental, but there's that five percent. Looking back, I don't remember seeing ligature marks on her neck. That's the first thing to look for in a hanging, deep marks in the neck that indicate cutting off blood flow to the brain. But I only learned about that later, when I went to an FBI seminar at Quantico. At the time, I just figured a little girl might not get 'em."

Without a trace of embarrassment, he added, "We should have insisted on an autopsy." A smile spread below R.D.'s mustache. "The reason I came here was, this might give me a chance to set things right. Even after all this time."

That afternoon, R.D. told a story he'd kept to himself for a decade and a half.

December 6, 1972, a Wednesday, began with a cool snap in the air. It promised a crisp, bright winter afternoon on Jefferson Hill Road in Fairdale, Kentucky.

At around ten o'clock that morning, Jake Miller, a police officer who lived across the street from the Rearden family, came over to help Virginia and Bud with some masonry on a chimney. Bud Rearden had redesigned their fireplace, part of a new addition to their house, but he had fallen ill before he could do the work. Jake offered his help for a modest fee.

All that morning, he laid bricks in the living room while Virginia baked in the kitchen and little Cynthia Elaine ran rampant through the house.

"This is my fireplace," she chirped as she jumped in front of the half-built hearth. Jake nudged her aside, but minutes later she came coyly back, laughingly insisting it was "her" fireplace.

Some neighbors complained that Cynthia Elaine was "too aggressive," but by and large, the golden-haired child was the darling of Jefferson Hill Road. She climbed over picket fences, got lost in other folks' yard, and, like her mother, loved to show off. Jake let the little girl amuse herself, steering her away whenever it looked as if she might get into trouble.

At two-thirty that afternoon, Jake stopped work. His shift at the police station began at three. Jake washed up in the Reardens' kitchen sink and then walked back across the road to change for work. The sky had grayed over, a gusty wind kicked up, and freezing rain pelted the mud puddles in the road. It was classic, dreary Ohio River Valley weather; a day where the damp got to you more than the cold and the clouds hung low and heavy over the treetops.

A few of the neighborhood kids had planned to go riding, but by early afternoon they all decided to stay indoors.

Substation Charlie sat just down the road from Jake's house, no more than ten minutes away. It was an old one-story brick building divided into an assembly room, where a couple of manual typewriters clacked away, and a roll-call room. The place was rarely busy. There were thefts of farm equipment and lawn mowers, and good ol' country boys getting together with the city boys and knocking heads. One man had been arrested for sodomizing goats, caught *in flagrante,* and that was the talk of the department for months. But otherwise, it was as sleepy a police station as one would expect in a sparsely populated hamlet like Fairdale.

Jake Miller checked in at 3:05. Five minutes later, he was responding to an emergency: death of a child at 10105 Jefferson Hill Road. There were five or six officers already on duty, but Jake drew the assignment. The incident had taken place directly across from his own house—at Bud and Virginia Rearden's.

Cripes, the thought ran through Jake's mind as he sped back up the winding dirt road, *I hope that little girl didn't get hurt in my chimney.*

When he swerved into the Reardens' drive, Jake saw fellow officer Bob Hamilton's cruiser back near the wooden one-story barn. Bob happened to be in the area and had beaten Jake to the scene. Jake jumped out of his cruiser, ran down to the barn, and found Bob in his blue uniform, bent over the rear seat of a jalopy Bud used for parts. As Jake got closer, he saw that Bob was giving mouth-to-mouth resuscitation to Cynthia Elaine.

Virginia's father, Christie Hoffmann, his glasses fogged with the damp, stood next to the car with Bud and Virginia. Christie held a sickle in his right hand and was breathing with an emphysemic wheeze. Bud looked beside himself, Jake remembered, but Virginia "wasn't too shook up."

Cynthia Elaine lay on the seat. She wore a blue snowsuit with red and white trim, mittens, and blue tennis shoes. She looked like a cherub dressed for outdoor play—except for a face as unnaturally pale as a wax figurine, and a streak of blood that seemed to have come from her ear. Her tiny chest puffed out as Bob forced air into her mouth, but she never resumed breathing.

Jake and Bob scooped the girl's body out of the wreck and laid her out in the backseat of the cruiser. Virginia jumped in the front passenger seat. Officer Hamilton kept up mouth-to-mouth resuscitation in the rear as Jake raced to Saints Mary and Elizabeth Hospital. En route, Jake radioed for a detective. Cases like this always needed some official looking into.

The attending physician at Saints Mary and Elizabeth Hospital pronounced Cynthia Elaine Coates dead on arrival. It was 3:55 P.M.

R. D. Jones, a young detective on his first death investigation, met Jake and Bob in the emergency room. They went to look at the body. R.D. remembered seeing "blue areas" around Cynthia's face and neck when she arrived, probably a burn from the twine, he figured. But his main concern at that moment was with interviewing the family.

Back in the hospital corridor, R.D. pulled Virginia aside and asked what had happened. Thirty-five years old, Virginia Rearden seemed to R.D. like an ordinary Fairdale resident. She was a heavyset woman with auburn hair and green eyes that looked at you with a cooly quizzical stare.

Virginia said she was going to take Cynthia Elaine for a ride on their pony, a "quarter-horse mule." When they got to the barn, the pony either broke free and got out into the yard, or, Virginia said, she might have gone to walk it around for a few minutes, since it had too much spirit.

R.D. noted that Virginia seemed to be telling more than one story, but he wrote it off to the trauma of the moment. She went on:

When she returned to the barn, Virginia said, she found her daughter hanging by the neck from some twine that was looped over a rafter. She immediately ran back to the house to get her father. He returned and helped cut the girl down. After that, the police came.

R.D. called Coroner Burchett from the hospital, but Burchett said he had a few more runs to make and asked R.D. to check in later.

That afternoon, R.D. drove up to Jefferson Hill Road to examine the scene. He sloshed through the mud to the barn and went into the north door, where bales of hay were stacked behind a riding tractor-mower, no more than three feet high. A child's footprint was visible on the little tractor. A cut loop of twine still hung from the rafter. R.D. noticed that the horse stalls occupied a different section of the barn, one not connected to the room where the girl had died.

He took a couple of photos, coiled up the twine, and went back to interview sixty-nine-year-old Christie Hoffmann.

Christie said he had been sitting inside the main house when he heard Virginia calling him. He poked his head outside to see what the fuss was all about. There was Virginia, standing in the yard yelling something about Cynthia and the horse. Christie came out and they hurried over to the barn—into the part where they kept the tools.

He looked inside and saw Cynthia hanging by her neck from some baling twine looped onto a rafter above the tractor-mower. It looked to Christie as if she was almost sitting on the mower. Christie said he pulled a sickle off the barn wall, cut Cynthia down, and carried her out to Bud's old car. He tried mouth-to-mouth resuscitation, but it was no good.

The whole story didn't quite ring right, R.D. thought. But accusing a mother of murdering her own daughter and staging events to look like an accident was not something he was going to even consider without compelling evidence. And Jake Miller was more than ready to vouch for Virginia's character.

R.D. closed his report:

> . . . possibly the victim was playing on the tractor and swinging on the twine and became tangled in it and slipped off the tractor. The victim was in a partial sitting position when Mr. Hoffmann found her. He told us that she was not breathing and he could not find a pulse or heartbeat. . . .

> Officer J. Miller lives across the street from the Rearden home. He told us that the family moved in approximately three years ago and he has known them for this length of time. He feels that by knowing the family the accident happened like the report is titled . . . an accidental hanging. . . . Detective Davis called Coroner Burchett and advised him of our report. He ruled the death was caused by

an accidental hanging and released the body to Hardy's Funeral Home.

On December 8, 1972, Cynthia Elaine Coates was buried in an unmarked plot at Resthaven Memorial Park.

"We didn't know about child abuse," R.D. explained. Keeney looked up from the file and the photos of the little mower-tractor and loop of twine. Fifteen years of waiting showed in R.D.'s face. He twined his thick fingers and went on: "The media hadn't sensationalized it. But I always sensed something was wrong.

"Virginia didn't seem upset. She was more unemotional, even kind of cold. And the weather that day was stormy, down about thirty-five and really raw. Around the barn, there were three or four inches of mud. I had to borrow a pair of boots from Bud Rearden just to go back inside to look around. Now why would a mother want to take her three-year-old daughter for a pony ride in the mud on a lousy, freezing day?"

After work that evening, while digging holes in his front yard for a line of evergreen shrubs, Keeney ruminated over R.D.'s report. Virginia's explanation of Cynthia Elaine's death caught his ear like a familiar tune, one that keeps looping back on itself.

He put down his shovel and stood back from the house to survey his work: a series of holes, eighteen inches in diameter, spaced at intervals of three feet. He thought of the overweight woman in Deana's last snapshot, and her unctuous voice on the phone with Bobbie. He pictured Virginia slipping the twine around the child's already-limp neck. Maybe she strangled her in a fit of anger, then called in her aged father and made him a witness to a staged accident.

But R.D.'s report contained almost as many inconsistencies as Dave Dungan's. In practically the same breath, he asserted that the girl "possibly" died of an accidental hanging, yet she was found in a "partial sitting position." R.D. had also taken care to note that Virginia herself gave two explanations of what she had been doing at the time the girl died. It felt like a lie, but it also had that familiar ring. She had talked her way right past the cops with a confusing tale once before. . . .

Keeney suddenly felt the facts lining up, falling into a coherent pattern. He yanked off his gardener's gloves and jogged up the stairs.

In a few seconds, he pulled Deana's "murder script" up on the computer. He punched in the details of Cynthia's accident and lined up the narratives on a split screen.

Virginia had told Don Smythe that "It got cold" and she went back to the car. Virginia told Bobbie on the phone that Cynthia had wandered into the barn saying, "Mommy, I'm cold."

Deana tripped and fell off a cliff; Cynthia, apparently, tripped and fell off a tractor. In both cases Virginia was at the scene because the girl wanted to go; it was *her* fault.

Both girls were dressed in blue; both were wearing blue shoes.

Both stories involved animals: sea lions, a pony.

Virginia reported both deaths and thus controlled the moment when the police arrived.

Both victims were DOA.

The accidents happened when the victim separated from Virginia just for a moment, and while her back was turned. Virginia never heard a thing, never saw a thing. She was just minding her own business.

In each case, Virginia had a convenient, and easily manipulated, witness on hand—Christie and B.J.

And with each death, Virginia had been standing just yards away.

Keeney closed his eyes and took a deep breath. *The narratives were the same.*

CHAPTER 12

BLOOD
RELATIONS

▼

Fall in Kentucky is a dependable season, clear and bright. The summer rains stop, the black earth begins to harden. Against skies as majestically blue as any in Colorado stand trees as brilliant as Vermont maples. The smell of decaying leaves crisped with frost permeates the air. Horses snort in their stalls, blowing clouds from their nostrils.

But the change of season did little to buoy Bobbie Roberts or Steve Keeney. On Sundays, Keeney caught sight of his client wandering amid the crowds in the Second Press Fellowship Hall. He would be planning a golf game or a dinner out with Wynn, when Bobbie's vacant expression floated by. They seldom spoke in church, but occasionally she called Keeney at home, and then she wanted nothing more than to talk.

It wasn't the insurance case or the police work that seemed to interest her. She preferred to reminisce about Deana or talk about how she still couldn't get her own life back on track until she knew the truth about her daughter. Or, she complained that Virginia *still* hadn't sent back Deana's things. Inevitably, the conversation circled around to the same words: "I just miss her so much."

Keeney tried to encourage Bobbie with remarks that the legal process had never won awards for speed. But he kept to himself the unpleasant thought that, had Deana been an Ivy League graduate, a politician's daughter, or a successful young professional, the case might have made the papers, motivated everyone to work more diligently, and ranked higher in everyone's roster of priorities. Triage mentality obviously held sway over the law enforcement machine, and Deana just didn't make the priority cut.

Things at State Farm also were moving slowly. Mike Hatch had called to explain that his investigators were still trying to find whether there were other insurance policies on Deana. Insurance companies must have informational clearinghouses, Keeney assumed. The job should involve cross-referencing beneficiaries and insureds like the Grantor-Grantee index for real estate. A five-minute computer search.

Hatch said the job wasn't quite so easy. Insurers had to be called, one by one, and there were literally thousands of them scattered across the country. He apologized for the delay, and mumbled something about the federal government limiting information banks to property insurance. Then he signed off.

And in spite of the suspicious similarities between Deana's and Cynthia's deaths, and the events that had occurred at the McCain insurance agency, nobody in the Monterey Sheriff's or DA's offices seemed to think they had enough evidence even for a search warrant.

Every day, Keeney hoped to hear a gravelly voiced homicide prosecutor or detective ask him to step aside while the professionals took charge. But with each call and each letter, even Donald Smythe seemed to be politely backing off.

Of course, Keeney reminded himself, the Monterey authorities, especially their District Attorney's Office, had plenty of good reasons to scuttle Deana's case. Indicting a person for murder implicated a host of political and economic considerations, the prime numbers in any prosecutor's calculus. The investigation alone would demand a massive investment of time and effort—cross-country flights to Louisville, hundreds of interviews, fees for expert witnesses—and, even so, all that trouble and expense would lead only to a risky trial. No eyewitness had crawled out from the redwoods along Highway 1, and none seemed forthcoming. This wasn't a simple stabbing or a shooting, where everyone agrees it's a murder and the only question left is, Who done it? The issue here boiled down to murder or accident, push or slip. The victim, too, was a drifter, or could be turned into one easily enough by a skilled defense attorney. Deana first left Louisville, then broke up with her husband to live with a jailbird. Who knows what else she had been up to?

And what trial lawyer could ignore the fact that Virginia McGinnis had talked her way past the Sheriff's Office twice already? On the witness stand, she would surely testify with the same convincing sincerity. The Monterey DA certainly knew that taking the case also meant exposing all the shortfalls of the sheriff's original investigation, an unfortunate circumstance that carried its own political liabilities—especially if they lost.

No, the McGinnis case certainly was nothing Monterey prosecutors would jump at.

Meantime, Keeney watched as his own unbilled time on behalf of Bobbie Roberts added up. Already, it ran to five figures, and right when B & A needed its partners to be bringing in major clients and billing long hours. It was just a matter of weeks before somebody pulled him aside and asked why his time sheets were shy a few dozen hours each month.

In a lengthy letter summing up every fact uncovered to date, Keeney began to prepare Bobbie Roberts for what seemed inevitable disappointment:

> Because I am very concerned not to get your hopes raised unrealistically that we will ever know, with any degree of certainty, exactly what happened on that cliffside, let me caution you again that deaths resulting from falls from high places are some of the most difficult ever to investigate and to establish exactly what happened. Although I believe we will do a creditable job of accumulating and analyzing the available documents, there are always "holes" in every investigation. For example, in this instance, the autopsy reports and photographs do not closely describe the external appearance of the body, the prescription medication found in her body was not quantified at the time of the initial investigation, the investigating authorities did not take photographs of the scene of death, and it may be that other omissions (such as a search of the site for possible weapons or an examination

of the clothing of the McGinnises) will leave questions that can no longer be answered. Nonetheless, as I trust you know, we shall do our utmost to fill in all the blanks we can.
Sincerely,

Steven H. Keeney
BARNETT & ALAGIA

While Keeney waited for the official word to come in, R. D. Jones kept working on Cynthia Elaine's death. He sensed that there was a homicide to be made, it was just a matter of perseverance. He ran Virginia's and Billie Joe's names through the Kentucky law-enforcement computers but came up empty-handed. Virginia's sons James and Ronnie Coates, however, seemed to have racked up juvenile offenses the way some people collected 4-H ribbons.

Jimmy's were petty offenses—drunk driving and assaults—the sort of roistering that some boys grow out of. But Ronnie's rap sheet brought back a memory from 1976. Ronnie, then twenty years old, had fled from Kentucky to California to avoid trial on charges of kidnapping, robbery, and burglary. R.D. had arrested the boy and hauled him back. Home in Kentucky, Ronnie was convicted of burglary 2d degree and criminal conspiracy.

Keeney whistled when R.D. called in with the police file on Virginia's boys. "I hate to say it, but it kinda makes sense," Keeney said. "You figure Virginia would raise at least one bad apple."

"Steve," R.D. said with a trace of professional condescension, "what do you mean 'one'? I think you've been inside those cushy offices too long. Remember, Coates was in jail when Deana died."

"Sure, but we don't know what for, do we?" Keeney asked.

"You don't think Jimmy Coates is going to turn out just as bad as his brother?" Keeney asked.

Is he kidding? R.D. thought. Since their first meeting, R.D.'s apprehension about this laced-up corporate lawyer had softened. But when he heard Keeney come out with remarks like these, he remembered what a greenhorn he was dealing with.

"Let's just put this down to experience rather than philosophy," R.D. said, closing the subject temporarily.

That afternoon, he called back. "Let me pass on the number of a fella named May. Just ask him about James Coates."

"Another of Virginia's husbands?" Keeney kidded.

"Nope. I just think you'll find his point of view enlightening."

Keeney reached Albert May at his home. Though ten years had passed, the man was still boiling about Jimmy Coates. "Yeah, I knew that boy," he ranted.

"Years back, my son was riding a ten-speed bike by the side of a road in Fairdale. Jimmy came hauling along in the back of a truck. He threw a rope out over the side like he was lassoing a steer! It wrapped around my son's neck, dragged him down the street, and left one hell of a rope burn. Could've killed my boy! Then that rotten kid goes off to California before the case came to trial. The court sent a bondsman out after him. But by the time he got back, my son decided to let the matter go."

While Keeney listened, he realized that R.D. was right. It was laughable, his trying to "lead" the Monterey police and solve Deana's case like some Mickey Spillane detective. Unfortunately, there didn't seem to be anyone willing to take over.

October 9, 1987. Bored.

Sarah West had been through the usual flurry of letter typing and filing at B & A, and the day now settled into a sleepy afternoon lull.

Sarah began to rummage through the Deana Wild file. The case was like an afternoon soap opera. It didn't hurt that the whole thing was surrounded by an air of secrecy, Keeney never breathing a word around the firm.

West had already read and reread Dungan's and R.D.'s reports and listened to the tape of Bobbie on the phone with Virginia. Today, she went back to the disc photos. Looking at the fifteen prints, she felt as if she were peering into the very world inhabited by Deana and Virginia McGinnis. The thought made her beehive hairdo stand at attention.

Clicked off in order, the photos seemed to make sense as part of a well-planned murder. In Sarah West's estimation, it was obvious what happened after Photo 11. One push by B.J. Then a scream as the girl, drowsy from drugs, tumbled down the rocks, scattering the sea lions.

But what had the McGinnises done afterward? She imagined the crafty woman and her pawn of a husband arguing at the cliff. Did they understand that a human life had just gone tumbling to its end? Or was it all just a question of money, with Deana a convenient vehicle?

Then Sarah closed in on the last four photos. Each one presented a meaningless, meandering view. Four shots of nothing in particular. Four frames fired off randomly, as if Virginia had wanted to finish the disc in a hurry. . . .

It was so exciting, Sarah West's breath came short. She pulled out Dungan's police report, just to be sure:

> Mrs. McGinnis had just completed taking their photo and Mr. McGinnis walked away from Wild, towards the parked car. He and his wife were walking when they turned around in the direction from where Wild and Mr. McGinnis were standing and Wild was nowhere to be seen. Both looked around and then walked back to the site. Neither could see her but looked slightly over the edge and saw a high heeled shoe over the edge about twenty feet below. They looked further and saw Wild lying on the rocks at the bottom of the cliff. The McGinnis' immediately went to the Coast Gallery to call for help. . . .

". . . *just completed taking their photo* . . . *immediately went to the Coast Gallery* . . ." If the McGinnises' story were true, then the last shot should be of Deana and B.J. together. Instead, there were four more unexplained shots, all of scenery that looked like Big Sur. If those pictures were of Seal Beach—and they certainly looked like the others—then *they must have been taken right afterward at the same spot.*

Keeney was away at a meeting, so Sarah West typed out a note and left it on his chair: "Steve, It would appear that the last four pictures on the Kodak disc negative were taken at the scene to finish the disc so that the pictures could be developed. Sarah 10/9/87."

Keeney came back from court late that day. After reading the note he called Sarah to congratulate her. Her insight punched one more hole in the McGinnises' story. Virginia hadn't raced breathlessly back to the Coast Gallery to alert the cops, as she had claimed. She took her time and snapped a few photos. Maybe to ensure that Deana really was dead.

I wonder just how long Deana was down there? Keeney mused.

Sarah West's discovery was only the start. When Deborah Cross of Big Sur, California, called, Keeney sensed that another real break in the case had come through. Cross apologized for taking weeks to get back in touch, but she had been out of the country on vacation for most of that fall, away from her job at the Coast Gallery down the road from the Seal Beach turnout. Keeney suspected Cross might become a pivotal witness: She was the first person Virginia had spoken with after Deana's death—apart from Billie Joe. Keeney asked every question he could dream up and scrawled a dozen pages of notes. Then he offered to send copies of the photos taken just before Deana's death in the hope they might trigger some memories.

"If this case ever goes to court," he said, "it always helps to get the story down while it's fresh. Mind putting your recollections down on tape?"

Cross agreed. Dated November 7, 1987, her verbal memo to Keeney lasted fifteen minutes:

> *I manage the Coast Gallery on Highway One in Big Sur.*
>
> *It was about quarter of five in the afternoon on that April day that a heavyset woman walked into the gallery. She was probably in her early fifties. . . . She was extremely agitated, nervous, and came around to the counter and said that a girl she had been with had fallen over a cliff nearby. . . . She could barely get the words out; she was breathing very heavily. I was as much concerned for the older woman as anything else. I didn't know if she would pass out or have a stroke on the spot or what. . . . She did not want to have a seat but she said, "Where can I call nine-one-one?" . . . She wanted to go back up to Seal Beach where her husband was at the time and I saw she was in no shape to walk, so I offered to drive her. . . .*
>
> *We arrived at the site. There was a man there—he was . . . informally dressed . . . probably in his fifties or so, slimmer, or more fit than she was. I recall that they said the girl had been taking photographs—it could have possibly been sea lions. . . . They are visible, they're perfectly visible from the parking area. . . . You can't hear them from your car driving north, so maybe they just saw the turnout. They were northbound as I understand it. It's an extremely dangerous left-hand turn; it is right on a corner. . . . Usually people stop there when they're going south. I don't know that they stop there so much when they're going north, since the turnout is so abrupt and there's really no view if you're north-bound. . . .*
>
> *Back to the conversation as I recall it. They had said that the girl had been taking photographs, that she tripped. She had high heels on, rather high spiked heels, and they had asked her on the ride north at the various points where they had pulled off the road to take photographs and just look at the view . . . to take her high heels off, that she would trip and she would fall. To please change*

into a pair of sneakers or just take her shoes off. And the woman said that she refused to do this. She absolutely said no, she wouldn't do this. She didn't want to take her shoes off and change her shoes and they had stopped several times along the road on the way north.

This happened to be the case evidently, and she lost her footing and fell. The woman also—I believe it was the woman who told me that, in a willful way—complained that they should have taken Highway 101, which goes up the valley and not the seacoast. She had wished they had done that but the girl had never been up the coast before. And so they wanted to take her up the coast to see the scenery. . . .

Another thing that the woman mentioned was how upset she was. How would she ever tell the girl's parents, her mother and father, what happened? She was extremely upset as to what she was going to say and how she was going to face them, and she became tearful. Not crying, not sobbing, but upset and tearful. The man was tense. I don't know how else to put it. He was not as emotionally upset, or well, he could have been. He just expressed it differently, I suppose, than she did. He seemed tense to me, and didn't really talk much. . . .

One thing I did when I got out of the car was to look over the edge. . . . You cannot see more than ten feet from the turnout circle to the edge of the rocks. Then it goes down quite vertically. There is a slight sloping shelf on which I saw a blue high-heel shoe . . . one only, nothing else, no disrupted soil. . . .

We were still on winter schedule, and the gallery closes at half past five, and I remember my concern wanting to go down and cash out and so forth and be there, yet wanting to stay with the couple until help arrived. I believe it was maybe quarter past five that I finally left. . . . So when the gallery closed at half past five, and I was on my way home north . . . I did see that help had arrived. . . . In any event, I was tempted to stop and I just didn't. I saw that everything was under control, or seemed to be, anyway. . . . And I also heard, almost as I reached my house, a helicopter heading south toward the site. . . .

I have done an extreme amount of, put a lot of energy into, this recollection and I will certainly continue to think about it and add whatever I can at the appropriate moment. However, this will be in the mail to you, Steve, on Monday. I know time is of the essence. You might try contacting the Sheriff's department. . . .

Keeney played and replayed the tape driving to work, to church, on his way to pick up Wynn for a date. Cross had added an entirely new set of disconcerting details to the murder scenario.

The turnout, according to Deborah Cross, was hardly ever used by northbound tourists, yet the McGinnises chose it after nine hours on the road, at a time when it was overcast, windy, and cold. Virginia made a point of telling Cross how upset she was about having to break the news to Deana's "mother and father." Yet if Virginia had been so concerned, why hadn't she phoned the night of the girl's death? After all, Deputy Coroner Dave Dungan had gotten Bobbie's phone number directly from Virginia. Virginia told Deborah Cross that *Deana* had been taking photos, while B.J. told Dungan that *Virginia* had been shooting.

B.J. told Dungan that he could see Deana's body lying on the rocks below, yet Virginia told Deborah that she could see only Deana's shoe. It also bothered Keeney that Virginia had acted as if Deana were *already* dead, even before the rescue crew arrived. And if Deana had slipped and fallen, why hadn't Deborah seen any soil disturbed around the shoe?

Virginia knows exactly what she's doing, Keeney brooded. She trickled out little lies here and there, kept people confused. Made sure no one person saw the whole picture. She did it with R.D. and she's done it in Monterey.

With two suspicious deaths—both victims who lived with Virginia and ate at her table—as well as a pattern of insurance claims, the world already seemed a darker place than Keeney ever suspected. Nice fifty-year-old mothers just weren't supposed to go around plotting murders. Then came the Coates boys' California rap sheets, courtesy of Donald Smythe, and the world turned on its head.

Unlike what R.D. Jones had found in Kentucky, there were more than just a few drunk and disorderlies.

Ronnie Coates's West Coast criminal career started out in Redwood City, with the warrant of extradition served by R.D. Within a few months, Ronnie was back, arrested on another burglary charge. Fourteen months later, on March 7, 1978, he pleaded guilty to receiving stolen property. One year later, it was a burglary conviction.

The list went on: On tax day 1980, San Mateo cops charged Ronnie with possession of drugs and a hypodermic. Before the year was out, he racked up three more narcotics arrests. On the last one, in December 1980, he was also convicted of felony forgery. In 1982, he was arrested for assault with a deadly weapon, burglary, and forgery. In 1983, he went to prison again on another burglary charge. Ronnie Coates, Keeney suspected, was a bomb on a short fuse.

Finally, he exploded. On August 29, 1985, Ronnie Coates, thirty years old, faced charges of murder, conspiracy, and assault with a deadly weapon. He was convicted on the assault charge and sent to state prison on a five-year sentence. While in the pen, Ronnie ended up facing still another assault with a deadly weapon charge along with a count of forgery.

Jimmy Coates's record proved no better. He was picked up for assault with a deadly weapon in April 1975 in Redwood City, California, and again on October 25, 1975. It remained unclear whether he was ever convicted of the charges. He was nineteen years old at the time. One week later, he was busted for sale of marijuana. That was dismissed, too. Then, over the next year, it was hit and run, then causing property damage, then burglary and receiving stolen property. Most of the early charges ended up dismissed or resulted in Jimmy spending short stretches in the city jail.

But on February 28, 1977, he shot and killed a San Francisco drug dealer and was convicted on the charge of second degree murder. While in Vacaville prison, a maximum-security institution in the California backcountry, his demerits included assaulting a prisoner. Later still, drugs turned up in his cell.

In spite of all that, Jimmy was paroled in August 1982. Within half a year, he was rearrested: receiving stolen property. Two weeks later he was up on burglary. This time, he got two years.

Most recently, in February 1987, while again on parole in San Diego, Jimmy was picked up for simple theft. With his record, he received sixteen months, a sentence rendered on March 20, 1987. He remained in city jail until April 1, 1987—the day Virginia paid for Deana's insurance policy—when he was transferred to state prison.

Keeney adamantly refused to believe in coincidences. Things happen for a reason, and the plain facts showed that Jimmy knew he'd be doing time when the insurance was bought. The whole McGinnis family knew he would be in jail weeks before Deana flew back from Louisville. Jimmy Coates's "rock-solid alibi" now began to look just as calculated as the purchase of the policy itself.

But that conclusion was overwhelmed by two other chilling revelations. First, Keeney realized, albeit belatedly, that the killer he was pursuing was different than any killer of his imagination: She was a mother. The idea undermined all his preconceptions, and it helped to explain why she was able to walk away from two suspicious death scenes.

More disturbing still, he understood that Virginia McGinnis was not just a murderer herself: *She bred murderers.*

Keeney thought that if he learned one more horrific fact about Virginia, he would burst into tears of sheer frustration. Didn't anybody care about the horrors this woman perpetrated? Apparently not. The time had come to take aggressive action to line up his sights.

There was only one place left to go: the Monterey District Attorney's Office. Like one of his exhaustive travel itineraries or corporate organization plans, he began assembling a document that would piece together every available detail: Exactly where Virginia and B.J. were standing when Deana fell; how Virginia steered Deana into buying insurance at the McCains' office; Cynthia Elaine Coates's death. He analyzed the elements of murder and discussed the legal requirements for a search warrant.

With copies of Deana's marriage certificate, summaries of interviews, newspaper clippings, rap sheets, transcripts of Deborah Cross's statement and Bobbie Roberts's phone call to Virginia, R.D.'s report on Cynthia Elaine Coates, and Dr. Barbara Weakley-Jones's analysis of the Deana Wild autopsy report, the memorandum totaled more than two hundred pages.

There were even lists of things that did *not* exist: such as any record of Virginia as a registered nurse in New York, Kentucky, or California.

Bound and indexed, his magnum opus went out to Donald Smythe with a cover letter authorizing that it be forwarded to the appropriate authorities. Even with all the remaining unanswered questions—and Keeney knew there were plenty—it was a thorough piece of detective work. When the DA read all the facts, Keeney hoped, the long haul would be over.

Shortly before the end of November 1987, a letter arrived from the Monterey County District Attorney's Office addressed to Mr. Steven H. Keeney, Law Offices of Barnett & Alagia. It had been preceded by a long period of silence. Keeney opened the envelope expecting to read congratulations on a job well done, and that the pros were stepping in.

The letter weighed in at a little more than a dozen lines:

Dear Mr. Keeney:

I have read over and thoroughly digested all reports concerning the above referenced subject which was forwarded to my attention.

All of the events which led to the demise of Ms. Hubbard-Wild only point to one reasonable interpretation.

However, our major stumbling block is criminal agency, and as I'm sure you appreciate, as derived from your letter, is proving to be a substantial obstacle. Investigation is continuing and if there is any more information that you would like to supply, please feel free to forward to my attention.

As you can imagine, I have a very heavy caseload, but I will do my best to get back to you within a reasonable time.
Sincerely,

Jon N. Yudin, Assistant District Attorney

Michael W. Bartram, District Attorney

P.S. Do you know if McGinnis also took out a life insurance policy on the deceased three year-old?

Half a page, riddled with confused sentences, in response to months of painstaking investigation all done as a favor to a woman in his church, came as the rudest sort of kiss-off. It felt like a hand-lotioned pat on the back. He knew that the local DA had no particular ill will toward him or Bobbie. There just seemed to be an institutionalized pecking order for bodies, one that didn't allow for hard-to-solve cases—except, perhaps, for the rare socially prominent victim.

The letter also didn't say how he was supposed to explain to Bobbie Roberts that the DA's Office wasn't interested in her daughter's murder. Even Jon Yudin, the assistant DA, agreed that the facts "only point to one reasonable interpretation." How could he write that, sign his name, then shrug it off? Was he really content to wait until an eyewitness caught Virginia in the act? And that phrase "criminal agency"? Keeney was a lawyer yet he wasn't even sure what it meant.

Remembering the day when he had broken the news to Bobbie Roberts about a life-insurance policy on her daughter, he began to prepare himself for another encounter: To explain to his one flesh-and-blood client that not only had her daughter been murdered but all their work notwithstanding, the killers stood a very good chance of getting away with it.

▼

PART TWO

ASHES,
ASHES

CHAPTER 13

MONTEREY

▼

In another law office, 1,800 miles from Barnett & Alagia, the picture was just as bleak. The only difference being, these attorneys had had their problems shoved down their throats by the local newspapers for months. According to the local press, the Monterey District Attorney's Office was a shambles of infighting, sexism, and favoritism, and its lawyers couldn't win a jaywalking case, much less a homicide.

The free-fall in Monterey morale had begun with the election of a new DA named Mike Bartram. During twenty years of prosecuting in Monterey County, Bartram had picked up a reputation as a trial lawyer's trial lawyer. He was not only a powerful prosecutorial presence, but also a man capable of compassion for deserving defendants. Legal talent aside, however, even staunch supporters agreed Bartram should never have become an administrator; he lacked the political savvy as well as the thick skin required to withstand the attacks inevitably aimed at public officeholders. Friends held their breath when he was voted in.

Enemies found their doubts vindicated from day one. Promptly after moving into his new office, Bartram picked his chief lieutenants, known in the county bureaucracy as assistant district attorneys. Even in making those simple appointments, Bartram managed to generate resentment. Instead of promoting career insiders, deputy DAs who had devoted a decade or more of their lives to trying Monterey offenders, he imported three old compadres, all of whom had long ago left the office for greener pastures.

Predictably, top prosecutors within the office grumbled. As one of their own, Bartram should have shown some loyalty. And going outside the ranks smacked of snobbery, if not outright insult.

Even before the tremors from the ADA appointments subsided, more trouble arose. Mike Bartram, rumor went, was having an affair with an attractive female deputy DA. Soon other deputy prosecutors started complaining that Bartram's woman unfairly garnered choice assignments.

To Bartram's mind, whom he slept with was his own personal business, and, as far as favoritism went, he vehemently denied the allegations. But the upstanding Skip Brauderick, one of Bartram's recently imported ADAs, felt otherwise—or at least saw a storm brewing. Brauderick cleared out his desk in June of 1987, only a few months after joining the office.

New hope arose among top prosecutors passed over in the first round of appointments. They waited for the DA to come around and elevate an insider to fill the new vacancy. As if to make amends, Bartram began interviewing up and down the staff ladder. But after the show of in-house interviews concluded, Bartram brought in yet another dark horse, a former Monterey deputy DA named Jon Yudin. When he installed Yudin as head of the Monterey office in August of 1987, staff resentment rocketed to a new peak.

In this unsettled atmosphere, Donald Smythe from the Sheriff's Office plunked down Keeney's two-hundred-page tome on Yudin's desk.

"The case needs to be investigated," Smythe insisted. "Something's rotten here."

Deana Hubbard's homicide case might have stood a chance of being actively prosecuted if in-house dissent were the only problem festering in Bartram's office. But it wasn't.

First came the murder case of *The People of the State of California* v. *Hart Silvierie.* The murder itself was a decade and a half old, yet it possessed enough inherent sex appeal to revive public attention the moment an indictment was filed. The case involved an attractive young woman found lying outdoors in stylish, upscale Carmel Valley, the cultural and financial center of Monterey County. An autopsy revealed she had had sex shortly before someone blew her away with a shot to the head.

For years, the case mouldered in the police tubs, clueless. Then, out of nowhere, an ex-con stepped forward and fingered Monterey local Hart Silvierie in the killing. Unfortunately, for Bartram's office, the case had ended in a hung jury and Bartram never sought a retrial. Editorials proclaimed the matter a prosecutorial boondoggle that should either have been shelved or won. Mike Bartram was zero for one.

While the DA's Office was still reeling from the *Silvierie* case, the Sheriff's Office brought in a new arrest, a real catch in fact: prominent Monterey County businessman Billie Leo Briggs. A month earlier, detectives discovered, Briggs had taken out a hefty life-insurance policy on a business partner. Then the partner's body turned up in the woods, his head half wasted by a shotgun blast. The case against Briggs was circumstantial but strong, or so the DA thought.

The DA's Office marched into court, hoping for a high-profile victory to obliterate the memory of *Silvierie.* The courthouse was packed. But when the sheriff's deputies took the stand, the case skidded out of control. Detectives had accidentally left the murder weapon in the sun for hours. Bits of blood and flesh on the barrel had dried to the point where they had become untestable. Then a government lab technician lost her original notes. Insurance policy or no insurance policy, the jury acquitted Billie Leo Briggs. The moment the verdict came down, newspapers screamed: Zero for two was unacceptable.

From all appearances, Bartram's self-confidence crumbled. Even supporters now complained they saw more of the DA's secretary than the man himself.

"He stayed behind a locked door, totally isolated from everyone in the city," recalled one prominent defense attorney. "I liked and admired Mike, I really did. But this was a disaster."

Deana Wild's case all too closely resembled both *Silvierie* and *Briggs.* It was a complex and circumstantial homicide, hampered by the passage of time and a subpar investigation by the Monterey

Sheriff's Office. (Indeed, the Sheriff's Office itself was still reeling from having one of its own members convicted of stealing property from the estates of recently deceased residents, as well as firearms from ongoing homicide and suicide investigations.)

ADA Jon Yudin viewed Deana's case as something akin to a recurring nightmare. Not that Jon Yudin was the sort to cave in easily—quite the contrary. A baby-faced, six-foot-four body-builder, Yudin came to the Monterey DA's Office via the Bronx, New York. And he brought his street-tough attitude with him.

"I'm not much of a detail person," Yudin once described himself. "I just go in there and fight. If I was a boxer, I wouldn't lose on a decision. I'd be carried out."

He had come back to the DA's office in August. When the McGinnis case came in, Yudin thought it was something he could "glom on to." But resources were scarce in the county. There was not enough money to put a single deputy DA on a case, let alone a full-time investigator. And the McGinnis case would involve travel back east, and a lot of man-hours.

"I was sure in my mind they had done it, that they'd killed her," Yudin said. "I can still picture reading the file three or four times, until two A.M. But we couldn't take it on."

CHAPTER 14

COLLECT FROM LODI, NEW YORK

▼

"Collect for Steven Keeney from Richard Coates," the operator chimed. Sarah West accepted the call, wondering what she would possibly say next.

She and Keeney had beaten their heads against walls for months trying to track down Richard Coates, the man listed on Cynthia Elaine Coates's birth certificate as her father. Of course, finding a man who might either be dead, in any of the fifty states, out of the country, or in jail, was almost laughably unlikely. Cynthia Elaine Coates's obituary referred to him as "Richard Coates of New York." Yet, her birth certificate stated Cynthia Elaine's birthplace as Palo Alto, California.

Keeney and Sarah searched California, Kentucky, and New York directories for Richard Coates. A few Jefferson Hill Road neighbors remembered that Virginia once said she had grown up in upstate New York near Ithaca, so they placed still more calls to operators in the various townships surrounding Ithaca proper. They bothered a lot of unrelated Coateses.

At one point, Keeney spoke with a woman named Margaret Coates who lived at a nursing home in the little town of Lodi. Margaret told Keeney she had a son named Dick who had once been married to a woman named Virginia. It sounded promising. In fact, it was the only connection that looked promising. Keeney asked Margaret to please have her son return his call, collect. That was weeks before, and one of dozens of messages.

A man came on the line: "Hello?"

"Is this Richard Coates?" Sarah asked.

The voice that followed sounded as if belonged to someone who had just crawled out of a moldy, twenty-year hibernation, even discounting the scratchy phone connection.

"This is Dick Coates. Steve Keeney in?" he croaked.

"Mr. Keeney's in court right now," Sarah answered, thinking fast.

"I'm at a pay phone."

Who knows if Coates will ever call back? Sarah thought.

"If you have a minute, sir, there are a few questions I'd like to ask you myself."

" 'f you say so," Coates answered.

By the time Keeney returned to the office, Sarah was on the verge of exploding with the pent-up news.

"We got her!" she said, her face flushed, beehive hairdo practically alive.

"Okay, Brains, don't keep me guessing." Keeney laughed.

"Virginia McGinnis," she said as she stood up from behind her desk and waved a legal pad. "Richard Coates called while you were in court, and if half of what he says is true, the case is closed. I've got five pages of notes you won't believe."

"All right," Keeney said, then nodded toward his office. "Let's take a look."

Half an hour later, Keeney leaned back in his chair and blew out some air. Then he turned and picked up the phone.

Margaret Coates answered. Could she relay another message to her son? Keeney asked. He wanted to speak with Richard as soon as possible.

"I think I could do that." The old woman meted out her words in unsteady syllables. "He's standin' right next to me."

A pause. Then Dick Coates took the line.

"Mr. Keeney, I know you been tryin' to dig me up. Now before I say one more gotdamn word, I want you to tell me what kind of gotdamn trouble my ex-wife has got herself into this time."

"Mr. Coates, that's a long story. I've been trying to reach you for—"

"I know you've been tryin' to reach me. That's why I called. Now, what kind of gotdamn trouble has Virginia got herself into? I haven't heard from her in twenty years and I don't want to muck up the gotdamn past." The man sounded like some mistreated dog ready to bite even a friendly hand.

"Mr. Coates, your ex-wife was standing at a cliff when a woman named Deana Hubbard Wild fell off and died. I represent that girl's mother. Now, if you have any information, either about Virginia, Deana, or about your daughter, Cynthia Elaine, I'd appreciate your sharing it with me."

"Okay, mister, now I know you're crazy. I thought you lawyers was supposed to know everything. I don't have no daughter. Never did. So you're wrong about the first thing you told me. And if you're investigatin' some kind of murder, why ain't you with the police?"

Keeney saw himself hitting another dead end, another wrong Richard Coates. Except, given what this fellow had told Sarah West, that didn't seem possible.

"How about sons? Ronald and James. Do you recognize those names?"

"Ronnie and Jimmy?" Coates's voice brightened with a flash of pride, then dulled. "They're my boys, all right. Last I heard, they was in prison, or jail. 'Course they only writ me when they's in trouble. But I still ain't got no gotdamn daughter."

"I hate to beat a dead horse here, Mr. Coates. But a girl named Cynthia Elaine Coates was born to Virginia in 1969 in Palo Alto, California, and your name's listed on her birth certificate as the father. Does that help your recollection?"

"No, it don't. The last time I seen Virginia was Christmas Eve 1966. I remember real well 'cause it was the last time we was actin' like what you might call husband and wife. Never had no relations with her since. Never been to California in my life. Never heard of no little girl. If that child was born two years after I last saw Virginia, you figger out how the hell I'm that girl's father. You're the gotdamn lawyer."

Keeney let it go. He had the right Richard Coates, although it was hard to reconcile the man's backwoods grammar with Virginia and her refined speech. He assumed the picture would become clearer over time.

▼

At first, when Dick Coates spoke about his ex-wife's interminable wrongdoings—and he listed scores of odd, even bizarre, events—he remained circumspect about details. He would hint at stories, then back off, dart up again to touch the memory, then run scared.

"Virginia always had a problem with stealin'," Coates said early on. "Stole every gotdamn thing she laid her hands on."

"Can you give me some examples, some of the things she took?" Keeney asked.

"If I told you every time she stole from me, we'd be talkin' for months."

"Did she shoplift?"

"I told you, we'd be talkin' for months," Coates would say, and then fall silent.

And so it went. Keeney had to remind himself that this man had been married to Virginia, and that every question reopened a wound. Whatever tales he had to tell probably involved the very things he wanted most to forget. Virginia, clearly, had not left him a happy man.

Ever since they broke up, twenty-one years ago, Coates said, he had lived alone in a lean-to outside a town that appeared as the merest dot in the Rand McNally atlas. He worked in local vineyards and timber stands and apparently never had more than a few dollars in his pocket on any given day. Some days, even some mornings, he sounded as if he had been drinking. Other times, he spoke with remarkable lucidity.

And, eventually, during one of a dozen phone calls, Coates's reticence turned. Keeney wasn't sure what set it off, but it didn't matter. Dick began recounting every detail of his life with Virginia, running on like a rusty faucet. As he listened and took notes, Keeney pictured Dick stationed at a pay phone on the empty Lodi main street, his truck pulled over to one side, his weathered figure leaning against the wall for an hour at a time, pouring out his life story to some stranger a thousand miles away.

The calls from Dick Coates grew more frequent, and Keeney started contacting other acquaintances and relatives of Virginia. Within weeks he had assembled a picture—albeit sketchy and uncertain—of Virginia's early years. And he began to understand what lay behind her sweet, ingratiating exterior.

CHAPTER 15

DIF'RNT

▼

"Ginger didn't have any friends," Nelson Eddy remembers. "Of course, who would want to get close to her, she smelled so awful? She was bigger than all of us, too, and a vicious bully. When she was eight years old, she stabbed me in the hand with a pencil after I pulled at her pigtails. I've still got the lead in my palm." He holds out a massive, callused farmer's hand, points to a dark splinter still visible through layers of skin.

TOMPKINS COUNTY, NEW YORK

The Hoffmann family quickly picked up a reputation as *different,* a word that Tompkins County locals—farmers, dairymen, timbermen, grapepickers, day laborers—pronounced with special emphasis, leaning on the first syllable, grunting the second: *dif'rnt.* It let you know they meant something more than just different. That was how locals talked in upstate New York in the 1930s and 40s: truncated words, sharp and barbed like the wire stretching between neighboring fields. And that was how word spread through Tompkins County on delicate subjects like the Hoffmann family.

Christie Hoffmann, a broad-beamed man with a scrub-brush of hair and a pair of black-framed eyeglasses that looked like a smudge, had left the United States Marine Corps a few years before moving to Ithaca in 1936. He had worked as a security guard in a Brooklyn bank, then moved on to the police department. But too drunk too often, Christie was soon out on the street, jobless, with a complaining wife, one noisy infant named Thomas, and another on the way.

In the Marine Corps, Christie learned a number of enduring lessons, chief among them raw survival. In the face of Red armies or the threat of world war, it seemed to Christie that about all a person could hope for was sticking it out on your own. "You can't dig up every hill of potatoes," he instructed his family, then promptly piled all their worldly belongings into a truck and drove to upstate New York to set up a dairy farm.

They arrived at a time when Tompkins County consisted mainly of quiet, rolling country. The Finger Lakes, Seneca and Cayuga, gleamed in granite beds carved by glaciers. Fields of corn and alfalfa continued along the roadsides and ended abruptly in deep woods. In winter, it was said that the temperature sometimes dropped low enough to bring tears to your eyes and freeze them shut. Water buckets left out turned to clear crystal. After a heavy snowfall, children skied into town on drifts that reached almost to the tops of telephone poles. In the remaining seasons, green fields specked with black and white Holstein cattle lay lush and open at the road's shoulder. Only the occasional truck lumbering along broke the country quiet.

Life in Ithaca was more rugged than peaceful. Some folks grew grapes and assorted produce, but dairy farming and logging accounted for most locals' livelihoods.

Christie Hoffmann, his wife, Mary Agnes, son, Thomas, and their new daughter, Virginia—nicknamed Ginger—crowded into a small wooden two-story house set back a few yards from Bostwick Road, an arrow-straight two-lane road leading up a hill above the town of Ithaca proper. The centerpiece of the Hoffmann house was a rank-smelling oil stove out of which climbed a pipe that hissed like a hot, black snake. Outside, a small red barn stood adjacent to the Hoffmann house, where the family's ill-kept herd of twenty-five cows shivered in stalls during the long upstate winter nights.

The house, the farm, and the cattle represented the length and breadth of Christie's dream.

The Hoffmanns no sooner arrived than they made their presence felt. In early fall, farmers harvested together, filling one another's silos with corn, hauling bales of hay. The traditional reward for a day's labor—besides lending a reciprocal hand when the time came—was a cool drink and some food at the family table. These were ancient rules, and it came only naturally that neighbors turned out to help at Christie's farm, and that Christie should lend a hand in return.

But as neighbors quickly learned, you never saw the inside of Christie's house, not even for a drink of water. The ornery fellow would stand outside with a cigarette in one hand and a beer in the other and not even so much as invite you in to sit at table. He was *dif'rnt.*

The Hoffmann yard, too, gave people plenty of fodder for talk. Mainly, it was the *animals.* Why in the world did ol' Hoffmann do it? Nailing stuffed bunny rabbits and teddy bears up and down the big oak tree in front of their house only to let them rot. Was he trying to scare the children?

And then there was the night he ran outside blind-drunk and fired off shotgun rounds at a tree until Sheriff Howard came and hauled him into jail, or his insane habit of pitching himself out of moving vehicles for no apparent reason. Folks agreed: He was *very dif'rnt.*

Only once in local memory did Christie relent and allow visitors past the front door. The family had agreed to host a 4-H meeting. But the festivities came to a screeching halt when Christie showed no intention of serving anything to eat, let alone allowing a single guest beyond the living room. It galled every hardworking local who felt he or she had a right to Hoffmann's hospitality.

The secrecy and the niggardliness and the stuffed animals rotting on the tree out front made it all the more notable when someone stumbled across the threshold and came out with a report of "what went on in there."

One blazing summer afternoon, a man hired to paint Christie's barn went to the front door of the house for a drink. He knocked. Hearing no answer, he went inside.

"You never seen such a filthy mess in all your life," he reported. *"And the smell in that place? It was like there was hogs livin' with the family. But the worst of it, they had the dogs doin' the dishes. They just put the plates down on the floor for the dogs to lick 'em."*

The fellow couldn't bring himself to take a drink after what he had seen, and nobody living in Tompkins County could blame him.

▼

As Ginger's brother, Tom, grew older, he picked up the family reputation for being *dif'rnt.*

"Tom would go over to Samson Air Force Base and pick up the month-old bread and candy and doughnuts and flour that the commissary doled out," one neighbor's son recalled. "People used it to feed the pigs. But the Hoffmanns *ate it themselves. Yes, they did.* I seen Tom with the old crumbs all over his face. He looked as big and sloppy as Junior Samples from 'Hee-Haw.' 'Course, Tom didn't care what he looked like, 'cause he was smart as anyone I ever met. He'd read a book as fast as he could turn the pages. Read every book in the Ithaca Public Library. Yes, he did. He was so smart, he didn't need to care how he looked.

"In 1952, we got TV and we'd go to Art Tuckerman's up the road to watch, and Tommy, he was the fastest with the quiz shows. Yessir, he was."

Although Dick Coates would never say so, Keeney came to understand that Christie Hoffmann and his brood stood for the low end of farming life.

Mary Agnes Hoffmann was known to put on airs that didn't fit her grungy existence. Folks complained that the woman acted "arty" and "high-handed," and that she bragged about visiting relatives in "New Yawk" and "New Jaw-zee." Worst of all, they gossiped, she carried on shamelessly behind her husband's back. She'd wait until Christie drank himself to sleep, then slip out of the house.

But the few people who did visit the delapidated old farm on Bostwick Road found themselves worrying most about Christie's daughter, "Ginger"—Virginia's childhood name.

Christie's brother Henry Hoffmann remembered his visits to the farm in the 1940s: "I'd come out and spend the summer when I was seventeen or eighteen. They had a rugged life, those Hoffmanns, especially Ginger. The house was always a mess, so I'd take her with me to the movies. I felt so sorry for her. I mean, you just hated to bring anyone to that house, it was so dirty. And then her brother, Tom, he used to take her back by the barn and mess with her. Sexually, that is. I'm sorry to say it.

"But then, Ginger was always kind of secretive. She'd hide places and just stay there. It seems like something was always on her mind. Kind of devious."

At school, classmates steered clear of the Hoffmann girl, as tall and strong as many of the farm boys, and equipped with a nasty temper.

She wore her hair chopped short in front and trailing into two long braids pushed back over her shoulders. Her large eyes had a distant look, a manner people took for aloofness. They started saying that Ginger took after her high-handed mother from "Jaw-zee."

"Sometimes Ginger would come in with these diamond rings and try to sell 'em," said Nelson Eddy, a former classmate who lived just down the hill. "They were probably fake diamonds, but that didn't matter. She acted like they was real and she could get 'em whenever she wanted. Us kids, we couldn't get a postage stamp to take to school, least of all Ginger Hoffmann. And I ought to know. I sat right beside her for seven, eight years. I figure putting on like she was a rich person, it was the only time she shined."

▲
FALL 1947
▼

"Hey, Ginger! Tom!"

Art Tuckerman's holler cut through the morning stillness. He pulled up his station wagon in front of the Hoffmann place and honked the horn, a signal at which the kids came tumbling out of the door and into Art's "school bus."

Seconds after the car horn, eleven-year-old Ginger came through the screen door. Most mornings, she wore a plaid jumper, a garment stained and restained so many times from her morning chores that its original pattern was mostly memory. And Ginger was usually yawning. Starting at 5:00 A.M. in the predawn dark, she milked the cows, carried pails of drinking water in from the well, and fired up the living room oil stove. Her brother, Tom, slept late—he was "one lazy dude," Nelson Eddy used to say—but he fell in with Virginia as she tumbled out the front door.

"Whew!" Virginia's schoolmates shouted when she climbed into Art's station wagon. "Cow manure and kerosene. Hold your nose, 'cause thar she blows!"

"Come on, honey," Art Tuckerman said, grinning and patting the seat next to him. "You can sit up here with me."

Next stop was down the hill and across the street at the Eddy farm for Nelson, even at eleven years old already burly and barrel-chested. Then, after hitting the bottom of Bostwick Road, they turned around, picked up Mary Baker, and finally headed up to school.

Education for the Bostwick Road kids meant the Colgrove School, a one-room shingled institution heated by a coal stove. From eight in the morning until three, their teacher, Mrs. Fisch, moved from subject to subject, trying as best she could to impart the three Rs to her twenty-odd students. Then, one by one as they reached their teens, her students went off to Ithaca High down in the city.

To her students, Mrs. Fisch was a legend. All day long—interminably, relentlessly, it seemed—she lectured or sat like a guard in her little office at the rear of the big square classroom. It was a wonder to all, and a subject of protracted debate.

"When does she do it?" they whispered.

"She doesn't do it. She just holds it."

"Go on! Nobody can hold it that long. 'Tain't human."

Then, one afternoon, one of the boys peeped into her office and learned the secret. Word spread instantly: "She pees into the coal bin."

During the morning ride, Ginger sat squeezed between Art Tuckerman and one of the other kids. She kept to herself, eyes darting out the window or fending off sneak attacks from the rear by some obstreperous classmate.

At some point, Art would manage to drop a free hand on Ginger's knee and work it up her leg. For a few tense moments, Mary Baker would watch in silence from the backseat as that large male paw crept up the girl's plaid dress. Then she would turn her eyes away. The subject was too frightening to contemplate, much less talk about—all the more so since Ginger never seemed to complain, and every morning she hopped in front at Art's beckoning.

Mary also spied raised red welts on Ginger's hands and arms. She and the other children could at least whisper about that: *horsewhipping.* But in rural New York in the 1940s, there was "discipline" and then there was "strict discipline." And all of it was considered private family business. What parent hadn't administered a spanking or even a strapping at one time or another? Besides, Christie Hoffmann—though too often seen nursing a can of Genesee cream ale in his front yard—let Ginger keep her own horse, a frowzy red and white creature named Pete. How bad a father could he be? Lord knows, a little strictness never hurt anyone.

Mrs. Fisch, nonetheless, kept an eye out for Ginger. She broke up fights when children piled on the poor thing in a game of capture the flag, and called a stop when their teasing whipped the girl into a frenzy.

Then the lunch-bag incidents started. Every day, somebody's brown lunch sack disappeared from under the coatrack near the bathroom. Mary Baker and Nelson Eddy, who both sat behind Ginger, were the first to catch on. They watched as Ginger raised a hand to excuse herself. With an eye squinting over her shoulder, she slipped somebody's lunch sack into her pocket before running to the outhouse. Moments later, she scurried back into class, wiping crumbs off her dress.

Soon enough, everyone figured it out, and they pointed their fingers: *"She filched the lunch bag! She filched it!"*

Mrs. Fisch took pity on a child who wasn't even given lunch by her own parents. She quieted the class with the order that there would be no laughing at Ginger Hoffmann. Everyone would have to break off a piece of whatever they had brought for lunch and share.

Ginger's stealing quickly joined the other subjects people didn't discuss.

▲
SPRING 1950
▼

"Well, I'll be jiggered."

The voice out in the barn belonged to Louie Petro, one of the dairy inspectors. Every month, Mr. Petro came around wearing his tan uniform and tested the milk.

"This product is near one-quarter water, Christie," he said. "What do you think you're doing selling watered milk to Dairy-Lea? That's criminal, for Crissake. I hate to do this, but I got to take you up to the board."

"Aw hell, Louie," her father protested, "let it go. It's just this once. I was short of cash, understand? It was only this one time."

"It ain't personal, Christie. But this is serious. Waterin' hurts every dairyman, apart from it's being outright stealin'. I got to think about the whole county."

"I'm asking you. I got the kids and the missus."

"Christie, if I give this the nod and the board finds out, I'm as good as fired."

"Louie, I'm asking . . ."

"It's no good."

"Sure. Figures." Her father's voice started to rise. "Some kinda friend you turn out to be, you and the frigging board. You don't give a damn about anyone else, do you?"

"Christie, I'm just—"

"Get off my property, hear? Get the hell off, you stinking, lousy son of a bitch!"

Ginger peeked around the corner and saw her father's raised fist. She slipped out of her hiding place, ran into the house.

That night, while Mary Agnes was away visiting relatives and Tom lay asleep in the next room, Ginger heard her father come in the living room downstairs.

"Ginger! Tom! Where the hell are you?" A crash was followed by some muttering. For a moment, everything fell still, then her father's slurred voice came up through the floorboards.

"You better be glad I'm too tired to whip you." His breathing turned wheezy. "Screw the board! Screw the world! Screw you kids! You just eat and eat, don't you? Stuff your fat mouths out of my pockets. Spoiled little princess and her fat-ass brother. *You hear me?* I'll tan your hides into shape tomorrow, you can believe that! Give you something to remember, you sunufabitches! Get out the riding crop and ride you two 'til the sun sets in China . . ." The voice trailed off, became less and less coherent. Ginger drifted into sleep.

▲
WINTER 1953
▼

Ginger's heart raced as she climbed on the last horse kept in the Hoffmann barn and bolted under a full moon. It was the eve of her sixteenth birthday in January.

Four days later, she slipped back into the house, past the hissing black stove and ran upstairs to bed.

While she was gone, Christie led a search party up and down the road. When he finally discovered Ginger safe and sound in bed, he exploded in a rage. Where the hell did you go? What came over your nasty little mind?

Again, people whispered the word *horsewhip.*

▲
FALL 1953
▼

Twilight. Two Tompkins County teenagers—Dick Coates and Bert Chase—were pitching hay up at Bert's barn about a half mile from Bostwick Road. Young Dick Coates had a small round head in which two bright blue eyes sat like a couple of blueberries pressed into a doughball. His nose was just a trifle long for a pug, and he possessed a busy mouth that often got him into trouble, though never for long. It was hard to take serious offense at disheveled Dick with his smiling, dirty face.

Dick's companion Bert Chase kept his hair neatly parted and his clothes in order—at least when he wasn't working the fields. But the two young farming boys never thought much about their differences. Sinewy around the arms and tough-skinned from logging, Bert and Dick were typical Tompkins County teenagers.

"Hey, Dick," Bert said, "lookee that!"

Dick spiked his pitchfork into the ground and leaned on the handle. The eastern portion of the sky, usually dark at that hour, glowed orange like an iron forge. They dropped their work and ran. *Fire!*

At the crossroads of Podunk and Bostwick, they looked downhill. It was the Hoffmann barn. Flames rose up through the roof and sent cinders spiraling into a black tornado of smoke. Christie Hoffmann stood in the road flailing his arms while Tom and Ginger ran in and out of the barn pulling out calves and cows, the animals' eyes rolling back in their heads. Dick and Bert sprinted down. With the fire starting to rage, there was not much to do apart from trying to keep the terrified animals from bolting and steering clear of the hot ashes blowing through the air.

A fire truck arrived minutes later, a dilapidated red dinosaur that moaned and whined with leaks from its pressurized water tank. Fire fighters formed a busy knot, spraying water, keeping the expanding crowd of onlookers at a safe distance, and herding the last of the animals, traumatized and bewildered, away from the barn.

Once the cattle were safely boarded up the hill at a neighbor's farm, people settled into a semicircle and watched the blaze.

Dick stood at the front of the crowd, close to Ginger. He knew Ginger by sight, but this was the first he had paid her any mind. Her long red-brown hair and large green eyes shone in the firelight; her face glowed hot with the excitement and sweat. Dick noticed her full figure, a firm young body tending toward plumpness. By Dick's way of thinking, she was ripe for the picking. And the look in her eyes, a darting, almost hungry glance, was more than enough invitation. He slipped one arm around Ginger's waist as she stared into the fluorescent embers and trembled at the cracks and reports coming from the burning rafters.

The barn fire lighted the road for half a mile in either direction, and by the time night set in, neighbors were still watching its dying gasps. Sometime after dark, the corner posts collapsed and the fire department stopped trying to save even a portion of the place. One by one, the posts gave way with the jerky, reluctant motion of a crippled animal, and the peaked barn roof floated to the ground amidst a shower of sparks. It was, by all accounts, a fire to remember.

Christie swayed, in a daze, as the last flames flickered out.

"The damn place's an albatross," he muttered. "First the Dairy Board, now this friggin' thing. Least I got in-surance."

He looked around for Ginger, but she had slipped off. Dick Coates was gone, too. "That slut," Christie muttered to himself. "If it ain't one fella, it's another."

For weeks afterward, Ginger's brother, Tom, went around Ithaca spreading a peculiar story. He kept telling folks that his sister, Ginger, had something to do with the barn burning down. He never said precisely how she had done it, but Tom said he was sure. Ginger refused to talk about it. She walked away from questions, with her head held high.

Rumors about arson had just begun to brew when two incidents brought the subject to an abrupt close.

One morning, a parent caught Tom "monkeying" with a little boy who lived along a paper route Tom ran for the Ithaca *Journal.* The subject was smoothed over when Tom quit newspaper delivery to take a job cleaning floors at Ithaca Hospital. But after his disgrace, he kept his thoughts about his sister's arson to himself. And people, in any event, seemed decidedly less inclined to believe him.

At the same time, a pair of insurance-company adjusters visited the remains of Christie's barn. The agents took one look at the damage and agreed to hand over a check, although in an amount utterly insufficient to rebuild the structure. As a result, no one ever bothered to find out exactly how the barn fire had started. But word among Ithacans—Tom Hoffmann's widow, Dick Coates, Christie's sister, and others—even thirty years later was that Ginger Hoffmann might have done it.

CHAPTER 16

GLUE FACTORY

▼

Still ice-crusted in places, Bostwick Road had softened here and there with a spring thaw. Mud season was due within weeks, and it would turn the Ithaca hillsides into brown ooze.

That afternoon, Ginger and Dick trudged up toward the house. At the crest of the hill, opposite the oak tree where a group of stuffed animals hung impaled and rotting, a pickup truck lifted something large and muddy up off the ground. A winch whined in the air. As the object rose into the air, stretching out to full length, the truck hunched down on its rear wheels.

Christie, red-eyed and smiling, leaned against a tree and took in the spectacle. The horse's carcass hung over the truck, streaks of blood flowing down the massive head from a shotgun wound the size of a quarter.

Ginger and Dick drew closer. Ginger recognized what was going on. All at once, she was running.

"Pete! What happened to Pete?" she cried, grabbing at Christie's sleeve.

"Had to shoot the damn beast," Christie puffed, wiping a hand through his nap of hair. "Ate too much and took up too much space. Time for the glue factory. Yessir, glue time for ol' Pete. Straight into jars." Christie offered a stained grin at the thought.

Ginger dug her fingernails into Christie's arm, her eyes wide. "Goddamn you, you bastard!" she screamed, sobbing. "Pete was *my* horse. You had no right! I hate you! Dammit all!! He was MINE!!"

With a swift jerk, Christie elbowed her away. Dick stepped in and put his arm around Ginger's waist. "Never you mind, honey," he soothed. "It'll be all right."

"He was mine! You . . . you . . . had no right!" she stammered.

"That's enough out of you, missy," Christie shot back. "You're spoilt too much as it is."

The sound of gears grinding into reverse cut their talk short. The horse's muddied body slid onto the flatbed and settled with a dull, thick sound. Dick Coates stood openmouthed. He had seen horses put down before, but Pete was Ginger's pet, as close to her as any friend. Christie must be desperate for cash, he thought.

The drivers packed up their tackle and started off. Christie stumbled back into the house, toting his rifle. Dick and Ginger watched as Pete's carcass disappeared behind a hump of road, jounced about in the rear of the truck like a sack of flour.

▲

FALL 1954

▼

Even by his own account, Dick Coates's wedding to Ginger Hoffmann—he was nineteen, she was seventeen—was short on romance.

"I knocked her up, then we got hitched," he told Keeney from the Lodi pay phone. "Over at the minister's house, Christie put on a little party with a piece of cake and some ice cream. There wasn't nobody there, just Christie, Mary Agnes, my dad and mother, Tom, and my little brother. Ginger told me that Christie had knocked her down one day and so she couldn't get pregnant. I found out otherwise, but by then it was too late."

They began married life by living with Dick's parents in the nearby town of Locke. The Coateses' two-story farmhouse was an old New Englander with the original hand-cut floorboards and low, narrow doorways. The building had been in Mrs. Coates's family for two generations. Dick and his mother were both born there.

Honeymoons being for the rich, Dick and his father went back to cutting timber three days after the wedding. Ginger joined Margaret Coates in minding the house, cooking, and helping haul lumber.

One evening that fall, as dusk settled, Dick and his father headed home from work. As they walked up the dirt drive, they heard Ginger's voice echo through the trees.

"I don't know what you're talking about," her voice rang sharply. "If you think that I—"

"You took it," a woman protested. "Your sticky little fingers! You're just a weasel, that's what."

"I don't have the slightest idea what you're talking about," Ginger answered. "If you lost your purse, don't come crying to me."

"Crying? You thief—"

The woman stopped just as Dick and his father appeared. She turned and pointed a finger at Ginger, who stood facing her, hands propped on her hips.

"I don't know which one of you's related to this weasel, but she stole my pocketbook and I want it back!"

"Now, ma'am, there must be some kind of confusion." Dick's father took charge and strode over.

The woman insisted otherwise and refused to take a single step until she got her bag back. Ginger said that she must be loony.

"We walked the road half the night lookin' for that danged thing," Dick recalled. "Finally found it right near our backyard. The bag had some money in it, and a change purse. But mostly the woman was upset about a picture of her dead daughter she had in there."

The woman snapped up her bag under her arm and stalked off. Ginger turned and walked back inside the house. Dick and his father faced each other silently in the yard, wondering what could have possessed Ginger to do a thing like that.

Dick let the subject drop. When all was said and done, Ginger was still his wife. He was not going to start off their marriage by siding against her. The whole thing had to be some sort of misunderstanding.

A few weeks later, just as the bag incident faded from everyone's mind, Dick stumbled across a steel vise lying in his driveway. It was a brand-new piece of hardware and whoever owned it, thought Dick, would surely come after it. Folks in Tompkins County were too poor to throw away a perfectly useful tool.

"Ginger!" he called up at the living room window. "What the hell's this thing doing' in the road?"

The screen door to the kitchen swung open and Ginger stepped out. She had on a pressed calico sundress, and her face was dabbed with makeup. Over the months she and Dick had dated, Ginger had begun to take care more and more with her appearance. She bobbed her hair, and, though she tended toward being overweight, she would never be seen in anything that hadn't been newly washed and ironed—right down to the lacy underwear she showed off to Dick. Some people called her snooty, but Dick felt proud of having so well-kempt a wife, and one who was hotter than a hellcat in the bedroom.

"It must've fallen out of a truck, Dick," she answered in her singsong voice. "Seems to me like you can just hold on to it. Finders keepers. That's the law."

"I don't know. Somebody's gonna come lookin'."

"Suit yourself, but I say keep it." Maybe she's right, Dick thought. He picked up the vise and took it inside.

Later that night, Dick asked again if someone hadn't driven through their yard and the vise bounced out. Ginger's face fell into a chilly smile. It was an expression Dick had come to recognize. It meant, Don't pry where you shouldn't.

But soon enough the signs became too obvious to ignore. Pounds of butter turned up in Ginger's coat when she came home from Fran Newhart's, the local grocer. She was starting to "show," so quietly slipping a few items into her baggy overcoat proved easy. Other times, a wad of dollar bills might mysteriously appear, or Dick would find a new dress hanging in the closet. And there was Ginger's mysterious supply of fancy lingerie.

Inevitably, one concerned neighbor came by asking about a vise left on his flatbed.

"I never knowed about her stealin' before we got married," Dick confessed. "Then everybody seemed to know about it. It hit me like a sledgehammer."

Everybody, it turned out, included Mr. and Mrs. Coates senior.

One day, the old man pulled his son aside. "Darn it, Dick, I'm not letting that wife of yours disgrace our house any more than she has already. You had to marry her, I understand that. But we're decent working folks and she's making fools out of all of us. She's got to go."

Dick loyally defended his expectant bride but succeeded only in working his father into a second burst of anger. "I know old man Hoffmann, he's a drunk and a thief who'd water his milk to line his own pockets at his neighbor's expense. That daughter of his isn't a whole sight better. You know as well as I do, the apple don't fall far from the tree." Mr. Coates sent the young couple packing with the parting salvo, "As far as I'm concerned, you can get out and stay out!"

The first snows of another rugged Ithaca winter had just fallen. Dick and Ginger turned up at the Bostwick Road doorstep, bags in hand, baby on the way, to stay with Christie and Mary Agnes Hoffmann.

▲
SPRING 1955
▼

Easygoing Dick Coates could live in close quarters with his wife's petty thefts and Christie's drunkenness, but he discovered that his bride had an even darker streak running through her character, and it was never a pretty sight.

One winter evening, Dick pulled his truck into Christie Hoffmann's driveway. Dick had been logging, hauling timber out beyond Lake Cayuga. Work ended, as always, when the light gave out.

Inside the house, Ginger, now well into her pregnancy, stood by the kitchen sink. She wore a pressed white apron over still one more dress Dick had never seen before, one that accommodated her swollen belly. From the look of the counters, she had been preparing dinner, washing vegetables and cutting beans with a large square butcher's knife.

"Where's the money you made today?" she asked as Dick slumped into a chair in front of the living room stove.

Dick picked through his pockets theatrically and, finding nothing, announced smartly, "Hell, I forgot all about it. But, shee-it, Donny'll pay me double tomorrow."

"No, he won't. You spent the money, didn't you?"

"Honest, Ginger. I just forgot. I'll get the money tomorrow."

Ginger's face settled into a vacant stare, her eyes glazed and hard. She was in that mood again, Dick understood, the mood where things usually got bad and the best strategy was to lay low. He turned his attention back to loosening his boots, and warmed himself by the stove.

Christie and Mary Agnes were away, the house was quiet, and in the heat of the oil stove Dick began to doze. Then, all at once, he heard steps running across the floor behind him. Rising out of a half-sleep, he turned and saw his wife—hair perfect, dress clean and pressed—coming at him with the butcher knife. Her pretty face had turned to a mask.

"Damn you, you idiot! Where's that money?" she shouted in a voice Dick scarcely recognized. Then the knife came past him in a downward swipe.

In one jump, Dick was up and backing toward the front door, tripping over his shoelaces.

Ginger turned to face Dick as he backed toward the front door.

"Now put that thing down," Dick said as he edged through the doorway. "I'm sorry, honey. I'll talk to Donny tomorrow. That's a promise."

Ginger didn't seem to hear. She lumbered forward and took another swing. Ginger, ungainly from her growing belly, lost her balance and tumbled over a coffee table. Dick scrambled outside and slammed the screen door between them.

"Ginny, easy now," he said, his voice shaking. "I'll get the money. Just put down that knife. You don't want to hurt anybody. *Put that thing down!*"

Through the screen, he saw Ginger pull herself up off the floor, straighten her dress, and wipe her palms. Then, once more, she snatched up the knife. In a clumsy lurch, she came at him, tearing at the screen with the blade.

Dick was not about to wait and see what would happen next. In the rearview mirror, he watched Virginia standing on the front porch, knife raised, her face lit red by the taillights of his truck.

▲

FALL 1955

▼

Dick and Ginger's first child, Ronald Albert Coates, had arrived the previous May. For a time after that, Ginger's temper seemed to have cooled. Dick was making good money working days for Dairy-Lea as a truck driver, and cutting a few logs "on the sideline."

By the following January (1956), he had set aside enough cash to move the family out of Bostwick Road and into their own home. They settled nearby in Newfield. A white, two-storied place with shuttered windows, their house sat back a few yards from Spencer Road, behind a neat rectangle of lawn. Newfield, like most of Tompkins County, was no more than a strip of civilization scratched tenuously into the wilderness. Not far behind the Coateses' new home, dirt roads meandered away into glens, hollows, and great stretches of rich woodland.

The Coateses rented their house from an elderly woman named Pierson who lived directly across the street. Mrs. Pierson charged the going rate of ten dollars a week. Dick's combined salaries from Dairy-Lea and moonlighting, totaling eighty-two dollars weekly, left plenty of cash for food, clothes, and outings to the occasional auction.

Around that time, Dick began to catch wind of his wife's sexual flings. It came as neither a surprising nor a cruel blow. Ginger had had a loose reputation as long as Dick could recall. For one thing, everybody in the area knew how Ginger Hoffmann lost her virginity: spending the night with *two boys* in a hayloft. Her girlfriend Betty Boyce, who chastely dated one of the culprits, was furious afterward.

"Jeez, Ginny," she gasped. "The whole town knows! How could you do this to me?"

"I can do what I want," Ginger said, and spun on her heels.

"Why you—" Betty started to say, but Ginger didn't seem to hear. She strutted away, pausing only for a glance over her shoulder.

After the two boys in the loft came Art Tuckerman, the school-bus driver. Dick Coates said he could never get clear in his mind whether it had been seduction or not with Art—Ginger sometimes said he had forced himself on her—but it didn't seem to matter, not given all her other notorious nightly meetings in the cornfields.

"Hell, Pete Gibbs used to sleep with Ginny once in a while." He laughed bitterly. "I caught him once when I came home early from drivin' a truck for Dairy-Lea. Saw footprints in the snow comin' right up to the back door.

"Must've run in the family, the way I see it. Ginger's mother was no better, that's for damn sure. She once grabbed me by the thumb and tried to get me in the backseat herself. Ginger was in front, but Mary Agnes woulda had me right there in the back if I'd let her. Never forget that night.

"And I never could be real sure if Ronnie was mine, even though he was what got us hitched in the first place. Now, when Jimmy come along a year later, I was pretty sure *he* was mine. But I could never *know*. Hell, Ginger was just a whore. She never did study for nothin' except to screw."

Dick took Ginger's promiscuity in stride, but her continually breaking the law sent him into a fury. One day, a new set of silver turned up at the house. "I knew better than to ask where this got-damn silver came from," he told Keeney. "I just wondered when somebody would come 'round looking for it."

Three days later, Ginger announced, "We're having Mrs. Pierson over for dinner tomorrow."

"Jesus, Ginger, you always called her an old bag," Dick said. "What's made you so friendly all of a sudden?"

"She's our landlady, and she deserves it," Ginger said. The subject was closed.

The following night, Dick came home to a table spread as nicely as he could recall. Ginger had obviously spent the day getting to-gether a real country feast: turkey, biscuits, gravy, a dinner fit for Thanksgiving. The silver, polished and shining, lay by the plates.

When Mrs. Pierson arrived, Dick felt a renewed flush of pride over his well-dressed young bride. All couples have their troubles, he consoled himself, ours are no worse than we deserve. They sat in the parlor and made polite conversation until Ginger called them into the dining room with the announcement that dinner was served.

"It was a fine sight. She really had me fooled," Dick said angrily.

Halfway through the meal, Mrs. Pierson looked up at Ginger and exclaimed, "You know, I had a set of silver just like these, but they disappeared from my back room last week!"

"Isn't that something?" Ginger smiled at her husband. "You never know, do you?"

"Ol' Mrs. Pierson knew them things was stolen," Dick told Keeney. "But people was afraid of Ginger, so no one did a gotdamn thing about it. That night, I batted Ginger for stealin', and she took me beside the head with a vacuum cleaner. That's when I took off again."

That same night, Dick ran into one of the few locals who con-tinued to hold his wife in high regard: Bert Chase, who had been working the fields with Dick the night of Christie Hoffmann's barn fire. Bert put an arm around Dick's shoulders and tried to get his pal to simmer down. Ginger might not be the most ambitious person in the world, but the gal did take good care of the home and the boy.

"You know," Bert said, "I've always thought of Virginia as a pretty decent woman. That's right. And you've got a family by her. Now be a man and get on home."

Dick and Ginger were still in Mrs. Pierson's house. Ronnie was now two, their second child Jimmy barely one. The intervening years had been filled with more bouts of infidelity, stealing, and violence.

People in Ithaca, Newfield, and Cortland all knew of uppity Virginia Coates with the sticky fingers. No one had ever witnessed anything quite like it: the big, brown-bobbed woman, neat as a pin, stealing anything she could get her mitts on. *Kleptomaniac,* a word hardly ever heard in Tompkins County, was now passed around freely. But the comments and the whispers he overheard drove Dick to distraction. Ginger had even gone to visit an old friend at school wearing a "new" fur coat that one of the teachers there recognized as her own. Ginger came home furious that she'd been made to give it back.

Slovenly and given to overdrinking, Dick was still a fundamentally honest sort. Being associated with the county's most notorious thief, Keeney sensed, tore him apart.

Dick said he never got over when Dutch Stolton stopped him on Main Street. "How d'ya like them new boots, Dick?" Dutch asked, smirking.

"I like 'em fine," Dick answered, trying to step past.

"Better not wear 'em to Baker's store." Stolton blocked the way. "That's where your wife stole 'em. Haw, haw!"

Dick slunk off, not knowing whether to tear out his hair, beat his wife, or just divorce her and start out fresh. And as the shame wore off, Dick hardened. He would come home, he said, "bat her one for stealing again," then settle in for the evening with a few beers.

Auctions ranked among the main social events in Tompkins County. People donated any and every spare household item or tattered piece of clothing to raise money for charity, church, or the fire department. Women baked and set up tables. Men got together and smoked their pipes. Sometimes a guitar or two would start picking out a tune.

Dick and Ginger stayed at one particular auction that December until midnight. When they came home, they pulled out blankets and slept near the stove in their living room. The upstairs floor stayed warm only by virtue of whatever heat seeped up between the floorboards, and tonight, with the temperature well below zero, they stood a better chance of staying warm by huddling right in front of the old oil stove. Dick fell asleep quickly, still wearing his flannel coat. Ronnie and Jimmy lay curled together in bed on the second floor.

Around two or three that morning, Dick snapped awake. Their mutt Dixie was barking furiously. Dick didn't need to turn on the light to see why. Across the room, a section of ceiling had caught fire. A ring of flames ate at the wallpaper and timber. Smoke drifted down and then was sucked up through a swiftly widening hole. Dick looked around, but Ginger was already up and gone. In this dry old place, there wasn't time to wonder about where she had gone. The children were sleeping upstairs.

Dick raced up the staircase, pulled the boys out of bed, and hauled them outside. Ginger was already there, watching as fire department trucks pulled in. Shivering on their square of lawn, the family watched fire fighters pour water through the upstairs window.

It took Dick a few days to begin wondering why Ginger hadn't been with him on the couch when he woke up. All he remembered was her face lit red, her eyes glowing just as they had the day Christie Hoffmann lost his barn to fire, some five years before.

And the fire itself was bothersome. It had started in a portion of the ceiling on the *opposite* side of the room from the stove. That just didn't square with the idea of an oil stove heating up the rafters.

Whatever its origin, the fire destroyed most of the ceiling, but the first floor remained salvageable. The family could have made do while carpenters came in to rebuild the place. But Mrs. Pierson insisted that they immediately find new lodgings. In her mind, the Coateses were probably responsible for the fire breaking out in the first place, and she had by no means forgotten the matter of the stolen silverware.

Once again, the family returned to Bostwick Road. Dick continued his day laboring. Ginger continued her shoplifting and promiscuity. The boys grew bigger.

On Friday, July 3, Dick came home to his family's newly rented place in Newfield. He found two hungry mouths and no Ginger. It seemed just as well. He had spent a few hours after work hanging around behind the Dairy-Lea milk house shooting pennies and drinking some beers. He had made ten cents, better than usual, and was in no mood for a row with the missus. Tomorrow, the Fourth, they would all go into town for the fireworks show. He fixed dinner for himself and the boys, then, nursing a can of beer, fell asleep on the sofa.

About eight o'clock, the phone rang.

A lawyer named John Ryan introduced himself. He said he was calling on behalf of a woman named Beverly Mulks who had been arrested in Cortland for passing bad checks. Mulks had given him this number to call. "Also goes under the names Virginia Coates and Mary Barnes," the lawyer added. "Are you related to the lady?"

Dick hopped in his truck and raced the ten miles over to Cortland, wondering along the way what in hell his wife had been up to this time. He arrived and found Ginger locked in a holding cell. The local justice was off for the weekend, so Ginger ended up spending the weekend in the tank. Dick brought over a few magazines to help her pass the time.

Monday, July 6, brought a few surprises. Police Justice Curtis Harris looked at the large-boned, well-dressed woman and read the charges. Eight counts of forgery, four of larceny. According to the police report, she had been on a check-forging spree through town and was apprehended on her way out of town. For Cortland, this ranked as high crime. Justice Harris saw no reason for lenience. He held the woman on one thousand dollars' bail, pending indictment by the grand jury.

Dick was still recovering from the shock when Ginger's attorney hit him with a bill for one hundred dollars, a retainer to represent his wife during the felony proceedings. Syracuse Bonding Company put up the cash and Dick and Ginger promptly left town.

Once they were home, Dick found the worst surprise of all: newspaper coverage. He had always feared Ginger's criminal habits were common knowledge. What he read left no room for doubt.

Ithaca *Journal*—July 6, 1959

CHECK CHARGE HOLDS WOMAN

A Newfield woman was in the Cortland County jail this morning after waiving examination on a charge of passing four forged checks totalling $195 in this village Friday afternoon.

Police Chief Thomas Davis identified the woman as Mrs. Virginia Coates. He said she first used the name of Beverly Mulks, Dryden RD 1, while passing the checks for $20 to $75 each on local merchants. He said she spent $68.50 on groceries, and the rest on clothing.

Local businessmen became suspicious of the amount of money the woman was spending, Chief Davis said, and she was arrested before she left the village. The merchandise was recovered.

Close on the *Journal*'s heels, the Syracuse *Post Standard* ran a similar article that mentioned that Virginia had been arrested "with the assistance of local businessmen, the bank and troopers and the BCI." To Dick, it sounded as if the whole town had risen up.

The event also had a weird significance for those who knew Ginger well. Dick recognized the name Beverly Mulks that Ginger had given the police. Blond-haired, voluptuous Beverly was hot stuff at Ithaca High School, the best-looking girl in the class. She stole half the hearts in town singing with a local C & W band. Dick grimaced at the thought of what people in Ithaca were saying now, Ginger Coates impersonating Beverly Mulks.

Two months later, Cortland's grand jury returned a twelve-count indictment against Virginia Coates aka Beverly Mulks, and she and Dick traveled back to the Cortland courthouse. This time, at least, Ginger's attorney, Jack Ryan, earned his fee.

On Ryan's motion, one count of grand larceny in the second degree was dismissed, and he managed a favorable plea bargain for his client. Virginia Coates stood before New York State Superior Court Judge Robert W. Sloan on October 5, 1959, and entered her plea of guilty to the remaining felony charges.

Judge Sloan placed Ginger, then age twenty-two, on probation for two years.

▲
SPRING 1960
▼

According to Dick, probation did nothing to cool his wife's ardor for theft. She still turned up unexpectedly with clothes, or food, or some trinket that caught her eye. It almost didn't seem to matter what she took.

Dick said there was one event he'd never forget. He kept a charge account at the Montgomery Ward store in Ithaca. That fall, a claims collector had stopped by the house demanding payment for an overdue eight-hundred-dollar bill. Ginger, Dick knew, was the only possible explanation.

"I called her everything but a white girl," Dick said. " 'Course, I didn't pay the gotdamn bill. I told the fella to take a walk."

Later that season, Dick and Louie Petro, another of the Dairy-Lea drivers, noticed twenty-five dollars missing from a cigar box where they pooled gas money. "We all figured she took it," Louie remembered. "She was just the sort of woman I wouldn't trust around any kind of money. But we never did nothin' about it."

A string of Christmas lights appeared in the Coateses' living room. Watches materialized on Ginger's arms and then vanished. Expensive wedding presents for their neighbors came out of nowhere, along with more food from Fran Newhart's store, even a set of operatic recordings from the Longines Symphonette Society. Another bill-collection agency telephoned, threatening to repossess the Coateses' furniture.

And their fights continued, usually with Virginia on the attack. Dick Coates started drinking heavily. The two boys were ill-behaved, and no one seemed to mind. Life for the Coates family in the quiet town of Newfield, New York, bottomed out.

▲
FALL 1961
▼

Once more, it happened at night.

Dick's logging buddy Peanut Everett was over at the house helping out. The two men had spent the better part of the afternoon planting a new vegetable garden. By sunset, Peanut, who was more intent on quitting than finishing, forgot to coil the garden hose.

After dinner, Peanut curled up on the living room sofa and fell asleep. At 5:00 A.M., Peanut woke up and sniffed the air. "Hey! Dick!" he shouted. "I think your house is on fire!"

Dick came tearing down the stairs and was hit by the ungodly reek of burning insulation. A cellar fire. The thought flashed through Dick's mind, There's nothin' down there that coulda burnt. He and Peanut scrambled outside and found the garden hose still screwed to the outdoor spigot. It took only a few minutes to run the hose into the cellar, and the fire sputtered out before it even singed the floorboards.

Sometime during the chaos, Ginger came downstairs with Ronnie and Jimmy. She stood by in her nightgown, keeping the children out of harm's way.

Dick and Peanut cleaned up the basement the next morning. Among the charred and wet debris, they noticed a small pile of spent matches under some electrical cord. Dick shook his head. He had just finished laying down that cord weeks before. It was brand-new insulated wire and there was no good reason for it to burn, at least not by accident.

Dick told Keeney he never confronted Ginger about it, or the other fires. What was the point? All he had were suspicions. And he didn't want her coming at him with a butcher knife again.

Nothing stood to be gained by confronting her. She seemed determined to claw her way through life. Dick said he should have seen it all coming, but by then it was too late. Jail time and probation hadn't impressed her, why should he expect a few words to work any better? The only place to go was out.

▲

WINTER 1966

▼

On Christmas Eve of 1966, Dick and Virginia broke up. They had enjoyed a few quiet years, but never entirely quiet. Ronnie was now eleven years old, running around in overalls and a work shirt, playing hide-and-seek in the yard with Jimmy, age ten.

Dick couldn't remember what his last fight with Ginger had been about—not that it mattered. Their marriage had been collapsing for years. Once more, they went at each other, aiming to draw blood. Dick screamed at Ginger to get the hell out of his house forever, and this time she went.

Lit by their Christmas window decorations, Ginger ran out into the snow. She took the boys, shoved them into the front seat of their truck, and tore off down the road.

For months, Dick heard only secondhand news about his wife. Word had it that she had moved back in with Christie at Bostwick Road, and that her mother, Mary Agnes, had gone off to live in California. Once, Dick glimpsed Ginger walking down Main Street, but he kept his distance.

The following year, in March, he read a piece in the Ithaca *Journal.*

ONE INJURED IN HOUSE FIRE

Fire leveled a two-story wooden-frame house at 903 Bostwick Rd. Sunday morning, resulting in a total loss of property and possessions for two families and the hospitalization of a mother of two.

Mrs. Virginia Coates was listed in satisfactory condition at Tompkins County Hospital today, there she is being treated for cuts and bruises to her face sustained when she jumped from [a] second floor window after lowering her children to safety by tying bed sheets together. . . .

The fire was discovered at 3:55 A.M. by Mrs. Coates who alerted the household and the Tompkins County Sheriff's Department.

It turned out Virginia landed on a fifty-gallon metal milk can, headfirst. Ginger had a way of being around when fires broke out. At least he wouldn't have to clean up after her any more.

But a few months later, a local insurance agent called, asking where he should send the check. "I told the man I don't have no gotdamn insurance," Dick said to Keeney.

"Then he says I'm owed ten thousand dollars because the Hoffmann barn just burned down! I told him again I didn't have no insurance. But he said he had a policy in my own gotdamn name. I didn't even know about it!

"Later that night, I called Ginny over at Chris Hoffmann's. She drove straight over in a Ford Mustang—don't ask me where she got the money for that gotdamn thing—and we had it out right in the driveway. She said that since she paid the premiums, she was owed the insurance money. But she was willing to give me one thousand dollars of it, since the insurance on the barn was in my name. I told her I'd take the money but she could go to hell.

"She got back in the car like she was going to leave. Then she turned it around and tried to run me down. I was layin' there in the snow watchin' her drive off ninety miles an hour. Never seen her again except to get my share of the money. Not that it made no difference. A few years later, what with the debts she ran up and the child support, I filed for bankruptcy."

CHAPTER 17

TAKING BUTCH
FOR A JOYRIDE

▼

My Lord, Keeney thought as he put down the telephone after one
more session with Dick Coates. The man rattled on like a tin can
dragged behind a car, but if even half of what he recalled were
true . . .

Coates's recollections also suggested a reason for killing Cynthia
Elaine: Dick had paid child support only on the two boys, Ronnie
and Jimmy. Cynthia Elaine, then, might not have been worth keeping alive.

But it was the larger picture that most deeply troubled Keeney.
How could Virginia have succeeded as long as she had? For decades,
she had glided past fire departments, insurance agents, police officers, and neighbors. They all suspected wrongdoing but they never
acted—other than once in Cortland, New York, when she went on
a spree of passing bad checks.

Virginia—Ginger—was clearly no master criminal. According to
Dick, everyone in Ithaca knew about her stealing. Shopkeepers
trudged over to the Coates house to reclaim their property; people

joked about her behind her back. Yet she was good enough at what she did. Insurance companies paid up. Police and fire departments missed clues or simply let things slide.

Yes, a portrait was slowly emerging and it led to one conclusion: If anyone was the type to buy insurance on a stranger and cold-bloodedly push her off a cliff, it was Virginia.

Keeney snapped back into the present, in his Castlewood study. He was a lawyer. He should be able to do something about a person who brazenly committed murder. The Sheriff's and DA's offices simply had to be made to understand how strong a case lay right in their file drawer. If Assistant District Attorney Jon Yudin felt that proving "criminal agency" barred bringing justice to Bobbie Roberts and Deana Hubbard, Keeney would meet Yudin's objection four-square.

While Keeney wrestled with the legal issues, R. D. Jones's unmarked cruiser rounded onto a long stretch of Jefferson Hill Road. Winter had brought a momentary slowdown in crime, and R.D. decided to take a spin up to Virginia's old haunt. He had reopened Cynthia Elaine's case, and applied for an order of exhumation for the girl's body. Now he wanted to nose around a little, talk to a few neighbors, and see whether the passage of fifteen years might not shed new light on an old worry.

R.D. also had a new concern: Virginia's second husband, Bud Rearden.

That inspiration had come, once again, from Sarah West. Cynthia Elaine Coates's obituary stated that she had been buried in Louisville's Resthaven Memorial Park. When West called Resthaven to confirm that Cynthia Elaine was indeed buried there, she discovered that Virginia's second husband, Sylvester "Bud" Rearden, Jr., had been buried in the same cemetery two years later. All the other Reardens, however, were buried at Louisville Memorial Gardens West.

To Sarah West's way of thinking, it sounded a little odd. Why just those two? Did they have something in common? Keeney and R.D. thought the connection seemed like another long shot, but given all that Virginia had done, they felt they had to run it down.

▼

R.D. drove past the Rearden place. The house had been rebuilt but the barn where Cynthia Elaine died stood in the same broad field out back. The neighbors, too, were still the same folks who had been living on Jefferson Hill Road ever since Fairdale emerged from beneath the swamp water. It remained an area where even lower-middle-class families could afford reasonably spacious homes in a green pastoral setting.

People remembered the old Rearden place: a two-story wood-shingled home with a large front yard surrounded by white oaks. It had a sprawling field out back that led to a barn where they boarded the family horse. First Sugar, an ornery half quarter horse, half mule that Virginia referred to as her "pony," and then Fancy, a part Arabian. The place was, in its way, typical Jefferson Hill Road. Everyone had a horse or two, everyone had a yard, everyone knew a little mechanics and carpentry, and everyone knew everyone else.

Gossip and suspicion about the Reardens still came cheap. R.D. took with a grain of salt the rumor that one couple who purchased the rebuilt Rearden home in the early 1980s had left within a week of moving in. They claimed it was haunted. R.D. had more serious issues on his mind.

Virginia's second husband, Bud Rearden, folks remembered, was something of an electrical Tom Swift. In 1955, on his seventeenth birthday, he had signed on with the navy, and rose through the ranks to become an electrical engineering technician PD 7556 "Sensitive." He developed an expertise in telemetry, collimation towers used for checking missile alignment, radar beams, TARTAR missile systems, and MK1 118 computers. When the high-tech spy ship *Pueblo* became the subject of international controversy, Bud was flown out as part of the emergency repair crew. At home, he designed the family's electrical and plumbing systems, and he had a reputation for being able to dismantle and reassemble most any automobile engine. Compared to Dick Coates, R.D. thought, Bud ranked as a sophisticated professional.

At the time Bud met Virginia, he worked out of a naval base in Port Hueneme, about a hundred miles north of Los Angeles. Virginia had moved out west to join her mother, Mary Agnes, who was working at a Veterans Administration Hospital in Menlo Park. Virginia took a "home nursing" job, attending to an elderly convalescent woman.

When Virginia met Bud, a trim, blue-eyed sailor who, like Dick Coates, was given to drink, they engaged in the courtship typical of two parents. They went on picnics, Bud bringing his three sons, Virginia her two boys and her infant Cynthia. Once, they all drove across country to visit Bud's relatives and former naval buddies in Falmouth, Massachusetts. On February 25, 1971, Virginia's divorce from Dick Coates became final, and the following June she married Bud.

Just after their marriage, Bud received a transfer to Louisville's Naval Ordnance Engineering Station, an "installation" that designed and built gun mounts. That July, the Rearden clan—now an entourage that included four grandparents and six children—moved into the house on Jefferson Hill Road in Fairdale, Kentucky.

Each Jefferson Hill Road local quickly took their measure in his or her quiet way. What neighbors learned about one another generally came by way of what could be observed through their parlor windows. And between the Rearden children, Virginia's parents, Bud, and Virginia herself, the neighbors had plenty to watch.

One woman recalled, "I first met Virginia in the fall of the year they moved onto Jefferson Hill Road. She was a little fat, but, even though she was overweight, I always had the picture of her growing up privileged.

"She dressed with a sort of studied, casual look: flared skirt and a sweater, that sort of thing. And the expensive objects in her home—they were like thousand-dollar wheels on a fifty-dollar car!

"There were pieces of jade, some silver service, a silk screen of the four seasons with jade and ivory insets. I asked Virginia how she got the money to pay for everything. She said that she had worked as a nurse in California for a convalescent woman who thought Cynthia was the greatest thing in the world, and the woman had left her things in her will. But it seemed strange, even then. Virginia told me that members of the family alleged undue influence and there had been a legal dispute. She told me about it just like it was nothing."

Terri Pullin, who lived two houses down and across the road, briefly dated Jimmy Coates. She was one of the few locals who clung to a good opinion of the Rearden family.

"Jimmy and me, we went to ball games, swapped stories about horses. The Rearden house seemed like a typical home. Virginia wore housedresses, had a jawline haircut, and was friendly toward all the kids in the neighborhood. Made us all feel welcome. She was always baking pies or a cake. Just good ol' country cookin'. She seemed like a real June Cleaver. It was, 'Come on in. Have a glass of chocolate. Stand before the fire.' That sort of stuff. When Little Cynthia died, Jimmy came over and said she had been hanged by a horse. But other than that, they was real normal."

"A couple of days after the little girl died, Virginia called me," Althea Boren, another of the Reardens' neighbors, recalled. Althea didn't care for socializing in the first place, but this particular intrusion struck her as more than just annoying. "She wanted to know if I wanted her daughter's clothes and toys for my daughter. 'What would you think seeing my girl playing outside in Cynthia's clothes?' I asked her. 'Wouldn't bother me,' she said. I told her I wasn't interested. The next day, Virginia put the toys outside in plastic bags for the garbageman."

No one had stronger recollections of the Reardens than Jake and Ina Miller. Jake and Ina lived directly across the street from the Reardens in a white-shingled colonial with a porch facing the road, an attached garage, and their own big barn at the rear. Jake had built the place board by board. He was twenty-six when he started, and since then had remained a fixture on Jefferson Hill—all the more so after he joined the Jefferson County PD in 1964.

After taking Cynthia Elaine to the hospital the day she died, Jake had grown into a beer-bellied, slow-moving redneck who wouldn't have minded hearing the term applied to him. He raised tomatoes in his backyard and shared them with his neighbors, spent his spare time expanding his barn, and never thought twice about living anywhere but Fairdale. An acquaintance once joked, "If you took Jake and multiplied him, that's Fairdale."

When R. D. Jones pulled up in front of his place, Jake came out to meet him, extending a callused hand.

"Jake," R.D. said as he got out of the cruiser, "you remember old Virginia Rearden? It looks like she might be in trouble again."

" 'f you say so. 'Course, it's only to be 'spected." Jake spoke with a backcountry accent that made each word sound as if it were chewed like a twist of tobacco, then kept in the pocket of his cheek for a few hours before being spit out.

"Let's sit down and talk this one over for a minute. Okay?"

Sitting on Jake's back porch, looking out at a winter field of bare trees, R.D. and Jake began reviving the stories that set tongues clucking up and down Jefferson Hill Road.

"Bud and Virginia seemed like real nice folks," Jake said, " 'course that was 'fore all them strange things started happening."

"You mean Cynthia Elaine's death?"

"That kinda seemed to start 'em. I don't know how many tales been told since. I remember coming over and there was the little girl lyin' in a car with a towel under her neck. There was a couple globs of blood on the ground, too. It tore up Ina, my missus, no end. She always said it seemed like it upset everybody but the mother."

Jake told R.D. that he had become suspicious about Virginia two years later when Bud Rearden died. That was when the "things" started happening.

"She and her mother told me they was nurses. I didn't know what they did for real. But they'd tell you right off they was practical nurses, liked to boast about it. Anyways, one night Virginia comes over sayin' Bud's dead. I ran back across the street and Virginia and her mother, they was the only ones in the house. The mother was in the bedroom washing and cleaning up the body. I remember thinking at the time, they shouldn't've touched the body, not before the doctor and the coroner had a chance to look it over. A few days later, Bud was buried and that was it."

Jake never got called to the Reardens again in his official capacity. But shortly after Bud died, Virginia came running over in the middle of the night.

"She said her house was on fire, and sure enough it was. The whole damn place, flames shooting out of the roof, sparks flyin'. They stayed over to our place that night, and we all stayed up watching the fire department working away. Those boys barely managed to save the house. Not that it mattered much." Miller let out a short grunt of a laugh. " 'Cause a few weeks later, the house burned again.

"This time, I knowed for sure something was wrong. The night before, I saw a three-quarter truck and camper out back there, and the family was loading it up with everything they could. Then the house burns all the way down and, one more time, Virginia comes a runnin' over in the middle of the night just like a bat outta hell.

"After that second fire, they left Kentucky. Nobody kept in touch. They just disappeared. I think I might've got a letter from one of the boys asking for a letter to get him out of the pen. But Virginia, she just sold the place, then up and left."

With a little checking around, R.D. traced the whereabouts of Virginia's three stepsons, Kenneth, Sylvester, and Butch Rearden. Kenneth and Dennis, the two oldest brothers, were now living in Texas. Neither son, now grown men, had much to say about Virginia apart from the same generalized suspicion already expressed by people R.D. interviewed on Jefferson Hill Road. But they said their brother Butch had stayed behind with Virginia, and that he knew all kinds of things.

Twenty-nine years old and married, Butch was working as an automobile mechanic in a small industrial town in central Pennsylvania when he got the call from R. D. Jones. Butch, with his wispy blond hair and slight frame, had a scrappy, smallest-of-the-litter look about him and a voice to match. But he also had a survivor's mettle.

At first, Butch was reluctant to rehash memories of living with Virginia. He said that even hearing Virginia's name made him uncomfortable, that she was one person he hoped he'd never have to remember. But when R.D. explained that Virginia might be implicated in a pair of murders, Butch agreed to talk.

"I'll tell you one thing," Butch's high-pitched voice cut in. "Something I've never told anybody except my wife."

"What's that?" R.D. asked.

"I never felt entirely comfortable about how my father died."

R.D.'s mouth pursed beneath his mustache. He thought of the cemetery where Cynthia and Bud had been buried. "All right, now. Tell me everything you know."

"Around the house, I always felt like a Cinderella," Butch began, talking around the subject. "Virginia favored Jimmy and Ronnie. They'd stay out all night drinking and raising hell, but I'd be the one who caught the yelling. You didn't mess with the Coates boys. If they beat the tar out of me, Virginia would still come to their defense. They could do no wrong in her eyes.

"Even if I caught hell all the time, I wanted to be with my dad—his name was Sylvester, but everyone called him Bud. What with his being in the navy and all, I never got the chance to know him when I was a kid, so I went to live with him and Virginia in Kentucky. I didn't care what *she* was like. Dad still had a lot of stuff to teach me.

"After my brothers left, to join my mom in Guam, Virginia slowly started working my dad against me. She kept tellin' me I was a no-good and worthless. And she would pull stuff around the house. Blame things on me and use them to humiliate me in front of my father. I spent one night sitting around the living room polishing every wrench in Dad's tool kit as a punishment for something I never did. Basically, she tried to drive me off just like my brothers. But I wouldn't go. I was stubborn.

"Then Cynthia Elaine died," Butch went on. "She was like a sister to me. I was at school that day. It was cold and rainy, and Virginia usually didn't go out to the barn alone. Once she got thrown and spent a week sitting on one of those rubber doughnuts. After that, she kept away from horses.

"Anyway, when I came home from school there was a police cruiser out front. I was totally devastated by it, but Virginia kept her composure. She kept the girl's picture facedown in the living room. And you just did not bring the subject up."

"How about your father?" R.D. tried to work the subject back around to Bud.

"Up until he started getting sick, we spent a lot of time together. Dad was a complete perfectionist. His head was like a vacuum. Anything gets near it, it'd suck it right up. We'd work on cars and electrical repairs around the house. When we built the new wing on the house, Dad wasn't satisfied with meeting city code. He had to exceed it. That's the kind of worker he was. Just meticulous. I'm not as good as he was," Butch said sadly, "but I'm close."

R.D. asked whether Virginia helped take care of Bud after he became ill.

"Sure, she took care of him," Butch said. "She'd even talk about being a nurse, but I never saw her going to work. But one of Dad's prized possessions around the Jefferson Hill house was this old Holly Crafter shortwave radio. Virginia said she was given it by an elderly lady in Palo Alto who she took care of. The woman died and left her the radio. At least, that's what Virginia said."

Finally, Butch related a story that he had kept to himself for the last thirteen years.

▼

"Butch," a faltering voice called from the first-floor bedroom, the room Virginia kept off limits to visitors.

This was the sickroom, the place where food was whisked in and out on trays, where a table littered with bottles of Darvon, Dilaudid, and morphine stood near the big rumpled bed, where the word *cancer* was whispered like a curse.

"Butch, come in here for a minute."

"Sure, Dad," Butch called from the good living room. The good living room, outfitted with all the best parlor furniture, was reserved for company. But Butch sometimes lounged there when no one else was around. That afternoon, Virginia had gone off on errands, and Jimmy and Ronnie were away, so Butch could do more or less as he pleased.

His older brothers were already in Guam, and his decision to stay on in Kentucky now lay more than a year behind him. Only recently, when Virginia yelled and screamed, called him a good-for-nothing or a half-witted idiot, had Butch begun to wonder whether the time hadn't come for him to go, too. Being with his father might not be worth all the abuse that came with being Virginia's stepson.

Cynthia Elaine's death was still fresh on everyone's mind.

Meanwhile, Butch's father was wasting away, his body becoming a mere stick figure with alarming speed. Butch could see the outlines of muscles beneath his father's rice-paper cheeks and in his cavernous temples. It was the face of a stranger.

"Butch," the voice persisted, "where are you?"

"I'm right here, Dad." Butch came into the sickroom, sat down by his father, touched his arm. Bud turned his head. It moved like a face on a pole.

"Good. Now, listen," he said in his insistent, crotchety way. "I'm not going to treat you like a baby anymore. All right?"

"I'm listening, Dad."

"You know what the doctors in the clinic said. That it's a matter of time for me. How much, nobody knows for sure. But I am going to die, and sooner rather than later." His father started coughing. Butch looked on, waiting. "Do you understand?" Bud said as he pressed his son's arm.

"Uh-huh." He did understand. His father was dying; everyone understood that. People visited, talking quietly in words like *prognosis* and *metastasis,* words he had never heard before.

"Go into my dresser, there." Bud raised a twig-like finger and pointed. "It's in the littlest drawer on the top right-hand side. Go on. There's a box with a spring lid inside."

Butch obeyed. He walked cautiously over to the dresser and slid open the little valuables drawer up on top. These were his father's private places. Opening them with permission, he felt as if he was doing something very adult.

He looked inside. Among some tarnished coins, wisps of tobacco, and scraps of paper sat a small blue jewelry box. He held it up for his father to see.

"Go on, bring it over here," Bud called out. Butch understood his father was allowed to be impatient. That was one of the privileges that came with being sick. "Hurry up. I might *be* dead by the time you get here."

Butch brought it over.

"Well, open it." Bud smiled reassuringly. "Go on. You'll like it."

A few clinging wisps of tobacco fell away as the blue velvet top sprung open.

"There they are," he said. "My gold tiger's-eye tie tack, cuff links, and ring. After I die, Butch, they're yours. Understand? I want you to have 'em. You know where they are now. So just come and take them."

"Okay, Dad. Thanks. I won't forget, I promise."

"Good." Bud's head sank back into the pillow. "Now put them away. I'm not dead yet, and I don't plan to go any sooner than absolutely necessary. Just remember to come and take them. You hear?"

"I hear, Dad."

September 7, 1974, Butch remembered, was a Saturday night. His stepbrothers, Jimmy and Ronnie, each a few years his senior, planned to hit the streets of Louisville as usual. Butch was staying home, also as usual.

Jimmy and Ronnie Coates, eighteen and twenty years old respectively, were coming into their own. Both weighed in as strong-armed country boys with sandy hair and deep-blue eyes that could take on a look of soulfulness, a look about a millimeter deep, but one that ensured a steady supply of girlfriends. Jimmy was clean-shaven. Ronnie wore a big unkempt mountain man's beard that he sometimes trimmed into a tangled goatee. Otherwise, they could have been a pair of face-stomping twins. They shared the same drugs, spent time outrunning the same cops, raised the same brand of hell.

Jimmy drove a modified 1966 four-door Wildcat with a souped-up V-8. The Wildcat had once led a useful life as Jake's police cruiser, then Jimmy bought it from Jake and transformed it into the ultimate joyride. With a driver cranked up on crystal meth, the Wildcat could outrun any state trooper's motorcycle along stretches of a state road known as the "Dixie Die-way."

That September, Jimmy was "traveling," as he called it, with a blond teenager from East Louisville named Debbie Williams. A cop's daughter raised around men with guns, Debbie shared her hard-riding beau's taste for the wild side. They cheered the professional wrestling matches at Louisville Gardens, lay on tombstones with cold cream on their faces, and drove the wrong way down highways at two in the morning while hallucinating on LSD. It was a good ol' time.

Debbie knew as well as anybody what Jimmy and Ronnie were capable of. But to a seventeen-year-old, the sheer machismo of their compulsive law-breaking was a turn-on. She had seen Jimmy tie a black man to the back of his truck, then drive down Jefferson Hill, hollering and screaming with sadistic delight as the man's knees were ground to the bone on the asphalt. Another time, he put a loaded pistol to a man's head, forced him to his knees, and then walked away smirking. "I was only kidding him," he said.

The evening of the seventh, while Butch was minding his father, Jimmy, Ronnie, and Debbie were smoking marijuana in a rusted-out trailer home in the Rearden backyard.

Around eleven o'clock, Virginia knocked on the door.

"You boys get out here on the double," she called.

Jimmy, Ronnie, and Debbie cracked the trailer door and stuck out their heads.

Virginia stood there holding Butch by one arm. Her face, as usual, was fully made up, and she wore a tight-fitting blouse, one that showed off her bosom. Her address might be Fairdale, Kentucky, but she dressed and acted like a city woman. That was Virginia's way, people knew: satin sheets in the bedroom, a new New Yorker sedan in perfect condition parked in front. She carried herself like the monarch of Jefferson Hill Road. "Champagne tastes, Kool-Aid income," people used to joke behind her back.

Butch had on a plaid hunting jacket and looked as if he was ready to go somewhere, though not entirely willingly.

Just the day before, Virginia had taken him aside and said, "Butch, your father isn't going to be alive much longer. You're a big boy and you should know that." Something in the way she spoke made the comment sound like a warning.

Jimmy and Ronnie came out and asked what was up.

"Here's twenty dollars, honey." She walked over and pressed a bill into Ronnie's hand. "I want you all to take Butch here for a nice ride." Her voice was sweet but firm.

"What's going on?" Debbie asked from inside the trailer.

"Mom wants us to take ol' Butchy here for a spin." Jimmy turned to Debbie, his slow grin exposing a set of stubby teeth. "Coughin' up twenny bucks jus' to make it worth our while. Shee-it, let's boogie."

"You boys show him a good time, now," Virginia called over her shoulder as she went back inside the house.

"Don't worry, Ma," Ronnie piped up.

The screen door slammed shut behind her. Butch stood awkwardly amid the three stoned teenagers as they yanked on their coats and warmed up their rebel yells. Something strange had to be going on. The only time Jimmy and Ronnie ever took him for a drive was to teach him how to smoke grass, and then they had left him two miles down the road.

"Come on." Jimmy grabbed Butch by the lapel and started to hustle him over to the car. "Do what yo' mamma say. Yee-ha!" Then he looked around for Debbie. "Hey, baby. Where'd you go?"

"Hold on," Debbie called from the front steps of the house. "I gotta take a leak."

"Me, too," Butch joined in, pulling loose from Jimmy. He ran to catch up with Debbie.

"Chickenshit," Jimmy yelled from behind. "Do it in the bushes."

As Butch climbed the porch steps, he overheard Jimmy ask Ronnie, "What do you 'spose Ma wants us to take Butch out so bad for?"

"Beats the hell outta me, bro. But twenny bucks is twenny bucks. I ain't gonna ask her."

The bathroom stood at the rear of the first floor, just off the kitchen, and opposite the sickroom. Debbie nodded through the open sickroom door to a bedridden Bud Rearden as she went in. He returned the greeting with a barely perceptible tilt of the head.

Butch waited outside the bathroom. He glanced in at his father and noticed a shiny object lying amid the collection of Dilaudid and morphine bottles on the side table. It was a syringe. Bud had been getting his antipain meds intravenously for some time now, he knew that. Virginia must be getting ready to give him another shot.

The Wildcat shot down Jefferson Hill Road, past the dark forms of trees overhead, past unlit houses and the silhouettes of barns, out toward the Dixie Die-way. Jimmy and Debbie sat up front, shouting at manic speed about where to spend their "chauffeur's money." Jimmy drove like a suicide, popping beers and pulling on joints as the car centrifuged around turns. Jimmy was crazy as a loon, Butch thought. He'd decided that long ago. But tonight, he focused on making it home alive. He kept imagining a head-on collision with an eighteen-wheeler on a midnight run.

It seemed miraculous that they weren't on stretchers, but at 2:00 A.M. they rolled back onto Jefferson Hill Road. The moon had set, the house lights were still on. The four of them crowded into the trailer, Jimmy pulling Butch along like a mascot. Ronnie flipped on the radio. Debbie started rolling another joint. The Coates boys were iron men, they could slug quarts of booze, drop acid, spark joint after joint and still outdrive the cops.

All of a sudden, someone was banging at the trailer door.

Virginia's voice called, "Boys, get out here! Right this minute!"

They peered out the small window vent and saw Virginia, hands on her hips. "Come on now, you kids. Hurry your behinds."

They piled out of the trailer.

"Butch," Virginia started in a friendly voice that didn't match her words. "I've got bad news for you. Your father's dead. He passed away just about an hour ago. Ma's in there cleaning up the body."

Butch felt as if all his blood had suddenly drained through his ankles. He wanted to throw up. His father, the only tie he had to Fairdale, in fact to anywhere in the world but Guam, was gone.

"No!" he shouted. "I don't believe you. I wanna see him."

He started to run to the house but Virginia grabbed him by the arm and held him still. A wispy sixteen years old, Butch was no match in size or strength for his stepmother.

"The coroner's coming soon," she continued in her controlled voice. "You're just going to be in the way. Now go inside and sit in the dining room."

Butch ran into the house, determined not to cry until he was well out of Virginia's sight. He felt an overwhelming desire to go see his father's body, but he obeyed Virginia. Everyone obeyed Virginia.

"Two or three days after my father died," Butch told R.D., "Virginia held the funeral. My brothers were never notified, or my mother. When I asked about my dad's will, Virginia just said, 'You're too young to understand what it says.' My real mom only learned about Dad's death when people from Social Security called her. Virginia never probated the will or gave me the cuff links, tie tack, or ring, or anything. She kept it all as far as I ever knew.

"I didn't stick around much longer. I left with the clothes on my back and a suitcase. Afterward, I heard that the house burned down, and that it was supposed to have been an electrical fire. That never made sense to me, either. My dad was so strict about everything being above code, he was always like that, a real perfectionist."

All through December, Keeney continued working on his memo to Jon Yudin. Convincing the DA to take the case had become a campaign and already his dossier had doubled in size from the original two hundred pages. But Keeney couldn't stop. He stayed up through the early morning hours, organizing, drafting, and redrafting until he felt he had put together an undeniable argument.

R.D.'s discoveries opened up another avenue: the possibility of a *third* murder.

"Six months ago, I would have said you were crazy." Keeney sighed after R.D. told him Butch's memory of Bud's death.

"I would've said so, too," R.D. answered. "But it wouldn't surprise me to see this thing get worse. Think about it. Can you name me one positive thing we've learned about Virginia? If Butch's story pans out, then we're looking at a real Angel of Death."

Soon enough, a stack of barely legible records from the Jewish Hospital in Louisville, where Bud had been treated up until his death, arrived at B & A. R.D. and Keeney read them over, squinting at the faded white-on-black print.

The hospital records disclosed that, starting around 1972, just before Cynthia Elaine's death, Bud began having treatments for back and arm pain. His chart from Jewish Hospital told the harrowing tale of the onset of cancer followed by vomiting, anorexia, wasting of the extremities, and intense pain. He soon required intravenous doses of Dilaudid, then morphine when the suffering intensified. The final entry, made just two months before Bud's death, stated: "Mr. Rearden is going rapidly downhill."

Peppered throughout the entries Keeney spotted a series of off-handed references.

"On 7/13/74, the patient's wife, a practical nurse, was given prescriptions for Dilaudid. . . ." *A practical nurse.* There was nothing wrong with the notion in general; all sorts of people had referred to Virginia's nursing. Still, according to Dick Coates, Virginia had no more than a tenth-grade education.

In the last pages of the report, the treating physician noted some irregularities in Virginia's nursing care: ". . . the Dilaudid has been stopped and the morphine has become the used analgesic, in a dose of 2 cc./three to four hours. This, according to his wife, is a total dose of 15 mg., but according to the discharge note of his old chart would equal 30 mg. . . ."

Had Virginia been tinkering with Bud's dosages? Did she want to put Bud out of his suffering, or out of the way? Passing herself off as a nurse certainly gave her a golden opportunity to speed his departure. Had she taken it? Or did she just have trouble figuring doses?

R. D. Jones soon came back with more hard facts, drawn from Bud's U.S. Navy file.

On May 11, 1970, Bud had filed an Election of Life Insurance Coverage form with the Federal Employees Group Life Insurance Program. It didn't name the amount to be paid in the event of death, but it certainly could have provided a motive for murder.

On June 28, 1974, Bud then requested that he be "placed in a leave without pay" status for a year because he had "been undergoing many medical tests and recently underwent an exploratory operation . . . and because I have exhausted all available annual and sick leave." The request was granted and became effective July 3, 1974—eight weeks before Bud's death.

At that moment, Keeney and R.D. realized, that with no income and an outstanding life insurance policy, Bud became worth more dead than alive.

The paperwork following Bud's death seemed to bear Virginia's distinctive stamp. Virginia promptly filed a Standard Form 2800 Application for Death Benefit with the Civil Service Retirement System. The peculiar way she filled out the form itself immediately raised questions with the navy's bureaucrats.

A memo from Ewing Davidson, Employee Relations Officer at the Naval Ordnance station, addressed to the U.S. Civil Service Commission Bureau of Retirement, read:

Standard Form 2800, Application for Death Benefits, was completed by Ms. B. J. Judson, a civilian representative of Mrs. Sylvester Rearden. . . . Ms. Judson insisted the SF 2800 be forwarded
as she had submitted without any corrections, typing or other
recognized responsibilities of this Division. Forwarded as is, with
this Division's awareness of whatever deficiencies are apparent.

There were more than a few "deficiencies," even to Keeney's
unpracticed eye. Virginia hadn't dated the document. More importantly, she had avoided straight answers to two yes/no questions.
The first asked "If an executor . . . has not been appointed, will one
be appointed?" The second asked, "If a guardian has not been appointed, will one be appointed?" A straight line had been struck
through *both* "yes" and "no" boxes on each question.

"She sure couldn't be accused of giving false statements," Keeney
said to himself. It was the same technique she had used in Deana's
and Cynthia's deaths: passing off half-truths, multiple stories, and
vague answers. Her usual smoke screen.

But Virginia and her "representative," Judson, did not stop there.
The government form asked, "If a guardian has been appointed by
the court for any of the children, give guardian's name." The answer
listed Virginia as guardian for Bud's sixteen-year-old son, Butch, but
the word *court* was scratched out. For "relationship to the child,"
Virginia wrote not stepmother but "widow."

"Kinda like 'mother-to-be,' " Keeney reflected. "Did she pick up
these tricks in the VA hospital?"

And then came the matter of the will. The naval form asked: "If
an executor or administrator has been appointed by the court to
settle the estate . . . give name." Again the word *court* was crossed
out and Judson's name appeared in the blank provided, presumably
as executrix. But how could there be an executrix without a court
order? Kentucky Trusts and Estates laws had been on the books
nearly two centuries.

A still different version showed up on the Form FE–6 Claim for
Death Benefit that Virginia filed under the Federal Employees Group
Life Insurance Program. This time, when it asked whether "a guardian has been appointed by the court for the estate of any minor
children," she scratched out *court* as before and wrote in the
word *will*.

But neither Keeney nor R.D. was able to locate the will. The probate court had no record. Bud's property seemed to have disappeared with Virginia, along with the proceeds from the two death-benefit claims.

Virginia knew the system—that much was clear. She understood how to slink through holes in the safety nets, how to work an insurance company, how to befuddle a bureaucracy. Moving across state lines helped, too. Reporting the incidents herself helped even more. Why shouldn't the police or the navy or an insurance investigator believe her? A married woman with children. They would *want* to believe her. A plain-looking woman, the neighbor next door. It was a natural, built-in bias. And it seemed as if for years, thirty years or more, Virginia had played it for everything it was worth.

"We make a pretty good team, don't we?" Keeney said one day as he and R.D. sat poring over hospital records. "Now let's see if we can snare Virginia."

CHAPTER 18

HARLOT
OF BABYLON

▼

That afternoon, Keeney was watching the Louisville skyline under a gray late fall sky from his office window. He tried to envision each of the deaths. The Louisville skyline faded; the Ohio River dissolved into a cliff edge. Deana tumbled down, bones breaking, a gash pouring blood over her head. Then the cliff became the barn where Cynthia Elaine's body dangled from a loop of twine. Wallpaper grew up to cover the raw wood walls and Virginia was standing by Bud Rearden's bedside. God, the horror of it all! he thought. She is utterly, coldly evil. Over the months, he saw that proving Deana's murder had grown into something more than a *pro bono* case. It had become a mission, almost a personal challenge.

The evolving murder script that had begun with Deana now extended all the way to childhood. He closed his eyes and saw young Ginger Hoffmann transfixed by the barn fire, slyly slipping school lunches under her coat, shoplifting pounds of butter, lighting matches in the cellar. He counted the fires. There were seven he knew of—four in Ithaca, one in Palo Alto which the McCains had

▲   BOBBIE ROBERTS AND HER DAUGHTERS, JANE AND DEANA.

STEVEN KEENEY   ▶

◀ DEANA POSED IN HER HIGH HEELS.

THE ONE PHOTO
TAKEN BY DEANA
ON THE ROLL. ▶

◀ DEANA AND B.J. AFTER THE
ELAVIL HAS TAKEN EFFECT.

DEANA AND B.J. AT THE
CLIFF'S EDGE MOMENTS
BEFORE DEANA'S MURDER. ▶

▲ VIRGINIA (FAR RIGHT) AT THE COLGROVE SCHOOL.

◀ VIRGINIA'S FIRST
HUSBAND DICK COATES.

VIRGINIA WITH HER SON
RONNIE IN ITHACA. ▶

◀ VIRGINIA IN FAIRDALE,
KENTUCKY AROUND THE
TIME OF CYNTHIA ELAINE'S
DEATH.

▲ THE FAIRDALE BARN WHERE CYNTHIA ELAINE WAS FOUND
HANGED.

◄ POLICE PHOTO OF THE SCENE OF CYNTHIA ELAINE'S "ACCIDENTAL HANGING."

▲ VIRGINIA AT A PARTY.

BILLIE JOE McGINNIS. ►

▲ VIRGINIA AND BILLIE JOE, WITH THEIR ATTORNEYS GARY EDWARDS AND ALBERT TAMAYO.

▲ SAN DIEGO PROSECUTOR LUIS ARAGON.

▲ JAMES COATES TESTIFYING AT THE PRELIMINARY HEARING.

THE TRIAL ON THE CLIFF
WHERE DEANA WAS
MURDERED. ▶

▲ R. D. JONES.

▲ CYNTHIA ELAINE'S EXHUMATION.

mentioned, two in Jefferson County. Then the bodies: Cynthia Elaine, Bud Rearden, Deana Hubbard Wild. God knows how many thefts, frauds, and bad checks she had tossed off along the way. Were there other mothers or children crying their hearts out over untimely deaths?

The incidents all had a sordid quality, a decaying feel like something best left outside the house. But now Keeney understood them as united by this furtive-eyed child raised on twisted love, chaos, and abuse, a girl who grew into an impulsive thief, adulteress, and murderer who passed herself off as the sweet lady next door. "A real June Cleaver," as one neighbor said. Given what he now knew about Cynthia Coates and Bud Rearden, Keeney found himself considering whether Virginia might not even be a serial killer.

Yet Keeney was lawyer enough to know to seek an expert opinion before he went back to the DA with any extravagant theories. Louisville Medical Examiner George Nichols recommended Emanuel Tanay.

"Tanay's one of the best forensic psychs in the business," Nichols told Keeney. "Works out of Wayne State University in Detroit. They called him in on Ted Bundy's case, so he's not exactly a greenhorn. If anybody can shed some light, he can." Bundy, Keeney recalled, was among America's most notorious serial killers, an all-American boy who left a trail of bodies.

That evening at home, Keeney looked up Tanay on a computer data base. Nichols was right: The man had sterling credentials. He had even spent time in Kentucky examining Donald Harvey, a nurse who set the current record for killing the largest number of victims.

As Keeney dialed Wayne State, he thought back to the "Mother Teresa" test he had once described to Bobbie Roberts. The real question, it now seemed, was not whether Virginia was Mother Teresa. He needed to know whether she might not even be the Harlot of Babylon. He lighted a cigar, listened to the rings, and thought, I'm way out of my league.

Dr. Tanay came on the line.

The son of Polish Holocaust survivors, Emmanuel Tanay came to the United States with a German doctorate and spent the following thirty-five years analyzing the psyches of killers. He spoke with a cultured Viennese accent that belonged to a movie caricature of Sigmund Freud, rolling his *r*'s and turning *s*'s into *z*'s.

Between pulls on his cigar, Keeney laid out the facts. It all built to one question: "Doctor, what do you think? Does this fit the picture of a psychopathic serial killer?"

Tanay took his time before delivering an opinion. When he spoke, his words were measured and serious.

"Basically, you have to start by dividing multicides into two groups: spree killers and serial killers. Spree killers are the ones who go into a crowded post office with a machine gun and mow down everyone in sight. They explode in a burst of rage and then cool off; maybe they won't kill again, ever. Maybe they commit suicide."

Keeney clicked his pen in and out. *Okay, she's obviously no spree killer,* he thought. *I suppose he has to go down his checklist. After all, the guy's a professor.*

"But *serial* killers," Tanay explained, "are an entirely different breed. They kill, cool down, kill again. It's a ritualistic, almost fetishistic act. Yet I must say, the odd thing about your case is that I've never heard of any *female* serial killers. And the woman's age places her well outside the norm. And there is another anomaly. There was a man acting with Virginia, but you say he's not the likely instigator. The problem is, psychopathic duos who kill together are also almost nonexistent."

Dr. Tanay's reputation was impressive, but still, dismissing the notion of a female serial killer so quickly didn't feel right. Keeney heard himself agreeing, but it was mainly to see what else Tanay had to offer.

"Doctor, how do you decide whether a person *might be* a serial killer, or even an 'ordinary' killer? Never mind gender. Don't they have certain ways they 'work,' or styles of operating, or maybe background experiences?"

"Given what you've told me, it sounds as if you're dealing with someone who is what we call 'organized,' and that type doesn't have a very strict conscience. This most recent death, the girl at the cliff, is not an impulsive or frenzied type of homicide. It was planned well in advance, step by step. And Virginia also does not sound like someone who kills for gratification. This is not a sex crime or a crime aimed at getting away with another crime, like rape or burglary. This appears to be more instrumental, goal-directed, to get results, if you will."

Right. She did it for insurance money. Keeney noticed his pen clicking again. *It's entrepreneurial.*

He looked up at the silhouettes of trees above his skylights.

Maybe experts didn't possess the golden keys, after all. So far he hadn't heard anything he could add to his profile of Virginia. Tanay went on:

"All the deaths you described—assuming they were murders— were convenient or profitable. For such people, taking a life, if it's convenient, is not associated with much inhibition. This kind of an absence of conscience flows from the childhood years. Lying, stealing, promiscuity—anything to achieve results—may be found in the early youth. Especially promiscuity, since some professionals associate the libidinal drive with aggressive drives. In either case, aggression or sex, there would be no strong sense of self-restraint."

Now we're talking, Keeney thought. Sticky fingers, rule-breaking sex, and layers of lies all fit Richard Coates's story. He reached for a sip of coffee.

"Such behavior is typical of a psychopath. We all desire forbidden things, but conscience stops us from acting on that desire. We see something we want in a department store, but we don't steal. Children may fear getting caught; adults fear damaging their relations with people they care about. It's as if we imagine a policeman standing at our shoulder. Psychopaths, if you will, don't have this built-in policeman.

"But there is another equally important trait. They're also readily bored, what we term 'underaroused.' Stealing and killing excite them. It reaffirms that they are *somebody*. For example, many children get pleasure from doing things behind their parents' back. Psychopaths have that same trait. They take pleasure from outwitting authority, police, et cetera. They find ways to assert themselves in the face of authority."

That's Virginia, Keeney thought. Ostentatious, controlling. She rubbed other people's noses in her crimes, like a dare.

Tanay's discourse continued: "Being an impostor—like posing as a nurse, for example—is another typical psychopathic trait. You steal somebody's identity, usually an authority figure's. It's very anxiety-provoking for most people to behave in that manner, but a psychopath does not usually have much difficulty with this. Having no conscience eliminates anxiety. And pulling the wool over people's eyes can be exciting."

An impostor! Keeney had been searching for the right word for Virginia's normal-seeming guise. *Masquerade* didn't get the right spin on it. Neither did *charade. Schizophrenic* went too far: There were no hallucinations or delusions that he knew of and Virginia clearly had not lost touch with reality. But *impostor* was a comfortable fit.

"But, Doctor," Keeney said. "Virginia may be a tough, promiscuous woman, but a psychopath's a big leap. Are there specific things I should look out for?"

"This, oddly enough, is where I think a number of such killers have an advantage over law enforcement," he answered elliptically. "They generally appear normal, even friendly. Most aren't even under any sort of treatment. So it's hard to spot them before they act.

"But it would seem you have some suggestive traits right in front of you. Sending the photographs to the girl's mother would go back to what I said before: playing with authorities, living dangerously— even showing off or taunting. And serial killers tend to select the same kinds of victims: the sick or the infirm. It depends on what they like, or rather fixate on, the most. Look at pictures of the victims; see if you can detect marked similarities.

"From what you've told me, and I mean by example only, there are two young females, each helpless in her own way. And, of course, her husband was bedridden at the time you say she may have killed him. You might look for other young women, or sick, weak people who died while in her reach.

"Serial killers also often develop routines: reporting their crimes, or killing with the same methods. It could be any sort of repetition, a kind of self-created ritual. And here is another area where they pick up their advantage. They have worked off the rough edges and are less sloppy than the average murderer. We expect pangs of guilt, but these people have no guilt at all. They appear remarkably normal.

"Finally, you also want to look for the *pace* of the incidents. Usually they escalate, getting bolder with each new success, and more arrogant. As a consequence, I predict you will find her early criminal career to be of the intermittent, nonconfrontational sort— shoplifting, petty frauds, that sort of thing. Then with success, she does it more and more, and the crimes get more serious, like arson, for instance. Once she is fully emerged and moves up to homicides, there, too, she will begin with stealth, then become increasingly brazen. In the end, she may kill so wantonly, it's as if she was asking to get caught, which, in fact, at some deep level, she may be."

Keeney thought of Deana's murder. Buying insurance the day

before you kill somebody, then lying about it to the police. It could be a real thrill for a disturbed personality. He asked Tanay to go on.

"Their conduct around others tends to be what is called 'grandiose,'" the doctor said through his thick accent. "The inflated picture of themselves they project originates in deep-seated insecurity. To compensate, they act with almost limitless arrogance. Their deepest images of themselves are so low, they border on self-loathing. Thoughts of suicide come to them, but the will to survive turns away the thoughts of killing themselves and aims the violence at other people."

"And those house fires?" Keeney asked. "Do they fit the picture, too? Pyromaniacs don't sound like killers."

"They aren't. But does she also have a problem with, uh, enuresis?"

"Excuse me?" Keeney asked, thinking Tanay's accent had somehow mangled the word.

"Cruelty to animals, bed-wetting, and fascination with fire. Enuresis is incontinence, bed-wetting. These three traits often are found together in psychopaths," he said. "A so-called triad. So, in answer to your question, yes. The fires fit in quite nicely with what we know about psychopaths. They all have to do, in some sense, with lost control. And control may be the key to this woman's personality."

Long after Keeney had thanked Tanay for his time, he sat looking at his computer screen. The sound of Christian battling Nintendo warriors drifted up the stairs. Now six years old, the boy's greatest fears were on the order of bogeymen in the closet. But Keeney understood he was bringing home something a lot scarier and a lot more real. Maybe seasoned cops get used to this, he thought, but not corporate lawyers. And if he started spouting off at B & A about chasing a serial killer, they would think *he* was crazy.

Still, in spite of Dr. Tanay's blanket remarks about there being no women serial killers, everything he had said fit the facts of Virginia's life to an extraordinary degree. It would have passed the test of Occam's razor with ease.

There was Virginia's rise out of dirt-poor Ithaca with a sexually and physically abusive brother, father, and school-bus driver. Being ill-fed and living in filth fueled her self-loathing. It also made perfect sense that she flashed paste diamonds to her classmates, then stole their lunches behind their backs. Promiscuity must have answered her need to feel important and to be loved. But quick and dirty relationships would only keep the anger within her smouldering. Occasionally, it burst out in ferocious episodes, but mostly she kept it buried below her sweet, kindly facade.

And so, shoplifting and passing bad checks along the way, she had quietly clawed her way up, trying to be somebody. She thumbed her nose at the world, daring it to catch her.

Posing as a nurse now loomed as a significant detail, as did preying on the helpless. They drew threads of connection between events separated by years and hundreds of miles. Even Dr. Tanay's comment about incontinence—enuresis—panned out.

Dick Coates had once passed along an old Hoffmann family story about Virginia. One night, Aunt Maggie, one of the relatives permitted in the Bostwick Road house, checked on the room Virginia and Tom shared as children. Maggie used to joke about how she noticed a terrible reek when she walked in.

"Tom, you throw up?" she asked.

"Nope," Tom's voice came from under the covers.

Maggie followed her nose up to Virginia's bed. She looked down and gasped.

When Dick first related the story, Keeney just shook his head. Now he understood it had clinical significance. It filled in one prong of Tanay's "triad." It was just an artificial construct, a theory. But when something fit this closely, and even predicted events unknown to the theorist, you had to take pause.

Three A.M. Christian's Nintendo game had been silent for hours.

Sitting at his computer amidst swirls of cigar smoke lit by the glowing screen, Keeney put Tanay's gloss on his portrait of Virginia.

He took a break and looked up at his reflection in the skylight, making eye contact with his reflected self as he stretched. At the edges, the image dissolved into darkness. The world is a strange place, he thought sadly. Taking Bobbie's case had pulled him away from his law firm, from dates with Wynn, and, more importantly, from his son. And Virginia's still out there, he thought. If she kills again, will I feel responsible?

▼

The following evening, Wynn Burkholder rang the bell at the Hill Road house, ready for a dinner out. She was primed for a romantic evening, her green eyes shining. Keeney met her at the door with an apology.

"I'm sorry, Wynn, but I need to finish up on Bobbie Roberts's case before we can go. Come on upstairs; it'll just be a minute."

Wynn followed him to his study, restraining herself from delivering a lecture on manners. The exquisite pleasure of watching Steve work figured low on her list of choices for the evening. Then she paused. She had never seen him looking quite so haggard.

"I hate to say so, baby," she said, putting a hand on his shoulder as he sat hacking at the computer, "but you look awful."

He kept his eyes on the screen. "I'm just a little tuckered out, Wynn. Nothing a good dinner won't cure."

"Steve"—she leaned closer—"I mean it. You better get yourself some rest."

Keeney knew she was right. In the weeks since Jon Yudin's letter had arrived, he had been eating compulsively and smoking cigars the way some people smoke cigarettes. His weight, usually around 180, jumped to 220, and his tailored suits now cinched where they once draped. He slept less, and worrisome dreams interrupted the few hours he did sleep. When playing with Christian or reading the morning newspapers or digging in his garden, the vision of Virginia moving into a new neighborhood and taking in a new "boarder" gnawed at him. And he wondered how many other bodies might be out there already.

He turned to Wynn, who stood looking over his shoulder, her arms crossed with a mixture of worry and discontent.

"I know it sounds absurd, but I think I've stumbled across a psychopathic killer," Steve said. "She was present at the death of her daughter, Deana Wild, even one of her husbands. On top of that, almost every house she ever lived in caught fire."

"Give me a break, Steve." Wynn frowned. "That's just not possible. People would catch on." She had heard Keeney talk like this before. Sometimes she felt he had a tendency to blow things out of proportion, orderly and detail-minded though he was. On the other hand, he was not the type to fritter his time away on nonsense. "If she's public enemy number one, why aren't the police doing exactly what you're doing right now?"

"I wish I knew. But part of the story is that she kept moving. She went from one state to another, she changed names, and nobody ever put the pieces together. I think I'm the first."

"Well then, why don't the police arrest her? If you ask me, you should be working on cases that will make some money."

Keeney turned and held Wynn's eye.

"Wynn, I could no more drop Bobbie's case than I could stop going to church. If I can put together an airtight case, they *will* arrest Virginia. And if they don't we can file a civil case for damages. Virginia may not have a dime to her name, but, either way, Bobbie gets her day in court, and the truth comes out. It's a question of perseverance, not money."

"I've got to be honest with you, baby," she said, walking across the study, running a finger along at the rows of neatly lined-up books. "I don't agree. People come into court and lose all the time, even when they're right. Innocent people end up getting hurt; guilty people walk out the door. It isn't a fair game, but that's the way it is.

"Well, Wynn," Keeney answered, "with any luck this case should be winding down in a matter of weeks. Meantime, how about that dinner?"

Keeney raced to finish his memo on Virginia. It felt like running the last five miles of a marathon over and over, especially with B & A's growing problems as an unsettling undertone. If he had tried, he could not have chosen a worse moment to invest time in a drawn-out, quite probably hopeless *pro bono* project. The firm was undergoing a wrenching reorganization. Lawsuits between dissatisfied partners had just been filed and they drained everyone's morale. During white-linen lunches, senior members murmured about lower profit margins, overexpansion, and client attrition. A few repeated the suggestion of selling off the firm's plane and firing its two full-time pilots. Keeney's hopes for a computer on every desktop were now on permanent hold. Even the name was changing from B & A to Alagia, Day, Marshall, Mintmire & Chauvin.

When pressed, Keeney could work at prodigious rates, researching, interviewing, organizing, writing, redrafting sixteen, eighteen hours a day. The world disappeared and the only thing he knew was his goal, gleaming before him in the dark like a diamond.

Above all, he had to answer Assistant DA Jon Yudin's doubts

about criminal agency—essentially a prosecutor's arcane way of asking for proof that an incident had an illegal cause. There was obviously nothing illegal about falling off a cliff, at least not all by yourself, Keeney thought wryly. To prove a homicide, you needed to show that someone intended to make the victim fall. The concept of criminal agency seemed little more than legal sleight of hand. If the people who were with Deana at the cliff stood to gain by her death, and the circumstances made slip-and-fall an unreasonable conclusion, then a jury would be entitled to find them guilty of murder. Circumstantial evidence, plain and simple.

In response to a follow-up call from Steve, Yudin mentioned five types of evidence he thought would resolve the problem: another insurance policy on Deana in which Virginia had a part; another murder involving Virginia; additional physical evidence in Deana's case; additional testimony in Deana's case; or proof that Deana's engagement to James Coates was a sham and that Virginia or B.J. actually knew it before buying the policy. According to Yudin, Cynthia Elaine's and Bud's deaths just weren't persuasive evidence, especially since they were inadmissible in a criminal trial.

The requests posed immense practical problems. Virginia had spent her life weaving through jurisdictions, hiding her crimes in files from State Farm to the U.S. Navy. Other bodies and other policies might be literally anywhere.

But the world had changed since Virginia began her career. Computers, modems, and faxes had turned state borders into abstractions. In this respect, Keeney hoped he had an advantage over police agencies who had missed their chances at catching Virginia in the past.

Virginia left Kentucky for California in 1975, Keeney knew. Mac McCain of State Farm placed her there as recently as 1985, when he wrote her homeowner's policy. In the search for more victims, that ten-year stretch in California seemed a good bet.

Keeney knew that insurance policies weren't organized into a data base—and Mike Hatch still hadn't found other policies on Deana. But death certificates were listed on computer. Unfortunately, California's registers held 2.2 million death certificates filed between 1975 and 1985. Looking at every one would be like reading the Greater Louisville phone book. It might take years.

He thought of Tanay's comment about Virginia's possibly being a habitual "reporter," the kind of murderer who always tells the authorities about her own killings. "Reporter" was a standard box on California death certificates. But even though Virginia's name appeared in the police reports of Deana's, Cynthia Elaine's and Bud Rearden's deaths, it wasn't on the death certificate.

Pass on that, Keeney thought. But instead of "reporter," why not use "manner of death"—either cliff fall or hanging—and the age and sex of the deceased—females less than twenty-four years of age? Sure it's a long shot, but then the whole case has been working against the odds. Virginia's name might turn up somewhere.

California sent back a list of *1,330 deaths* and asked whether he wanted to see all the certificates—at seven dollars each. People falling off cliffs really were like snowflakes in a snowstorm! Keeney recalled. And he was not about to ask Bobbie Roberts for money she didn't have. After narrowing the search to San Francisco and San Diego, the number pared down to a more manageable thirty. The California registrar sent the certificates along. None mentioned Virginia's name.

It was hardly surprising. Even more frustrating than surprising. After all, Deana's certificate didn't mention Virginia's name at all. Her death wouldn't have stood out from the pack any more than, say, Shelley Anne Shirey's, an unmarried eighteen-year-old who "lost balance, fell into cliff crevice to rocks and water below." Hours of work yielded nothing.

But Keeney kept attacking each of Yudin's elements with methodical persistence. Running a criminal investigation felt something like a game of lawyer's hide-and-go-seek. The case dovetailed, shot off in a dozen directions. Thank God I've at least got R. D. Jones to bounce ideas off of, he said to himself.

At last, Keeney summed up his findings. His memo to Jon Yudin took the form of a five-hundred-page document eventually known around the Monterey Sheriff's Office as "the book." Part case file, part biography, it spanned thirty years and three thousand miles, and dealt with every issue Keeney could fathom.

The "book" began with a thirty-six-page profile of Virginia. It started in late 1953, when she first met Richard Coates at a fire on Bostwick Road in Ithaca, New York, and ended on September 18, 1987, with the entry "Virginia and B.J. McGinnis refuse to take lie-detector test about Deana, saying it is on advice of attorney."

After that came a legal brief dissecting the fine points of criminal agency, Keeney's collected correspondence, a list of evidence that a search warrant might uncover, and summaries of the Coates boys' rap sheets.

The rest of the "book" consisted of exhibits: obituaries, newspaper clippings, hospital records, marriage and death certificates, interview transcripts, police reports, fire department and bank account records, mortgages, Deana's insurance policy, the photographs at the cliff, Barbara Weakley-Jones's analysis of the autopsy, and the California death certificate computer search.

Along the way, Bobbie Roberts had turned up Deana's letters to her Aunt Betsey, none of them mentioning an engagement to James Coates, indeed not mentioning his name at all. In a purse Deana had left behind during her visit to Louisville in February, Bobbie found two letters written to Deana from a convict named Donald Dale Moore. In grossly misspelled words, Moore seemed to explode the notion that Deana could possibly have been engaged to James Coates.

One letter, postmarked January 12, 1987, began: "Hi sweat heart how are you doing is every thing ok . . . i reley need you to be strown an sure of what you want, and if you reley want to gett maried to me 'lett me tell you' youre on as soon as posible. . . ." The letter became Exhibit 26.

Finally, on the evening of December 10, 1987, Keeney stood in the B & A hallway, watching as copies of the "book" addressed to Smythe, Yudin, R. D. Jones, State Farm, Sergeant Brown, and Bobbie Roberts came up from the B & A publishing section, churned out after hours in between paying jobs. The bound documents with their neatly tabbed exhibits all but buried Sarah West's desk. Keeney eyed the hallway to make sure he would not have to explain to one of his partners what this bulk mailing was all about.

Sunday. Keeney sat in the sanctuary of the Second Presbyterian Church. The worshippers' summer whites were replaced by dark winter flannels.

From his pulpit, the minister looked across a congregation of well-to-do Louisvillians and recognized, even in the shining suburb of the East End, a low mood. Economic recession had recently hit the area. Once-busy stores in the heart of downtown near the venerable old Brown and Seelbach hotels were boarded up. Unemployment lines were longer, and a lackluster holiday shopping season had hit local businesses hard. Christmas was days away, but the winter blues had arrived early.

The minister tried to lift everyone's spirits. "In your darkest moments," he said, "look up, for your salvation is at hand."

Seated in the midst of a crowded holiday audience, Keeney tried following the minister's admonition. He looked up. Staring at him from the place where salvation belonged, he saw his law firm in a shambles, the case against Virginia McGinnis costing him months of work without the slightest indication of victory, and Bobbie Roberts, her hopes raised, then dashed.

And what if I'm just dead wrong? The idea was something he didn't like to consider. But here, in church, the thought of falsely accusing a woman of murder—*multiple* murder—hit him with a terrible power. Already, he was paying a personal price for his one-man crusade. Wynn thought he was going overboard. His partners needed his time on money-making matters. Christian sat in front of the TV instead of on his father's lap.

But the case had taken on a life of its own. And in an odd way, Keeney felt he was doing what any good lawyer should do. Until the official word came through—and he hoped that would be soon—prayer, work, and study seemed the best and only hopes.

Study helped answer a number of questions about Virginia.

Keeney called the FBI and was informed by a resident psychiatrist that there were roughly nine traits characteristic of "organized" killers: 1. planned offense; 2. a targeted stranger as victim; 3. submissive victim; 4. restraints used; 5. crime scene reflects control; 6. aggression prior to death; 7. body hidden; 8. weapon not present; 9. transports victim or body. Deana's murder hit seven out of the nine points. Cynthia Elaine's and Bud Rearden's could each score six.

Indeed, Virginia fit all the other criteria Keeney could lay his hands on: The American Psychiatric Association's *Diagnostic and Statistical Manual of Mental Disorders* (third edition—revised) with its twenty-two diagnostic criteria; Hervey Cleckley's sixteen-point clinical profile in his classic work *The Mask of Sanity;* and William and Joan McCord's six criteria listed in *The Psychopath: Origins of Crime.*

Many respected authorities discussed the possibility of organic brain damage in psychopathic killers. Keeney knew Virginia had been beaten, and Dick Coates used to talk about a car wreck that knocked her out and left her with a permanently injured arm. He also considered Virginia's fall from the second-story window in Ithaca during a fire back in 1967. She hit her head on a steel milk can and wound up in the hospital for two weeks, her face bruised and scarred.

Professionals, in fact, had written pages and pages suggesting other contributing factors: Diet, addictive behavior, self-medication, and aggravated health risks headed the biological section alone. But Keeney had a hard time attributing premeditated murder solely to a whack on the head or to poor nutrition. At that rate, the world would be overflowing with killers. Thankfully, they were a rare breed.

Still, Virginia McGinnis bore more than a loose similarity to a textbook serial killer. "This was what computer people call a 'hit.' And a hit, and another hit, hit after hit, and hits to come," Keeney wrote after plowing through all the standard references. "Nothing else described Virginia's life and Deana's death with such remarkable accuracy."

Then he ran across a series of works that exploded Dr. Tanay's confident generalization that serial killers were exclusively male: *Ladies Who Kill; The Criminology of Deviant Women; Lifers: The Stories of Eleven Women Serving Life Sentences;* "The Female Serial Murder," in the *Journal of Police and Criminal Psychology;* and "Women Who Kill," in the *Archives of General Psychiatry.* History offered only a handful of examples, but they were to be found. Most disturbing of all, a good many of the women bore a powerful similarity to Virginia.

Hazel Doss, known as the "Giggling Grandma," went to prison in Oklahoma in 1955 after poisoning five of her husbands and collecting insurance on each one. Salie Jean Matajke, who passed herself off as a nurse for the elderly and helped herself to their checking accounts, killed four people in New York City in the 1940s. The list went on: Faye Copeland, age sixty-nine when convicted of five murders in Missouri; Velma Barfield, fifty-two when executed for five murders in North Carolina in 1984; "Ma" Belle Gunness, about fifty when she disappeared, leaving at least fourteen corpses butchered and buried on her Indiana farm.

Finally, Keeney came across the cases of Marie Frazier Hilley and Dorothy Gray Puente, two murderers whose lives could have served as early warnings for the likes of Virginia. Hilley, born in 1933, poisoned her husband, mother, mother-in-law, and daughter (who survived) as she traveled from state to state. Like Virginia, Mrs. Hilley had been arrested early on for passing bad checks, and also found herself present at numerous unexplained house fires. She was fifty years old when convicted of murder.

Dorothy Puente's story came even closer to a perfect fit. She was convicted of check forging at nineteen (Virginia was twenty-two) and had been married four times (Virginia, three times). Puente supported herself by lying about being a registered nurse and caring for the elderly (as did Virginia). To her friends, she was known as a kindly landlady with a penchant for flashy jewelry (again like Virginia). And then, in 1988, investigators unearthed seven bodies in the backyard of her Sacramento, California, home. Puente was fifty-nine years old at the time of her arrest.

Dr. Tanay's profile was more in line than he would probably ever know. Marie Hilley, Dorothy Puente, and Virginia McGinnis were all dead ringers.

CHAPTER 19

A PERFECT CHRISTMAS GIFT

▼

Fresh out of prison on early parole, James Coates turned up in San Diego in early December. Among his first actions as a free man was to hire attorney Bill O'Connell to pressure State Farm about paying up on Deana's life-insurance policy. And Bill O'Connell knew exactly how to lobby the right people.

On December 9, O'Connell sent Monterey Detective Don Smythe a letter, concluding: "You advised me that the investigation is still on-going, and although you had reason to believe it was merely an accident you had to follow up on certain items. . . . I shall follow up with you in January should I not hear from you sooner."

O'Connell then contacted Mike Hatch to warn that he was considering filing a "wrongful denial of life insurance" lawsuit against State Farm.

When copies of the letters caught up with Keeney in Louisville, he sensed a showdown in the offing.

Bobbie Roberts flared when she heard the news: "How dare he try to collect on my own daughter's death! His mother *murdered* her. It's just crazy."

"I understand," Steve counseled, "but remember we don't have any real case against Jimmy Coates. He was in jail when Deana died, and he never went to the insurance company. We might be able to show he was aiding and abetting the crime after the fact, since the claim was in his name. But, right now, we can't prove a thing."

The moment Bobbie left his office, Keeney called Hatch to warn that Bobbie would vigorously oppose Jimmy Coates getting even a dime of the insurance money.

Hatch answered in the unencouraging voice of a man who has seen a lot of cases derailed. "Steve, this has been going on a long time. We can't stall this forever. We're giving our investigation one final push, but then we'll have to make some hard decisions."

Hatch added that two experts in fraud—Diana Rael and Doug Camphuis—were already in the field conducting taped interviews. To coordinate their efforts, Hatch had assigned one of the company's top investigators, a former Georgia Bureau of Investigations agent named Ken Goodnight. Goodnight, Hatch said, either would make a "federal" case against Virginia or drop it with honor.

"That sounds like a reprieve," Keeney said.

"We'll see," Hatch said bleakly.

Keeney understood Hatch's cynicism. Just because State Farm had beefed up its investigation, that didn't mean he, or even the police, would have ready access to their findings. Quite the contrary: State Farm's field agents took a vow of confidentiality. And Hatch must have watched State Farm's detectives run parallel to the local authorities plenty of times before. Sometimes they uncovered useful information missed by the police, only to leave the case midstream once their own business interests settled. Sometimes the police showed enough sense to subpoena their files. Either way, State Farm's interest began and ended within the four corners of their contract. If they could bail out on a technical point—lies on Deana's health questionnaire or challenging the insurable interest—Hatch would deny liability on the policy and direct all the accumulated reports into the nearest locked filing cabinet.

Bobbie Roberts's potential interest in the proceeds of the life-insurance policy gave her a toehold, but that was about all.

When State Farm's investigator Ken Goodnight contacted Keeney, they started off like two dogs circling and sniffing one another. Had Goodnight been put on the case to scuttle Bobbie's claim? Keeney wondered. Or was he out to preempt a lawsuit by Bobbie against State Farm for selling the policy in the first place?

"Stop me if I'm wrong about what the scrape marks down Deana's side might mean," Goodnight would say. Or, "If I try to interview Jay Wild, will I be getting into anybody's way?"

It was a slow process, but Keeney and Goodnight came to an understanding. Goodnight, in fact, was the first insurance company employee Keeney ever heard say that State Farm never should have written Deana's policy.

"State Farm is so big and there are so many people working here, they just screwed up," Goodnight apologized. "They were just processing paper. Most of the management people, they're businessmen. They don't have any experience with investigations. They don't want to think their policyholders are crooks."

"It's nice to hear somebody say that," Keeney said. "Now, how about pooling some information?"

"That might be arranged."

Chief among the tidbits Goodnight slipped Keeney was the official version of Virginia's largest documented insurance claim. To Keeney, it read like Dick Coates or Jake Miller revisited.

In June of 1985, Virginia coowned a house at 828 Weeks Street with her mother, Mary Agnes, in a run-down section of Palo Alto, just east of San Francisco. On the evening of the twenty-third, a neighbor heard an explosion and called the fire department. Fire fighters managed to save about half the house, and in the blackened remains, they found potent evidence of arson: "a 2 gallon can of gasoline that was empty, in the kitchen." But the report ultimately found "insufficient information" to determine the precise cause of the blaze. State Farm assessed the damage at eighty thousand dollars and, for reasons not documented in Goodnight's file, chose to rebuild the home rather than pay outright.

A month later, 828 Weeks Street caught fire again. This time, the fire department failed to save even a part of the house.

Fire inspectors overhauled the area, and again "found a one gallon gasoline can in the house leading to the assumption that this fire was caused by an incendiary act." Their report ended with the reassuring comment that the "gasoline can was turned over to the East Palo Alto Police Department." Yet no official action was ever taken.

Not surprising, thought Keeney. Fire departments investigate arson, not the police. Somebody was covering his rear end on that one.

Goodnight, meanwhile, had dug up the name of Doreta Green, a next-door neighbor, in the Palo Alto files. When his agents went by her house in 1988, Green proved to be the most reliable witness on the block.

"Oh, I remember Miss Virginia and Miss Mary, all right. Miss Virginia told me she was a registered nurse," Green said. "Told me she worked at the VA. The first time the house caught on fire, I was having a birthday party. We heard the explosion and called the fire department. My friend ran over and broke through the window to see if anyone was inside. But there wasn't anybody in the house.

"The next day, Miss Virginia and her mother showed up. She said they'd gone to Las Vegas.

"Now the Hoffmanns had these dogs, a Doberman and three Pekingese. A week or so later, we heard them all cryin' outside. They were lying in the street, foaming at the mouth and breathing hard. We called the pound. They came and said the dogs had been poisoned. Had to take 'em away. *Just poisoned.* Terrible thing.

"Then things got stranger. A while after the dogs died, the Coates boys, Ronnie and Jimmy, came and took a lot of stuff out of the house and drove off with it on a truck. Miss Virginia said her mother was a dealer in antiques, that's where all the furniture came from. She had jade and these painted silk screens and statues.

"That night, my boys called and said, 'The house is on fire again!' From what I hear, Miss Mary and Miss Virginia got the insurance money."

Even though the official cause of the second fire was determined to be an "incendiary act," State Farm ended up paying the Hoffmanns $127,255 to cover the loss. Who could have been so blind? Goodnight wondered. Then he looked at the State Farm file. *He* had been working at the SRU right at that time. Those fires slipped past us too, he thought.

Keeney recognized all of Virginia's traits. There were the same references to the jade, and the same midnight preparations just before a blaze broke out. He even recognized another fact that might fill out Tanay's sociopathic triad: cruelty to animals—the poisoned dogs. Dick Coates, too, had said Virginia was "meaner 'n hell" around animals.

At last, the team of investigators Keeney envisioned had begun to galvanize around him and new facts were coming in steadily. Smythe was keeping the case open, R. D. Jones called in to say that he had started tracking down new leads in New York, and State Farm's staff had swung into full gear.

That afternoon, he wrote Bobbie Roberts to deliver the hopeful news:

Dear Ms. Roberts:

It appears that my December 10, 1987 letter has sparked some further attention to this matter both in the Monterey County Sheriff's Office and at State Farm Insurance as well as with Sergeant Jones of the Jefferson County Police Department's Violent Crime Unit.

I talked with Detective Smythe of the Monterey County Sheriff's Office today. He agreed to undertake four of the inquiries that were set out in my December 10 letter. . . . Detective Smythe also advised me that he had gotten a call from a special investigator at State Farm Insurance who said he wanted to meet with Detective Smythe in California in mid-January. . . .

I also talked with Mike Hatch, of State Farm Insurance today. . . . Mr. Hatch indicated that in addition to Mr. Goodnight, the company had put two of their special fraud people on the claim in California. . . .

Finally, I spoke with Sergeant Jones of the Jefferson County Police. . . .

In short, it looks as though we might be finally bringing this matter to a head and can anticipate some decision-making by the various authorities in the latter part of January.

I wish you and your family a happy holiday filled with good cheer and the blessings of the Christmas spirit.

Regards,

Steve Keeney

It was, Keeney thought, a perfect Christmas gift.

Bobbie Roberts decided to give herself a present of her own during her holiday break. Dreams of Deana falling and of a couple standing on the cliff still invaded her sleep. She wanted to see the scene for herself.

Late in December, Bobbie got out of her car and looked across a flat blue expanse of Pacific Ocean from the Seal Beach turnout. Big Sur was truly magnificent, she thought. Immense cliffs careened down to an angry blue Pacific. Vultures circled overhead and dove through the breathless space. The place had a prehistoric quality—the sight of some dinosaur poking its scaly head out of the water would fit right in with the rocks and the raw cliff faces.

She smelled the air, rich with aromas of aloe, sagebrush, rosemary, sea salt. Just a few hundred yards out, she spotted the spouts of migrating gray whales. There was no sign of human life anywhere except for an A-frame pitched below the northernmost curve in the road. Down below, on the sandy inlet formed by the crotch of a canyon, a family of sea lions lolled in the sun. Deana had been so alone in the world, she thought.

Looking around the turnout, she tried to imagine her daughter's death. Did Deana scream when she fell, tumbling down the rocks? Did she wonder why, why are you doing this to me? Bobbie hoped it had all ended quickly.

Within a week, the Seal Beach turnout had another visitor.

Ken Goodnight knew this was an important moment and he didn't want to waste first impressions. No other investigator had visited the site since the Monterey Sheriff's team retrieved Deana Hubbard's body from the foot of the cliff. Nine months had passed, along with rainstorms, high winds, natural erosion, and the effects of tourism. He knew he wouldn't find a piece of clothing, a cracked-off fingernail, or a bloodstain. But he could still get a feel for the place, something he could recall when he read through reports in his glass-box office back in Normal.

Not the sort to ponder the beauty of a spring day, Goodnight was nonetheless impressed with Big Sur. The power of the waves, the steepness of the cliffs, the pristine coastline. He imagined Deana having the time of her life.

And Virginia and B.J.? Where were they looking? No doubt, their eyes were focused on Deana's reactions, or on the roadway to the north. Had the drugs kicked in? Did she suspect anything? How long should they wait until they cashed in on the policy?

Oh no, Goodnight thought. State Farm really blew this one! If only someone at underwriting had noticed what was afoot. But nine times out of ten, underwriting meant simply a quick phone call to verify the answers on the form; basically, asking the same person the same questions twice. If they had only done a better job, Deana might still be alive. Not that the Monterey Sheriff's Office had all that much to be proud of. The ragged fingernails should have caught the pathologist's eye at the autopsy.

Goodnight took out Photo 11 from his pocket and compared it to the scene in front of him.

Deana seemed to have been standing at the northern edge of the turnout. Goodnight walked over, stomped his feet on the gravel. It felt solid enough. Unless something had changed radically in the past year, he felt sure the ground hadn't crumbled under Deana's high heels.

The angle of the cliff where she last stood with B.J. was also not anything close to what Goodnight had imagined. The cliff didn't actually begin as a cliff at all. It started out as an easy slope, barely enough to ski down if it were covered with snow. About fifteen yards down, a real cliff dropped away, but there were plenty of intervening bushes and protruding rocks to latch on to.

Virginia's story about a noiseless slip and fall made even less sense now that he could see the scene. A body would need momentum to reach the point of no return. It might even need to be dragged.

He glanced around one last time and took in the empty blue spread of ocean. This was Deana's final view of the world. It was a beautiful, horrifying way to die. He listened to the wind blowing up the hillside, as if the scene of Deana's murder would speak to him or whisper some answers. But the only sound was the roar of the ocean and the braying of sea lions on the shore below.

CHAPTER 20

RIVERBOAT GAMBLER

▼

As the cardboard doves and holiday wreaths came down from B & A's walls, murder and arson were not the only crimes being worried over in partners' offices.

One piece of news went up like a tree catching fire: Charles Barnett, son of founding partner Barney Barnett, and a powerful figure within B & A, was arrested by the FBI as he walked through passport control in New York's Kennedy Airport. It happened just months after his father died. Agents searched Charles's briefcase and found allegedly stolen documents relating to the purchase of oil by B & A client Ashland Oil Company from the National Iranian Oil Company. The documents were said to show that Ashland had committed fraud.

For the past ten years, National Iranian had battled with the corporate giant Ashland Oil over seven tankerloads of oil worth an estimated $283 million. Ashland got the oil, National claimed, but never paid the tab. They said it was a simple case of nonpayment. But with stakes that high, no claim ever stays simple.

As news of Charlie Barnett's arrest spread from office to office, partners surmised that Charlie must have been been set up. "How many briefcases do you think they checked for stolen papers at the airport that day?" they joked nervously.

But the joke had hardly begun circulating when the United States Attorney for the Southern District of New York announced Charlie Barnett's indictment on thirty-nine counts of conspiracy, bribery, and wire fraud. The prosecutor charged Barnett and a former Ashland Oil chairman with conspiring to sell documents proving Ashland Oil's fraud regarding the National Iranian Oil sale. The price for the documents was said to be in the millions of dollars. Partner's .offices were rocked to their windows. With hundreds of millions of dollars' worth of oil at stake, the case had generated endless quantities of work. For years, in fact, it had been a money-maker and helped to fuel B & A's expansion. Barnett's indictment, even unproved, amounted to an ugly blot on B & A's reputation.

Within weeks, Keeney and his partners read their firm's name in grimly speculative newspaper articles. One judge suggested that Ashland Oil retained the right to seek reimbursement of fees paid to B & A during the 1980s. The firm thus looked at a potential *triple* loss. One of their largest clients out the door, disgorging a small fortune in legal fees, and spending another on their own defense. Coming so close on the heels of his father's death, the thing was a disaster. It could hurl them all into bankruptcy fast enough to singe their three-piece suits.

Almost overnight, B & A's associates began giving notice, preempting their being fired. The firm dropped from 160 attorneys to fewer than 100 in a matter of months. Partners, Keeney among them, thought about looking for more hospitable surroundings. They quietly met colleagues from competing firms with an eye to forming new alliances, and year-end bonuses were the last thing on anyone's mind. Hanging on was the best one could expect.

Through force of will, Keeney ignored worries about the future and cranked out the work at hand. His railroad bankruptcy had finally gone through, a judge in federal court having carved up the assets among a pride of hungry creditors. Now a hotel partnership wanted to pool assets to get a city development bond, but they needed to know the tax ramifications. There was still plenty of work in which to lose himself. . . .

▼

January 15, 1988. Keeney was grinding through the bond documents when Assistant DA Jon Yudin called. Keeney's five-hundred-page book had gone out five weeks earlier.

"You've really done a superb job," Yudin began. "The people in my office here are quite impressed. You must have put in a tremendous amount of time."

Yudin sounded sincere—but regretful. Keeney steadied himself for what was coming: another pat on the head.

"The problem is that we still don't have enough to go on," Yudin said. "I've spoken to the DA and several others. The consensus is that we don't think we'd get past a preliminary hearing on the murder charge, much less a trial. We wouldn't even be able to get a search warrant. We still need a witness or another body.

"The only other option is to exhume Deana and examine the corpse. It's really a slender reed, Mr. Keeney. I'm sorry."

Before Keeney knew what had happened, Yudin signed off. Keeney took pride in being able to control his emotions, to remain poker-faced when things turned against him. Many people, including a number of Wynn Burkholder's friends, even felt vaguely suspicious of his self-imposed calm and his deliberate way of speaking. But at this moment, Keeney wondered whether it wouldn't feel better to rip the phone out of the wall and kick it through his plate-glass window.

He had assembled reams of evidence, and directly confronted Yudin's concerns. Why wouldn't Monterey take a ready-made homicide? The least they could do would be to execute a search warrant.

Yet, within five minutes, Deana Wild's death was written off as "too hard to prove." The sufferings of Dick Coates, Bobbie Roberts, and Butch Rearden were relegated to the junk heap. Keeney recalled his optimistic letter to Bobbie Roberts, sent just a few weeks before: ". . . it looks as though we might be finally bringing this matter to a head and can anticipate some decision-making by the various authorities in the latter part of January."

Well, the authorities had made their decision and now Keeney would have to explain to Bobbie why he hadn't seen it coming.

He had to figure out the next step before he called. Having come this far, he refused to accept defeat.

Time now loomed large as a threat to any sort of case against the McGinnises. It was as if a series of alarm clocks, all set to go off at different times, ticked away simultaneously. The statute of limitations for a civil lawsuit against the McGinnises was one year from the date of Deana's death. The criminal statute of limitations for insurance fraud was two years. State Farm itself might decide to award Deana's life-insurance proceeds to James Coates at any moment.

The only part of the case that could survive much longer was murder, which had no time limit. In every one of the fifty states, you could prosecute a person for homicide no matter how much time has passed—five minutes or fifty years. But in Virginia's case, that didn't seem likely at any time.

Ticking alongside all these clocks was Keeney's personal meter set at $150 per hour. The time invested on Bobbie Roberts's behalf now amounted to a sizable chunk of his yearly billing, not including the out-of-pocket expenses, phone calls, printing, and secretarial time. And now, with Monterey out of the picture, there was no clear end in sight.

The annual B & A partners' meeting was coming up in just a few months, and with it, the yearly review. Every partner's numbers would flash up, one after the other, on a screen above a boardroom table. Dollars "realized," dollars in the bank for advance payments, dollars "sourced" for all the business each partner brought in. Dollars and more dollars. These weren't "points" for doing good, or teaching seminars, or training young attorneys. But in the eyes of the firm, the columns of figures added up to a measure of each partner's "success." *Pro bono* work was not encouraged at B & A.

Keeney's work for Bobbie Roberts also had not brought in dollar one. His fellow law partners might not exactly stand up and cheer for that performance—not during the hardest of hard times at B & A. At the rate things were going, next year's partners' meeting would probably be held in Fellowship Hall instead of Palm Beach.

Perhaps it was time to drop the Bobbie Roberts *pro bono* crusade, concede failure, and cut losses, Keeney considered. Even if he sued the McGinnises in a civil court, he probably wouldn't recover more than a fraction of his own accrued time. People who kill for a $35,000 life-insurance policy probably do not have vast assets worth seizing in the event they lost a lawsuit.

He had promised Bobbie they'd learn the truth about Deana's death. Well, they had come closer than he ever dreamed. No one would ever fault his diligence if he quietly pulled out now.

▼

That evening, Steve tucked Christian into bed. They had just watched a run-of-the-mill cops-and-robbers TV show. Steve noticed Christian flinch at some of the more brutal scenes. You never knew what would affect young children. One day, they're drinking down gallons of death and destruction, then they're scared of the dark.

"Dad," Christian asked as Keeney tucked in the covers, "could you stay in the room for a while?"

"Okay, Christian." He smiled indulgently. "What's on your mind?"

"I'm just scared. Those bad guys on TV." He pulled the blankets up to his chin.

"Is that all?" Steve laughed as he sat down on the bed and stroked his son's head. "There are police officers working twenty-four hours a day, seven days a week, every day of the year, and their job is to catch bad guys and put them in jail. I wouldn't lose any sleep over bad guys sneaking into my room at night. More than likely, the police can take care of them without your help."

"You mean like in Monterey, with the woman who did all those things? They'll catch her, right?"

Just the other night, Keeney had told him a little about the McGinnises. It was one story he could bring home. Murder was a lot easier to explain to a six-year-old than a corporate merger. But now he wondered whether telling Christian was such a wise idea. He wanted to say, "Yes, like in Monterey." But in his son's bedroom, telling a lie felt wrong.

"It's my job to lose sleep over that one," Keeney said as pulled the covers away from Christian's wide eyes. "Let's say prayers and then we'll both get some rest."

Keeney kept his word. After putting Christian to bed, he went down to the kitchen, fixed a new pot of coffee, and stayed awake watching dawn open up the day. The kitchen was a quiet, comfortable place where he could unwind and follow his thoughts.

There were plenty of obvious reasons for dropping the investigation. He had rehearsed them already, worn them smooth like a worry stone.

Instead, he thought about why he had become a lawyer in the first place, the reasons he had left the seminary and stepped into the courtroom. Technical fascination played a large part. The law could be like an enormous logic puzzle, as complex as you cared to make it. Strange as it sounded to some people, Keeney *liked* solving the problems of corporate taxation. And like all law students, he was also seduced by the notion of doing justice. He had wanted to see his ideas applied, to right wrongs, to protect innocent victims, to leave the world a better place than he found it. That was the siren song that draws thousands into the profession every year. One of his law professors once told him, "The law is light." Keeney never agreed entirely with that truism, but it certainly captured some of the allure. Serving justice was more than an abstract ideal; it offered a way to navigate through life.

But these days, the common theme in his work at B & A seemed to be money. One client was looking for tax loopholes; another complained they had wrongly lost money in a business deal; his own firm diligently hustled bucks. Was money the fuel that made the legal world spin on its axis? And, if so, was that the world he wanted to inhabit for the rest of his life?

Wordsworth, one of his favorite poets, had written, "The world is too much with us now ... Getting and spending, we lay waste our powers." One hundred and eighty-one years old, the lines still inspired him, and people were still making the same mistakes with their lives.

He hadn't thought in those terms for years—not since marching in Chicago, or writing radical rhetoric in college.

"Wrongful death, Mr. Keeney? I thought the DA was the only person who could bring murder charges."

Keeney had reached Bobbie Roberts at home, after a school day. A long time had passed since their last call and he suspected Bobbie was beginning to lose patience with the legal process. At the mention of this new legal theory, she positively bristled. They had been over the idea before, but at the time it had been only a remote possibility.

"Wrongful death isn't a murder charge," he explained. "It's a civil case where all you can win is money. Nobody goes to jail; that's for criminal matters. You don't even have to prove a civil case beyond a reasonable doubt. You just have to convince a judge or a jury that the McGinnises *probably* caused Deana's death. If it makes you feel any better, civil cases are my area. That's one place I feel right comfortable."

"I just don't know," Bobbie said. "Deana's dead. Money won't bring her back. And you said yourself that these people probably don't have a dime. What about just waiting to see what the district attorney does?"

Keeney balked. He closed his eyes as he delivered the bad news.

"Well, Bobbie, the DA says he still doesn't feel there's enough evidence to arrest the McGinnises or even to get a search warrant."

"What about the insurance policy?" Her steady, homeroom voice faltered. "And the drugs in her blood? And all their lies? It doesn't make sense. Don't they care that my daughter was murdered?"

"I know, Bobbie. But we both have to accept their decision even if we don't like it. Now, let me give you some reasons why you might want to sue the McGinnises."

"I don't want to hear any more reasons. This is just going in circles and I think the system stinks."

"Bobbie, if you sue, we can subpoena the McGinnises' bank records, compel them to turn over the last of Deana's belongings, the ones Virginia never returned. We can take sworn statements from everyone. I'd have a chance at cross-examining them under oath on the witness stand. Maybe even another witness or an insurance policy will turn up.

"Of course, you'll have to take the witness stand, and cross-examinations can get rugged. More than likely, they'll put Deana's character on trial. You may not want to hear some of the things they dig up: sex, drugs, whatever skeletons she had in her closet. It's a lot like they do in rape cases. Somehow, they'll try and blame it on Deana. But the longer we keep the case alive, the better. That's what it comes down to. It's your call."

Just as the silence started to turn awkward, Bobbie spoke up. "Deana's got nothing to hide. She never did drugs or anything like that. But still, Janie and I need to decide this together."

"I don't mean to sound harsh, Bobbie, but you've got until April first. After that, the statute of limitations bars your claim for good. Give me a call when you're ready."

After Keeney put down the phone, he sensed that the whole conversation sounded familiar, like a replay of their meeting more than half a year ago. Why should things go any better now?

With the possibility of a civil lawsuit now on the horizon, Keeney kept gathering information. A Monterey indictment was out of the question, but he could still cement his connections with Ken

Goodnight. State Farm, Keeney knew, had file drawers full of information.

Bit by bit, Ken Goodnight had been revealing what State Farm had been up to all these months, and their efforts were impressive indeed.

Once Virginia laid a claim on the policy—just a week after Deana's death—State Farm swung into action. Investigators fanned out across California, working any angle that might extricate the home office. There had been dozens of interviews, every one taped and transcribed. The file already added up to many hundreds of pages.

One group of investigators tried to uncover any false medical information provided on Deana's application. Rumors about Deana doing drugs had surfaced, and a lie on the application would render the policy void and get State Farm off the hook. With the same end in view, agents also looked into the question of Deana's true relationship with James Coates.

But neither avenue of investigation panned out as far as State Farm's interests were concerned. Apart from rumors passed on by junkies who barely remembered Deana's name, there was no proof of drug use. And Deana's system had been clean when she died— excluding the Elavil.

The question of the engagement, too, boiled down to Coates's word against State Farm's. No one the agents interviewed had ever heard Deana talk much about Coates. The only thing people agreed on was that Deana and Jimmy had known one another for a few months before Jimmy went back to prison. Most of their acquaintances were hard-core drug users and cons, along the lines of Coates himself. A whirlwind romance was possible, but the odds were stacked against it.

In fact, one of State Farm's investigators was tempted to say that the "engagement" smelled as badly as Jimmy Coates himself. Just after Coates turned up and made his claim for the insurance proceeds, he had tracked Jimmy down for an interview.

Thirty-one years old, needle-scarred Jimmy Coates offered the investigator a rabid cellmate-from-Hell stare. To each question, Jimmy resorted to a pat response: He and Deana had been engaged. His mother had written him a letter breaking the bad news just days after the accident. Now that Deana was dead and buried, he wanted the thirty-five grand. Beyond that, he preferred to remain silent.

Keeney and Goodnight agreed Jimmy Coates probably knew more than he was letting on. "Why call your attorney right off if you've got nothing to fear?" Keeney asked. "Why not just wait for the right decision to come down?"

Goodnight said he'd thought the same thing. Murder, after all, was nothing new to James Coates.

State Farm had also unearthed a few background details about B. J. McGinnis, and they were not any more comforting. Forty-seven-year-old B.J. turned out to be something of a small-time swindler. The man had spent a good many years with the navy traveling the world. He left the service after being arrested for forgery and serving time in a United States–run stockade in Germany. Once discharged, he went to San Francisco, where he blended into the gay scene and racked up a string of arrests for small-time forgery.

One acquaintance parted with an old photo, a professional portrait. It showed B.J., his mustache trimmed to pencil thickness and hair slicked down the middle, nonchalantly leaning his head on one hand. Behind him hung a roll-down backdrop painted to look like bookcases filled with leather-bound volumes. B.J. wore a pastel shirt and vest, and his hands were decked out with gold rings. Keeney thought he looked like a sad, silly man, a failed hairdresser who fancied himself a riverboat gambler.

One of B.J.'s past male lovers told State Farm investigators he could never understand why B.J. went with Virginia. "Billie, I told him, you can't marry that woman, you've been gay too long!" But Keeney did some further digging around and found out that B.J. and Virginia were indeed married—at the Wedding Bells Chapel in Carson City, Nevada, on April 14, 1984. Indeed, it was far from B.J.'s first marriage. It was at least his *fifth.*

One of B.J.'s marriages lasted all of three months. Another ended with the ex-wife hiring a lawyer to recover her possessions.

"I think I see the pattern," Keeney said to Goodnight during a late-night phone call. "B.J. met Virginia in the VA hospital where they both worked. He spotted her as one more woman whom he could bilk. After all, she had a taste for flash. B.J. probably thought she had money," Keeney said with a note of pity. "He probably realized too late just what lay behind that facade."

At last, Goodnight revealed that State Farm had something close to a smoking gun in its files.

Just weeks earlier, on January 12, Virginia and B.J. had shuffled into the office of Bill O'Connell, James Coates's lawyer, to meet with a State Farm investigator named Diana Rael. O'Connell had made it his business to keep an eye on anything that might keep the insurance proceeds from his client, so the interview took place in his San Diego office.

Virginia and B.J. nodded curtly as they came in. Diana Rael took a close look. Virginia was a large woman, probably pushing two hundred pounds. Her graying hair was pulled back in a ponytail that exaggerated her large square face with an unusually high forehead and wandering eyes. She had a small nose set above a mouth that curved downward like an inverted smile or a hung horseshoe. But it was her eyes, cold and distant, that stayed in Rael's mind.

B.J., on the other hand, looked limp. He had the familiar face of a one-time joker now consumed by worry.

Keeney got a transcript of the tape. The first thing that struck Keeney was that, throughout the two-hour interview, neither husband nor wife offered any pretense of feeling for Deana. Virginia never so much as mentioned missing her son's "fiancée" or feeling responsible for allowing the tragedy to occur.

The only display of emotion came when Diana Rael asked, "Why would you want to put up somebody you hardly know?"

"Hardly know?" Virginia sounded offended by the question. "Well, doesn't everyone owe something to other people? I've had people help me in the past, I don't know about you personally. . . . I had lost a daughter; she was not a substitute—nothing ever brings back someone you lose through an accident or through death, whether it be a child, or a parent, or whatever—a friend. But she was a very nice person in my opinion. And if she was going to marry Jim, she's—she appeared to be sincere that she wanted to go to school, and we took her basically at face value. We didn't want to see a kid turned out on the street someplace." No one ever "suggested" that Deana was a "substitute" for Cynthia, Keeney ruminated.

Keeney and Goodnight also noted that a few details of Virginia's story seemed to have changed with time. She now recalled taking Deana down to Mexico for a day trip, even though she originally said she wanted an insurance policy to get a visa for her. One more lie for her to explain on the witness stand, Keeney thought.

Investigator Rael told Goodnight that when she turned to B.J., he broke into a cold sweat. He mumbled answers and even then rarely went beyond monosyllables. When truncated replies wouldn't suffice, he hid behind a screen of evasions and memory lapses.

RAEL: How were you notified of the policy issuance for Deana?
B.J.: I don't know.
RAEL: By phone or by mail?
B.J.: I don't know.
RAEL: You didn't take any phone calls?
B.J.: I rarely answer the phone, and I rarely ever go to a mailbox.
RAEL: How long were you at the cliff site?
B.J.: Fifteen, twenty minutes. . . .
RAEL: And . . .
B.J.: We don't remember just how long we were there, it was . . . we'd just taken some pictures.

Everyone agreed that B.J. sounded heavily coached. They could practically see Virginia's fingerprints all over his testimony. She had the man squirming in her grasp.

When pressed about Jimmy's engagement to Deana, neither Virginia nor B.J. had much to say:

RAEL: Who knew about the engagement?
VIRGINIA: They had made the statement that when Jim got everything straightened up, that they planned on getting married.
RAEL: Okay. Did they ever make a formal announcement to the family?
VIRGINIA: No. It was just between themselves.
RAEL: Okay . . . but you knew?
VIRGINIA: Deana had said to me that she planned on getting married.
RAEL: Did she notify her family?
VIRGINIA: No.
RAEL: And she hadn't mentioned anything about her husband?
VIRGINIA: Nothing. We never knew the girl . . . had been married.
RAEL: Did they set a specific date for the wedding?
VIRGINIA: No.
RAEL: Even a month?
VIRGINIA: No.

RAEL: And during the time that James was incarcerated, did [he and Deana] communicate?

B.J.: Not to my knowledge.

RAEL: Do you know why [Deana never visited James Coates in prison]?

B.J.: She didn't want to contact him like this. You know, she just didn't, and I didn't discuss it.

Toward the close of the interview, Rael went into two new areas, questions she hoped the McGinnises might not evade so easily.

Virginia had told both Dungan and Smythe that on April 2, 1987, she, Deana, and B.J. had planned to drive up to B.J.'s sister's place in Santa Rosa, just north of San Francisco. Rael had discovered from neighbors that at the time, Virginia owned a dog named Tsunami.

"How long was your trip planned for?" Rael asked.

"Approximately four or five days maximum," Virginia said.

"And who would be feeding your dog while you were gone?"

"We'd kenneled her," Virginia answered, easily.

"Do you know which kennel?"

"No, I really don't."

"Is it in Chula Vista?" Rael pressed gently.

"Now wait a minute," Virginia suddenly seemed to recall. "We didn't even have a dog at that time. We'd picked up an Akita, but we did not buy her until mid-April."

Rael tried to keep a straight face as Virginia passed off the blatant lie.

She then asked about the claim form Virginia filled in. There were three signatures on the document—Virginia's, James Coates's, and the semi-legible name of a witness. Rael knew Virginia had signed Coates's name—she held a power of attorney for her son that allowed her legally to sign for him. But Rael wanted more information on the witness. "Did you fill out this claim form?" she asked.

"Yes, I did."

"Who is the witness? I can't identify that."

"That's not my writing," Virginia answered, hesitantly.

"Well, yeah, I know, somebody else signed it, but who witnessed it for you? A friend? Neighbor?"

"Oh!" Again Virginia perked up with another sudden recollection. "Alice Kissane . . . our next-door neighbor."

"Your next-door neighbor?"

"Yeah, it took me a moment."

After Rael's interview, investigators went to Virginia's neighborhood in search of the witness. It took a little longer than expected to find Mrs. "Kissain," largely because her name had been misspelled on the form. Alice Kissane was an elderly woman who had only a passing acquaintance with the McGinnises. She took one look and confirmed the investigators' suspicions. People don't misspell their own name. The signature was forged.

C H A P T E R 2 1

HAEUSSINGER

▼

The two men rode together, one in front, one in the rear. They talked intermittently as they wound through eight lanes of San Diego traffic. Physically, they resembled one another, although neither would have appreciated the comparison. Both were tall and sandy-haired, with square faces and refrigerator builds. The man in the rear was balding, but both their foreheads were lined with high-relief Southern California creases, a sign that both men made their livelihoods prowling San Diego's seamier precincts.

Robbery Detective Jack Haeussinger sat in front and drove. He kept a revolver tucked into a leather holster, sweat-stained and smooth, hidden beneath his tweed jacket. He whistled cheerily, a habit that grated on his passenger's nerves.

In the rear seat, James Coates sat and watched the squat San Diego houses roll by. In addition to a pair of jeans, cowboy boots, a denim shirt, and an outsized mustache, Coates wore a pair of chrome-plated handcuffs that locked his arms behind his back. He also wore an expression not unlike that of a married man exasperated with his spouse's bad habits.

But Haeussinger was in a good mood and wanted to talk. He shot Coates a smile via the rearview mirror.

"Tough break, Jimmy. Watch yourself or next time probation's gonna slam you even harder. You ain't exactly shinin' like a diamond in a goat's ass."

"Been slammed before, Jack. Vacaville ain't no big deal."

"Yeah? I know a guy out there, found himself with a three-hundred-pound cellmate named Bubba who likes blow jobs. You might luck out."

"Be out in eight months with good behavior. I figger I can take care of myself."

"Don't forget to tell your mom to send your toothbrush," Haeussinger said, keeping an eye on Coates's reaction. Before making the bust for parole violation, Haeussinger had heard from Jimmy's parole officer that, on top of being a killer, Coates was wanted for a second interview by a State Farm investigator named Diana Rael. The case had something to do with a life-insurance policy bought by Coates's mother, and Haeussinger couldn't resist doing a little digging to see what was up.

"You leave her out of this, you hear?" Jimmy snapped, sticking out his stubbled chin as if it were some sort of weapon. "Ma's got her own business to worry about."

"Hit a raw nerve?"

"Some lawyer's trying to sue her for murdering a girl out here. Shit! She can't believe it. Murder? I mean, me and Ronnie, we could take on something like that, but Ma—"

"You and Ronnie?" Haeussinger asked, checking Coates's face. He didn't look like he was kidding.

"Yeah," he said. "*We* coulda. But not Ma."

Jimmy really is a sick puppy, Haeussinger thought. He squinted at the man's face. Coates's arrogance wasn't even slightly diminished from sitting hog-tied in the rear of a police cruiser. He still looked smug—smug and dangerous.

"So, who's this lawyer?"

"How the hell do I know? Some clown out in Louisville. Says she killed my ol' girlfriend for insurance money. It's a load. Ma ain't never been in the can."

"Louisville?"

"I'm still trying to figure just who *is* this guy. Not that I care. My girl died by accident, and I'm owed the insurance money. That's a proven fact. Thirty-five thousand. I may be goin' back in, but I got a helluva lawyer who'll keep at it."

A Louisville attorney chasing after Coates's mother for a California homicide? That was a new twist. The story could be a product of Jimmy Coates's warped imagination, Haeussinger thought. But then again, Haeussinger liked exotic stories.

Love of the strange had drawn Jack Haeussinger to the police department in the first place. San Diego generated plenty of crime, both strange and routine. With its regular Hell's Angels' head bashings, street-gang shoot-outs, thriving prostitution, and Mexican drug trade along El Cajon Boulevard, and its strip joints filled with thousands of sailors pouring through town just off three-week tours at sea, there was no shortage of odd cases to sate his appetite. Haeussinger also liked working alone; ten years for the SDPD and he still possessed maverick instincts.

"Louisville, Kentucky," Haeussinger repeated out loud. He'd track this country lawyer down and see what the shouting was all about.

CHAPTER 22

BETTING THE HOUSE

▼

Keeney didn't know whether to laugh or cry at the call from AmEx Insurance Company. Coming so late after Bobbie had asked him to look into the very same matter as a small favor, it seemed almost funny. But the adjuster could point to chapter and verse.

"Ms. Roberts's insurance policy covers only burial costs for children 'in school,' 'not married,' and 'up to nineteen years of age,' " the adjuster's mechanical voice explained. "Deana fails to qualify under even one of the requirements. The company's decision has nothing to do with Deana's death certificate or the coroner's report, Mr. Keeney. Those are the terms of the policy."

As the adjuster went on about the various clauses, Keeney tried to keep from laughing out loud.

Had he only ordered a copy of the contract a half year back, he would have cleared up Bobbie's question in ten minutes. He might have offered her a few words of condolence, then said that he would see her at the pastry table in Fellowship Hall. Instead, this shortcut had steered him into a case that lately had him worrying about whether the Coates boys might not decide to visit him or Bobbie in Louisville. He thanked the adjuster for passing along the information and apologized for the misunderstanding. "Just shows some things are meant to be," he laughed to himself.

Yet it seemed as if every aspect of the case was going seriously off track. For one thing, time virtually had run out with both Monterey and State Farm.

Just a month ago, O'Connell had written a letter to the Monterey police that tried to force a decision exonerating the McGinnises and releasing the life insurance money:

> Dear Detective Smythe,
>
> I am informed by the McGinnis family that they have been reinterviewed by officers from your department, and that they once again cooperated fully. . . .
>
> Given that the persons present at the scene with Deana have been interviewed and reinterviewed, have cooperated fully, spoken with officers at all times without asking for counsel to be present, etc., I feel it is time to conclude this investigation. Your delay in doing so is holding up the settlement of the insurance claim, and has so held it up for almost a year. Let's bring the matter to a conclusion now. File charges, or make the proper conclusion that the incident was an accident.
>
> I feel it is time to take legal action in the courts to protect my client and his interests. . . . By copy of this letter, I am informing the insurance carrier of my intent to litigate this claim, and follow up with a bad faith action, unless this matter is resolved within the next twenty (20) days. . . .
>
> I am told that your office is pursuing this case only because of pressure from Deana's family. . . .

Within weeks, Keeney feared, Monterey would officially rule that Deana's death was accidental, and State Farm would have to pay James Coates every dime of the policy money—plus damages for bad-faith denial of life insurance.

It made him sick at heart. He had brought Bobbie Roberts closer to the truth, all right. But he had let her down in every other way. She would end up infinitely worse off, forced to live with the knowledge that her daughter's killers had wriggled through cracks in the system and would soon be living off the profit.

▼

March 8, 1988. The day would have marked Deana Hubbard's twenty-first birthday. Bobbie Roberts chose the occasion to telephone Keeney at his office in B & A. He had been looking out at the skyline under a bright spring sky that nonetheless looked bleak to him.

"I want to go ahead with a wrongful-death case," she said. "I want to see those people face up to what they did." Keeney listened to her words with an uncomfortable sense of déjà vu. Nonetheless, he was willing to press ahead.

After the call, he set up a rough calendar. April 2, 1988, marked the first anniversary of Deana's death and the cutoff date for a civil case against the McGinnises. That left only four weeks to engage West Coast counsel, draft a complaint, and file it in court.

He went to get some coffee. On the way, he passed a number of recently vacated offices littered with papers and half-filled boxes. B & A felt like a ghost town these days. "You could fire a shotgun down the hall and not hit a thing," Pete Lazar had joked.

Within the week, Monterey attorney Chuck Warner agreed to take Bobbie's case on a contingency-fee basis, with Keeney as lead counsel. Bobbie offered Keeney the customary lawyer's one-third. He saw no reason to refuse. It wouldn't amount to much, anyway. One third of any money they got would go to Keeney, and Warner would take a third of Keeney's third.

Together, he and Warner drafted a three-count complaint alleging wrongful death, negligence, and assault and battery. It was revised, fact-checked, and filed with the Superior Court of the State of California for the County of Monterey on March 30, 1988, at 3:07 P.M.—two and a half days before the statute of limitations expired.

Serving the McGinnises with copies of the complaint marked the next critical step. Chuck Warner said there would no problem. But Keeney was experienced enough to know that over the years lawyers had made serving the defendant with a legal complaint into a devious art form. "Knock and leave with" (just toss the complaint to whoever answers the door at the defendant's house) and "sewer service" (throw the thing in the gutter and lie about it in court) became well-recognized tactics in below-the-belt legal gamesmanship.

"I want actual service in this case," Keeney insisted to Warner.

"Get the Sheriff's Office to help you, or a professional process server, but no shortcuts. This may be the prelude to a murder case. It's gotta be slicker than a greased weasel."

"All right, all right," Warner said. "One way or another, we'll find 'em and slap 'em."

Keeney had barely put the phone down when Sarah West buzzed him again. A detective was waiting to speak with him on the other line.

"Steve Keeney? Detective Jack Haeussinger from the San Diego Police Department." The man sounded as if he enjoyed saying his name, chewing on each syllable like a leather thong—How-zin-jur. "Don Smythe up in Monterey says you're behind all this murder talk about Virginia McGinnis. I thought I'd call and see what you know."

Keeney mulled for a moment before answering. Jack Haeussinger was a totally unfamiliar name. Detectives from other cities don't just call up out of the blue, do they? It sounded wrong. The voice could belong to Jimmy Coates, coming to harass him about the insurance proceeds. Jimmy was a dangerous character, as likely to shoot you in the head as shake your hand. Keeney thought of the boy Jimmy had lassoed from a speeding truck, and of the drug dealer he had killed. And here I'm sitting in my office, Keeney thought, waiting to be picked off like a milk bottle on a fence.

On the other hand, the call could be a break.

"Detective," he answered. "I'm sorry to ask, but could you give me your number at the station house so I can call you back." He figured if Haeussinger were a pro, he would read between the lines.

"Your option, Counselor," the leathery voice said. "But you'll find out I'm on the up-and-up." Keeney checked out Haeussinger's status with the San Diego PD and returned the call, considerably relieved.

"Seems you're getting a reputation with the Coates boys," Haeussinger said. "Jimmy tipped me off to you."

"That's not exactly what I need to hear right now," Keeney answered. "I was just thinking about taking my number out of the phone book."

"Don't worry. Ronnie and Jimmy are in the can. Of course, taking a few precautions won't hurt. You own a pistol? But that's not really my business, is it?"

"Detective, maybe you could start with telling me what *is* your business."

"I spoke to Don Smythe and an investigator who works for State Farm, a gal named Diana Rael. They say you've been doing your own investigation into Virginia McGinnis. Now, I know the Coates boys; they're about as cold-blooded a lot as you're likely to scrape up around here. So I figure, Mamma's not going to be Betsy Ross.

"Smythe tells me he's got some problems getting this over with the DA. But if his case is as strong as he says, then it's politics that's standing between you and an indictment, not evidence."

"All right, you've got my interest, Detective. But where can you take it? I spoke to Jon Yudin and I didn't come away all that optimistic."

"A good homicide might be something I can put on a plate for our local DA, even the AG. Play the two off each other, if one doesn't bite first."

It sounded fine, but wasn't Haeussinger overlooking one fundamental problem?

"I hate to sound like a lawyer," Keeney interjected, "but what about a little detail called jurisdiction? Deana was murdered about five hundred miles north of San Diego County. Hell, I'd take the case to *our* local DA here in Louisville if it were that easy."

"It don't matter that the body's not in our county," Haeussinger said. "At least if you'll accept an opinion from an untrained legal mind. We know that the McGinnises bought the insurance policy in Chula Vista. That's inside San Diego County limits. If they bought the policy as part of a conspiracy to kill the girl, then we've got jurisdiction over the conspiracy and the homicide. You're banging your head against a brick wall in Monterey, and all you're going to get is a headache. You don't really think they're going to stick their necks out on this one?"

"Why don't you tell me what you've got in mind?"

"You send me whatever you've got on the case. I'll run it down on my own time and see if there's a homicide to be made. If there is, I'll personally take it to our DA Ed Miller's office."

Keeney didn't know what to make of this character. Haeussinger sounded like some Clint Eastwood–style hotdogger, but also like someone who would gnaw on the bone. He certainly didn't operate like most police officers Keeney had encountered. He could be either one of San Diego's finest and bravest or a renegade whose name on a case file amounted to a kiss of death. And if San Diego started to look into the matter and then dropped it, Monterey would blackball Keeney for shopping the case to competing jurisdictions.

"I'm gonna have to stew on this one for a few days," Keeney finally said. "Talk it over with my client. She's the one who's going to be living with the results."

"Have it your way, Counselor," he signed off. "You just send up a flare when you realize I'm right."

May 1, 1987. Chuck Warner, local counsel in Monterey, called in to B & A with unexpected news.

"Congratulations!" Warner announced. "You won."

"What are you talking about?" Keeney sat up and grabbed a pen. "Did the judge set an accelerated-motion schedule?"

"No, seriously. You won. On a technicality, if you want to call it that, but you've got your judgment." Warner paused, waiting for a reaction. "I thought you'd be thrilled."

"Chuck, just tell me what happened in court." Keeney was in no mood for joking. They had finally gotten the McGinnises into court, it seemed, and now his lead man in California wanted to kid around.

"Okay, okay. Here it is. B.J. and Virginia were living at separate addresses. A process server from the Sheriff's Office tracked them down and served them personally. B.J. was staying with his sister in some nursing home; Virginia had a place up in Contra Costa County. We served 'em in person *and* via U.S. mail."

"And?" Keeney's pen started clicking.

"That's it," Warner said brightly. "Nothing. They had three weeks and they never answered. They never even showed up in court. Total default. Judge William Wunderlich, one of our former prosecutors, entered judgment for Bobbie Roberts. You won. Boom."

Keeney's voice fell. "Chuck, that's unbelievable. Totally unbelievable. I never thought I'd be so put out to hear I won a case."

"What are you talking about?" Warner asked. "This is a victory. You should be delighted."

"Yeah, but *nobody* defaults wrongful-death cases, Chuck. At least nobody innocent. Their deadline came and went without a whisper." He took a sip of coffee; things with Virginia just kept getting curiouser and curiouser.

"Well, it happened," Warner said. "And now you can walk into court and demand a monetary judgment, no questions asked."

"That's just it. Sounds to me like they didn't want to say anything about this case on the record, no matter what."

"So?"

"So, they're guilty as sin and they saw us coming. Now we don't get to ask them question one. Except . . ." Keeney paused, took another sip from his cup. "Except if we go after their assets. They're betting the house on this one—if they have a house. What do you say we find out?"

"Well, first we've got to wait for a hearing to place a dollar figure on Bobbie Roberts's loss. Then we can chase after assets. But I agree, it's the best shot we've got."

"Let's try to get a jump on the hearing and do a little checking around. Start with Virginia's home: title, book value, etc. She's certainly the type who responds to money. What do you say?"

Warner said he'd stay along for the ride. Keeney thanked him and they signed off.

Only one thing seemed clear now that the McGinnises had defaulted. It was either go with Haeussinger or wait for a ghost witness to change Yudin's mind. On May 11, 1988, one final copy of Keeney's book, now swollen by the latest updates into a six-hundred-page tome, went out to Jack Haeussinger, Investigator, San Diego Police Department.

The subject of the next annual partners' meeting did not bring much joy to the partners at B & A, even though it provided a respite from the angry turf wars among departing partners, and incoming details of Charlie Barnett's battle with the federal prosecutors in New York.

Pete Lazar led the discussion and tried to keep the mood light. After discussions about budget versus location, Lazar suggested the Scottsdale Princess Hotel in Phoenix, Arizona. A joyless silence filled the room as Lazar lowered a hand onto the table, signaling that the resolution had passed. Not that the Princess was a second-class operation, but it symbolized the end of an era at B & A. Farewell to the Breakers in Palm Beach!

"While we're on the subject of accommodations," Keeney spoke up. "I was hoping to get a suite adjoining my own for my date, Wynn Burkholder. You all know who Wynn is by now." A few heads nodded in reply as Keeney's glance traveled up and down the boardroom table. "I'll pay for it out of my own account, but I thought I'd square this with you all first."

Through the fall and winter, Wynn had been the one stable part of Keeney's life. They spent afternoons with one another's children—Wynn had two: Mark and Kelly—and even started to become something of a family. Taking a vacation together, away from the kids, seemed the natural next step.

Before any of Keeney's colleagues could respond, an emergency call for Pete Lazar drew the meeting to a close. "Sorry, Steve," Lazar said as he headed for the door. "Let's take that up next week. Meeting adjourned."

The reality of the Arizona partners' meeting was still sinking in when Keeney heard a knock on his office door. He opened it and found one of the firm's elder statesmen, Hugh Stark, standing in the hallway. Stark looked his usual overly serious self.

"Steve, there's a problem we need to discuss—privately," he began portentously. Stark's white head of hair reminded Keeney unsettlingly of his father, as did the impassive set of his jaw. Had his net realization slipped that low? Keeney felt a twinge in the pit of his stomach.

"Sure, Hugh. Come on in, take a seat." He motioned to a pair of chairs at a coffee table in the wing of his suite.

"It's nothing I bring up lightly, Steve," Stark said, walking in but resolutely not sitting. "There's just one word for it, really."

One word. Keeney racked his brain. Billing? Hours? Profits? Nothing jumped out at him. Except that Stark really could be a pompous ass. Couldn't the man just say what's on his mind?

Keeney finally opted for something softer: "I give up, Hugh. Let's have it straight."

Stark's eyes focused into two blue bullets as he pronounced, "Fornication." He paused to let the weight of the word sink in.

Keeney knew better than to laugh. Both he and Wynn were formally divorced, entering their forties with three children between them. What century did Stark think he was living in?

"You mean Wynn?" he asked at last, his voice cracking.

"I don't think I have to explain any further," Stark concluded before turning to leave. "Adjoining suites, indeed! I trust you'll reconsider." The door swung shut behind him.

Keeney returned to his desk, speechless. Half-heartedly, he picked up the phone to call Wynn at her office and explain that he'd be going to the partners' meeting stag. He started to dial, then stopped.

He looked around his office. Papers all but carpeted the floor. At home, his study didn't look any better.

He thought of Christian shuttling between two homes, and of his own compulsive eating and smoking and coffee drinking. Wynn seemed the one bit of unequivocal good in all this chaos, even if she did think that chasing the McGinnises was a fool's errand. She had tried to coax him out of his bad habits, had even gotten him to watch his weight.

Hugh Stark might be a prude, Keeney thought, but he's responsible for one of the best decisions I'll ever make.

Fornication. The word echoed in Keeney's mind as he and Wynn walked aboard the *Bonnie Belle,* one of Louisville's paddle-wheel steamboats. Along the riverfront, a few cars lazed across the bridges leading over to Indiana as the sun burned gold into the late-day sky. But the deck of the *Bonnie Belle* was deserted.

"Steve, are you sure we're not on the wrong boat?" Wynn looked around at the postcard-perfect scene. Then her eyes fell on the single table, flanked by two chairs and topped with a silver champagne bucket holding a bottle of Roederer Cristal and a dozen roses. She knew Keeney well enough to know how the rest of this script would read. She had seen it before.

Within ten minutes, the bottle was open and they were steaming toward the Ohio Falls, engaged to be married. Under a rising half-moon, Keeney saw the pieces of his life start to pull together. Along with thoughts of a new family, he imagined offering one choice word to white-haired Hugh Stark at the upcoming partners' meeting in Phoenix: *fornication.*

Across the country, Jack Haeussinger was up late reading Keeney's book. It was a first-class piece of work in Haeussinger's opinion, although typically, he also thought it was lawyer's overkill.

"You take the insurance policy, the photographs, and Virginia's statements that she never heard of an insurance policy on Deana," he grumbled. "There's your case. All the pathologist's opinions and taped phone conversations in the world can't build you a better homicide than that."

All through June, he put in calls to Ken Goodnight and Diana Rael at State Farm, Don Smythe in Monterey, and R. D. Jones in Louisville. Everything checked out. Then, one afternoon, Haeussinger took his copy of Keeney's book and his own twenty-page report, climbed in his blue cruiser, and drove into downtown San Diego from his station out in the Eastern Division.

Jim Pippin, chief of the DA's Superior Court Division, was just returning to his desk from lunch at a local Mexican joint named Los Quatros Milpas but affectionately nicknamed by the police officer regulars as "The Fly." A plate of chorizo and rice with a side of hand-rolled flour tortillas, all washed down with a Tecate, had left Pippin feeling logy and undisposed to an interruption.

At the sight of Haeussinger's six-foot-two frame filling his doorway, Pippin managed a friendly, if forced, greeting. He knew exactly what Haeussinger had in mind and he wasn't relishing the idea. Pippin had plenty of murders on his docket already. San Diego saw close to four hundred homicides per year, that on top of tens of thousands of burglaries, robberies, rapes. Close to 600,000 warrants for failure to appear in court remained open. Why should a busy office bust its butt to take a case that's going nowhere? One out-of-the-jurisdiction homicide in such a morass didn't so much as raise a hair on the back of Pippin's neck. But after eighteen years of trying criminal cases for the DA, Pippin knew that law enforcers had to stick together.

"Same old murder, Jack? I told you last week, we've got cases coming out of our ears here," Pippin said in his deliberate drawl. "The last thing we need is some orphan from Monterey."

Pippin liked Haeussinger. The guy was a cutup with his battery of expressions and his Dirty Harry attitude. But he was a *robbery* detective, a good one admittedly, but still a robbery cop. Pippin doubted he had ever handled a homicide from start to finish in his life. And, counting phone calls, this was his *sixth* time making the rounds of the DA's office with his "great homicide." *The case is solid. The Louisville lawyer's done one hell of a job. The perp's a regular dragon lady without an ounce of compassion in her.* Pippin had practically memorized the lines.

And each time, Haeussinger went on longer, getting more heated up. Now, here he was again, leaning over Pippin's desktop, the gravel grinder in his throat shifting into low gear.

"This guy Keeney's hung in there like a trooper for a year without getting paid one lousy simoleon. How many lawyers are crazy enough to do that? You owe it to yourself just to read his book and check out my report.

"Besides, it'll be a nice feather in your cap if you guys make a homicide that Monterey wouldn't even touch. Think about it."

Pippin reflected on Haeussinger's words in the afterglow of his Mexican heartburn. Here was a cop getting the door slammed in his face. If the DA's office at least went through the motions, Pippin hoped Haeussinger would back off. He didn't think he could take another one of these visits.

"All right, Jack, you win. I'll give it a look."

"Fine, I'll call you next week to discuss the plans for arrest."

"I said I'd read it, Jack. Then we'll talk."

Keeney had expected a call from Mike Hatch and Ken Goodnight ever since he read James Coates's lawyer's letter threatening a wrongful-denial lawsuit. He was hardly surprised when they telephoned in tandem to explain State Farm's next step: They were bailing out.

"We'll probably never know for sure what happened on that cliff," Goodnight said. "The investigation's gone on longer than anyone could have predicted, and still there's no real hope of clear resolution."

Keeney said he wished it could be otherwise but admitted that State Farm had already gone beyond the call of duty.

"Not that we're going to cut Coates a check," Hatch hastened to add.

In a legal maneuver known as federal interpleader, State Farm was going to pay the insurance proceeds to the federal court, "sue" everyone with a potential interest, then ask the judge to decide who got the money. State Farm would wash its hands of the whole mess, and protect itself against any wrongful-denial lawsuits.

Hatch and Goodnight then signed off for the last time.

The only good news, Keeney decided afterward, was that James Coates might just might be fool enough to try and claim the money. That meant going to trial, and then he would have a chance at cross-examining Coates, or his mother, under oath.

"Steve, got a minute?" Peter Lazar asked as he passed Keeney in the B & A hallway. Lazar's deadpan delivery made it plain that he had something on his mind more serious than the Scottsdale Princess.

"It's about Charlie Barnett," Lazar said as his door swung shut. "They're leaving him out to dry."

"Seriously, Pete," Keeney objected. "Charlie's in trouble, but with a good defense team he's got a fair shot at acquittal."

Lazar waved a hand derisively. "I don't mean the U.S. Attorney's Office, for Chrissake. *We're* leaving Charlie out to dry. No defense fund, no rallying support. Just complete disassociation. The capital partners cut him loose not ten minutes ago."

"But why?" Keeney asked, dumbfounded. "We're like a bunch of Eskimos pushing the old folks out to die on icebergs."

"That's just the start," Lazar continued bitterly. "We're also cutting a dozen partners. You're not on the list, but you'll be hearing about it, probably reading about it, too."

"A dozen partners," Keeney repeated.

Making partner was supposed to be a lawyer's apotheosis, the pot of gold justifying the long haul through law school, bar examination, and serving as an associate. You were set for life. In the firm's directory, attorneys' names were followed either with an *a* for associate or a *p* for partner. The line around the firm was that every lawyer wanted his *a*-ness turned into his *p*-ness. For weeks after his own ascension into the elite, Keeney felt as if he were cloaked in a solid-platinum security blanket.

"I'd do a little checking around the job market," Lazar advised. "We can buy some time with accounting, but in the end there'll be more bloodshed. We're hemorrhaging already."

Keeney thanked Lazar and headed back to his office.

So this is how the brethren of partners stand up for one another when times are hard, Keeney thought. Kill or be killed.

He looked back at a career of creating and defending paper creatures, moving blocks of money and stock. His trophies were marble mementos and acrylic "tombstones." One read: "$12,000,000 1984–1985 Lease Transaction." He felt proud of is accomplishments, but none of them filled him with the sense of purpose he felt in chasing down Virginia and in helping Bobbie Roberts. This case had brought back a taste of his youthful idealism, both familiar and welcome.

Keeney pulled out a yellow pad and began to write:

MEMORANDUM: To all Partners
RE: Steven H. Keeney—Resignation

That fall, Keeney wound down his affairs at B & A. There were his accounts, valuing his goodwill with prized clients, percentage of year-end bonus. But Bobbie Roberts's case hadn't faded away. Alongside State Farm's interpleader action, Keeney started preparing Bobbie to testify in California, "woodshedding" her for an upcoming hearing on damages.

"Basically, you have to boil down a twenty-year-old's life to a certain number of dollars," Keeney told Bobbie.

"The out-of-pocket expenses are simple. Your and Jane's counseling costs; the cross-country trip you took last Christmas to look at the site; funeral expenses; moving from the Fincastle house. On top of that, you try to give the court a verbal portrait of Deana, of what her loss means to you in personal terms. The California courts call it 'hedonic' damages."

It was a job only a lawyer could view as routine.

And the frustration was palpable. Virginia McGinnis had committed cold-blooded murder and walked away from it without so much as a slap on the wrist. That was just fundamentally wrong. The judge could award Bobbie Roberts a million dollars—and if Virginia didn't have any assets to seize, it meant only a paper victory. Keeney still wondered if there were other mothers out there, mourning the loss of a child or a relative who had died at Virginia's hand. How many other "patients" she had nursed. It didn't seem likely that Deana was Virginia's first kill. She and B.J. had planned the crime for over a month and brought off the paperwork and the interviews with a cool, practiced hand.

They're still out there, Keeney kept thinking. It made the fall of B & A, that legal powerhouse, feel unexpectedly small.

CHAPTER 23

OPERA IN THE BARIO

▼

By the end of July, Deputy DA Jim Pippin decided he had to do something with Haeussinger's homicide. It had sat staring at him from across the room for too long. One afternoon, he carried the mass of paper into the office of one of their middle-level prosecutors, Deputy DA Luis Aragon. Pippin figured Aragon was the studious sort of guy who might actually read the thing.

"Hey, Luis, I got something for you. Read it and tell me if it's a homicide. Some civil attorney in Louisville says it might be. The Monterey DA says it's not. Take it home and see what you think."

Seated behind a desk buried in trial prep notes, Aragon listened to Pippin and then frowned.

His first thought was that whoever put the thing together must be some kind of jailhouse lawyer or just a plain old loon. There were plenty of monomaniacal ex-cons and attorneys running around, writing tomes on "burning issues" or imaginary conspiracies.

But Jim Pippin was his superior. He insisted Keeney was a bona fide attorney, and that one member of the local PD thought the case had some merit. Aragon decided he would take the file home and figure out a way to get rid of it diplomatically.

Luis Manuel Aragon had been trying cases at the San Diego DA's Office for eight years, but he was by no means their top man. There were many days, in fact, when he looked around his office and wondered at how he had ever managed to climb as high as he had.

Aragon grew up in Calexico, a town of no more than ten thousand situated a few miles north of Tijuana, just inside the U.S. border. His father had started out working the fields, then moved to the broiling Imperial valley, where he found work as a smelter for U.S. Gypsum. While Mr. Aragon endured what he called "heat upon heat," his wife educated their nine children—Luis was the youngest—in subjects from Latin poetry to opera. Mariachi blared from other bario tenement windows, but Mrs. Aragon ensured that her home was filled with Puccini and Wagner.

After graduating from Calexico High School, Luis took the first chance to leave: Yale College, then Georgetown Law School. Coming back to the San Diego Prosecutor's Office in 1981 marked a sort of homecoming. Notwithstanding his Ivy League education, Aragon prided himself on still being able to roll up his sleeves with farmers from the border. And the DA's Office—its powerful clout and political intrigues aside—required daily contact with hookers, junkies, cops, and salt-of-the-earth human beings. His job kept him nicely suspended between sky and earth.

Aragon knew he was not a natural trial attorney. His courtroom demeanor came across, initially, as unimposing, even meek. He had a narrow, lightly pocked face, a spray of fine black hair, and a trim but desk-bound figure. It all emanated sincerity but not power. So, too, his voice, which, when raised to a crescendo, wavered slightly.

Yet Aragon made the most of his special blend of professionalism and folksiness, of Ivy League and Calexico High. To juries, he carried a straightforward message: We're just going by the book here, folks. If nice, mild-mannered Luis Aragon believes the defendant did it, how can you possibly acquit?

Eventually, he got around to reading Keeney's book. Saturday morning, he was lounging in bed in his pajamas. Having run out of excuses, he got a cup of coffee, turned on the bedside lamp, and propped the tome on his knees. He stayed in bed the rest of the day reading, then picked up where he had left off the next morning.

He could hear the defense already: "Members of the jury, my client has never been convicted of a crime. She's fifty years old. And she reported the death to the police on her own. When all is said and done, this is a purely circumstantial case!" But Aragon knew how to turn the line to his advantage. "Members of the jury"—he had said it a dozen times before—"circumstances don't lie. People do."

Monday morning, he called Jim Pippin.

"Jim, I was reading the thing all weekend. I think we've got a homicide here."

"What needs to be done?" Pippin asked, masking his surprise.

"Well, that's the problem. Keeney represents the dead girl's mother, and he might be working an angle of his own. I'm going to need six months with a full-time investigator. Then we can decide about jurisdiction and whether we've got a triable case."

"All right," Pippin said warily, "let's go across the street and talk to the DA." He hoped Aragon was not about to throw away his reputation on some cockamamy case slapped together by a Louisville Slugger.

Aragon's telephone call from the San Diego DA's Office that afternoon seemed to Keeney to be a miracle. He had all but given up on Jack Haeussinger. But Aragon remained cool.

"We're simply investigating here," he cautioned. "I want to make that clear. Whether we'll be able to make a case or file charges depends on what we find. But you and Ms. Roberts should know that the case hasn't gone completely stale."

"I guess my own feelings are clear," Keeney said. "For now, let's leave it that if there's anything Ms. Roberts or I can do, just ask."

Throughout the fall and winter, and then into the spring of 1989, Aragon and DA Investigator Scott Lawrence tracked down leads. Jack Haeussinger volunteered for the assignment, but that was not to be. Aragon had to ensure a smoothly working unit and he quickly learned that, for whatever reason, bad blood existed between Lawrence and Haeussinger. It forced a choice, and in the end Aragon chose FBI–trained Lawrence.

He and Lawrence, a blond thirty-year-old with a squat, linebacker's build, trekked from California to upstate New York to Kentucky and back, interviewing Art and Cleo McCain, Dick

Coates, Ken Goodnight, Donald Smythe, R. D. Jones, Bobbie Roberts, and dozens of other potential witnesses.

It took only a few weeks before Aragon and Lawrence realized the full extent of the case. It reached further than even Keeney's book implied. Everyone who knew Virginia seemed to have been waiting for someone to come along and ask. But Aragon couldn't get sidetracked by other remote misdeeds. He had Deana's homicide as his primary responsibility.

Deana's character might form a pivotal issue if the case ever went to trial, Aragon understood. Would she really have asked to buy life insurance? Was she a clumsy, reckless soul prone to accidents? Was she a druggie who might have foraged through Billie Joe's medicine cabinet and gobbled down whatever pills she found? And what had been her true relationship to James Coates? The inquiry led from Bobbie Roberts's house in Louisville through some of the most drug-infested precincts of San Diego. The further he dug, the more Aragon became sure that Deana would inevitably become the focus of the trial.

But all that would be later. In the meantime, the DA's team subpoenaed State Farm's files and ran rap sheets on the McGinnises. Deana's blood, kept frozen in the coroner's lab, was retested for Elavil levels. Pharmaceutical experts were consulted. Scott Lawrence rappeled down the cliff with a video camera, trying to re-create the trajectory of Deana's fall. Using triangulation, he determined the height of whoever had snapped the last photo of Deana and B.J. at the cliff edge. Aragon discovered that Virginia and B.J. had no source of income other than Virginia's small disability check from the VA.

Information quickly piled up, thousands of pages' worth. And almost everywhere they looked, Aragon and Lawrence kept finding signs that the Louisville lawyer had preceded them. In December, Scott Lawrence went to the Eagle Crest Hotel to dig up records from Deana's stay there. The owner directed him to a back room filled with dust-covered guest ledgers. Lawrence pawed through the pile until he came to the volume for fall of 1986. As he opened the book, a slip of paper fell out. "11/10/87. Call Steven Keeney," it read.

Eventually, Aragon decided that a good case could be made against Virginia and now he needed to wallow in the feel of the thing. He flew out to Louisville to join Scott Lawrence. By the end of their first day, Aragon had interviewed Steve Keeney, Bobbie Roberts, R. D. Jones, and a group of Deana's friends. He wanted to be in Deana's house, eat her food, meet her peers; get to know the victim.

The next day, he and Lawrence headed their rent-a-car toward Lexington to speak with Deana's aunt and uncle. A dreary, damp afternoon drizzle crept in and turned the day prematurely into evening, but that was no reason to stop working.

"Where's Deana buried?" Aragon asked Lawrence impulsively. They unfolded a map of the city and turned their car down a rain-slick highway toward the cemetery in Lexington.

A few shrubs and trees populated the broad field of graves, but otherwise Aragon and Lawrence sloshed across the lawn alone. Deana's small granite headstone looked lost amidst hundreds of others. It wasn't a pauper's grave, but it seemed quietly anonymous, much like Deana herself. Who could know that this girl had been the victim of a treacherous act in one of the most beautiful places on earth? Aragon thought.

The rain started to pick up, and Lawrence said he wanted to head back to the car.

"Go ahead." Aragon nodded. "I'd kinda like to be alone with her, anyway."

Aragon was not a churchgoer, but he practiced his own homespun religion. The courtly prosecutor lowered his head, drops of rain now rolling down his glasses and blurring the words on the granite slab until they became illegible.

Half out loud, he said, "Deana, this is a very difficult thing for me. I don't know what will happen in the case. I believe Virginia is guilty, but I don't know if a jury will agree with me. I need your help. All I can give you now is a prayer."

The rain accelerated, falling harder and harder until the sound of Aragon's voice became lost in the rush.

▼

PART THREE

THE
ICE LADY

CHAPTER 24

DRAWING THE NET

▼

Bobbie Roberts walked to the witness stand in Monterey. The last few months seemed to her to have gone by in a state of suspended animation. The McGinnises still had not responded to the civil complaint. Keeney now occupied a new, one-man office and was even more overwhelmed than usual. State Farm had completely stopped its investigation. And Aragon still had not arrested the McGinnises.

Bobbie testified for an hour that day, never losing her prim, schoolteacher's poise. The defense table, where Virginia and B.J. should have been seated, stood conspicuously vacant and made the square, modern courtroom feel out of balance. With no defense lawyer to interpose objections or cross-examine her, the story of her life with Deana came out in a smooth stream.

"Have you been to the scene of the incident?" Chuck Warner asked when Bobbie reached the end of her narrative.

"Yes, I have. I did that Christmas. Yes, sir."

"Why did you go to the site of the fall?"

"I kept having dreams," Bobbie said, "and trying to visualize each

223

night what it looked like and everything. I wanted to get the facts; I wanted to straighten up in my own mind exactly what it looked like, and I did."

At the close of the hearing, Judge Wunderlich took over the questioning.

"Was your daughter—I can't tell quite from that picture what your daughter's size was. Was she a woman of full stature?"

"Yes."

"In other words, she wasn't very short or very, very tall?"

"Yes, she was very tall. She was five nine."

"All right. Approximately what was her weight at the time of her death?"

"I would say one thirty, one thirty-five."

"Was she a person who had problems with balance?"

"No, sir."

"Was she involved in athletics when she was a younger girl?"

"She was a swimmer."

"And was she coordinated well?"

"Yes." By the end of Wunderlich's questioning, the notion of Deana being a clumsy incompetent vanished. She was clearly a healthy, physically fit young woman. A good defense attorney could have raised a host of questions—the dizzying effects of Elavil combined with the high heels, the possibility of dangerous gusts of wind. But the McGinnises had opted out.

"And it's your understanding," Wunderlich went on, "based on the investigation, that on the first day of April they get an insurance policy on your daughter's life, and on the second of April she falls from a cliff in Big Sur?"

Bobbie Roberts put a bitter edge to the innocuous words: "Absolutely. Yes, sir."

Chuck Warner called Keeney at the end of the day. It was evening, Kentucky time.

"A total success," Warner cheered over the telephone. "Two hundred eighty-five thousand dollars in damages and a judicial record you can bank on. Especially Wunderlich's impromptu remark at the close. I wrote it down word for word, it's so good. He was a former prosecutor here for twenty years before he became judge—"

"Chuck, spare me the flowers," Keeney said impatiently. "I want news. What did he say?"

"Got a pen?"

"Chuck—"

"All right, all right. Wunderlich turned to Bobbie and said, 'Ms. Roberts, I'm very sorry for what happened. It's a tragic fact of life in Monterey County that we have an incredibly beautiful stretch of coastline to the south, but it also, unfortunately, from time to time is the situs of incredibly violent and despicable conduct.' How about that? Our former prosecutor as much as said they murdered Deana."

Keeney spoke with Bobbie Roberts that night while she rested at her hotel room. She sounded tired, Keeney thought, but he heard some settling down in her voice.

Was Virginia smiling right now? Keeney wondered that evening after congratulating Bobbie. He looked up through his study skylight at an ascendant crescent moon.

Judge Wunderlich's pronouncement in Monterey would give Bobbie Roberts a dose of comfort but little else. The McGinnises could ignore the wrongful-death judgment and go on living just as they had for years. Even the San Diego DA had yet to seek an indictment. They were just investigating.

Yes, murder, forgery, and possibly arson seemed to be the McGinnis family businesses, and they were frighteningly good at them. Virginia probably counted on Deana's death to be her meal ticket. Denied that, she simply moved on. Virginia had collected insurance in Ithaca, Louisville, and San Francisco, Keeney knew, and he suspected she would probably do it again now. Her son James Coates, meanwhile, stood a better-than-even chance of collecting the money. Judge Wunderlich hadn't found *him* guilty of anything.

One way or another, her scheme might well work out.

While Keeney envisioned the McGinnises' fugitive life, Scott Lawrence and the DA's investigation team spent the months of July and August documenting it. They tried to keep B.J. and Virginia under twenty-four-hour surveillance, although, right off, they met with complications. It turned out that Billie Joe and Virginia had left town a few months after Deana's death. They had gotten an instant divorce, then went their separate ways.

Lawrence led the group that traced Virginia. She had moved twice in the interim and had also gone back to using the fifteen-year-old name Rearden. The investigators eventually caught up with her at a two-bedroom tract home at 282 Shoreline Drive in Pittsburg, California. It was a simple suburban one-story with an attached garage; the place seemed built to blend into the plain, suburban neighborhood.

The agents kept up a vigil from an unmarked car parked across the street. In the course of one of the hottest summers on record, they spotted Virginia leaving the place only twice. Newspapers piled up on her front porch. The front door might just as well have been nailed shut. Either she knew someone was watching, Lawrence figured, or she had bizarre habits.

From the surveillance vehicle, he snapped photos of Virginia the first time she ventured out. Lawrence eventually got one clear full-face shot of her carrying a bag of groceries along a brightly sunlit street, small dog in tow. The photo wasn't for trial evidence. Lawrence had to be sure he was shadowing the right woman.

Rule one at FBI training school was, Be sure you've got the right person before you make a bust. Nobody laughed off a lawsuit for false arrest. And Lawrence had nothing more than descriptions from State Farm, and Photo 5, the fuzzy rear-view snapshot of Virginia and B.J. taken at the cliff edge.

The second time Virginia went out, Lawrence trailed her to a Social Security office. From there, she went to a storefront check-cashing business. Through the plate-glass window, he watched her sign a piece of paper and collect cash. He wanted to go in afterward and inquire about the check, but he couldn't run the risk. "Hey, Mrs. Rearden, some cop was in here wanting to know about that check you cashed." That wouldn't do.

Virginia had already handed off the insurance claim to James Coates like a piece of hot jewelry, cut ties with her coconspirator, and then left town. She would run at the slightest hint of trouble. For now, the game was to watch, to wait, to patiently draw the net closer.

There was another reason to lay low. People continually said they were "scared to death" of Virginia and her family. In particular, one of B.J.'s ex-lovers from San Francisco, Kirby Meyer, said he had been concerned about B.J.'s safety around Virginia ever since the two had gotten married. When Lawrence tracked him down, it became obvious that B.J. might be in danger if anything tipped Virginia off.

"What's your opinion of Virginia?" Lawrence asked Kirby.

"To be honest, I wouldn't put it past her," he said bluntly. "I mean I wouldn't put it past her, bumping someone off, insurance money . . ."

"Uh-huh," Lawrence assented quietly, trying to draw Kirby out.

"You know, you know, B.J. had a stroke last November?"

"Yes, sir."

"Okay." He took a deep breath. "I believe Virginia has books about all kinds of pills and things. Knows what reactions are and uh . . ." He stopped himself.

"What do you base that on?"

"Well, I feel she may have caused B.J. to have a stroke. . . . When I'd be down there to visit, B.J. appeared to me—all the time I would see him at the house while she was around—like he was on his ass, bombed, drunk. And I'd see him and it didn't seem like he was drinking that much. . . . And I feel she'd been drugging him. And I think she may have caused him to have the stroke because, while he was here and since he's been away from her, it's gotten better. And then B.J. also told me that she had gone to the store to get him a prescription of pills. This was just, I guess, before they'd split up. And she comes back and hands him the bottle of pills and her name's on it."

"Her name's on it?"

"Her name's on it. And he said, 'This isn't my prescription.' She said, 'Oh, they must have just made a mistake at the pharmacy.'"

"Uh-huh."

"Well, evidently he didn't take 'em, but, I know, I mean . . . There was her mother's death."

"What do you know about that?"

"The mother's house burned down in East Palo Alto. And I heard it was arson. I think even B.J. or Virginia told me that. And she was living with them in San Francisco. And then they moved. She bought the house in—the mother bought the house in San Diego. That's what I was told."

"Okay, go ahead."

"And then, the mother passes away three months after she bought the house, of a heart attack. And the mother's body was cremated almost immediately. So I start, you know, I start thinking things."

Lawrence made a note to check out Virginia's mother's death. If Kirby Meyer was correct, that made body number four.

"Did B.J. ever tell you he thought his life was in danger?"

"Uh, no. But he didn't feel comfortable. I mean, I told him his life was in danger. Well, anyways, after he moved away from Virginia, I called him on his birthday. And he told me he was going down there and spend a week and get some of his clothes. I told him, I says,

'I think you're nuts.' I said, 'You go down there, you may not come out alive.' And I was, I, you know, thinking, maybe she has an insurance policy out on him."

"What did B.J. say to this?"

"Well, as far as B.J. knew, told me, he said no, she didn't have insurance out on him. Well, anyways, he thought about it and he didn't go down."

Lawrence kept thinking of Kirby Meyer's fears as he sat watching Virginia's quiet home from his unmarked car.

At the same time, the other half of the DA's team circled back to the Bay Area's backwoods to follow B.J. After the divorce, B.J. had gone to live with his sister Eve Williams in a hospice she operated for a small group of mentally incompetent patients. Eve's home sat at the end of a long dirt road marked with a hand-painted sign warning DEAD END. The investigation team decided it looked like some sort of "Hole in the Wall Gang" hideout. Everyone started to wonder who B.J. feared most, Virginia or the police.

Thursday afternoons, San Diego District Attorney Ed Miller regularly reviewed the week's list of pending matters in his large office across from the Criminal Justice building. He made it his practice to sign off on every indictment and to follow every significant investigation.

This particular Thursday, Luis Aragon, Scott Lawrence, a group of trial supervisors, and the DA himself were weighing the results of *In re: Deana Hubbard Wild.* Aragon had put on a two-hour presentation using slides, graphs, time lines, and videos. It was a minitrial, the final step before the office committed itself to an indictment. After Aragon finished, the assembled group looked up, clearly troubled. The combined experience of all the men in the room amounted to eighty years of criminal trial work, yet everyone drew a breath at the scope of Virginia's activities.

Ed Miller broke the silence. "Are we ready to issue?"

"I called Jon Yudin in Monterey this morning to give him one last shot. He said, 'Go ahead, our office can't make the case,' " Aragon answered.

"What kind of sheets do these folks have?" Like any good

prosecutor, Miller wanted to know his suspects' criminal pedigrees.

"That's one problem with the case, sir," Aragon answered. "Virginia has a couple of recent petit larcenies—for stealing cigarettes, I think. But that's it unless you count a forgery conviction from 1959. B.J.'s a practiced forger, but he hasn't been in for years. Basically, they're clean. If they take the stand, I won't have any priors to use on cross-exam."

Miller's expression narrowed. The budget, as always, was strained, and this matter wasn't even strictly from their jurisdiction.

"You want it, Luis. It's your baby," he said. "Just remember, we're looking at close to a million-dollar outlay to convict these folks."

Aragon felt he owed the DA at least one caveat before he filed the murder indictment. He placed as a mere middle-level deputy. Plenty of other prosecutors down the hall had trial records that considerably outranked his own. This would be the biggest case of his career.

"Mr. Miller," he said through a dry throat. "You know, I can't guarantee we'll win."

Miller looked up as if to say, What do you mean "we"? Instead, he asked, "Well, Luis. Is this a homicide or isn't it?"

"I can guarantee it's murder. I just can't guarantee we'll win. You know Monterey's opinion. If we lose, I can just picture the editorial." Aragon put on a whining voice as he canted, "Our DA doesn't have enough to do here in San Diego. He has to go around picking up other jurisdictions' cases, spending our money, and then losing."

Miller's face was calm, but Aragon saw the effect of even the imaginary attack register in the man's eyes.

By September 15, 1989, both arms of the DA's arrest team were poised to strike. Thirty officers, members of the Pittsburg, California, PD and DA's offices, the San Diego PD and DA, and the Sheriff's offices for each county, all joined in. Animal Control came to deal with Virginia's dog, and CPR and Medics were on hand in case B.J. suffered a stroke.

At 9:35 A.M., Virginia answered a knock on her door. Detective Jack Haeussinger stood on the threshold, a line of police officers at his back. He looked Virginia in the eye and smiled ever so slightly. It was a moment Haeussinger had waited for ever since he had read Keeney's book and started bugging Jim Pippin at the DA's Office.

Aragon decided Haeussinger at least deserved the honor of person-ally busting the "Dragon Lady," as he liked to call her.

Virginia looked much the same as in the photo Scott Lawrence had taken and as in Photo 5. An overweight woman in unexceptional polyesters, high, square forehead, and wide, green eyes that looked out from behind a pair of pink plastic glasses.

"Virginia McGinnis," Haeussinger announced, "I'm placing you under arrest for the murder of Deana Hubbard Wild."

Her jowly face froze over as an investigator stepped up and handed her a search warrant. In a cordial voice, one at odds with her daunting expression, she invited the squadron of officers inside.

As investigators photographed and inventoried Virginia's posses-sions, Haeussinger sat Virginia down on her sofa and explained, "All right, Ms. McGinnis, you're being charged with causing the death of Deana Hubbard Wild. You understand that?"

In her sugared voice, she said, "Yes, I understand."

"You're being charged in San Diego," Haeussinger went on. "And there's going to be a long drive down there."

Virginia's eyes fluttered as she explained that she had been seen by her personal physician two days ago, and asked whether she could bring her medications along. Haeussinger wanted to know whom she had been seeing. Virginia answered that she was unsure how to spell the man's name.

"Let's have a look at the meds," Haeussinger said.

She went to get her purse and pulled out four brown prescription bottles. Haeussinger read the labels. They were all out-of-date and should have been used up, if taken as prescribed.

"I tell you what," Haeussinger decided. "Here's a couple of Exce-drin. We'll keep the pills."

"Caraway!" he called to an investigator. "Read the lady her rights."

"I'd like to speak with an attorney," Virginia quickly interjected.

Aragon and Lawrence went to supervise B.J.'s arrest personally. He was far and away more likely to confess outright than Virginia, and a confession could lock the case in tight.

While Jack Haeussinger was knocking at Virginia's door, Scott Lawrence was telephoning B.J. at his sister Eve's hospice. Eve Wil-liams answered and put B.J. on the phone. Lawrence explained that he was a police officer looking for a friend of James Coates's, asked if B.J. would mind going over some pictures. In a weak but friendly voice, B.J. invited Lawrence to come on up. They could go to a diner down the hill and talk.

Aragon agreed to wait down by the diner with the rest of the team. When Lawrence and B.J. arrived, they decided, Aragon would make the bust and start asking questions.

Minutes later, Lawrence was at the hospice. He and B.J. talked briefly at the door, then started driving down the scrubby brushland road. As they rode along, they made small talk. So far, so good, Lawrence thought.

All of a sudden, Lawrence spotted two police cars headed toward them, with Aragon in the lead vehicle. *Couldn't these guys keep their pants on ten minutes?* Lawrence groaned to himself. One tip-off could leave him shot and bleeding, and B.J. running into the bush. He had to think of something to say.

He looked over at B.J. and asked, "Who are these guys?"

"There's a guy up the road. He's a lawyer," B.J. said. "Must be here to see him."

Lawrence pulled to the side of the road and hailed to the on-coming cars.

"You lost?" he yelled, giving Aragon a wink.

"Yeah. Where's the main road?" Aragon leaned through the window, trying to get a good look at B.J.

"Just follow me. We're headed to a diner."

The caravan of cruisers ambled down to the highway and pulled in at a small burger joint. Scott and B.J. got out and walked over to the officers who now stood outside their own cars.

"Billie Joe McGinnis," Lawrence said, "this is Deputy District Attorney Luis Aragon. I believe he has something to tell you."

"Mr. McGinnis, you're under arrest for the murder of Deana Hubbard Wild."

Billie Joe looked as if the air had been knocked out of him. Then, after reading B.J. his rights, Aragon quickly followed up with, "Do you wish to make a statement?" He wanted to catch B.J. at his weakest moment, a time when he would confess without thinking too hard about new lies, or lawyers, or Virginia.

Aragon could see the fear in B.J.'s eyes and in his pursed mouth. He felt sure B.J. was on the verge of confessing. Aragon waited quietly. But nothing happened.

"I'd like to speak with an attorney," Billie Joe finally said with an effort.

It wasn't long before Bobbie Roberts and Steve Keeney also got to see the faces of Deana's killers. Shortly after the arrest, reporters snapped a pair of photos that hit the front pages of newspapers in Louisville and San Diego and generated a wave of local television news stories.

Wynn Buckholder took one look and made up her mind. "They did it," she said, waving the newspaper.

Bobbie Roberts's face hardened. "My God! She looks evil, doesn't she?"

Keeney stared at the shots, put them down, picked them up again. "I hate to say it," he said, "but they look the part."

In the photo, Virginia cocked her head over her right shoulder, looking aslant at the judge, as if she were figuring, What have they got on me? The charms she possessed when she married Dick Coates and Bud Rearden seemed to have faded. In a loose-fitting blouse drawn around the neck with a string, she cut a disheveled, round-shouldered, and almost obese figure. Her hair fell in strings, and a subzero look in her eyes increased her forbidding air. If any emotions ran through her, they lay packed deep below a grim surface. She seemed to Keeney to embody Tanay's theory of a woman consumed by self-hatred.

B.J. stood by her side, looking more lost than evil. He had broken out in a painfully itchy rash on the drive down to San Diego after his arrest and it left him sweaty and exhausted. He wore the same metal-rimmed glasses Keeney knew from the photos at the cliffside and his silver-brown hair was still neatly parted. B.J. did not seem to have absorbed the fact that he was up on charges of murder, conspiracy to commit murder, forgery, and insurance fraud. Or that his codefendant was a woman who had kept him living in a poisoned stupor.

Just prior to the McGinnises' arraignment, Keeney and Monterey cocounsel Chuck Warner discovered that Virginia had sold her Chula Vista house for close to $200,000 and used the proceeds to buy the tract home in Pittsburg where she had been arrested. Keeney suggested that Aragon ask for bail of at least $2 million, enough to prevent her from using the house for a 10-percent bond and getting out of prison. Aragon took the lead and asked for $5 million, assuming the judge would engage in the usual horse-trading with defense counsel.

The arraignment judge listened to Aragon describe the extraordinary circumstances of Deana's death at Big Sur. He paused. Then, with a cast-iron expression across his face, he set bail at $5 million for each defendant—full cash only. Newspapers quickly discovered that the figure ranked as the highest bail ever set in a California State court case.

Whatever else happened, the McGinnises could now be easily found.

At last they're off the streets, Keeney thought. But his relief was incomplete. After all, the Monterey Office had felt there wasn't enough evidence even to obtain a search warrant. And Aragon would have to prove her guilt beyond a reasonable doubt.

The State of California lodged Virginia in Las Colinas prison, a correctional facility half an hour out of town in the scrubby San Diego desert hills. Aragon's position on her case remained uncompromising: no offers, no deals, plea to the charge. Not that Virginia showed any desire to cooperate. She offered neither explanations nor protestations of innocence. Just a cold stare across the courtroom.

As a result, she spent her pretrial months, months that multiplied into two years, sharing a cell with a series of accused murderers. But though her silence was complete, Aragon still hoped to use her words against her.

"Jailhouse ratting," a prisoner spilling their guts to a soulmate, is one of the prosecutor's most notorious tools. Even a few stray remarks to a cellmate can undo a defendant's carefully crafted version of the crime. Aragon couldn't work on Virginia directly—he had nothing to offer her in exchange for a guilty plea—but he hoped her cellmates might have something to contribute.

He instructed Scott Lawrence to keep tabs on everyone who spent even a few hours with Virginia. Betty Broderick, a socialite who shot her ex-husband and his new wife to death as they slept in their elegant beach house, spent months alone in a cell with Virginia. From what Lawrence gathered, Broderick probably knew Virginia better than anyone else. But Broderick, who faced a double homicide charge, was not exactly in the state's good graces herself, and her apparent mental instability made her an unreliable source.

Another prisoner who briefly shared a cell with Virginia claimed that Virginia had told her that B.J. was the one who had actually pushed Deana off the cliff.

Scott Lawrence excitedly reported his find to Aragon. This was tantamount to direct evidence.

Aragon heard the details and debated whether the witness would not do his case more harm than good. Using the cellmate's words meant having to sever Virginia's and B.J.'s cases—trying two cases instead of one—since the statement pitted one codefendant against the other. And the informant, a heroin-addicted prostitute who wanted a reduced sentence in trade for testifying, might not even be believed by the jury. Aragon wavered, then decided just to pass the information along to B.J.'s and Virginia's attorneys. He could live with a circumstantial case. He just hoped he could find the right jury.

As Virginia sat in Las Colinas, B.J. stayed in the San Diego Criminal Court holding pens, a crumbling, dark four-story annex to the San Diego Criminal Justice building that dated from 1950. Its forty-foot walls and slow-moving cameras on all four corners had roughly the same effect on downtown San Diego as the gallows once had in downtown London.

For health reasons, B.J. remained isolated from other prisoners, billeted in a cell of the sort that sets prison reformers on rampages. From the northwestern corner of the building, it looked out on a small strip of cement sidewalk and a wedge of sky. The claustrophobic circumstances of his confinement seemed to contribute to a steady mental and physical decay.

B.J.'s flagging morale gave Aragon reason for hope. He might fill in the "black hole" in Virginia's life from 1976 through 1986, offering the key to other deaths or missing persons. Or he could just turn and say who had done the pushing at Big Sur.

But there was one obstacle standing in the way of a confession: B.J. was terrified that Virginia's boys might harm his sister Eve. Just after the arrest, Scott Lawrence phoned Sarah Tabor, long-time friend of B.J., Virginia, and Eve, and taped the conversation. Although she had been interviewed once before by State Farm, this time Sarah decided she had to fess up.

Sarah told Lawrence she had never liked Virginia from the moment they met: "She's too sweet and juicy and then you, you can feel it, this coldness in her eyes. I really have the feeling that B.J. was afraid she would have somebody harm his sister Eve. . . . That was right from the beginning. He said, 'Honey, they're mean.' "

"So, B.J. said he was afraid that—?" Lawrence prodded with an open-ended question.

"That she would hurt Eve. And he told her, 'You be careful.' He said, 'She's a vicious person.' And he said, 'I'm afraid that she might have somebody hurt you.' "

"Well, now why would they? I'm not following you," Lawrence asked. "What did he base that on?"

"I think because he said the boys were so bad, that they were on dope and everything. And that they got a kick out of, of some of the bad things they did. I think it's the oldest guy was drinking. And it seems to me like he said that he admitted he had murdered somebody and gotten away with it.

"I remember B.J. coming home because he got so deathly sick that he couldn't stand it anymore. And when they were in San Francisco, he came home and he told me then that he thought she was poisoning him. I tried to get him not to go back." Sarah paused. Then she sighed. "He went back."

"Now why would she be poisoning him? I mean, they were newly married. Correct?"

"Right. And she found out that he didn't have the money that she thought he did. Because she told me once that she never would have married him but she thought he was wealthy."

Scott Lawrence thought back to Billie Joe's series of short-lived marriages, the women he probably married for their money. It all made sense. The whole marriage boiled down to one bloodsucker trying to drink the life out of another. No wonder they conspired to kill Deana. They had struck out trying to scam one another.

"What did B.J. say about when Virginia's mother died? Mary Hoffmann. What'd he tell you about her death?"

Sarah seemed shaken by the simple mention of the subject.

"Oh, boy. I really hate to say. He thought she did it. I'm not, I know I shouldn't say that, but he was terrified. He wanted to leave her then, but he didn't."

"And what did he tell you?"

"The reason he thought that was because the night before she died, Virginia had talked to the son. He was living there at the time.

He was out of prison again. And she sat him down and she talked to him. She said, 'Now, son, I know you love your grandmother very much, but she's an old woman and she could die at any moment.' And he said she died the next day."

Lawrence had spoken to R. D. Jones and knew that Virginia had given Butch Rearden an almost identical warning just before Bud Rearden died. One way or another, Virginia seemed to leave her signature on every death.

Lawrence tried to dig for some concrete details. "Now why did B.J. say that that scared him? I mean, if she was ill, then maybe she was just saying that—"

"If she thought it was going to be over that night, why didn't she have her in the hospital? She had insurance, this was my thinking. . . . And what astonished us is, is when they called me, she'd already been cremated, and that was the following day."

"Did B.J. say that they, once Virginia's mom had been discovered dead—did he say who discovered the body, who called the pol—?"

"Virginia."

"Virginia did? Did he say how she acted or what she did?"

"No. That's just it. She's very, very cold. I believe that she mentioned that sometimes her mother gave her own insulin shots and sometimes she gave them."

"Did Virginia ever tell you she was a nurse or medically trained or—?"

"She didn't say she was a nurse. She said she had done some private duty sitting for—she said it was for a well-to-do lady."

Lawrence probed further, but Sarah's well of recollections started to run dry.

She apologized. "I really don't know, because he said he didn't know a lot that Virginia did and he said she kept so much hid. He said she was a strange woman. But, you know, there's a lot of things Virginia had that he didn't know about. And he said, she'd come in with a new dress on when she was going out with a friend or something and he'd say, 'Well, where'd you get that dress? That looks new.' 'Oh, no I've had this rag stuffed back in the closet for years.' "

Lawrence thought Sarah's last comment sounded like Dick Coates revisited. *Don't pry where you shouldn't . . .*

▼

Even given B.J.'s fear of the Coates boys, Aragon did his best to leave open the possibility of a negotiated plea. He could no longer talk to B.J. directly, since he and Virginia now had court-appointed lawyers. Albert Tamayo of the Public Defender's Office drew Virginia's case. B.J. received the services of Gary Edwards.

Aragon knew of Gary Edwards from his successful private practice in San Diego. Edwards was a gentle, vaguely handsome gent with a soft-spoken manner that could seduce a jury the way a cocker spaniel wins morsels at a dinner table.

With B.J.'s case, Edwards took a relaxed stance. From what he sussed out, his client had a fair shot at an acquittal. How much hard evidence could the authorities point to as far as B.J. was concerned? Going with Virginia to the insurance company? A few comments at the cliff? The Elavil prescription? Photo 11? After that, they had nothing. A jury might pour out its wrath on Virginia, but B.J. could be passed off as a weak-willed stooge manipulated into doing his wife's dirty work, and win their pity. Accepting a deal, on the other hand, meant certain jail time. Given B.J.'s age and declining health, it also meant dying behind bars. A complete acquittal was the only alternative.

Still, Aragon took every opportunity that came along.

"Everyone knows Virginia masterminded the plan to murder Deana," he cajoled Edwards during a break in one of the many pretrial hearings. "Your client can make peace with his Maker before it's too late. He can clear his conscience and hope he lives to enjoy some freedom."

"Hey, Mr. Aragon," B.J. called from across the room.

Aragon spun on his heel. Defendants almost never spoke to DAs with that friendly a tone. B.J. was sitting at the counsel table, waving a postcard from Paris confiscated from Virginia's house under the search warrant.

"You know what I think, Mr. Aragon? I think we need to investigate where this postcard came from. Let's see about arranging a trip to make sure."

"You bet, B.J.," Aragon retorted. "So long as Gary Edwards pays for it."

Aragon tried to rekindle Edwards's interest. "We're prepared to offer a plea to manslaughter with a reduced sentence. Otherwise he's looking at L-WOP [life without parole]."

Edwards went to whisper with his client. Aragon watched the

conference and thought he spotted a glimmer of trust in B.J.'s eyes. It seemed as if B.J. was steeling himself to open up, checking in one last time with his internal counsel or the spectral threat of Virginia.

Then B.J. lowered his eyes and mumbled a halfhearted refusal: "No. I just . . . I'm not interested." It was over, Aragon knew. B.J.'s face seemed to close, like a door slamming.

That pathetic, weak-willed soul felt alone, Aragon imagined. He and Virginia stayed in separate prisons fifty miles apart, yet she continued to manipulate him. Had State Farm approved B.J.'s life insurance policy, he might have been the next to die. B.J. probably sensed it, too. Yet, like so many people, he continued to obey Virginia.

In the months surrounding the McGinnises' arrest, Keeney found himself overwhelmed. He had long since bid good-bye to his comfortable B & A quarters, large salary, and to Pete Lazar and Sarah West. Now he faced the task of running his own practice.

It took an immense amount of planning, all the more so for someone who had always worked in established firms. Keeney brought along a few small commercial clients to start with, but pretty soon he had to start casting about for business—that, and hire paralegals and secretaries, pay the rent, balance the books, and somehow make time for teaching Sunday school and preparing for his marriage to Wynn.

If he needed reassurance that he had left at the right moment, he found it that November in David Margolick's *New York Times* "At the Bar" column:

> If anyone symbolizes the stability of the nation's lawyers, it is supposed to be the president of the American Bar Association. But as the troubles facing the current office holder, L. Stanley Chauvin Jr. of Louisville, attest, he can also represent the turbulence. . . .
>
> But more than most law offices, [Chauvin's firm of Barnett & Alagia now renamed Alagia, Day] has over the past 15 years mirrored wider changes in the profession over which Mr. Chauvin presides.
>
> First the firm grew exponentially . . . growing from single digits to 140 lawyers in a decade. It opened branch offices the way McDonald's opened franchises. . . .
>
> But now . . . the firm has come to represent another side of the

bar, the firm that grew too big, too fast. Since January [1989], 50
lawyers have left or been laid off. A lease on spacious new quarters
has suddenly been cancelled. Branch offices are bleeding. . . .

But at least to some degree the firm proved jerry-built. There
were all the usual battles, over turf, input, authority, money, ego,
perquisites, without any institutional glue binding everyone together. Mr. Barnett died a few years ago. Last year, his son was
indicted on bribery charges. . . .

Mr. Chauvin had finally put the firm on the map, though not
quite as his colleagues had anticipated. . . .

Keeney hoped he had internalized some of the lessons from
B & A's rise and fall. He now wanted to start a "human-scale"
practice. One where clients had faces instead of corporate charters,
and where he no longer had to worry over his partners' ethics. When
he finally signed a lease for a new one-man office, he had Bobbie
Roberts's files wheeled over in two chin-high cabinets. He looked at
the immense set of pleadings and transcripts and knew that, even if
indirectly, she was in part responsible for the new direction of his
career. She was the only client who had ever said, "My heart is
broken." Her case had pulled him out of a blithely serene existence.
And, of course, Keeney didn't believe in coincidence.

But the case was far from over. Bobbie's interests now spread in
all directions, and each aspect had to be handled so as to avoid
tripping over the DA. As a result, he remained in almost daily
contact with Aragon.

Publicity became a potentially dangerous issue. Television, radio,
and newspaper reporters started calling in surges the minute the
McGinnises were arrested. The San Diego *Union,* Monterey *Herald,*
Louisville *Courier-Journal, The National Examiner,* TV tabloids like
"Inside Report," and others all wanted to run stories on the "Evil
Couple."

Bobbie instructed Keeney to make "everything" public. She
wanted the world to know. Aragon cautioned that inflammatory
press could hurt his chance of impaneling an impartial jury, maybe
even require a change of venue. On the other hand, one well-placed
article might flush out a hitherto unknown witness.

Not that anyone had much choice in the matter. Keeney had been
a newsman and he knew the press was going to run the story
whether or not he cooperated. After conferring with the San Diego
DA and Police Department, as well as the Kentucky Bar Associa-

tion's Ethics Committee, Keeney and Bobbie agreed to a few carefully selected interviews.

The resulting publicity, along with a wave of defense investigators, succeeded in bringing old acquaintances out of the Kentucky backwaters. First, Jimmy Coates's ex-wife, Debbie Abell, saw Virginia's photograph on television and called Scott Lawrence. She said she had vivid memories of the year she spent living with Virginia and her son Jimmy and wanted to talk.

Scott Lawrence found Debbie still living in Louisville, not far from where Coates had left her. Outside the house Debbie shared with her children and her parents stood a dilapidated station wagon plastered with bumper stickers declaring, PROUD TO BE A TEAMSTER RETIREE; GO BRALESS—IT'LL PULL THE WRINKLES FROM YOUR FACE; and I'D SLAP YOU BUT SHIT SPLATTERS.

Scott knocked on the peeling front door.

Like her car, Debbie Abell looked as if she had racked up considerable mileage. Her blond hair had dulled and her complexion smacked of a bad diet. When she saw Lawrence's badge, she trembled like a scared rabbit but invited him inside. The place smelled to Lawrence like a dog kennel that hadn't been cleaned in months.

After the usual preliminaries, Lawrence turned on his tape recorder. He began: "It's my understanding that you were married to Mr. Coates."

"Yeah, unfortunately," she answered in a sour voice. "It was either in the year of 1975 or '76. . . ."

At the time, Debbie said, she was seventeen years old and had just given birth to a baby girl who wasn't Jimmy Coates's child. In reply, Lawrence simply asked her to tell him what she knew about Virginia and Jimmy and not to guess at answers.

"Right. No, I wouldn't, 'cause I'm scared to death of his family, anyway. . . . Jimmy done some awful things to me when we were together. Tied me to a bed for two days, pulled a gun on me. Just horrible things like that."

Lawrence nodded, watching the woman's eyes carefully. He wanted to be sure she wasn't putting on a show just to get back at her ex-husband. She looked genuinely fearful.

"When we were dating, it was fine. He opened the car door, and said 'Please.' After we got married—Bam! It was like Dr. Jekyll and Mr. Hyde. He even started telling me about a girl he raped back in Fairdale. Anything that wasn't right, he'd do it. . . . He's crazy. He really is." Debbie's voice started to quaver. "He can put on one side, then another."

Lawrence asked Debbie what she knew about Virginia.

"After we got married," she said, "we started having hard times. I had a baby girl named Jackie who Virginia was crazy about.

"This was just after the house in Fairdale burned down, right before Christmas. Jimmy, Ronnie, me, Grandfather Hoffmann were all living in three rooms at the Alamo Plaza Motel. Virginia was there, too. She walked around in mink coats and had these diamond rings. Her taste was the best. She had to have the best of everything. It was satin sheets and money is no object. Every hair was in place and she had a real stern voice. What she said *went.*"

Lawrence tried to pull Debbie Abell's thoughts into some kind of order. "So you say that Virginia liked Jackie. What do you base that on?"

"Because it was strange for—Virginia is a really strange woman. I mean she is like a black widow spider to me and I was scared of her. She more or less seemed like she was starting to control me, with Jackie. At the time, I was so scared of the woman, it was awful."

"Why? Why were you afraid of your mother-in-law?" Lawrence asked.

"I don't know." Abell's eyes opened wide. "It was just something . . . she controlled you. There was a way that she could. There's just a way the woman is."

Lawrence asked again about Abell's daughter, Jackie. "Did Virginia ever express any desires to you to, let's say, legally adopt or take care of the child?"

"Yes," Abell said almost offhandedly. "She offered me five hundred dollars for her."

"Five hundred dollars?" Lawrence repeated, hoping for some elaboration.

"Uh-huh. That sticks real well in my mind, because now I think, gosh that's so cheap, five hundred dollars."

"Now when you say she offered you five hundred dollars for the child, basically it already is her granddaughter. Would you explain what's behind that."

"I didn't see it as a granddaughter relationship. That's another thing," Abell skittered off on a tangent. "My mother came in and took Jackie out of that house, and, when she did, all kinds of stuff got started. Virginia went crazy. She ended up calling the police, taking them to my mother's house, demanding, wanting Jackie back. Said that when she got Jackie back, that more or less, she wants to . . . wanted to take Jackie to California with her, while me and Jimmy and the grandfather stayed here in Louisville for at least three months."

"Why three months?"

"I don't know. She never went into detail on anything. There was never a reason why she did the things she did. Just that she did them."

"Did Virginia ever encourage you to get life insurance?"

"Yes." Abell's voice slowed, her thoughts coming together. "Now, I'm not real vivid about it. I know that she brought it up, wanting me to get insurance on Jackie. Not me and Jimmy, just her. At the kitchen table, it just popped up, you know, about insurance. She asked if Jackie had any, and I said no."

"Was this medical insurance or life insurance?"

"Life insurance, I believe, because I had medical insurance on her. . . . That's why I contacted y'all 'cause that's, you know, seeing her on TV and then hearing about the insurance policy, you know, it makes me sick to think she'd hold my daughter. I know that a lot of mishaps happened, too, when she lived here. Her house burnt down; her husband died; her little girl died; she wrecked her truck. She would come in with mink coats, diamond rings. I mean, it was just really strange."

"Where would she get the money for mink coats and diamond rings?" Lawrence asked.

"She would say that either a airplane pilot would buy it for her or a lawyer or a doctor, you know, someone high up there with the money. She'd say these men would buy them for her."

"You think that was probably true?"

"No. Because I never seen any of them, and when she went out she wouldn't be gone for very long."

"Let me get back to the part where Virginia offered to buy the child. Who else knew about that?"

"Jim, but I doubt if he'd own up to anything, you know. The grandfather, the grandfather was there."

"Whose grandfather?"

"Hers. This man knew what was going on."

"What do you think was going on?"

"I don't know. . . . I just had a feeling about the insurance, her collecting insurance off everything because she was coming up with too much money."

"Can you think of any reason, back then, why she would purchase life insurance on your child?"

"Yeah, she wanted to kill my child. . . . I mean I'm just bein' honest with you."

"Why do you think Virginia wanted to kill the girl?"

"I don't know. Money? She was obsessed with having beautiful things. You know there wasn't a thing she didn't own that wasn't the finest, or there wasn't nothing she didn't buy that wasn't."

Lawrence looked over his notes, checked the tape recorder, and thanked Debbie Abell for cooperating. As he stood up to leave, Abell burst out, "I don't have to come to California, do I?"

"I don't know," Lawrence answered. "It's up to Luis Aragon, the deputy DA, to decide."

Abell's face twisted as she cried, "Oh, Lord! Because I'm scared to death of these people."

That fall, while Scott Lawrence traipsed back and forth across the country, Steve Keeney and Wynn Burkholder were married. The ceremony took place in the Second Presbyterian greater sanctuary. Christian, now seven, sat in the audience beside Kelly and Mark, Wynn's children.

The day before the wedding, Wynn arrived at her house, a brick three-bedroom in the spacious green suburb of Saint Matthews. She and Steve had decided to keep her place and sell his, hoping to ease the transition for Wynn's two children.

From halfway down the street, Wynn saw a moving truck the length of a football field blocking her driveway. She knew Steve had sold the Hill Road home just days ago, but the sight of three men in jumpsuits unloading an endless series of boxes onto her lawn brought the reality home.

Inside, her husband-to-be stood by, puffing on a cigar and directing the relocation of his library. There were more than five hundred boxes of books, each lettered and numbered. For lack of a better place, the overflow sat in the living room, turning it into a warehouse.

Wynn realized that she was looking squarely into her future. A few of her friends continued to be put off by Steve's workaholism and his need to plan every step of his life. And Wynn didn't know what to think when Steve handed her a twenty-five-page itinerary for their honeymoon, complete with a rundown on each golf course, restaurant, and beach in the area. Everything he did seemed to be attacked with the same almost maniacal energy and marksman's focus. But even the doubters admitted he may have mellowed in the last year. Beneath the pinpoint-cotton exterior, there was a rare and loving loyalty. It didn't matter if it was rambly old Dick Coates or Bobbie Roberts or the San Diego DA, Steve Keeney made a point of giving everyone his all.

Since her own divorce, Wynn herself had helped build a successful office-decor business from a single telephone and answering machine, all while raising her two children. Taming this three-piece workhorse seemed a worthwhile new challenge.

She knew to start with the little things, so cigars were the first order of business.

"Steve, honey, you're not going to light that ugly thing, are you?" she asked as the NO SMOKING sign on their honeymoon flight out of Louisville blinked off.

"This superb hand-rolled pre-Castro Cuban?" Keeney smiled, looking up from the cigar he had just pulled from a leather case. He met Wynn's stare, searching for a complicit smile. Instead, he faced a solid steel wall. In an instant, he knew it would all be over. But out of self-respect, he had to go down with the flag flying.

"This is no ordinary stogie, Wynn. In restaurants, people come up and say, 'I usually hate cigars, but that one smells so nice. It reminds me of my granddad when he smoked.' "

"My father didn't smoke cigars," Wynn said. "The only thing a cigar reminds me of is a phallic symbol for men who need to make up for something they're lacking in another department."

"Well," Keeney rejoined, "as Freud once said, 'Sometimes a cigar is just a cigar.' "

A second, firmer look from Wynn told Keeney that she meant business.

"Maybe I can give away the rest of these as presents." Keeney sighed, sliding the five-dollar beauty back into its case.

▼

The honeymoon was short, but when Keeney returned to Louisville, he found a number of people already anxiously awaiting his return.

First Jay Wild called. He was still tearful over Deana's death. He was also a little scared, recently having heard talk that some people thought he might have been involved in a plot to kill his own wife. Keeney calmed Jay down and told him he had nothing to worry about. At least he loved her, Keeney reflected.

The next caller, Debbie Williams, was not as easy to deal with. Her phone message said it was an "emergency." Keeney called her back, but Debbie insisted they talk in person.

She showed up at Keeney's new law office, still shaking after her interview with defense investigators. A wrung-out blond with an unstable tilt to her yellow-green eyes, and accompanied by a non-identical twin sister, Debbie said she was probably in danger. Keeney asked the twin to wait outside.

The moment the door closed, Debbie started in.

"The public defender people said they were with the DA, but they're not," she said in a flat southern twang broken by weird, giggly laughs. "They went to where my mother works and scared her. That's how they found my place. I told 'em I can only incriminate Virginia."

The public defender's conduct didn't come as news. Jay Wild had complained about the same deception. Keeney could easily imagine a defense investigator flashing a badge and saying, "I'm with the PD's Office." It would be up to the witness to ask whether that meant Public Defender or Police Department, and the Public Defender's investigators could be the last ones to volunteer their true affiliation.

"Me and Jimmy Coates were what you might call boyfriend and girlfriend in Louisville back in 1972," Debbie continued. "We had one son together named Little Jimmy. I met Jimmy the night after Cynthia Elaine died. When we first met, he had bought a '65 Buick Wildcat from a police officer named Jake who lived across the street. There wasn't a car in the county could catch him."

Debbie let loose another strange laugh and then recounted the night Virginia sent her, Butch Rearden, Jimmy, and Ronnie out for a joyride, the night old Bud Rearden died.

"She never would let Butch come out ridin' with us. It was always, 'Butch, get in the house!' Then, tonight she says, 'Here's some money; now you all go for a ride.' I seen she was gettin' Bud's medications ready, fillin' a needle.

"We had fun that night," she remembered. "When we got back, we went into the camper and told ghost stories. All of a sudden, we heard somethin' just hit the side of the camper. And Jimmy and Ronnie said, 'What the hell was that?' The next thing we know, Virginia opens the back door and stepped in the camper. She said, 'Sylvester'—we called him Butch, but she always liked to use fifty-million-dollar words—'Sylvester, your father's dead.' The kid started cryin' and I started boo-hooin' 'cause I lost my father and I knew what kind of experience that can be. And this woman, she never shed a tear. Not all through the funeral, or in the limousine, or nothing'. Matter of fact, after the funeral, the first words out of her mouth were, 'That kid Butch is out of here.'

" 'Course when Mr. Rearden was dying, Virginia was seeing another man that worked at the Marathon station at Third Street . . . or was it Taylor Boulevard?" Debbie's memory fuzzed out momentarily, but Keeney was hooked: Her story exactly matched Butch Rearden's.

"How do you know she was seeing another man?" Keeney prompted.

"When we went over to Tom Wallace Park, Jim and me, we saw his mom in the park with a man, parked in a Chrysler, putting her clothes on. That's when Jimmy said not to say nothin'. He said, 'Everybody needs to get somethin' sometime.'

"I said to myself, Virginia, you really are a slut. Your husband's dying of cancer at home and you're out making it with some guy in your car. Her hands were down between his legs. They were making out. We were watching, but she never knew. To be honest, I think she killed Bud."

"Why do you think that?" Keeney pressed.

"Well, the day before, I seen her windin' this big grandfather clock she had in the house, and I was real interested 'cause I never seen one before. After Bud died, I told Virginia it weren't ticking no more. She said, 'Yes, the grandfather clock stopped at two o'clock, just like it did when Cynthia died.' I mighta believed it then, but not now. 'Cause I'm thirty-three years old. You'd have to reach in there and stop the pendulum."

Keeney asked Debbie what she knew about Cynthia Elaine's death.

"Once or twice she brought that up—but just once or twice. Her mom told him she wanted to go out and play cowboy and Indian and the little girl had put the noose around her neck and climbed up on a rafter and jumped." She paused, then let out another of her odd trilling laughs.

"When I talked to Virginia about that, it was a real cold reaction. It was like you open up an icebox and step into it. That was a hush-hush topic. When I asked a second time, she slammed her fist down on the table and said that wasn't to be talked about.

"Later on, she gave me a glass of tea. I got groggy and fell asleep on the living room sofa for hours. When I opened my eyes, Virginia was slappin' me to wake up. I came home sick and stayed nauseous for two whole days."

Keeney looked down at Debbie Williams' hands. They were clutching a purse and trembling as if she had Parkinson's disease.

"Virginia's safely behind bars," he said. "And you don't have to talk with the public defender if you don't want to. There's nothing to be nervous about."

"Somebody broke into my trailer this Easter," she replied, not the least bit comforted. "I was in the hospital when it happened. All the drawers were emptied."

"Have you called the police?"

"Filed the report Easter weekend," she answered. "But they didn't get my Smith and Wesson forty-one. I've got that right here." She patted her purse with her unsteady hand.

"I'm glad you called the police," Keeney said warily.

"Little Jimmy's on the verge of a complete nervous breakdown," Debbie started up again, seeming to have forgotten her pistol. "He's afraid his dad's gonna do something to me. He would. Jimmy said he killed some dumb Mexican out in the desert back in '85. Used to boast about it. When Jimmy was here in town just a few months ago, he talked about taking Little Jimmy back with him. 'Over my dead body,' I told him. 'That can be arranged,' he told me."

James Coates in Louisville just a few months ago? That was a distinctly unpleasant thought. Keeney realized he was still a sitting duck if Coates ever wanted revenge. Just keep taking notes, he told himself.

"Jimmy and I split up right after I had Little Jimmy," Debbie Williams prated on. "He come over with this new gal, Debbie Abell, and I put my fist through the wall! I never married him; Debbie Abell got that honor." She laughed.

Debbie said Virginia wanted her to move out to California with her baby daughter but she wouldn't go. Virginia told her she'd make it worth her while.

"Tell the truth, I never did care for Virginia. I wouldn't trust that woman as far as I could pick up an elephant and throw it. For instance, when the girl died out in California. That's a real good for instance, I think.

"Jimmy called me the other day. He was telling about his mother being arrested and I told him, 'I know, I read about it in the newspaper.' He said, 'Shh, Debbie, we can't talk about it 'cause the phone's tapped.' I asked him anyway, 'Jimmy, is it true about your mother, did she really kill that girl?' He just laughed that cold, mean laugh of his and said, 'What do you think?' I said, 'I think in all honesty she did it.' Then he said, 'Listen, I can't talk. I'll call you from a pay phone.'

"Next thing I know, the phone rings and it's Jimmy again," Debbie said. "I asked him about Virginia. This time, he told me, 'You're right. We planned it. Deana was bucking; she wanted to leave. Mom and B.J. drugged her and dragged her up to the cliff. B.J. couldn't get her over the edge by himself, so Virginia had to help." Debbie paused, looking as if she was on the verge of tears. Then she added, "Now that I know, that makes me involved, don't it?"

"What did you say after that?" Keeney dodged the subject.

"I told Jimmy I wanted to see him, but he said, 'Shoot me a kite,' you know, jail talk for send me a letter. That was about the last thing I remember him telling me."

Keeney breathed a sigh of relief when Debbie Williams left without pulling out her .41.

Later that day, he called Luis Aragon and passed on Debbie Williams's information. Under ordinary circumstances, he would have thought Debbie utterly incredible. But where Virginia was concerned, Keeney had long since suspended disbelief.

He realized that he once lived with the assumption that evil would never touch him, as if he were a creature happily prospering in a terrarium world. But these days, he felt as if he were inhabiting two parallel worlds. There was the sunlit world of his new family, his law practice, and his church. Alongside that was a netherworld where sinful mothers raised murderers, and children died of "accidental hangings." And the lines of distinction had begun to blur.

CHAPTER 25

"P.S. THE DOG IS FINE . . ."

▼

At 2:30 P.M. on February 26, 1990, Luis Aragon pushed a shopping cart full of evidence into Department 9 of superior court. He offered the usual lukewarm "Good morning" to Gary Edwards and Albert Tamayo, and wheeled over to join Scott Lawrence at the prosecution table, where Lawrence sat marking exhibits. All sides were present and ready for the McGinnises' preliminary hearing.

The McGinnises sat side by side behind the defense table, their left wrists handcuffed to chairs. A pair of yellow legal pads lay open on the table before them.

Aragon and Lawrence were still marking exhibits when Judge Kasimatis announced, "You may proceed, Mr. Aragon."

The Honorable Nicholas Kasimatis had drawn the McGinnis case from a random court-assignment lottery. Aragon took Kasimatis's presence as a sign of good fortune. He knew the judge's long, kindly face, his silver halo of hair and half-moon glasses. When Aragon explained that the government's first witness was still occupied marking exhibits, Kasimatis patiently replied, "All right. We'll wait for him, then."

The preliminary hearing, as practiced in California, is usually a brief affair. In about three hours, the state puts on a skeleton case, just enough evidence to show that the defendants should be held over for trial under their current bail. The DA tries not to tip his hand. The defense takes a first crack at witnesses whom they will cross-examine in earnest at trial.

Luis Aragon, however, saw no shortcut through the case. The evidence formed a cat's cradle of details, and he was not about to chance leaving out any crucial strands. From the time he answered "Ready to proceed" until he rested, eleven prosecution witnesses testified for a total of two and a half days.

Scott Lawrence went first. With his beefy build constrained by a tweed jacket and a red tie, he could have been a star football player dressed for a college interview. In taut testimony, abristle with terms such as *telephonic conversation* and *photostatic representation,* he gave a sketch of the remote coastal spot where Deana fell to her death. Then he ticked off the principal exhibits: photos, a map.

Albert Tamayo, Virginia's public defender, cross-examined first. Aragon had never tried a case against Tamayo but he quickly picked up that Tamayo possessed the trial lawyer's natural advantage: a favorable first impression. Copper-skinned, almond-eyed, and with a shag of tar black hair, he cut a handsome figure in his perfectly pressed tan suits. Outside the courtroom, he was a passionate athlete, which showed in his noiseless step and physical self-possession. At forty, Tamayo retained the bright and motivated look of a hungry advocate.

But to Aragon's surprise, Tamayo took only a few halfhearted verbal swings at Lawrence, then sat down. Gary Edwards, consistent with his theory that B.J.'s best hope lay in keeping a low profile, was content to sit and watch.

Technical testimony consumed the remainder of the day.

Dr. William Hoops of the Monterey Coroner's Office defined the term *basal brain laceration, minutes* that had appeared in his original autopsy report. Deana died, as Hoops put it, from a single "deep cut type of thing through the pons in the cerebellum, which is a very vital area." He explained that *minutes* meant Deana had died within minutes of the injury.

Catherine Hamm, a toxicologist from the San Diego Coroner's Office, testified that in 1989 she detected "trace" amounts of amitriptyline and nortriptyline in a preserved sample of Deana's blood—0.02 micrograms of drug per milliliter of blood. It was barely enough to register on her high-tech gas chromatograph, she said, but the drug was unquestionably present.

All afternoon, Bobbie Roberts sat at the rear of the courtroom on a polished wooden bench, surrounded by a small group assembled for her benefit. Her brother had flown in from Lexington to join her. A couple from the San Diego chapter of PMC—Parents of Murdered Children—also came to lend support. The following day, they all knew, Bobbie would testify.

But Bobbie hardly noticed her companions. She couldn't take her eyes off the McGinnises. Keeney had prepped her for everything but this, the most harrowing part: seeing her daughter's killers in the flesh.

The woman from PMC kept telling Bobbie that everything would be all right. The woman herself had testified at the trial of a man who had raped and murdered her thirteen-year-old daughter, and that criminal was ultimately sentenced to Life Without Possibility of Parole.

Bobbie leaned over and said, "I just want to see them pay for what they've done." She hastily apologized that it wasn't "a Christian thought," but three years was a very long time to wait for justice to move its hand, and this was only the beginning. "So many things could still go wrong," she said anxiously.

The following afternoon, Aragon announced, "The People call Bobbie Roberts."

Dressed in a somber blue suit and cream silk blouse, Bobbie walked to the witness stand. She seated herself, scrupulously avoiding eye contact with the McGinnises. Aragon gently led Bobbie through Deana's youth, the girl's learning deficiency, and her elopement with Jay Wild in September of 1986. Then he played the tape of the call to Virginia McGinnis she had placed from Louisville years earlier.

As the judge listened, Bobbie let her eyes drift over to Virginia and Billie Joe. The sight of the couple, handcuffed to a chair, made her feel both furious and vengeful. Virginia turned her head away, seeming more bored than intimidated. Her demeanor seemed to say that the criminal case was a mere inconvenience that would be over soon. B.J. stared into space with an empty, glazed look.

After the tape had finished, the defense lawyers engaged in only a cursory cross-examination and Judge Kasimatis excused Bobbie from the stand. With a nod, she started down the steps of the witness box. At the last step, she hesitated, casting a glance at Aragon. Then, with a single slow movement, she collapsed.

Two court officers ran over and lifted her by her arms. She swayed uneasily but managed to say, "I'm all right, really. I'm sorry."

After Art and Cleo "Mac" McCain, the State Farm agents who had sold the insurance policy, testified, Aragon put on his one "surprise" witness.

Robert Brian Lyke was a slight, spry man with a well-trimmed beard and a birdlike preciseness of manner. Although he held a master of divinity degree from Princeton Seminary, Lyke worked at the Esalen Institute, a New Age community known as home of the human potential movement. Esalen offered a life abundant in massage, yoga, meditation, and philosophy set along a stunning stretch of coastline. In 1973, Lyke had signed on as the institute's dishwasher; he was now administrative general manager. After reading about the McGinnises' arrest in the Monterey *Herald*, Lyke had called the DA's Office.

That afternoon, he described how he had been driving south along the coast with his wife and children when they noticed the Big Sur ambulance team at a turnoff. It was April 2, 1987. A member of the volunteer ambulance crew himself, Lyke pulled over to offer assistance. Members of the Search and Rescue team were already over the edge looking for Deana.

"I was told that someone had fallen off the cliff and it wasn't determined whether she was alive or dead. They weren't able to get to her because of the steepness of the area. . . ."

Spotting Virginia and B.J. in their car, he went to lend moral support. As he walked over, Lyke noticed a blue shoe lying near the cliff edge.

"It seems inconsequential in a way, but this blue high-heeled shoe bothered me, the fact that the shoe was lying where anybody could have picked it up. And I guess I put myself in the position of someone who, if I had lost someone that was close to me, over the cliff, I would not have sat in my car. I would have been out. I would have been eager to find out what the fate of this person was."

Lyke went on: "After I heard from the men in the Sheriff's Search and Rescue squad that, in fact, they found the victim had died, I went over to the McGinnises. I said, 'I'm sorry. I have to tell you that she is dead.' . . . And what I read on their faces was relief rather than grief."

Virginia's large hands wrote busily. B.J. shifted stiffly in his chair.

Court recessed for the evening.

Virginia rode the prison bus back to Las Colinas; B.J. was escorted to his holding cell. Bobbie Roberts left, hugging her brother's arm.

At the rear of the courtroom, a man with a blond mustache and suntanned face swung out of his seat and headed out the door along with a group of elderly courtroom regulars. Detective Jack Haeussinger had been watching for the latter part of the afternoon, "keeping an eye on Luis," as he put it.

Driving his blue unmarked cruiser home, he mused over the day's events. Only in California can you put a New Age minister on the stand and bring down the house, he thought. Jack Haeussinger did not have much use for New Age aroma therapy or lotus sitting. By his book, you also didn't need a parade of experts waving their Ph.D.'s to tell you that the ol' gal did it.

Still, he had to admit, Luis was putting on a good show—for a lawyer.

The prelim was proceeding more or less according to Aragon's plan. An expert in clinical pharmacology testified about the dizzying effects of Elavil. Deputy Coroner Dave Dungan recited how Virginia and B.J. had denied knowing about any insurance policy. Donald Smythe took the stand and recounted his interviews with the defendants in Chula Vista. Tamayo harped briefly on the whereabouts of Deana's second shoe. It had been lost. Smythe admitted he knew about the insurance policy but hadn't felt there was enough evidence for an arrest. Gary Edwards barely left his seat. At this juncture, Aragon's only concern was how few questions the defense seemed to be asking. In any event, it was too late to rethink his strategy. He was down to his last witness.

James Coates had been anything but pleased to receive a subpoena to appear in superior court—especially from the hands of Jack Haeussinger. For Coates, the last year had been spent shuttling in and out of Vacaville prison, a place that felt like the inside of an oven during the summer, and was filled to the rim with pimps, gang members, and psychos. Whenever he made it out to the street, he went to shoot dope in hotels where hookers went screaming down the corridors, the head never worked, and the plaster on the ceiling looked like a dried-out tortilla. All along, he kept waiting for his $35,000 from State Farm.

Aragon called Coates as a witness for one purpose only: to "neutralize" him. If the state locked him to a story, Coates might even help the prosecution. And it avoided unpleasant surprises down the line.

Seated in the witness stand in his embroidered cowboy shirt, worn boots, and jeans, Coates, lanky and muscular, affected a balding Johnny Cash look.

"Mr. Coates," Aragon began as sternly as his voice allowed, "you are the son of Virginia McGinnis, the lady who is sitting in court this afternoon?"

Leaning back in the witness stand a few degrees, he answered, "Yes."

"Did you know Deana Hubbard Wild?"

"Yes."

"When was it that you first met Ms. Wild?"

"October '86, approximately."

"Where did you meet her?"

"First time I seen her was at Frankie and Leslie's."

The questions continued in the same vein. Coates testified with a wired, jailhouse jumpiness, spitting out terse answers as he sat cocked back in his chair.

Aragon readily picked up that Coates's idea of courtroom savvy was to try and blur the facts.

"What did Ms. Wild tell you about her status: single, married?"

"I wouldn't have—I can't answer something I don't know. Not at that time I didn't know. When I first met her I didn't know she was married. I learned that at a later date."

"When did you learn she was married?" Aragon kept after a solid answer.

"After we were seeing one another," Coates hemmed.

"You tell us you met her in about October of 1986?"

"Mid-October or so, yes." Coates hawed.

"It was not until January of '87 that Ms. Wild told you that she was married?"

"Approximately, yes. I'm not good on exact dates."

Coates claimed he had asked Deana to marry him in January, after dating for two to three weeks, although they hadn't set a wedding date. He added that he gave her an engagement ring, an heirloom handed down from his grandmother.

"Did you see her show the ring to your mother?"

"Not that I recall, no."

"Did you see her show the ring to B.J. McGinnis?"

"Not that I recall."

Aragon paused before asking the next, critical question: "What was your reaction when you found out that your mother had taken out life insurance on Deana?"

"I don't recall."

Aragon was stunned by the coldness of Coates's answer. He had at the very least expected a perfunctory show of emotion. "Were you happy about it?" he asked.

"I don't recall. I wasn't happy about too much of anything at that time. I was on my way back to prison or I was in prison."

"When was it that you learned you were the primary beneficiary on that life policy?"

"I'm not sure of the exact date."

Aragon picked up People's Exhibit 19, a letter from Virginia to her son, written while he was in prison, dated April 3, 1987. He walked toward the witness box. Coates knew what was coming, and a flicker of insecurity lit in his eyes.

"Yeah," he said. "I gave Don Smythe that letter. I believe you have a copy of it."

Suddenly, a low rumble rose up through the floor. Luis Aragon turned, still holding the exhibit. Then he looked up. The courtroom walls and ceiling began to roll, slowly at first, then in waves, as if they had turned to liquid. "Oh, my God!" "Oh, no!" a group of voices in the rear gallery exclaimed simultaneously as an earthquake pulsed through San Diego, shaking every building within a hundred-mile radius.

Bobbie Roberts jumped to her feet, then doubled over, clasping a handkerchief over her face to stop a nosebleed. Virginia and B.J.

leaned forward, testing their handcuffs against the arms of their chairs. Judge Kasimatis stood and spread his arms, admonishing people to remain calm. In his black robes, he hovered behind his bench, swaying like an angel of death.

Then, all at once, it stopped. The walls regained their solidity. The ceiling again hung firmly overhead. Bobbie Roberts ran to the bathroom.

Judge Kasimatis, a seasoned San Diegan, settled himself and calmly returned to the business at hand: "Let's continue."

Aragon read the letter while Coates nodded his grudging acknowledgment.

> Dear Jim,
>   Just a short note to say we are fine. Enclosed you will find a $50 money order for your books. Also some stamps. Let us know where you can have a care package. Call us when you can.
>   Last Thursday 4-2-87 we were going up Highway 1, coast (near Big Sur) and had stopped at a lookout point and took some pictures, and to see the view. Deana was with us and slipped and fell down the cliff. . .

The letter ended, "P.S. The dog is fine and we are okay."

Coates insisted that he hadn't learned about the life-insurance policy until "one, two, maybe the next letter."

"Did you ask them how Deana could have fallen?" Aragon kept at him.

"Not at that time, no. I don't believe I ever did."

Coates's continuing, easy dismissal of Deana's death pushed Aragon to a rare show of anger: "This was the death of your fiancée, sir! Did you have an interest in finding out exactly how she died?"

"I was told already how she died," Coates said.

Aragon sat down. "No further questions."

Albert Tamayo walked briskly back and forth in front of the witness stand, pivoting on his heel. Under his gentle cross-examination, James Coates explained that prisoners commonly confer power of attorney on friends or family once they face an extended sentence. He hastened to add that Virginia had taken out insurance on him and his brother, Ronnie, fifteen years earlier. Cross-examination ended in minutes.

Gary Edwards never left his seat.

Before Coates was permitted to step down, Judge Kasimatis turned to ask some questions of his own.

"Mr. Coates, what was the charge that originally sent you to prison?"

"Which time?" Coates faced the judge with an aggressive set to his jaw.

"Well, how many times have you been to prison?"

"Been to prison four times," Coates said, biting off the end of each word. "It's irrelevant, isn't it, what I been to prison for?"

"Well, you know, sometimes we get to inquire into these things, and this is one of those times." Kasimatis offered a cast-iron smile. "What were the charges?"

"Murder." Coates sounded almost proud.

Kasimatis couldn't conceal a double take. "Murder?" he inquired, peering at Coates over his half-moon glasses. "What else?"

Coates's pride suddenly turned to anger. Just when things looked safe, the judge wanted to peep into his record. He quickly replied, "Burglary, holding and receiving, and petty theft."

"Burglary?" Kasimatis asked.

"Four fifty-nine, four ninety-six, and four eighty-four with a six sixty-six prior." Coates rattled off the charges with the speed of a police dispatcher.

"The last return to prison for what?" Kasimatis asked.

"Four eighty-four with a six sixty-six." The numbers were delivered in another burst; Coates seemed electrified.

"Are you still on parole?"

"Yes, I am."

"Okay, then, Mr. Coates." Kasimatis turned away with ill-concealed distaste. "You may step down; you are excused. You may leave or you may remain."

Coates wheeled around the edge of the witness box and headed for the door, his arms and legs pumping. As he passed his mother, seated by the center aisle, he clapped his free hand around hers, his bear paw against her pudgy white mitt, and said under his breath, "Call Ronnie tonight, Ma."

Aragon rested his case.

Tamayo offered neither witnesses nor argument. Edwards made a brief plea that the People had failed to show his client Billie Joe was an "active participant."

Kasimatis listened politely, then delivered his findings without hesitation.

"The Court is more than convinced that each defendant has shown sufficient complicity in the whole scheme to warrant a bind-over on the counts as charged. . . . Clearly, the conspiracy is shown by numerous overt acts which are alleged and which have been shown by the evidence to more than raise the Court's suspicions concerning the defendants' complicity in this very terrible premeditated murder. . . .

"The amount of bail previously fixed will remain. Court will recess at this time."

That afternoon, Aragon found three messages from Keeney. They shared congratulations and agreed that Judge Kasimatis's impromptu remark—"this very terrible premeditated murder"—bode well for the trial. It was also the second vindication of two and a half years' work. But ample cause for concern remained. Aragon hadn't learned anything about the shape of the defense, yet both defense lawyers had just spent more than two days listening to all of his pivotal witnesses. They knew everything about his case; he still knew nothing of their defense.

CHAPTER 26

DEATH DENIED

▼

Trial was set for June 1990. Keeney assumed that meant preparing Bobbie Roberts, encouraging Dick Coates to cooperate, tracking the McGinnises' assets, and coordinating with the DA. Other than that, he would remain a sideline observer.

Then Aragon called.

"We've made our decision about penalty, Steve," he said. Keeney sensed a certain urgency in Aragon's voice.

"Go on, Luis."

"Drugging a girl and shoving her off a cliff to collect insurance is about as terrible an act as I've seen in nearly ten years of prosecuting. I wanted to get your reaction before you read about it in the press. As you know, this is murder for profit, a 'special circumstance' under our homicide statute. I know you may not agree, but we will be seeking the death penalty against both Virginia and B.J."

Aragon understood that both Bobbie and Keeney were members of a church that had taken a public stance against the death penalty. And the last thing his office wanted to see was the victim's mother or her attorney criticizing the decision in the news and citing Scripture in their support.

Keeney wasn't sure how to answer. He couldn't speak for Bobbie Roberts, but what about his own feelings?

Virginia and B.J. should be convicted, that much was obvious. But *killing them*? As far as he was aware, executions did nothing to deter killers. And the cost of appeals, stays, and habeas corpus petitions in the average death case easily overran the expense of lifetime confinement. True, it wasn't his daughter the McGinnises killed. Yet he couldn't let the DA's decision slide by without comment. Keeney asked for some time to think things over before the DA went public. Aragon said he could take a few weeks.

Keeney went at the problem with all the zeal and rigor that only a churchgoing tax attorney could muster. He called his pastor, contacted the head of the Presbyterian Church USA Criminal-Justice Project, and opened scholarly texts. As always, he wrote his analysis on the computer, late into the night. In spite of his new marriage and expanded family, Keeney's marathon work habits remained unchanged.

To his mind, the plain language of the Old Testament was unequivocal on the subject of execution. In Genesis, as God blesses Noah and his sons, entering into the covenant with them, He decrees: "Whoever sheds the blood of man/ By man shall his blood be shed. . . ." The words were a simple application of the *lex talonis*— "an eye for an eye"—which numbered among the most ancient legal codes.

Even the Sixth Commandment, "Thou shalt not kill," did not mean "No capital punishment." As any lawyer knew, statutory terms are subject to precise definitions. The active verb in the Sixth Commandment is the Hebrew *r-ts-ch*, which, according to the scholarly majority, best translates into English as "to murder," *not* the colloquial "to kill." Elsewhere in the Old Testament, the term refers specifically to premeditated murder. Thus, "Thou shalt not kill" more properly translates as "Thou shalt not murder"—that is, kill without legal authority. If that was not clear enough support for capital punishment, the entire Pentateuch lists no fewer than seventeen offenses that merit death. So much, it seemed, for the Old Testament. It was simply a question of defining terms.

But Jesus' teachings still needed to be reckoned with, and the waters of the New Testament were a good deal muddier. Even diehard opponents of the death penalty admitted you had to read the Gospels "synoptically" to find support for a strict antideath penalty position. The question ultimately came down to whether Jesus repudiated *lex talonis* in his famous admonition in the Sermon on the Mount to "turn the other cheek." Was he advocating a practical, but optional, approach to dispute resolution, or was He repealing the *right* to seek commensurate retribution? It posed a thorny legal issue.

Context, as any lawyer knew, is everything. Elsewhere in the Gospels, Jesus explicitly offers support for the Old Testament laws. In Matthew, Jesus says, "Do not think that I have come to abolish the Law . . . not the smallest letter, not the least stroke of a pen, will by any means disappear from the Law until everything is accomplished." Surely *lex talonis* and the Mosaic Code were larger than "the smallest letter."

And, Keeney noted, Jesus never argued against capital punishment at *His own* death-penalty trial or crucifixion! Presumably, He would have said it conflicted with God's will, even if only for the sake of His two fellow sufferers at Golgotha.

Arguments advanced by Presbyterian leaders in a 1985 church resolution didn't take the debate much further. One rationale read: "The use of the death penalty in a representative democracy places citizens in the role of the executioner: Christians cannot isolate themselves from corporate responsibility, including responsibility for every execution, as well as for every victim."

That was a mouthful. It reminded Keeney of an old Presbyterian saying: "Where the elders are unanimous, the decision is wrong."

As best he could judge, the Bible as a whole neither prohibited nor required state-sanctioned execution. He personally opposed the death penalty, and he considered the heart of the Bible to be love and mercy rather than law and justice. But, clearly, Scripture was not the strongest pillar on which to rest the argument.

The United States Supreme Court, too, had ruled the death penalty constitutional in a 1976 case named *Gregg* v. *Georgia.* Keeney disagreed with the decision, but he was not the first lawyer to chafe against the High Court's reasoning. As a Supreme Court justice once wryly remarked, "The Supreme Court isn't final because it is right. It's right because it is final."

Still, lowly California law offered some practical reasons why seeking the death penalty might be ill-advised in the McGinnis case. In fact, certain provisions made Keeney wonder whether Aragon had fully weighed all the implications.

Once the McGinnises faced the death penalty, they instantly became entitled to two "death qualified" lawyers and four investigators apiece. They would also have access to a limitless, undisclosed budget. That meant four lawyers and eight investigators versus Luis Aragon and Scott Lawrence.

There would also be *two* trials: a "guilt phase" and "penalty phase." In the penalty phase, the jury would decide between sentences of Life Without Possibility of Parole or Death. The entire proceeding would run up a bill in the neighborhood of a million and a half dollars. Add the automatic appeals under the especially strict standards for judging death-penalty trials and federal habeas corpus petitions, and the figure doubled—all out of taxpayers' pockets, and all aimed at killing Virginia and B.J. McGinnis.

As a practical matter, California hadn't executed anyone since well before the *Gregg* case came down, fourteen years earlier. Why go to all that trouble with a fifty-three-year-old defendant when the effective result is life imprisonment, anyway? For $1 million, you could buy a small island and strand the McGinnises there with a lifetime supply of food. The balance could be put into a fund for the homeless, or education, or crime prevention. But that was no answer to a prosecutor who needed to make concrete decisions about a pending trial.

One week later, with all parties hooked up via conference call, Aragon explained his position. Bobbie Roberts's answer came quickly: "They killed my daughter, Mr. Aragon. You do what you think is right."

"Luis," Keeney spoke up, "you're sure you want to take on the extra attorneys and investigators that come with a capital case? I may be a country lawyer, but four against one just doesn't seem like a fair fight."

Aragon laughed. "Thanks for your concern, but you built the case. You ought to know there aren't any holes in it."

"If you want to make it a death case, and my client agrees, I won't object. But I also won't complain if you plea-bargain the death penalty away to get the whole truth."

▼

Within days of the DA's announcement, two new "death qualified" attorneys joined the defense team. Albert Tamayo shared Virginia's case with Juliana Humphrey, a voluble young attorney with a special facility for the technical points of criminal law. Gary Edwards and Elizabeth Barranco, another seasoned trial lawyer, handled B.J. Both new appointees promptly asked the court for more time.

In Superior Court Department 22, the Honorable Bernard Revak listened to argument on delay.

Through some backroom shuffling of cases, Judge Revak, who had been a superior court judge only two years, found himself assigned to the McGinnis case. Revak welcomed the assignment. He loved conspiracies—the more complex, the better. During twenty years as a prosecutor in the San Diego DA's Office, he had tried dozens of them, one year being named California Prosecutor of the Year for winning a homicide where no corpse ever turned up.

The son of a Baptist preacher, Revak seemed to have picked up a knack for fire and brimstone. Colleagues at the DA's Office said that when Bernie was on a roll, his tall figure strutting before a jury, you could hear his voice four or five courtrooms down, even with all the doors closed. Now well into his fifties, his temperament seemed to have been mellowed by the California sun. Instead of glowering from the bench, he tended to lean back in his chair, head tilted to the ceiling, eyes closed behind his rectangular glasses. When he did speak, his wide brown mustache seemed to mute every word.

More than a few deputy DAs offered Aragon condolences. Judge Revak ran a gentlemanly courtroom, they said, but his notion of fairness amounted to dividing every dispute with a sword of Solomon. And deputy DAs thought that after the blade fell, the defense often got the larger share.

Revak heard out all five lawyers on the question of delay. Then he pushed the date ahead *five months:* October 1990.

For the second time, Keeney worried over Aragon's tactical sense. Here he was, taking on twice the legal firepower and saddling himself with what now amounted to a one-year delay since the McGinnises' arrest. The DA could have tried the case today. Time would only blunt everyone's energies and weaken witnesses' resolve.

Then came a series of legal maneuvers that twisted Aragon's stomach into knots and jacked Keeney up to a new level of concern.

First, the defense moved to exclude from the trial all evidence of the deaths, fires, and insurance claims in Virginia's past. Those incidents were never proved as crimes, they insisted. They added up to nothing more than highly prejudicial speculation.

The motion itself came as no real surprise, some of the events being twenty years in the past. But the question in Aragon's mind was, *How much* would be kept from the jury?

"Well, Mr. Aragon"—Judge Revak turned to the deputy DA—"I've read the briefs. I'm still not convinced why all these prior acts should come in." Aragon knew that all of Virginia's other "accidents" and insurance policies put her "accidental cliff fall" story into a revealing context. Without them, a jury might well find a reasonable doubt about Virginia's and B.J.'s guilt. Accordingly, he had spent the day before putting together what he thought was a compelling argument:

"Your Honor, if you are in a coffee room and there is a Coke machine and for some reason you are upset and you say, 'By gosh, I'm really upset I didn't get that raise,' and you bang that Coke machine and out pops a Coke. A totally innocent act. You get—you take the Coke and drink it. Well, you are in the same room about a week later and you are dying of thirst and all you have is a dollar and the change machine doesn't work. You want that Coke, and you recall, Well, you know, I banged it. So out of an innocent act grows an experience, a learned event.

"What Virginia learned, even admitting that there was no wrong done in those three other deaths, she learned what happens. And she learned most importantly that the authorities don't investigate. And, in fact, as we know in this case, this case was treated as an accident. There were no photographs taken. There was an autopsy done. And that's about it. There was almost no investigation. It was only after other factors were learned that, in this case, an independent non-law-enforcement person, Mr. Keeney, got involved. So the lessons that were learned in the prior deaths were instructive. And that is the probative act that shows method of operation, and knowledge of insurance."

Judge Revak nodded, his eyes still closed behind his glasses. Then the sword fell. He said he agreed in principle but felt compelled to exclude everything but the insurance claims made while Virginia lived in Chula Vista—the wind and water damage, the burglary, and the truck theft.

"The other facts are just too prejudicial," he said. "They don't tend to prove they pushed that girl off the cliff. And that's what this case is all about."

True to form, however, Judge Revak spread the pain evenly across both sides. Virginia's past would not come before the jury, but neither would Monterey's failure to prosecute. Aragon had moved to preempt its mere mention at trial. Another law-enforcement agency's opinion of a case, he argued, had no bearing on the facts of guilt or innocence.

Revak agreed.

Keeney heard the results of the latest round of hearings and marveled at the criminal-justice system's belief in blinders. In a civil case, you could put in all sorts of evidence about character, about the circumstances of an event. But in a criminal case, where the stakes were higher, a jury was given *less* information. The twelve peers trying Virginia and B.J. would never learn that, as recently as a year ago, members of the Monterey Sheriff's Office still believed they did not have even enough evidence for a search warrant, or that Virginia had a strange propensity for being present at accidents. For better or for worse, Deana's murder would be tried in a vacuum.

In spite of his partial victory, Aragon left Department 22 troubled. He didn't like the expression on Judge Revak's face as he delivered his rulings. Did Revak think Virginia was innocent? Or was Virginia's sixth sense about how to manipulate bureaucracies going to help her wriggle through the mesh again?

When the October trial date arrived, B.J.'s counsel Gary Edwards apologized that he had just started a kidnapping trial that might last at least six weeks. Aragon fumed. Edwards should have consulted with the court, especially before trying a much more recent case. The timing seemed suspiciously convenient.

"We're canceling Bobbie's plane reservations," Aragon told Keeney. "Judge Revak's given the defense another three months. We're looking at December."

The delays continued. Edwards's trial dragged on an extra two months. The December 1990 date became the January 1991 date. The January date became the March date. To Keeney, the process began to seem like some Kafkaesque courthouse routine with double-talking lawyers who never get anything done. Wynn kept reminding him of her own low opinion of courts.

As the battle over trial dates continued, Aragon was also skirmishing with the defense on another front. Nine months after the McGinnises were arrested, a criminal law reform bill called Proposition 115 passed into law. It became effective on June 6, 1990. Known as the Victim's Fair Trial Act, Proposition 115 aimed at evening the odds in criminal trials. In particular, Aragon hungrily eyed a provision entitling the DA to so-called reciprocal discovery from the defense.

"Discovery" boils down to swapping eveidence before a trial. Previously, California criminal discovery was a one-way street. The DA had to give the defense virtually everything in its files well before trial. Defense attorneys, on the other hand, could wait until their witnesses actually took the stand before giving the DA a peek at their prior statements. Disgruntled prosecutors called the time-honored practice "trial by ambush." Proposition 115 made the obligations run in both directions. It was also a "retroactive" rule change, which meant it applied even to defendants on the eve of trial.

"This might be a real break," Aragon told Keeney. "A chance to find out just where the defense is going." Keeney wasn't so sure. Ample precedent for reciprocal criminal discovery existed in other states, and the United States Supreme Court had long since ruled the practice constitutional. But he didn't savor the idea of Bobbie Roberts's daughter's murder being a test case under a new statute—and too much time had already been burned up with motions.

As it turned out, B.J.'s attorneys easily sidestepped the new law. They told Judge Revak they simply didn't have any notes or reports whatever. Aragon sputtered: It simply wasn't possible for two lawyers to defend a man against a homicide without generating notes of interviews with witnesses or experts. But Edwards and Barranco swore they had nothing.

Virginia's lawyers, Albert Tamayo and Juliana Humphrey, had their own blunt strategy: They refused to comply. Aragon, once again, was incensed. His office had already turned over more than ten thousand pages of reports and transcripts to both defense teams. Even more to the point, the law was the law, and he could not respect any attorney who deliberately flouted it.

Judge Revak ordered the defense to comply with Proposition 115. But by December 1990, Tamayo and Humphrey still had not turned over any discovery whatsoever. Revak repeated his order, then threatened sanctions. This time, Virginia's lawyers appealed. They claimed they were willing to take the issue to the U.S. Supreme Court if necessary.

Judge Revak glowered and Aragon wrung his hands in despair, but they both knew the defense had everyone hamstrung. Revak had the power to order Tamayo and Humphrey to trial. He could even refuse to let them put on witnesses whose statements weren't turned over to the DA. But no appeals court in the country would ever uphold such a murder conviction.

Virginia's defenders had stumbled onto a foolproof way to buy a year's delay, maybe more. Keeney saw tears of frustration in Bobbie's eyes as he explained the situation.

While the murder case inched forward, Keeney continued to hammer on the civil issues with only marginally more success. Monterey counsel Chuck Warner had dug up the deed to Virginia's new house and promptly encountered problems.

"She saw us coming," Warner groused.

"How so?" Keeney asked. "Just slap a lien on the property, sell it at auction, and Bobbie will get her due."

"Yeah, but we can't sell *Ronnie Coates's* house."

"The fox sold it to Ronnie?"

"From what I can figure, Virginia *gave,* and I use the term loosely, the place to her son. The quitclaim deed went through on August 11, 1989, just three days after our default judgments were recorded in the county abstracts. She saw us coming as clear as day. Now we've got to go back to court and prove that the transfer was a fraud to prevent us from satisfying the judgment for Deana's death. Not bad for a woman who doesn't even have a high school diploma."

"Okay, Chuck." He sighed. "You know what the next step is. I'll slip you a complaint to set aside the 'gift' of the house."

Keeney felt as if a witch had just ridden out of the closet on a broom and shot him a wicked smile while taunting, "Catch me, catch me if you can."

"Hey, Steve, have you heard the news?" said the voice on the phone.

"Pete Lazar! How's B & A?"

"Never mind the firm, this is too important. I was driving and when I heard the radio, I nearly hit an embankment."

"Okay, Pete, so I'm out of the fast lane. What's up?"

"Stan Chauvin showed up in Chicago the other day to pass on the ABA presidency to his successor. He checked in at the Hyatt Regency Hotel and the next morning he went down to the vault. Next thing, he's phoning the police saying that fifty-five thousand dollars in hundred-dollar bills is missing from his hotel safe! He swore he locked the money away just last night."

"What was Stan doing with a bankroll like that?" Keeney gasped. "Did he stop believing in banks?"

"That's just it. Nobody knows what Stan was doing. He called a press conference, but then he winged it. Didn't even confer with us about what to say. I just heard him tell reporters that the money didn't come from a client, but the source *might* consider himself a client, so he wasn't at liberty to say."

"Well, I guess that's one more reason to be in solo practice. At least I can trust my partners," Keeney said. "I'll look for it in the papers."

By fall of 1991, Keeney and Chuck Warner had moved to void Virginia's gift of the house to Ronnie. But a California judge froze the case pending the outcome of the criminal trial. Keeney argued that he was merely trying to collect on a judgment he had *already* won in Monterey. Legally, the murder case was irrelevant. But the local judge wasn't interested in "fine points."

Then, Bobbie Roberts and James Coates came head-to-head over the State Farm insurance proceeds in the federal interpleader case. Virginia and B.J. had both been served with papers asking them to assert their interest in the policy, but neither answered. Jay Wild bowed out, too. In the end, it was mother versus "fiancé." And Bobbie said she'd be damned if she'd let Coates see a dime of the money.

Keeney reminded Bobbie that there was no longer any point in taking her claim to trial since James Coates had been examined by the DA on the record. It would simply cost both sides thousands of dollars. "Why not give the money to charity?" he suggested. Bobbie agreed, but Coates refused the offer.

Swallowing her pride, Bobbie acceded to the only other solution short of trial: Divide the proceeds. Keeney passed on the offer of settlement.

After protracted wrangling, Coates agreed to take $7,500, a figure representing the accumulated interest on the policy. Bobbie got the remaining $35,000 and gave the standard lawyer's one-third to Keeney and Warner. Since she didn't have a contract with Keeney, she didn't have to pay. But Bobbie felt it was the right thing to do. And with four years' of uncompensated work behind him, Keeney was not about to turn down a little largesse. His take roughly covered the long-distance telephone bill.

Bobbie celebrated when she got the check, but her joy was restrained. The cash felt filthy, and she tried not to think about the fact that Virginia's deadly scheme had succeeded—even if only in part. Day by day, court by court, Virginia and her sons were wearing everyone down, playing hide-and-seek in the law's labyrinth. Already it had been an agonizing four years. *How will this awful thing finally end?* Bobbie kept thinking. She didn't think she could bear the sight of Virginia and B.J. walking out of the courtroom scot-free. But at this point it was all too easy to imagine.

On November 14, 1991, Luis Aragon called Keeney at work. Keeney immediately detected a hollowness in his voice.

"I just came back from court," Aragon said. "Revak knocked out the death penalty."

Keeney paused. When he answered, he spoke with the distant, slow-motion voice he fell into when things went seriously awry. "Now why would he do that? On what grounds?"

"Prosecutorial misconduct."

Keeney could sense Aragon's morale collapsing.

Without the death penalty, the case would have been tried long ago. Instead, the prosecution now faced the largest defense budget allowable under law and double the number of lawyers: all for no good reason. Given enough time, the lesson seemed to be, something will screw up royally.

The alleged misconduct, Aragon explained, had started innocently enough.

B.J. was always a secondary figure in the DA's estimation, a puppet manipulated by Virginia. The man's life history, so far as it mattered to the State's case, could be written in one succinct sentence: B.J., an uninsurably unhealthy man, conspired with Virginia to murder Deana Wild.

Aragon knew little beyond that, and B.J.'s history of forgeries; he didn't need to. But during the months of pre-trial delay, he decided to close off a few possible defenses. One possibility involved the claim that he and Virginia never heard a sound when Deana fell. B.J. and Virginia had stuck to that story in interviews with Don Smythe, Dave Dungan, and State Farm's Diana Rael.

What if B.J. were hard of hearing? the thought occurred to Aragon. It was a long-shot defense, but why not make a preemptive strike? Aragon subpoenaed records from Sonoma County Hospital, where B.J.'s sister said he had been treated.

The DA's subpoena requested that all documents be sent directly to Judge Revak in double-sealed envelopes. But request or no request, one day a package arrived at Aragon's office, return address Sonoma County Mental Health.

Aragon opened it and read. Then he showed the documents to his newly appointed cocounsel, Anna Long, a rookie prosecutor sent by Ed Miller to help even the score against the defense. The medical records said nothing about a hearing problem. In fact, they said nothing about physical health at all. They were B.J.'s psychiatric records, and they were forbidden to the DA under the psychiatrist-patient privilege.

Aragon shouldn't have read them, but fortunately, he decided, there was no harm done. The records—all from 1985—contained pages of irrelevant personal material. Only one comment made Aragon uncomfortable. The remark involved B.J.'s fear that Virginia might be trying to poison him. It was a damning assertion, and arguably related to the Elavil in Deana's system. But Aragon had already heard the same conjecture from B.J.'s friend Sarah Tabor. Keeney had, too. Even B.J.'s new death-qualified lawyer, Elizabeth Barranco, mentioned poisoning in an offhanded statement to the court. Aragon believed he hadn't learned a thing.

On the other hand, he knew he had to act fast. Courts are unforgiving when prosecutors break the rules, even inadvertently. First, he turned the records over to Judge Revak. Then he telephoned Elizabeth Barranco to explain the situation. Their conversation was as short as it was bitter. Within days, the entire defense team all howled about prosecutorial misconduct and moved to dismiss the entire indictment. As an alternative, they moved to recuse Aragon from the case—which would buy them at least another six months' delay.

The DA's Office filed a voluminous reply. Judge Revak, one more time, ordered all the parties into Department 22.

On November 12, 1991, Aragon and Long appeared with special

counsel. Aragon felt sure the storm would blow over. He hadn't learned one new fact from his mistake; he hadn't wanted the records in the first place; he had even gone to the length of informing both the court and the defense lawyers.

Judge Revak disagreed. After a morning of testimony from both Anna Long and Aragon, he delivered a stinging ruling.

"I think there has been misconduct," Revak said, his face assuming a dour expression. "I don't think Mr. Aragon deliberately subpoenaed psychiatric records. . . . I think he was looking for medical records. . . . And I'm a firm believer that his intention was to have these records delivered to the court and not to take receipt of them. The problem is, he received them. Not only did he receive them, he opened them. Not only did he open them, he read them. Not only did he read them, he passed them on to somebody else to read and then discussed them. . . .

"I think the clerk or whoever mailed these out made a bad mistake, didn't read the subpoena. . . . But the question in my mind is what's the remedy. I clearly don't think dismissal is in order. I'm not going to recuse the district attorney. But I think the remedy I'm going to fashion is as follows:

"I don't think it's just an idle statement that Mr. McGinnis has been compromised. Now Mr. Aragon says that he learned nothing new in there, and I think that's a little self-serving. I can't agree with that statement because I've not read it anywhere else. . . . And there is one comment in the records that I can tell you is an explosive, explosive comment. It is a devastating statement in my mind, particularly with Mr. McGinnis in a penalty phase.

"Here's my ruling: I'm going to strike that aspect of the case that calls for the death penalty as to both defendants. I know it's drastic. I think you have a right to appeal my order. I just think that in fairness to these defendants who have been waiting now for years to get this case to trial, who are facing the death penalty, that . . . I don't think Mr. McGinnis can have a fair trial insofar as the penalty phase is concerned.

"And furthermore, I think that there is an awful lot in there that rubs off on Ms. McGinnis and I can't erase it. I wish it had never happened. But the damage has been done, and I think the only proper remedy is the one I just described."

Aragon left the courtroom dazed. He had built a reputation as a fair-dealing, conscientious prosecutor. Now, through a county hospital's clerical error, he was branded with misconduct, and the case had suffered its second major setback. Virginia and B.J. could still be sentenced to Life Without Possibility of Parole, but, clearly, the defense had won a major victory.

"This is easily the worst day of my life," Aragon said to Keeney.

"It wasn't you, Luis, it was the court," Keeney consoled. Yet as he spoke, he silently worried. Virginia's defenders were handily whittling the prosecution's case down to the bone.

CHAPTER 27

A BRIDGE
IN LODI

▼

"Steven H. Keeney?" a sheriff in a green uniform asked.

Keeney had just returned to his office, a small suite in the Kaden Tower office building just outside of downtown Louisville. The sheriff was standing outside his door.

"Yes, sir?" Keeney asked.

"Subpoena from San Diego Superior Court. Sign here."

Keeney unfolded the papers and read. An order from Judge Revak under the Uniform Act to Secure Attendance of Witnesses from Without a State in Criminal Proceedings commanded him to bring his files to San Diego and testify. The attached affidavit bore the signature of Virginia's lead counsel, Albert Tamayo.

Keeney conferred with Bobbie Roberts and Luis Aragon that evening. They all agreed the move was outrageous. Keeney had nothing to hide from the defense; in fact, his book had long since been given to Tamayo and Edwards along with Xeroxed copies of his telephone log and notes. But the thought of being compelled to fly across the country and give aid to his client's daughter's killers incensed him.

Keeney fought the subpoena at four extensive hearings in Louisville over the following month. But eventually he bowed to the will of the court. He could have appealed the final ruling, but that would only have given the defense fodder for still more delays.

Before leaving for San Diego, Keeney called R. D. Jones to see whether there was anything he might need from the DA.

"Nothing I can think of," R.D. said. "But, if you don't mind my asking, are you taking any protection?"

"You mean the Coates boys?"

"Well, they're both out on parole and they know who's responsible for Mom being locked up. You might consider getting a permit for your forty-five."

"I'll check the exits from my hotel room, R.D. Thanks for thinking of me."

Keeney opted against taking a gun. Nevertheless, R.D.'s words haunted him as he and Wynn checked into their government-issue San Diego hotel room. That night, a Pacific storm rolled in. Monsoon rainfall beat against the glass so hard, it sounded like handfuls of gravel. Steve and Wynn slept only a few hours.

Testimony lasted two days. Tamayo marched through Keeney's book, then scrutinized his daily notes, phone call by phone call. Wynn sat in the rear of the courtroom, watching her husband get the third degree, all for having tried to do the right thing by a lady at church. What she saw tended only to confirm her cynicism about criminal courts.

Not one new fact came out. But Tamayo seemed bent on more than learning the facts. He did his best to attack Keeney personally, as if Keeney had concocted the entire case out of a brilliantly rich imagination. Referring to a note that said, "J.M.; cleaning him up," Tamayo asked, "You didn't like Jake Miller's statements to you, they didn't fit with the theory that you had. Is that right?"

"How in the world could you say that?" Keeney answered. Tamayo pressed with a dozen more questions, but the evidence of manipulation he hoped to find never materialized.

At another point, Tamayo paraded the fact that Keeney told news reporters he did the case on a *pro bono* basis, yet he took money from Bobbie Roberts's insurance settlement. Keeney agreed that he got some money but explained that it was a gift. There had never been any contract, bill, or demand for payment.

Toward the end of the day, Tamayo still hadn't shaken Keeney's story. In desperation, he turned and asked, "Isn't it true you've been charged with a felony?"

Keeney sat motionless for a moment. This was a crude, personal assault; the unproved "felony" had been brought by his wife over a child-support dispute. The charge was dismissed in the end.

In a solemn voice, he answered simply, "Yes."

The following day in court, Tamayo argued to Judge Revak that Keeney should remain under the court's subpoena as a potential defense witness. "I think this idea that a *pro bono* lawyer could, out of the goodness of his heart, prosecute and investigate this case needs to be destroyed as a myth," he insisted. The Louisville attorney, Tamayo concluded, concocted the case for self-aggrandizement, publicity, and money. A book was in the offing, as were TV offers. The man stood to profit by his client's demise.

Keeney left San Diego on notice that he might be called as a witness *for the defense.* Before departing, however, he took the opportunity to express his disgust.

"I came into this case believing it was an accident. I *hoped* it was an accident. It looked like an insurance claim for burial insurance. And I waited until the last possible minute to file a wrongful-death claim. . . .

"Much ado has been made about money in this case. All I can tell you is that if any of you want the money that I'm getting out of the case, I would welcome you to change positions with me today. In fact, if I had known what I was getting into when I started this case, I would have welcomed you to change positions with me then.

"It includes no fewer than three civil litigations. Those were supported by costly, multi-year, cross-country investigations. Every call was a toll call. It wasn't like working a Kentucky case. And that doesn't even begin to reflect the staff work like Ms. West and others who assisted in the case, or coordination of our counsel in California and Illinois. . . .

"As I sit here and look at my wife in the back of the courtroom, sometimes I wish I hadn't done it, but I think it was the right thing to do.

"But you all didn't want to stop there. You also wanted to see if you could slur my character. It's not material to the case; it has no relevance. But you *wanted* to go further. . . .

"We teach by example. And in this merry-go-round of pleadings and hearings and pitiable subpoenas, we have not taught the law that we dedicated ourselves to. My client's daughter is dead. And if the meticulous care that is shown to the rights of the defendants were extended to my client, that would be one thing. But it has not been so here. . . ."

All through the pretrial proceedings, right up to the day of jury selection, bad luck continued to haunt the prosecution.

First, there had been Deputy Niemi. While tracking down witnesses, Aragon learned that Deputy Sheriff John Burke had recovered Deana's body with the help of another deputy named Richard Niemi. To the best of anyone's information, Niemi had never been interviewed about the case. Maybe he had noticed some blood on the McGinnises' clothing, Aragon hoped, or broken fingernails at the surface of the cliff.

The sheriff's roll call administrator offered Aragon Burke's services but said that Niemi was "unavailable."

"This is a homicide investigation." Aragon's voice stiffened. "He doesn't have any choice in the matter."

"I'm sorry, sir. Deputy Niemi committed suicide just a few months ago." Aragon quickly apologized.

Days later, Aragon learned that James Coates's former girlfriend, Debbie Williams, had recently attempted to kill herself. She survived, but her instability led Aragon to eliminate her from the witness list. Soon, Aragon and Keeney began harboring the bizarre worry that perhaps some other witnesses might not make it to the trial.

They did not have to wait long. Izetta Ramsey, a scheduled witness for the DA, died.

Three months before jury selection, Dick Coates jumped off a bridge in Lodi onto a dry creekbed seventy-four feet below. He left a note behind erasing any doubt: another suicide. The news came in December via the Tompkins County Sheriff's Office.

At the time, Aragon was still debating whether to call Dick as a witness. Keeney wondered whether the fear of traveling to California—Dick Coates had never even been on an airplane—and of confronting Virginia after twenty years had accelerated the man's undoing.

That evening, he called Dick's mother, Margaret, at her nursing home to offer his condolences.

"Dick's health was bad." Margaret sighed. "He'd been sick a long time. His legs were bothering him."

"I'm so sorry," said Keeney. "I remember he said he'd been out of work. But we were talking about how we looked forward to seeing each other, maybe in San Diego."

"Yup," she cut in. "It's a terrible shock."

Keeney wanted to ask more about the death, and about what Dick had said in his note. He wanted to be sure it really was a suicide. James and Ronnie Coates were both out on parole again and they were eminently capable of taking care of their mother's problems.

"Did you see the note?" he asked cautiously. "Was it in Dick's handwriting?"

"Yup. Probably was," came the unencouraging answer.

Probing further would feel like trespass, Keeney decided. "I can't tell you how sorry I feel," he said. "I'll miss hearing from him. You know, I was just wondering if he'd call for Christmas. Now I know."

Over the hiss of the circuits, Keeney heard her quiet breathing.

"You'll be in our prayers, Margaret. I hope you can still have some joy and peace."

"Thank you," she said. "I'm going to Lilly's. She has a begonia for me."

"Thanks for talking with me." Keeney put down the phone.

Kindly, tipsy old Dick Coates, fifty-six years old at the time of his death, had been his keyhole into Virginia's past. Just to be helpful, he had relived the worst days of his life, and all he ever got out of the deal was pain. In recent months, investigators of every stripe had knocked on the door of his Lodi lean-to. Unaccustomed to receiving visitors, Dick had called Keeney more than once wondering what to do. Dick Coates deserved a better end, Keeney thought.

And still the death toll wasn't over.

Jury selection began in late November 1991. Aragon had waited more than two years since Virginia's and B.J.'s arrest. At last, he thought, the case was going to be tried. The sight of a few hundred jurors crowding the courtroom seemed to clinch it.

At 6:00 A.M. on December 2, Aragon was awakened by a phone

call. In the past week, they had winnowed the jury pool and were now down to talking with individual prospective jurors. Trial would kick off after the first of the year.

The call came from Aragon's wife, Julie, a reporter for the San Diego *Tribune.* She wanted to get the information to her husband before it hit the radio.

Minutes later, Aragon called Scott Lawrence and Anna Long for a quick huddle before the day's session.

After Judge Revak called the courtroom to order that morning, Aragon broke the news.

"Your Honor, the People are informed that Billie Joe McGinnis died between two and three A.M. this morning. The tentative diagnosis is pneumonia. An autopsy is scheduled for either tomorrow or the next day."

A shocked stillness filled the room; death seemed to follow Virginia's shadow.

What more was there to say now? Aragon considered. Edwards and Barranco could pack up their attaché cases and head back to their offices, fully content. Their delays had resulted in multiple victories. Having died before trial, Billie Joe McGinnis would remain cloaked forever in the presumption of innocence. And there was no longer any hope of learning the whole truth from Virginia's co-conspirator.

Tamayo and Humphrey looked at their client. Her square face came alive for a moment. Her eyes fluttered behind the thick glasses she wore to court every day. Her down-turned mouth pursed. Then she settled back into her imperturbable posture.

Revak excused the panel of prospective jurors but refused to delay the case. The trial date of January 6, 1992, remained firm.

Keeney rushed to reach Bobbie Roberts before the local press descended upon her. This was no time for her to blurt out, "At least Billie Joe McGinnis won't be killing any more little girls." Anything she said might be played back at her in court by Virginia's defense team.

When the Louisville television news crew arrived at Bobbie's house, she was ready. "I express my deepest sympathies to his family," she said. "Now he's going to the Ultimate Judge. The Judge who knows everything. I pray for his soul."

B.J.'s death left a vacuum in the case that Aragon, Anna Long, and Scott Lawrence scrambled to fill. Aragon and Long needed to assess, first and foremost, whether B.J.'s statements could still be used against Virginia. Scott Lawrence tracked down everyone in the jail system with whom B.J. kept company in the hope that the ailing prisoner might have made a dying declaration or left behind letters, notes, or books in which he scribbled a confession.

But other than discovering that B.J. had died of AIDS-related pneumonia, Lawrence found nothing new. B.J. had languished in his decrepit prison cell for two years, guarding his right to remain silent to his final bitter moment.

Virginia had triumphed again.

Albert Tamayo and Juliana Humphrey agreed to comply with Judge Revak's order on Proposition 115's reciprocal discovery just days after B.J.'s death. The California Court of Appeals had denied their appeal and they decided not to press their luck in higher courts. The material, they promised, would be arriving at the DA's Office within days.

"Is this it?" Aragon exclaimed when a packet as slim as a newspaper arrived from the Public Defender's Office. He expected boxes full. The defense team consisted of three full-time investigators and two attorneys working the case for years, traveling to Louisville, Ithaca, San Francisco, and scouring San Diego. The prosecution had diligently provided the defense with an amount of background material unusually large for any but a major white-collar prosecution. Yet here, in response, they were handing over forty-five pages of notes and a list of thirty-three potential witnesses, a list that still included Steven Keeney.

Their "compliance," Aragon knew, amounted to a cheap move to appease the judge and force everyone to trial. That final salvo made one fact plain: Tamayo and Humphrey planned to try the case by street rules.

▼

The final detail to be wrestled into place was by far the most colorful. All along, Aragon had argued that the only way a jury could fairly decide between "an oops and a push"—between accident and murder—was to visit the cliff itself, five hundred miles north. To make the trip truly worthwhile, Aragon added, witnesses would have to testify at the scene. It promised to be expensive, time-consuming, and a logistical headache. No jury in history had ever traveled so far. Unprecedented problems of traffic control, lodging, and transportation needed to be addressed. But it was necessary.

Revak turned to Tamayo and Humphrey, the look on his mustached face amounting to a mute plea for a reason to avoid this quagmire. But the defense enthusiastically agreed.

Aragon and Anna Long exchanged surprised glances. They had visited the site many times. Every juror, they thought, would understand that Seal Beach was not a "one false step and it's all over" cliff edge. Deana simply couldn't have slipped and fallen silently to her death. But the defense team's ready assent turned Aragon's confidence to queasiness. One side or the other, he knew, had badly miscalculated.

C H A P T E R 2 8

BIG SUR
REVISITED

▼

By the afternoon of January 6, 1992, Luis Aragon faced fifteen jurors—eight men and four women, and a trio of alternates—in a
windowless, wood-paneled San Diego courtroom as he began his
opening statement. The jurors were mostly middle-aged, evenly divided between men and women, and, with one exception, all white.

Their faces projected an attitude of critical expectancy. Judge
Revak had warned them that the trial might last two months. Aragon knew they would demand a mighty good reason for being pulled
out of their lives to sit in silence eight hours a day listening to four
lawyers battle it out.

Virginia appeared to have taken pains to look her best. That morning, before the jury filed in, she made a grand entrance in a brilliant
teal blue dress. Her hair, dyed chestnut, and freshly combed and
permed, hung lightly around her face like a Clairol ad. Touches of
makeup softened the forbidding look in her eyes, and streaks of
rouge gave some cheer to her cheeks. She had gained weight since
her arraignment and now looked truly obese. But the "evil woman"

from page one of the San Diego *Union* nonetheless managed to assume a motherly persona. She kept her hands folded in her lap and offered the jurors nervous smiles as they filed in.

Aragon stood before the jury and read from his neatly typed opening statement. He wore a navy blue double-breasted suit over a crisp white shirt, the clothes in which he had been remarried just a few months ago. But, as always, his professional aura was offset by a shy smile and a few straying wisps of hair he regularly pushed back into place.

"This is a chilling case of deception and greed," he began, taking care to make eye contact with each juror through his square glasses. "This is a case of a young, unsophisticated twenty-year-old woman from Kentucky who had fallen in with the wrong crowd. But how did Deana Hubbard Wild end up four hundred feet from the top of Seal Beach in Big Sur on April the second? The evidence will show you very clearly that we are not here by accident."

In just over one hour, he explained the State's theory of the crime. The McGinnises lied about an engagement with James Coates in order to insure Deana's life. They drove her up the coast on the pretext of a sight-seeing trip, slipped her some Elavil, then threw her off the cliff. Virginia used a power of attorney to try to collect the money in her son's name. After that, she and B.J. covered their trail with a series of lies.

The case had not changed substantially from the narrative in Keeney's book. Aragon had recruited some additional experts on topology and toxicology. A few members of the Sheriff's Department would attest to a range of inconsistent statements by Virginia and B.J. about who stood where just before Deana's death. But ultimately, he followed the script Keeney had written after-hours while his law firm disintegrated: the Elavil, the McCains, the insurance policy, Deana's low IQ, Virginia's phone call with Bobbie Roberts. The simplest explanation of the greatest number of facts: Occam's razor.

"Deana trusted," Aragon said slowly, scanning back and forth across the jurors' faces. "It was that approach to a not-always-kind and -safe world that caused Deana to make some big mistakes in her life. The biggest mistake being when she accepted Jim Coates's invitation to move into the defendant's house in January of 1987. Jim Coates had already been convicted of four felonies, had spent most of his adult life in and out of state prison. But that didn't matter to

Deana, because all she needed to be your friend was for you to be nice to her. She took things at face value. She took people at face value."

Aragon read the letter Virginia wrote to James Coates, breaking the news that his "fiancée" had died. After reading the closing line— "P.S. The dog is fine . . ."—Aragon quipped, "Thank heaven for that." A few jurors smiled back. He sensed he had set the right tone.

Aragon waited a few moments in silence after reading the letter, then closed with a brief exhortation: "This was no accident. In spite of the defendant and her husband's best efforts to obscure the truth, you will find the truth. In spite of everything they did to convince everybody in the world that this was an accident, you will come back and state to one and all that the defendant is guilty of premeditated first-degree murder for financial gain."

Everything about Albert Tamayo, from his trim surfer's build to his immaculate suit, contrasted Aragon's semi-rumpled image. He spoke with an air of extreme reserve, and he moved soundlessly, displaying exhibits before the jury and calmly gesturing with an open palm.

Up to that moment, Aragon still had no clear notion of where Tamayo planned to take Virginia's defense. He and Keeney had batted around ideas for hours but, given how little they had to work with, had come up empty-handed. Insanity was out. A psychiatric examination, in fact, had never even been mentioned by the defense. The only other possibilities were accident, suicide, assisted suicide, "B.J. did it," "Steve Keeney framed Virginia," or pure reasonable doubt.

Tamayo's witness list included experts on "coefficient of friction," human memory, and forensic toxicology. Keeney remained on the list, as did Deana's natural father, two neighbors of Bobbie Roberts's, a group of State Farm bureaucrats, and five ex-cons from San Diego. If one strategy connected them all, Aragon couldn't find it. He sat cross-legged in his chair as Tamayo spoke, poised to catch any hint of a coherent theory exonerating Virginia.

"In this case, you are going to hear about two stories, two tragedies," Tamayo said, speaking to the panel with the voice of a concerned citizen—one more contrast to Aragon's emotional plea. "The first tragedy involved Deana Hubbard's fatal fall, the fatal accident that occurred on April 2, 1987. The second tragedy involved my client, Virginia McGinnis, and the accusations and the blame and the innuendo she's suffered since the investigation in this case began. . . ."

Deana's life in San Diego pulled her downward in a spiral of rampant drug use and promiscuous sex, Tamayo said. "Over a period of two and a half to three months, she left Kentucky as the country girl the district attorney describes, and became a dope user and dope dealer. That you'll find out later on. But for a brief period, she experienced some civility, and that was with my client, Virginia McGinnis. And that's when we get into the second story, the second tragedy in this case. . . .

"Virginia has been victimized by the circumstantial evidence which the district attorney describes, and by the coincidence of time. An insurance policy was taken out before Deana's death, and, because of that, we now have a murder." Aragon sensed the jurors' attention quickening; he knew Tamayo was offering them a comfortable way out. Fifty-year-old mothers normally don't go pushing young women off cliffs.

"There will be no contest with respect to many of the facts," Tamayo explained. "What we will contest is the interpretation of those facts."

It was only natural that Virginia should think Deana unmarried, Tamayo went on. Jay had been on the U.S.S. *Kitty Hawk* for most of the fall, and Deana was off picking up men at bars and dealing drugs. She had reverted to calling herself by her maiden name, and started to fall in and out of relationships where marriage always seemed a possibility. By the time Deana stood at the cliff edge, she was "depressed, almost suicidal."

Witnesses from a San Diego "subculture" of drug dealers and felons would tell the jury about the "real Deana": "Bones" Sherman, "Pinto" Steve, Frank and Leslie Garcia, and her former lover Donnie Dale Moore. "In fact," Tamayo said, "Donnie Moore knew Deana by her reputation and didn't care whether she was married, because, as he says and will say—these are his words, not mine—'She would fuck everything including a rattlesnake.' "

The men and women of the jury looked back at Tamayo openmouthed. Aragon wanted to jump to his feet and object. Even if everything Tamayo said was true, Deana's sexual habits were no defense to a *murder* charge. But by linking it to the question of whether Virginia might have thought Deana a married woman, Tamayo had found a way to make her sex life arguably relevant. The DA was calling Deana's engagement to James Coates bogus. The defense, therefore, had a right to show that Deana behaved like an unmarried woman. Aragon opted to stay in his seat, gambling that Tamayo's crude attack would alienate the jury more than it would harm the State's case.

Then Tamayo's focus shifted to the hidden hazards of Seal Beach. "It's very windy there," he said. "And it's very cold even in the middle of summertime. But it's not only steep, which is the obvious danger. It's also dangerous because of the surface—which is not so obvious.

"They arrived there on April second and, like tourists, they started taking shots. Nothing looks professional here. It looks like it's just made by a couple of tourists. There were no warning signs. People will testify that sometimes the wind gets so strong that they see rocks being blown upward. Even for a person who is careful, careful about their lifestyle, careful about their habits, it's a very dangerous place. . . ."

This all suggested that Tamayo had weighed in for proving accident. Deana, with her alleged drug habits and casual approach to sex, was certainly not careful about her lifestyle. But then, Aragon wondered, how did that jibe with the suicide theme hinted at moments ago?

"David Dungan will testify in this case," Tamayo went on, referring to the man who wrote the Coroner's Register for Deana's death. "And his report is very interesting. Dungan had the benefit of all the information from the pathologist. He also knew that there was amitriptyline and nortriptyline in her system. The only thing he didn't know was about an insurance policy. That was the *only* factor he didn't know about. But his conclusion yet was"—Tamayo picked up a page and read—"'In the initial and subsequent interview with the McGinnis', I found nothing to even slightly indicate foul play.'"

Tamayo's opening lasted close to ninety minutes. It was the longest he had given in ten years of defense work. But by the time Tamayo sat down, Aragon still felt no closer to understanding the defense's theory.

Meanwhile, Juliana Humphrey kept up a quiet patter with Virginia, whispering together and rubbing shoulders like friends at a coffee klatch. They made an unusual pair. Humphrey's brown hair fell about her rounded face in disarrayed cables, and brightly intelligent eyes shone from behind a pair of glasses that tended to slip down her nose. Virginia could have been this young lawyer's doting, overweight aunt. "Such a lovely girl," she might have said. "And so talented." Juliana Humphrey also suspected that, at this moment, she was closer to Virginia than anyone else in the world.

"I can't understand where Albert's going," Aragon told Keeney that evening. "First he hands over the skimpiest discovery materials imaginable. Then he excludes Virginia's past from the trial, knocks out the death penalty, and generates a two-and-a-half-year delay that ends with B.J. dead. It would at least be nice to know what he planned to argue. But he's raised every defense in the book."

Keeney laughed. "Albert Tamayo walked into the courtroom stark naked!"

"You think so, Steve?" Aragon found the Louisville lawyer's easy manner a soothing antidote to the stress of the courtroom, but it didn't square with what he had heard in court that afternoon. "I've asked around and Tamayo has a reputation for being incredibly meticulous."

"I'm telling you, Luis, he doesn't have a theory. It's a smoke screen."

"Well, I'd like to agree with you, but underestimating your opponent is fatal. And I know for sure he made headway today with his comments about Dave Dungan's report."

"I can't argue with you there. And I guess I should be glad you sound concerned. But you're going to win."

Aragon decided to change the subject. Too much confidence had a way of bringing bad luck.

The opening days of trial were bathed in tears. The first seven prosecution witnesses comprised a sort of eulogy to Deana. Aragon knew that the jury needed to get to know Deana's life before they could feel her death. Bobbie Roberts, Deana's sister Jane, Deana's aunt and uncle Russell and Betsey Abner, Jay Wild, and two of Deana's high school friends from Louisville each offered a portrait of the Deana they knew. Not one left the stand dry-eyed.

Bobbie Roberts testified first. She told the sad tale of her daughter's life, beginning with the learning disability and ending at Seal

Beach. Though she had recited it a dozen times now, pain still showed in her uneasy gestures and forced smile. Over objections from defense counsel, Aragon played the taped phone call between mother and murderer.

Admitting the tape into evidence at trial posed a subtle legal issue. California and Kentucky viewed "one-party consent" tapes differently. One-party consent laws allow any one person to tape-record a call to an unsuspecting party and then use the tape against them in court. In Kentucky, such calls are legal; not so in California. Bobbie was in Kentucky when she placed and taped the call, but Virginia answered in California.

Judge Revak decided the jury should hear it.

For sixty-six minutes, Virginia's singsong voice filled the room. She explained how she had lost a daughter, too, and that when Deana disappeared at the cliff she and B.J. never heard a sound.

Aragon watched as Virginia scrawled across a yellow pad and tapped Juliana Humphrey on the shoulder to exchange a few words. When the tape finished playing, Aragon noticed Virginia's expression settle into that peculiar look of calculating repose. She tilted back her large head and raised a finger to her chin. She had it all scoped out, she seemed to be saying. In that single moment, Aragon felt he saw the killer peering out from beneath the grandmotherly mask.

Deana's girlhood friends Laurel Peak and Lisa Troutman took the stand and recounted their Louisville memories. All during high school they hung out in a pack, the two reminisced. Their weekends consisted of camping trips where they foraged through the brambles in a nearby piece of wilderness known as Sleepy Hollow.

"It was pretty rough terrain. And we didn't stick to the basic path," Lisa Troutman recalled. "We went out there sometimes at night. And Deana, she was real good. She was the best one out of the group. We had a nickname for her. We called her 'Deanbo,' from 'Rambo.' "

Laurel Peak added that none of the girls liked to get too close to one particular precipice at Sleepy Hollow, a sheer drop-off above a deep pool of water. "We were all too big chickens to get three feet away from the edge of the cliff."

Most of the girls enjoyed a beer here and there, Laurel said, but drugs were definitely out for everyone. Laurel even remembered Deana starting out with a wine cooler at parties. By midnight, she would still be nursing the same half-finished bottle.

Sergeant R. D. Jones next made a brief appearance to play the jury a videotape of Sleepy Hollow. Aragon set up a TV monitor to give the jury a short visual tour of the cliffs and crumbling rock paths where Deana and her friends walked and played without a fatal slip or fall.

After the lights came back on, Deana's husband, Jay Wild, a twenty-six-year-old ex-navy man, took the stand. He leaned toward the microphone and struggled to speak through his tears. With his blond hair cut into a Davy Crockett raccoon cap, his bearded face took on a boyish quality, but sadness had left its scars in a smile that never fully opened.

"Nothin' could get Deana down," Jay said, "nothin'."

He then told the jury a story each member already knew in one form or another: the story of a navy marriage.

"The very next day after Deana and I arrived in San Diego I had to report to the base and they flew me out to the *Kitty Hawk* on a chopper. I didn't know that I'd have to go to the ship the next day," Jay said, shaking his head. "I think it was going to be somewhere around two and a half, two weeks."

Overnight, Deana became the local fixture known as a "West Pac widow." The malls were filled with teenaged wives lost in a big city, their husbands at sea in the Western Pacific with the "West Pac" naval group. A few jurors in the front row nodded sympathetically.

Jay testified that when he got back from his tour of duty, Deana came to meet him at a local club. "She came in and, you know, hugged me, gave me a kiss, and asked me if I was ready to go. She said she didn't want me to go back to the ship. She hated to see me leave. I told her I really didn't have much choice."

The next time Jay came back, he said, he took Deana to the Royal Apartments and rented her a room. For three months, up until December 1986, Jay was at sea for all but two weeks.

"I think everybody in the navy feels the same way. You know, she wanted companionship and friendship and love. But by January, it was over. She wouldn't come back to me. There wasn't anything left for me to do but go on. She had left me a note saying that if I wanted a divorce she wouldn't stop me, but I had never talked to her about a divorce before that."

Jay said he learned of Deana's death while back on the *Kitty Hawk* in the Gulf of Oman. Seven or eight hours later, he flew to Oman and from there into L.A. He called the mortuary in Monterey, they released the body, and Jay flew home to Louisville.

Deana's uncle Russell Abner made perhaps the deepest impression on the jury. Russell was a granite-faced man, a hardened Kentucky truck driver with steel-colored hair and a weather-beaten face. He walked with a cane and spoke in sentences delivered like short, hard punches.

But when Russell Abner started to testify, his stoic bearing gave way. Twice during forty minutes of testimony, the hard-bitten trucker was rendered speechless by tears.

"I considered Deana as belonging to me," he said. "She went to church. She kept her room clean. And at church she would baby-sit for the preacher's daughter. During summertime, we told her, when she got up, we told her what to do. And when we come home, she'd done it."

"Do you think that Deana trusted people?" Aragon asked.

"Yes. That was her problem," Abner said.

"Why do you say it was her problem?"

"Well, as long as you were good to Deana, you could talk her into anything."

Tamayo used cross-examination with each of the witnesses to reinforce his own theory of a "San Diego Deana" who ran from her husband, experimented with drugs and sex, and held herself out as an unmarried woman. Bobbie admitted that Deana had once stolen checks from her and tried to cash them at school. Laurel and Lisa recalled that, back in Louisville, Deana hung around with an older man who tended to drink too much. Russell Abner seemed to contradict Bobbie Roberts's statements about Deana's learning disability when he insisted that Deana had no trouble in school.

With Jay Wild, Tamayo went through memories the young widower surely wanted to leave behind forever. He lingered over the day Jay found a strange man sleeping in his bed when he came back from his third cruise aboard the *Kitty Hawk*. Deana wasn't at the apartment, Jay insisted. But innuendos of infidelity hung thick in the air.

Tamayo then asked Jay whether he hadn't suspected Deana of using drugs.

Jay Wild's reddened eyes narrowed. He answered slowly and deliberately, commanding the courtroom: "Deana—never—used—drugs."

At the end of the second week of trial, a pair of corrections officers escorted Jimmy Coates to the stand. Coates had recently violated parole again, but the return to prison only seemed to have hardened him. For two full days, he slouched in his hospital green prison-issue garb, testifying with the same cocky attitude he had at the preliminary hearing.

Judge Revak kept Coates's murder conviction from the jury. Like Virginia's past, this bit of truth was "too prejudicial." But Aragon ensured that the panel immediately learned about the many felony convictions that had kept Coates in prison for twelve out of the last fifteen years.

Above all, Aragon hoped Coates's presence would convey one subliminal message to the jurors: To believe Virginia, the matronly woman seated at the defense table, is innocent, you have to believe she wanted *this man* to collect money in the event of Deana's death. He began by asking Coates how he earned his living in late 1986 when he met Deana.

"I was probably dealing drugs or something along them lines," Coates said in a speech slurred by recent dental surgery that left him with an ill-fitting pair of dentures. "But I never do no drug activity around my people," he assured the jury. "I didn't tie off and fix in front of 'em. I would go in the bathroom and lock the door, you know. . . . But when I'm on the streets, all I do is narcotics, okay? I'm a dope fiend."

Coates hewed close to the tale he had spun at the preliminary hearing. He met Deana in mid-October and they started living together at Virginia's house by early January. Sometime that month, he gave her a ring to cement their engagement.

"You tell us that your relationship with Deana was casual in 1986. And you had known her about two weeks in January of 1987," Aragon stated. "Why the rush to ask Deana to marry you?"

"Well, I liked Deana. I knew I was going back to prison, and I wanted some boneyard visits and a runner. You know, 'congenial' visits."

Aragon tried to bait Coates: "So you believed you knew Deana well enough to spend the rest of your life with her?"

Coates mugged for the jury as he answered, "Marriage is a crap-shoot, you know, as far as I'm concerned. It either works or it doesn't. At the time, I believed it would have worked. She did, too."

Coates's testimony, in its way, was honest—a quality Aragon found unsettling. The jury might well believe that Coates actually had been engaged to Deana. The man said he wanted a steady supply of sex and drugs in prison; that seemed in character. He wasn't offering up some absurd fiction about wanting to reform, get an honest job, and raise kids in the suburbs.

Better move on to motive, Aragon thought.

"You tell us that you weren't bringing any money into the house in January of '87. Is that true?"

"Yes."

"And Mr. McGinnis, he wasn't bringing any money into the house in 1987. Is that true?"

"No, he wasn't."

"And Deana wasn't working. She wasn't bringing any money in. Is that true?"

"Correct."

"And the money that your mother had was from disability? Is that true?"

"That's correct."

"Is it safe to say that money was pretty tight in the McGinnis household in January of '87?"

"As far as financial things were. I guess, yeah."

"Was there money to spare? Was there money to spend on things other than the necessities of life?"

"In the household? No."

When Aragon shifted subjects to the insurance policy, Coates leaned back defensively in the witness box. His tone was curt: "Mom asked me about the life insurance and what I wanted done. And I asked her to take care of it. I just said, 'Take care of it.' Period."

"Did you ask her how much the policy was for?"

"I probably did ask for the policy, but I don't remember."

"You didn't have much interest in it?"

"I never did. I offered to give it all to charity." This, Aragon knew, was utter nonsense, and he could easily prove so.

"Which charity did you make that offer to, Mr. Coates?" he asked, letting Coates improvise details.

"You'd have to talk to my attorney, Mr. O'Connell. I believe he has it all in writing with Bobbie's attorney and Mr. Keeney."

"Did you offer to give any of this money to Deana's family in Louisville or Lexington?"

"Well, Bobbie was really bein' kind of a bitch about the situation, so I didn't offer her nothin'."

After eight hours of questioning, zig-zagging across every detail of his "engagement" to Deana, Aragon turned Coates over to the defense. His lies about wanting to give the policy proceeds to charity, he hoped, would destroy Coates's standing with the jury—not to mention his callous reference to Bobbie Roberts.

Juliana Humphrey cross-examined. Whenever Juliana spoke in court, she made much of her hands—pointing, stroking her chin, gesturing in large arcs. But today she kept her examination of Jimmy Coates low-key and pithy. This dope-shooting felon was Virginia's flesh and blood. It wouldn't take a jury long to figure that a person with Coates's mentality might not be the product of your ordinary mom.

Instead of trying to discredit Coates, or even to rehabilitate him, Humphrey used him to tar Deana's character. The worse Coates looked, she seemed to figure, the worse Deana looked. And the less the jury would accept the DA's characterization of Deana as an innocent girl from Kentucky. From there, it would be only a short step to believing she could have committed suicide or just stumbled in one reckless and fatal move.

In his jailhouse argot, Coates unabashedly explained that he spent most of 1986 and early 1987 fixing heroin, four or five times day.

"My number-one priority was shootin' dope and bein' with women," he said, reveling in shocking the middle-aged, middle-class jurors. "It was the most important thing in my life. If it came down to giving money to my mother or 'gettin' well,' I'd get well."

Deana never injected any drugs, he admitted. "That's one of the things I liked about her a lot. I would rather support my habit than her habit. I get more." But he and Deana would pop pills together or smoke dope. Coates added that he didn't mind supplying Deana with pills, since they were a dime a dozen.

Humphrey let Coates pour on the "terrifying dope fiend" routine with one final attention-getting question: "Mr. Coates, if you had a choice between heroin and sex with a woman, which would you pick?"

"I'd pick that outfit in a heartbeat." Coates smiled.

"An outfit of heroin?"

"That's right."

Aragon looked over at Virginia, expecting some sign of emotion. Here was her son testifying about fixing heroin at her own murder trial, but he saw nothing beneath her cold, green-eyed stare.

"Okay, Mr. Coates," Humphrey pressed on, "how much money did you get from the insurance policy on Deana Hubbard?"

"I'm not sure of the exact amount. I know it was over five thousand that I got personally, plus my lawyer got his issue."

"You didn't give any of that to your mother, did you?"

"No, I didn't."

"Basically, you spent it, didn't you?"

"Fast," Coates said, gloating.

"What did you spend it on?"

"A good time . . . a lot of drugs. I invested a little bit and turned that over and kept on going. I was seven, eight months, I guess, rolling pretty good with my paycheck and that."

"You invested some of it in drugs, and sold it to make more?"

"Yeah. I bought two pieces, turned it over and fixed out of that and did my methadone, and went to work every day, and shot dope every day and cocaine and sold drugs."

Humphrey decided it was time to bring Coates's testimony to a close. Like any good trial lawyer, she had saved her strongest point for last.

"Was B.J. ever involved in trying to make a claim on Deana's insurance proceeds?" she asked.

"No. I hired my attorney Bill O'Connell myself."

"Your mom didn't find Bill O'Connell, did she?"

"No. I just picked him."

Humphrey sat down and cast a sidelong look of success at Aragon.

Aragon always felt a knot in the pit of his stomach when Humphrey cross-examined. She had a way of turning damning facts to her own advantage, and she had just done it with Coates. If Virginia wanted the insurance money badly enough to kill Deana for it, her cross-examination implied, then why sit back and let her dope-fiend son get even a piece? Obviously, Virginia didn't care about the money. And what kind of good, clean-living, Kentucky girl *chooses* to live with Coates? Both of these questions, Aragon knew, sprung from facts that came from his own witnesses' mouths.

At 5:00 A.M. on the morning of January 17, the twelve jurors and three alternates were herded into a chartered plane, flown to San Jose, then bused fifty miles over to a hotel in Monterey. From there, they boarded the same bus and headed down the coast to the site of Deana's death.

Everyone had trouble concentrating on the testimony during the following two days, since the trip to Seal Beach was ushered in with perfect azure blue Northern California weather. A cloud or two lazed across the sky, the temperature hovered at seventy-five degrees, and the Pacific sparkled so brightly, it seemed to be showing off. The coastal cliffs to the north and south cut knife-edged silhouettes down to the sea. If the earthquake during James Coates's testimony at the preliminary hearing was the rumbling of an angry god, this seemed to Aragon to be a blessing. In any event, he knew, it would be a pivotal moment.

The cliff itself had been turned into one immense courtroom exhibit. Voices of prosecution witnesses were broadcast from radio microphones over speakers set at each end of the turnout. The boulders at the cliff edge bore large blue numbers for easy reference. Below the edge, Day-Glo markings indicated where Deana's shoes and body had been found.

The place was standing room only. A court stenographer sat with her stenographic machine beside Judge Revak. The jurors squeezed shoulder-to-shoulder in folding chairs facing the ocean. A sound crew mixed microphone levels from a remote board near their van while a videographer tagged after witnesses. Each pair of lawyers spread out their notes on folding tables. And Virginia took her place between her attorneys, just yards from the spot where Deana had fallen to her death five years earlier.

As if to downplay any danger, Aragon and Long both wore full business attire and leather-soled shoes or pumps. Humphrey and Tamayo, too, played to their version of the scene. Juliana wore jeans and cowboy boots. Tamayo sported an ostentatiously white pair of sneakers—an advertisement for requisite caution and sensible shoes on this deadly bluff.

Jurors kept their sunglasses on. The lawyers would have worn them, too, but hiding behind shades was no way to win trust. Instead, they tried the case squint-eyed, examining witnesses against a backdrop that extended miles out to a blue and white horizon. It was one of the most strange and magnificent courtrooms ever convened on the face of the planet.

The DA's witnesses—four officers and two civilians—testified with requisite formality. Scott Lawrence demonstrated where each of Virginia's snapshots was taken. Lawrence then posed Aragon and Long in the exact positions where Deana and B.J. had stood in Photo 11: Aragon's hand on Long's back, his leg cocked, body ready to spring forward and push her to her death. They held the pose and let the cliff edge at Long's feet speak for itself.

Deborah Cross, the woman who managed the Coast Gallery, recounted how Virginia had come huffing in, almost apoplectic with worry about a girl who had fallen. She demonstrated how they had come back to the scene and looked in vain for Deana's body. Along the way, she said, Virginia told her that she didn't know how she would break the news to the girl's mother—who Virginia said was a "good friend."

John Burke, dressed in his olive drab Sheriff's uniform, detailed the rescue procedures. It was impossible to see from the top where Deana's body had come to rest, Burke said. This statement would later stand in stark contrast to Virginia's remark to Mac McCain that she saw Deana "down among the seals," and her statement to Deputy Coroner Dave Dungan that she saw Deana's body "lying on the rocks."

Burke then climbed down the edge of the cliff and placed an electric blue high-heeled shoe in the spot where he had found Deana's first shoe five years before. The videographer followed as each juror went to peer down the rugged incline.

Aragon took in Virginia's reaction with a kind of clinical interest. Even here at the scene of Deana's death, her green eyes, magnified by her eyeglasses, remained impenetrable. Occasionally, she managed a distant smile, but otherwise her face settled back into a half-vacant, half-malevolent gaze.

The remaining witnesses—Deputy Richard Schmaltz, Sheriff Jess Mason, Donald Smythe, the New Age minister Robert Brian Lyke—all added their pieces to the picture. Taken together, their testimony boiled down to one unified impression: the McGinnises seemed strangely unmoved for people who had just lost a close friend in a tragic accident. There were no tears, no worried frowns, not even an anxious question. In Deborah Cross's words, it seemed like "a *fait accompli.*"

Tamayo reserved the bulk of his cross-examination for San Diego. But he was not about to leave before driving two points home.

Six times—once with each witness—he gestured toward Grimes Point at the north and asked whether an A-frame house that jutted out just below the road level had been in the same spot back in 1987. Everyone agreed it had.

The inference was obvious: Would the McGinnises be so stupid as to commit murder in plain view of someone's living room? Aragon had accused them of a well-executed month-long murder plot. Surely they would have chosen a more secluded location.

Tamayo then drew the jury's attention to a six-inch metal stake poking through the ground just a few feet from where Deana and B.J. had posed for the final snapshot. The Big Sur locals readily agreed that the stake had been there in 1987. In fact, they recalled it being a few inches taller. . . .

When the second day of open-air testimony came to a close, Judge Revak allowed the jury to inspect the turnout on their own. Aragon's heart sank as he watched each member of the panel walk up to the rusty stake Tamayo had pointed out and tap it with their shoes. The stiff and corroded metal rod blended in perfectly with the ruddy ground. If the jurors were looking for a reasonable doubt that Deana's death was accidental, they could find it right at their feet.

While jurors poked and tapped at the ground, Judge Revak walked over to Virginia, sitting alone at the folding table, her lawyers conferring over the day's events at the far end of the turnout.

"You can stay here and observe," he said to Virginia. "It's all part of the case."

She looked back and ground out a few words: "Get me out of here." Revak signaled to a pair of corrections officers, who discreetly escorted her into a waiting squad car. Revak looked again and saw Virginia wiping tears from her eyes. Testimony at the cliff site was over.

▼

Back in the sealed courtroom, Aragon laid out more facts in painstaking, graphic detail. He used over a hundred exhibits—videos, slides, documents blown up to poster size—and put on twenty more witnesses. By now, he hoped, the jurors would care enough about Deana herself to be willing to absorb a few weeks of technical analysis.

Handwriting expert Sandra Homewood described the signatures of Alice Kissane on the insurance-claim form as inartful forgeries crafted with the classic backward slant of "disguised handwriting." At Homewood's request, Virginia had provided handwriting exemplars, writing her own name side by side with Alice Kissane's. Projected against a screen in a darkened courtroom, the samples unmistakably matched the signature purporting to be Kissane's.

Homewood delivered her conclusion in one sentence: "I was able to positively identify Virginia McGinnis as having written all of the printing on the claimant form."

That's one count down, Aragon thought contentedly. All along he knew that proving forgery was a foregone conclusion. But that also didn't mean much. If convicted on that count only, Virginia faced a sentence that amounted to Time Served.

Cross-examination lasted less than five minutes, but Tamayo did his best to weaken Homewood's impact.

"You asked Virginia to actually go ahead and do the exemplars?"

"Yes, I did," Homewood said.

"She made no attempts to disguise her handwriting in any way?"

"Nothing significant, no."

Tamayo retired to his seat, letting the inference hang in the air: Why would a guilty party cooperate?

Art and Mac McCain's testimony lasted for three grueling days.

Aragon took both father and son through the same narrative they had told to Steve Keeney, various State Farm agents, Scott Lawrence, the Monterey investigators, and Judge Kasimatis at the preliminary hearing. Aragon had the red-flag memo Mac had attached to Deana's and B.J.'s insurance application enlarged into a poster and placed before the jury.

While they described the events in their little Chula Vista office, Aragon felt a profound sadness descend over the courtroom. The jury was beginning to visualize Virginia grimly pursuing her prey.

And for the first time, perhaps, the ugliness of Deana's murder became palpable.

To Albert Tamayo, the McCains represented targets to be taken down. During cross-examination, he took Art McCain through Deana's application process, emphasizing that Deana herself voluntarily answered more than two dozen questions and signed the policy herself. Art next admitted that Deana, in fact, supplied almost all the information on the application and had mutely expressed her assent at naming Jimmy, Virginia, and B.J. as beneficiaries. He also agreed that Deana gave her last name as Hubbard, not Wild, and described her marital status as "single."

Aragon felt each answer as a solid blow to his theory about a sham engagement. Deana certainly knew how to say "I'm married and my last name is Wild." But she hadn't.

Before sitting down, Tamayo asked Art McCain whether Deana was free to change the beneficiaries whenever she wanted. Art admitted that she was free to change them at any time. Points in the defense's favor seemed to be adding up quickly.

Aragon had warned Mac McCain that he would be attacked more viciously that any other witness. Tamayo did not disappoint. He began innocently enough, going over minute details of the insurance transaction: where Deana had been sitting; exactly how Virginia had "grabbed" the insurance policy; and her demeanor when she announced Deana had died.

At regular junctures, Tamayo interrupted the flow of events to ask, "You remember these events vividly even though they happened *five years ago*?" He drew out the last words each time he asked the question.

Each time Mac McCain patiently repeated that he remembered the events as if they had happened yesterday.

Finally, Tamayo forced the issue: "This is something that you and your son had talked about over and over again after these events transpired?" Tamayo asked.

"Yes," McCain agreed.

"But you referred to a number of things my client said, and you quoted her verbatim. Do you really recall her comments word for word after five years?"

"I don't think I'll ever forget her words," McCain said.

"But since you heard those words, you've been interviewed by a number of people—police officers, State Farm investigators, the district attorney's investigators—and you've talked about these events over and over with your son, Art, and your secretary, isn't that correct?"

"Yes," Mac McCain repeated.

"Mr. McCain," Tamayo pressed, "you mentioned that there were a couple of statements Virginia made on her way out the door when she had picked up the policy. One of the questions was, 'Now this is in force, right?' Is that right?"

"That was the question."

"But Mr. McCain, that's a fairly common question asked by most people who take out life-insurance policies?"

"Yes," Mac hemmed. "Yes, it is."

"Okay." Tamayo glanced at the jury. "And when Virginia asked the second question, 'Does this policy cover accidental death?' you replied 'No.' Is that correct?"

"That's correct," Mac said.

"Did you explain it any further?"

"No," Mac answered. "No further questions were asked."

"And that was the last you saw of Virginia on that particular day?"

"That's correct." Mac nodded. Aragon noticed the jury studiously taking down his words in their notebooks. McCain had explained during direct examination that by "No," he meant, "The policy doesn't pay double indemnity for accidental death." But Tamayo was not interested in unspoken subtleties.

During the following day, Tamayo brought Mac McCain's cross-examination to a head.

"Yesterday, you talked about your concerns about this policy on Deana Hubbard," Tamayo said. "You told us that one of the reasons for your concern was the McGinnises' prior claims. Do you remember that?"

"That would have been an additional reason," Mac agreed.

"But the main reason was the beneficiaries and those things shown on the application." Tamayo's voice started to rise.

"Right," McCain answered cautiously.

"Because of the concern about the insurable interest?" Tamayo pressed, his voice still up.

"Correct."

"What else? What else caused your suspicions?"

"The previous record. Right," McCain said hesitatingly.

"Well, isn't it true that the reason you didn't want to send this binding was because you thought that if you issued this policy, Deana would be *killed*?" Tamayo was almost shouting as he finished the question.

McCain took a breath before answering, "That was in our mind. Yes."

Tamayo hit the point again. "You were concerned that this was a person who, if this policy was issued, she would be killed. *She would be as good as dead!*"

"I didn't say that," McCain answered, backing off. "That was a concern of mine, though."

The courtroom fell silent as Tamayo followed out his argument.

"Yet given that feeling you had that she was going to be killed, your response was, I'll go ahead and send the policy nonbinding."

"That's correct."

"And the only follow-up that we had was this little piece of paper stapled to an envelope with a little red flag drawn on it? There were no other efforts other than this one phone call to Stan Sodomka. Correct?"

"Correct," McCain agreed.

"And your response to that, rather than making a phone call back to State Farm protesting it, was to give the policy to the individuals who came in and to take their check. Correct?"

McCain looked uncomfortably at Aragon as he answered, "Correct."

"What about *re*submitting it to Stan Sodomka? Did you ever think for a moment that maybe Stan Sodomka may have misunderstood what you talked about?"

"I don't think he did. We talked to him on the phone."

"And it was very clear to you at the time you told Sodomka you were concerned that this girl was going to be killed? You had no doubt that Stan Sodomka understood what you were saying?"

"That's my thought, right."

"Is Stan Sodomka the *only* person you could have contacted at State Farm regarding your feelings and suspicions?"

"He was at the top." McCain's expression hardened, but Tamayo kept after him.

"How much more effort would it have been to make a simple phone call or write a memorandum or a letter involving your suspicions on the life of a girl?"

"I don't think it would have accomplished anything."

"You just gave up and decided, Well, it's the life of a girl. I suspect she's going to be killed, but—" Tamayo let the half-finished question stand unanswered. The only inference could be that Mac, in fact, never suspected a thing.

After the McCains, a series of expert witnesses dutifully took the stand. A civil engineer introduced a scale map of the overlook. Deputies from the Search and Rescue team drew in the approximate fall path of Deana's body, the original location of each of Deana's shoes, as well as where the McGinnises told them they last saw Deana before she fell.

With each of the witnesses, Tamayo pursued the same line of questioning: "Big Sur is a pretty dangerous area, isn't that right?"

The witnesses concurred. People get injured there all the time, they said. Especially when they try to climb down the cliff face.

Aragon decided that the argument had just enough value that he needed to counter it. Tamayo's experts on "coefficient of friction" might be able to tie together these stray comments into a credible defense, and of course there was that six-inch stake at the scene. Aragon asked officers Burke, Smythe, Mason, and Schmaltz the same question: "Have you ever in your years of working the Big Sur area known a person to fall off the top of Seal Beach overlook?"

"No" was the unanimous response.

Tamayo chose to force the issue. Halfway through John Burke's testimony, he asked Judge Revak to excuse the jury and the witness. With the courtroom cleared, Tamayo pointed out one major assumption underlying the People's case:

"Burke is testifying that, in his experience, never has there been a fall from the top. Well, it's not relevant here, because no one's arguing that Deana was at the very top. We don't know where she was—unless the district attorney is going to bring forward a witness to testify that the only way this could have happened is a fall from the very top."

Judge Revak agreed that the absence of falls from the top of Seal Beach, standing alone, didn't prove a thing. But he added that all of Tamayo's questions about Big Sur being a dangerous place might have left a false impression in the jurors' minds. He would allow Aragon some latitude.

With Burke back on the stand, Aragon circled gingerly around the issue.

"Was there any physical evidence that allowed you to believe that you were rappeling down in the fall path?"

"There was brush that was bent back," Burke said. "There were little signs of where somebody or something had moved the dirt or the granite out of the way, like somebody walking across a wet field. I've been to enough tracking schools in my tenure to know how to track people and stuff like that. Broken brush, rocks missing, turned-up earth, blood . . ."

"At what point did you see physical indications that, based on your training and experience, caused you to believe that you were on the right path?"

"Fifteen feet," Burke answered.

"From the top?" Aragon asked

"From the top. Or less."

It was a victory for the prosecution, Aragon thought. He had pinpointed the site of Deana's fall to within ten or fifteen feet from the surface of the turnout, and thus reduced the possibility that Deana had hiked well below the top. But by the end of trial, he came to regret ever asking the question.

Alex Lutzi, an investigator with the DA's Office, had executed a search warrant at Virginia's home in Pittsburg, California, at the time of her arrest. On the witness stand, the strapping young officer testified with the eagerness of a new recruit. Yet all his energies turned up only three even remotely incriminating items: a Kodak disc camera; a thick reference book entitled *Drugs*; and a copy of Deana's birth certificate. Otherwise, the place was clean; just an ordinary home.

On cross, Tamayo asked Lutzi about the extent of his search. It encompassed all of Virginia's papers and bookshelves, even her bedroom dresser. Yet the sum of the damning evidence he found was these three items.

Dr. William Hoops, the now-retired pathologist who conducted Deana's autopsy, testified next. Given his advanced age and the passage of time, Hoops had no recall of the actual exam; it blended in with the thousands he had done in his thirty-year career. When shown photographs of Deana's battered hands, he said he didn't notice anything unusual. Aragon rephrased the question, trying to get comments about the broken fingernails into evidence, but Hoops wouldn't budge.

This was an utterly unexpected setback. The condition of Deana's nails tended to prove that she had clawed for her life at the cliff edge, and, therefore, must have screamed for help. It flatly contradicted Virginia's story about not hearing a sound. But if the jury accepted Hoops's word, the photos were as innocent as a manicurist's advertisement. Aragon had no choice but to press on.

The next expert witnesses walked through the Elavil issue unchallenged. Two forensic toxicologists testified that they had tested Deana's blood and urine—once, days after Deana's autopsy, and, again at the San Diego DA's request in 1989. Both tests detected amitriptyline and nortriptyline, the component drugs in Elavil. A pharmacist from Kaiser-Permanente brought in records to show that B.J. refilled his prescription for Elavil on February 20, 1987. Dr. Sidney Zisook detailed the effects of Elavil, the unsteadiness, blurry vision, and feelings of nausea that accompany even small doses of the drug.

Their testimony, well grounded in fact, appeared open and shut. Tamayo gave them wide berth.

When Scott Lawrence came by Martha Grant's house looking for information about Deana's death, the young mother of three was happy to oblige. The McGinnises, her next-door neighbors in Chula Vista, had worried her for years.

On the witness stand, Grant emanated a kind of armored sincerity. She had an attractive face, even-featured, blue-eyed, and framed by blond bangs and a neat white blouse. But she also wore the firm expression of a woman determined never to be duped.

She recalled the Thursday in April of 1987 when the McGinnises left to drive up the coast. Virginia had come by her house at the last minute and asked Martha to take in their mail while they were gone.

"Was there any mention made of Tsunami, the dog?" Aragon asked.

"I did ask about the dog and was told that they were going to leave the dog in the backyard with food for him."

Grant said she didn't think much about the conversation until a few days later when she saw Virginia and B.J. standing in front of their house.

"I was pulling in my driveway," she testified. "I walked down to check the mail, and B.J. and Virginia were standing near their gate and I was very surprised to see them. I was thinking that they were going to be gone much longer. We spoke for a few minutes. Virginia said that a friend's daughter fell off a cliff and they didn't feel up to finishing their vacation." Aragon let that last phrase sink in.

On cross-examination, Tamayo pressed Grant about her neighbors.

"The McGinnises were pretty good neighbors, weren't they?"

"Yes," she answered.

"They weren't real loud neighbors, were they?"

"No."

"Always kept the yard up?"

"Yes."

"Never parked cars in front of your house?"

"No. They were nice neighbors in that way."

"Probably ideal neighbors, wouldn't you say?"

"Yes," Grant said with a trace of reluctance.

"They wouldn't talk to you about everything in their lives, then, I take it?"

"They talked about a lot of personal things that I don't think anybody should discuss with somebody else," Grant said, practically begging for a follow-up question.

Tamayo steered clear. "They kept their lawn clean and mowed, didn't they?"

"Yes," she said.

"In fact, they were basically your ideal neighbors, isn't that right?"

"Well . . . yes."

Aragon had no questions for a redirect exam and so Martha Grant stepped down from the stand.

That night, she tossed in bed. She never got to speak her mind and that kept her stewing. Somehow, in the heat of the moment, Tamayo had transformed the McGinnises into "ideal neighbors." And in Martha's opinion, nothing could have been further from the truth.

She came back to court the next day, hoping to set the record straight.

"They were liars," she told Aragon privately, catching him during a break in the case. "B.J. hung around all day in the front yard drinking. He'd come up to me and brag about being an ex-army psychologist and about going with Jimmy to strip clubs." Martha's face twisted into a look of supreme disgust.

"He even boasted about the orgies he and Virginia had in their Jacuzzi. He told me I was lucky we had such a tall fence between our houses. My husband and I got to the point that we'd pull our car up to the garage, open the carport, drive in, and wait for it to close before getting out. We were that afraid of them. And I'm sure their son Jimmy was the one that broke into their house and stole all that jewelry."

When court reconvened, Aragon called a sidebar conference. He argued that unless Grant was allowed to retake the witness stand, the jury would be misled. Revak warned that Aragon was flirting with a mistrial if Grant got into any of the McGinnises' unsavory private habits or speculations about a robbery. All she could do would be to explain that the McGinnises were *not* ideal neighbors.

In the end, Martha Grant left Department 22 even more frustrated than the day before. Her sanitized testimony barely scratched the surface about the goings-on next door. But at least she had tried.

By early February, Aragon had made it down to his last two witnesses. He was too exhausted to feel sure of how to read the jury. He knew he had made every point he set out to, but Tamayo and Humphrey had pounced on every hole. The jury, he suspected, would be deliberating for a full week, maybe more. He worried briefly over his decision not to call Debbie Williams, who could testify about Jimmy Coates saying that Virginia told him she had murdered Deana. But it was too late. There was nothing left to do but follow the script.

Diana Rael, a pixie-haired investigator for State Farm who wore a snappy blue suit and bright silk scarf, looked as if she belonged more in the public relations office than the criminal investigations bureau. But that impression quickly dissolved when Rael played a tape of her interview of Virginia and Billie Joe McGinnis in January of 1988 at Jimmy Coates's lawyer's office. On the tape, she smoothly drew out Virginia's contradictions and lies without ever tipping her hand.

"Regarding the insurance for Deana, how did that come about?" Rael's voice crackled from the tape recorder.

"Initially . . . we . . . had gone in," Virginia answered. "My husband had gone in to get some insurance. Deana was with us, and Deana said, 'What am I, chopped liver?' And I looked at her, I said, 'Deana.' And she says, well I have insurance, . . ."

"How were the beneficiaries decided?"

"Deana decided that she wanted Jim to be beneficiary and she says, 'I guess you and B.J.' "

Aragon hoped that the tape proved at least one thing beyond a reasonable doubt: Virginia lied as easily and smoothly as someone giving directions to the supermarket. She lied about who named the beneficiaries, about Deana wanting life insurance, about the kennel for her dog, and about Alice Kissane's signature. And why would she lie unless she had something to hide?

Every night, Keeney had been conferring with Aragon, getting regular updates and honing trial strategy. Before eight o'clock Louisville time, he paced his house in a state of nervous preoccupation, smoking cigarettes and polishing off two or three tall-boy cups of coffee. The intense mood was nothing new; during trials, he often lived in a fog bank. He liked to tell friends how he once walked straight into a swimming pool—cigar, wristwatch, suit, and all—while practicing a closing argument.

But trying a case long-distance ratcheted him up to another notch of preoccupation. He thought up objections not made and questions unasked, worried over Tamayo's shifting line of defense. Two years earlier, he would have welcomed the Monterey DA stepping in and running the prosecution. Now, relegated to the sidelines, he realized he wanted nothing more than to try the case himself. He felt like Tantalus, tormented at his infernal dinner table by dishes of food that moved out of reach at the last moment. This must be Attorney Hell, he thought. For lack of being able to help in person, Keeney sent Aragon a slew of memos. Thirty pages on Elavil. Seventy pages on suicide and "assisted suicide." A short treatise on Dr. Elizabeth Loftus—one of the defense's experts.

"Steve, calm down. You're like a caged animal," Wynn scolded as he wandered through the kitchen and nearly elbowed a cake on a platter. "You'll drive us all crazy, and there's nothing you can do."

"What? Oh, sorry," he answered vaguely as he refilled his cup of coffee. "By the way, did Luis call?"

Aragon had been simultaneously underoing his own anxieties. He worried about Mac McCain telling Virginia that the policy *didn't* cover accidental death, about Virginia cooperating with Sandra Homewood, about Deana's behavior in the insurance agency, about

Virginia's allowing her son to get the insurance money. And he still fretted over the cliff-site visit: the stake and the A-frame posed real problems. After all, he worried, even the Big Sur Search and Rescue team had initially bought Virginia's story. He kept thinking, one side or the other had miscalculated.

Deputy Coroner David Dungan, however, was the witness Aragon worried over the most.

Dungan looked out from the witness stand across an audience of news reporters, lawyers, observers, and bailiffs, with a sheepishness rarely seen in career police officers. *'I found nothing to even slightly indicate foul play.'* The line had eaten at him ever since the McGinnises' arrest. Having spent six and a half years as an officer with both army intelligence and police, and four and a half years with the Monterey Coroner's Office, Dungan had too much professional pride to quickly forgive himself that error.

His brown eyes, looking out above his narrow-shouldered frame draped in a loose-fitting corduroy jacket, made him appear doleful, almost like a man waiting for the gallows. And he appeared visibly tense, as if someone had asked him to pull a length of rope as taut as possible as long as he remained on the stand.

Aragon knew Tamayo would attack Dungan's testimony every bit as hard as he had Mac McCain's—although that was precisely because Dungan could so thoroughly damn Virginia.

Under Aragon's questioning, Dungan testified that he interviewed Virginia and B.J. behind the coroner's substation in the Monterey twilight of April 2. He had gone through his usual list of questions, obtained Bobbie Roberts's phone number from Virginia's personal phone book and gotten Deana's purse from the trunk of their car. The McGinnises then described how, after taking snapshots and heading back to their car, they eventually looked over the edge of the cliff and saw Deana's body lying on the rocks.

Dungan went on: "I always ask, in every kind of case, including natural deaths, about the mental state of the deceased and the existence of any insurance. I always phrase the question in the same manner regardless of the type of investigation. I always ask, and I asked Mrs. McGinnis, 'Do you know of the existence of any insurance on the deceased or that the deceased may have taken out on herself?' I was told by Mrs. McGinnis that she did not know of any.

I then turned to Mr. McGinnis and asked the same question and he said, 'No. I don't.'

"I then asked if I could take the camera and develop that film. I remember promising Mrs. McGinnis I would return the camera."

"What response, if any, did you receive?"

"I was told I couldn't have the camera right at that time, that the photographs would be developed and a copy would be sent to the Coroner's Office later on."

Dungan then described directing the couple to a nearby motel where they could spend the night. The following morning, he called to go through the same questions.

"Nothing deviated from the previous day's information," he said. After a few wrap-up questions about never receiving Virginia's promised snapshots, Aragon sat down and held his breath.

Tamayo began cross-examination by reviewing some innocuous subjects: Dungan's inventory of Deana's possessions; exactly where Dungan had been earlier that day; how much time had elapsed from the time of Deana's death until their interview.

Dungan answered politely but cautiously. He knew what was coming. It took Tamayo only a few more questions to get to the heart of his inquiry.

"You ask about insurance in every death you investigate. Is that your testimony?"

"Yes, sir."

"Whom do you ask that question of?"

"Number one, the persons who are with the individual when the event occurred—immediate family members, maybe close friends."

Tamayo stepped forward, squaring off with Dungan. "You never really did ask that question, did you?"

Dungan paused. Aragon saw the jurors's pens poised to take down the answer.

"Yes," he said. "I did ask that question."

"You asked that question because it was pretty important to you?" Tamayo asked with a note of sarcasm.

"That, and other questions," Dungan countered.

"Because it's so important, you never included it in your report?"

Dungan restrained himself and answered simply: "That's correct."

"You never referred to the question," Tamayo snapped back. "You never stated the question. And you don't have any answers to the question in any of your reports. Yet this was an important question for you?"

Dungan fell silent; Tamayo kept at him.

"Didn't you just testify that you know your report is going to be read and reviewed by the pathologists and the coroners in your county?"

"That's correct."

"Something as important as that, something you would ask not once but twice, you didn't include on any of the subsequent pages of your report?"

"Amendments to the report can be made later on as the information is fully developed," Dungan answered defensively.

"Right." Tamayo spun toward the jury. "And did you include that information on any amendment?"

"No, I have not," Dungan answered, trying, remain confident in the face of an answer he knew to be inadequate.

"Deputy Dungan, you never told Detective Don Smythe about this question and answer involving insurance until it was important to you, a year and a half later?"

"No. That's not correct," Dungan fired back.

"You knew about the insurance about two or three weeks after the incident. Isn't that right?"

"It was several weeks after. At that time, I notified the investigations division."

"And yet you never talked to Smythe about that question and answer?"

"I certainly—well I don't know if I spoke with Detective Smythe," Dungan hemmed. "But I know I spoke with his supervisor."

Tamayo looked confidently at the jury as he sat down. He knew he had given them still one more reason to find a reasonable doubt.

Dungan, looking a good deal more pale than when he had begun testifying that morning, thanked the court and walked down the center aisle to the exit at the rear.

Aragon glanced around the courtroom, past the 105 prosecution exhibits that lay scattered in stacks. Then he consulted with Anna Long and, once more, panned across the jurors' faces.

"Your Honor," he said, rising to his feet, "the People rest."

CHAPTER 29

JUNKIES, INSURANCE EXECS, AND HIRED GUNS

▼

Joyce Braden set a peculiar tone for the first week of the defense case. A stringy-haired, nearly emaciated blond dressed in a stained shirt and ragged jeans, Joyce took the stand and immediately began crying. Her hands shook, an affect explained when she revealed that she was currently following a regimen of methadone.

Joyce told the jury that Virginia put her up back in 1975 when she and Jimmy Coates were going together. They used to steal things from the house so they could buy drugs, Joyce said, but Virginia never asked for a penny in recompense or in rent.

Aragon waited for the story to tie in with Deana, but it never did. Joyce ended by saying that she and Jimmy had talked about getting married ever since she met him. "I always thought we would some day," she said sadly.

Anna Long whispered to Aragon: "The real purpose of Braden's testimony seems to be, Here's one girl who Virginia *didn't* kill."

Aragon smiled back. He knew he could make use of a witness like Joyce Braden.

Cross-examination consisted of three questions. "You believed that at some point you and Jim Coates would get married," Aragon asked. "Is that right?"

"Yes," she sulked.

"Did you discuss that with Virginia?"

"Yeah. I believe I discussed it with her. And I believe she thought someday it would happen."

"When you had those discussions with Virginia, did she suggest that the two of you go out and buy some *life insurance* on you?"

Joyce Braden sobered herself out of her teary state. With unexpected vehemence, she answered, "Never."

The next three witnesses all were middle-aged men in gray suits and with gray, nondescript faces. Their brown hair was cropped short, and two of the three sported mustaches. These gentlemen represented the State Farm bureaucracy, the people Mac McCain said he had relied upon to make the right decision about issuing Deana's policy. It was immediately obvious to the jury that a rejection letter from any of these three might have saved Deana's life, if it was indeed murder.

Stan Sodomka, the man Mac McCain referred to as being at the top of the ladder, testified that he had been with State Farm for twenty-five years. When Deana's and B.J.'s policy applications came across his desk, he held the position of Regional Life Health Manager.

Sodomka remembered the applications only distantly. He recalled speaking with Mac McCain, but he wasn't clear on whether Mac had focused on Deana or B.J. The conversation, apparently, was just one of the half dozen or so Sodomka had every day with agents throughout Southern California.

Tamayo pursued the point: "If an agent called you and said that he believed the insured on a policy was going to be killed, would you notate that to go along with the file?"

"I would either notate that or immediately take it to the underwriting superintendent and say, 'You need to pay close attention to this.' "

"Do you remember words to that effect coming from Mac McCain?"

"No."

Under further questioning, Sodomka agreed that B.J.'s numerous health problems posed obvious obstacles for the underwriters. Deana's policy, on the other hand, looked like an excellent risk. Sodomka personally gave B.J.'s file to Life Underwriting Superintendent Mike Kalish. Deana's file, however, was funneled to Peter Kay, a man much lower in the State Farm bureaucracy.

The inference came out clearly: McCain never mentioned any suspicion about Deana's murder. He red-flagged *Billie Joe's* application because the man posed a health risk. Now, in retrospect, McCain was trying to tie the red flag memo to Deana's application, in all likelihood to pass blame on to State Farm.

Aragon knew that all the cross-examination in the world couldn't break Sodomka. But in a handful of questions, he attempted to undermine some of his impact.

Sodomka agreed that he had never received a call from Mac McCain on any other life-insurance application during the nine years he had headed up State Farm's Southern California office. And he did indeed recall Mac being "concerned in general" about the McGinnises. It was a marginal recovery, and Aragon knew he hadn't undone the damage, but he had nothing better to work with.

The next of the carbon-copy insurance executives was Mike Kalish, the Life Underwriting superintendent in the Costa Mesa office. Juliana Humphrey had Kalish detail the steps of underwriting a policy—essentially evaluating the risk of insuring an applicant.

"I normally do not underwrite this small an amount of an application, my being the superintendent," Kalish said after finishing his lecture on insurance risks. "But my boss, Stan Sodomka, brought Billie Joe's file to me. In general, he indicated there was a concern expressed by the agent. I remember when Mr. Sodomka brought me the application, there was either a phone-call record or a memo attached." This, clearly, referred to Mac McCain's red flag memo.

"Billie Joe's policy was ultimately declined," Kalish concluded. "I believe it was declined for medical history."

"Was it declined because this particular applicant was going to kill another applicant?" Humphrey asked.

"Oh, no, no," Kalish assured her.

Aragon couldn't do much more with Kalish than he had with Sodomka. Communication within State Farm's gargantuan operation had broken down and Mac McCain's red-flag memo parted company with Deana's policy the minute it went from Sodomka to Kalish. From then on, Mac McCain's concerns faded into the woodwork—until they proved all too true.

Still, Aragon found one point that helped return the focus of the trial to Virginia, who seemed to have been lost in the petty battles over who told what to whom, and when. "Mr. Kalish," he asked, "directing your attention to the medications section of Billie Joe McGinnis's insurance application, is there any area or question regarding what medications, if any, the applicant is prescribed or taking?"

"Yes."

"As you review that, do you see any notation that Mr. McGinnis was prescribed and/or taking Elavil or amitriptyline or nortriptyline?"

"No, it does not indicate that anywhere."

That was one more argument Aragon could make in closing: Why lie about Elavil when you've listed a host of other illnesses?

Of all the insurance men to come before the jury, Peter Key gave the strongest impression of having had his lifeblood sponged out of him by reams of paper. His drawn face, jaundiced-looking eyes, and scruffy beard brought to mind a downtrodden Dickensian clerk, or Bartleby the Scrivener.

Under Juliana Humphrey's questioning, Key explained that he had worked for twenty years as a State Farm underwriting specialist. He said it was his duty to evaluate the risk on life-insurance policies, but he couldn't recall reviewing Deana's policy. Small wonder: He reviewed 150 to 200 insurance-policy applications *per day*.

Deana's policy, quite obviously, had been business as usual. Key never spoke to Stan Sodomka, Mike Kalish, or Mac McCain about a single detail. He didn't recall seeing a red-flag memo. He didn't check to see whether Deana and James Coates were actually engaged. And he never heard a concern that Deana's life was in danger.

The one action Key took was ordering a "life history" on Deana, a procedure that involved a single telephone call to the McGinnis house by yet another State Farm functionary. Virginia had taken the call. She explained that Deana was out, and proceeded to answer all the questions in her stead.

"We assume that the information on the application is accurate," Key admitted.

"Regarding the status of the fiancé," Humphrey asked, "do you usually check to make sure the folks are really engaged?"

"No, not for this amount of insurance."

Aragon now saw exactly how the defense had positioned itself. Key's spotty recollections served to reaffirm the likelihood that Mac McCain was initially concerned only about B.J., who posed an obvious health risk.

In cross-examination, Aragon did what he could to turn the argument on its head. Key should have been the bulwark between Deana and her murderers, he implied. Instead, the man had behaved like a machine simply because the face value of Deana's policy was so small.

In 1987, Key said, State Farm required a medical exam only for applicants buying more that $250,000 in life insurance.

"As you are doing your evaluation for State Farm, is the issue of cost-effectiveness in your mind?" Aragon asked.

"Yes."

Key agreed that reviewing both Deana's application and life history took between eight and ten minutes. It was Deana's death warrant signed, sealed, and delivered by assembly line.

That evening, Aragon and Keeney conferred as usual. Aragon sounded troubled, the energy drained from his usually upbeat voice. Keeney tried to encourage him, even though he had to agree that the State Farm witnesses were damaging.

"Why doesn't anyone remember Mac McCain's worries about murder?" Aragon wondered aloud. "I believe Mac's telling the truth, but it's strange."

"Well," Keeney suggested, "if I were State Farm, I surely wouldn't want to admit that I went ahead and wrote a life-insurance policy on a girl I suspected would be murdered. Maybe that helps to blur their recollections. Of course, I'm just guessing."

"I don't want the *jury* guessing," Aragon said, then changed the subject. "Any chance of you coming out to watch?"

"I'd like to be out there," Keeney said. "But Tamayo might take a shot at putting me on the stand. I'm still subject to his subpoena."

"If he puts you up, he's crazy. During cross-exam, I can ask you how you got suspicious in the first place. That'll open Pandora's box—the fires, Cynthia Elaine, Dick Coates, everything they've fought to keep from the jury. My only fear then would be a mistrial."

"I know. In fact, I kinda keep hoping he might just be foolish enough to try it. Still, there's no point in giving Tamayo a free shot at me." Keeney paused, then asked, "By the way, how're you all holding up?"

"It's getting long. I'm bushed; Anna's bushed. I just hope the jury can keep paying attention. Of course, now that we're into the defense case, maybe I *should* hope they fall asleep," Aragon joked.

"*You* sleeping?" Keeney asked.

"Oh, sure," Aragon laughed. "A good eight hours a night. Just like you, right?"

The next group of defense witnesses gave the jury their own versions of Deana's story from the day she set foot in San Diego. Some anecdotes seemed so peripherally related to the case, they drew smirks from the jury. But in all they traced the downward trajectory of the girl's lonely life just as Tamayo had promised.

Lillian Lawrence owned an apartment where Deana stayed after Jay Wild first went to sea. Deana was to have lived with Lillian for two weeks, but she ended up leaving within days.

"I asked her to leave," Lawrence said. "I have two small kids and she was doing things that I just didn't like in my house."

"Did you see her doing anything on the day that you asked her to leave?" Tamayo asked.

"She was kissing our best friend, Louie Sciano. . . . The next morning, he came back and apologized to me."

Aragon had no questions, but he sensed the image of Deana playing around just after her newly wed husband went to sea had its effect on the jury. And yet, those facts had no business in a homicide trial.

Next came Helen Schoellen, a doddering, elderly woman who had lived one door down from Deana at the Royal Apartments in the seedy El Cajon district of San Diego. She spoke in a hazy, almost dreamlike voice, attributable to medications she took for a thyroid condition.

Schoellen mistily remembered the one time she went to Deana's apartment. "I smelled a lot of marijuana there," she said.

"She looked like she was all alone, not a friend in the world. She kept talking about home; she kept talking about her husband. She wanted him to hurry back from overseas. . . . The last time I saw Deana, she was heading toward a car full of rowdy people, with the radio up loud."

Aragon had no questions.

Deana's self-professed boyfriend Donnie Dale Moore made, perhaps, a worse impression on the jury than even James Coates. The black clothes on his stick-figure frame accented a pair of darting black eyes. And his sallow, sunken face had lost all life; it looked as if it were a mask made of old leather. Aragon thought Moore came across like every mother's nightmare.

"Now, when did Deana come to live with you and your family?" Juliana Humphrey began.

Moore looked up and answered, "I don't remember dates or any of that, tell the truth. At that time, I was way out there. I was doing whatever I could get my hands on, pretty much. Mainly amphetamines."

Eventually, Humphrey coaxed Moore into remembering some details other than his drugs of choice. He had met Deana in September of 1986; she had moved into his parents' house the same day.

"Did you know whether or not she was married?" Humphrey asked.

"Didn't know. Didn't care. Did not see no ring." Moore spoke like a man who had nothing left to lose.

"Did there ever come a time that you talked about marriage?"

"I believe we had at one time."

"Did you know at that time whether she was already married?"

"She told me she had *been* married."

"Did that concern you, that she might still be married?"

"Not in the least bit. It's not against the law until you do it." Moore's mouth spread into a creased grin. "Besides, at that time I didn't have the money to marry nobody. Mainly we were just hangin' around the house and sellin' drugs."

Aragon objected to Moore's last remark and Judge Revak struck it from the record, but it was too late to erase its impact on the jury. If the jury wanted to believe Deana sold drugs, they now had a reason, however shaky.

Moore went on to say that he and Deana stayed together at his parents' house until he went back to prison that fall. Humphrey introduced as exhibits the letters Moore wrote Deana where he talked hopefully about getting married once he finished his sentence. These were the same letters Bobbie had found in Deana's purse and passed on to Keeney.

The whole tale bore an uncanny resemblance to Deana's relationship with James Coates. Here were *two* hard-core junkies and felons living with their parents and dealing drugs to stay alive. Both took Deana home for a month or so, and both said they talked with her about marriage even though they knew she was already married. It suddenly made Deana's engagement to James Coates look all the more plausible. And it destroyed the image of Deana as the cookies-and-cream Kentucky girl who frolicked in Sleepy Hollow.

Aragon thought that still didn't explain why Virginia bought life insurance on Deana. He could concede that issue to the defense, allow Deana's character to be trashed, and still prove murder. But if he surrendered even one part of his case, how could he expect the jury to trust him all the way to a conviction?

The defense portrayal of Deana came to an end with a pair of witnesses: Frank Garcia and "Bones" Sherman. Like Donnie Moore and James Coates, both were drug users with major-league rap sheets, and their proffered testimony—stories of Deana's numerous affairs and her drug dealing—seemed aimed more at dragging the DA's "country girl" through the gutters of San Diego than at exonerating Virginia.

To Aragon's mind, these witnesses were called for one purpose only: to assassinate Deana's character. Out of the presence of the jury, Aragon tried to preempt the witnesses even from taking the stand. Tamayo and Humphrey argued hotly that if Deana were portrayed as moving from one intense relationship to another, the jury would be more likely to believe that she held herself out to the world as an unmarried woman, thus undercutting part of the DA's case.

Judge Revak replied with an argument that, as usual, split the difference:

"I don't think that whether someone sleeps around is evidence of whether they're married or not, or that it's conduct necessarily inconsistent with being married," Revak said. "We all know married people who sleep around. Some of them happily married people. I'm not going to let this jury hear a bunch of witnesses take the stand and say 'I went to bed with Deana. I went to bed with Deana.' "

Drugs, however, were another matter. On that issue, Revak ruled that if Deana had a history of taking drugs, it increased the likelihood that she had taken the Elavil voluntarily. Whether Tamayo had the evidence was another matter, but Revak wasn't going to cut off that line of questioning.

Bones Sherman and Frank Garcia were both permitted to testify about Deana's supposed rampant drug use. As it turned out, however, neither witness had much to say. They had seen Deana smoking marijuana and had heard her talk about taking "crystal meth," but neither of them ever actually saw her take a pill of any sort.

Still, one message came across: Criminals and dope addicts seemed to be Deana's chosen milieu.

Aragon watched for changes in Virginia's demeanor as the defense case moved toward its conclusion. He was looking, in particular, for hints of whether she would take the stand.

It seemed to him impossible that anyone accused of throwing a young girl off a cliff would *not* testify. How could a person sit for two months, listening to witness after witness, and then ask the public defender to say to the jury, "It was an accident"? Her own taped voice formed the backbone of the DA's case. She *had* to testify.

Over the last two years, Aragon had prepared more than eight hundred questions; he planned to keep her on the stand for days. But defendants almost always testified last, and Tamayo had yet to use his battery of experts.

The penultimate phase of the defense involved the Elavil in Deana's blood. Tamayo attacked the issue with a surprising vigor—surprising given that Virginia and B.J. admitted keeping the drug around the house. Aragon began to wonder whether Tamayo hadn't run amok, attacking parts of the DA's case simply because it was feasible.

Susan Giorgi of the Institute of Forensic Sciences testified that she had tested Deana's urine at the request of the Monterey Coroner's

Office back in August of 1987. Tamayo had the report blown up to poster size and placed on an easel before the jury. Typed clearly at the center of the page, it stated 0.00 mg/ml (micrograms per milliliter) of amitriptyline and 0.00 mg/ml of nortriptyline.

Aragon and Long knew about the report. Giorgi's test, in fact, had been performed at Keeney's urging years ago in order to quantify the amount of Elavil in Deana's system. During cross-examination, however, it came out that the amount of the drug in Deana's blood was substantially below the sensitivity of the equipment used at the Institute of Forensic Sciences.

Aragon, in fact, had already shown the jury results of another, highly sensitive test done on Deana's blood in 1989. That test detected 0.02 mg/ml of amitriptyline and trace amounts of nortriptyline.

Nonetheless, Tamayo pressed forward. Dr. James Meeker, a Ph.D. in forensic toxicology, tested a sample of Deana's blood in April of 1991. Using sophisticated and "self-validating" dual-column gas chromatography, Meeker also said he was unable to detect any of the components of Elavil in Deana's blood.

On cross-examination, Anna Long pressed Meeker about performing a test on a four-year-old sample. But Meeker held firm. He refused to admit that the drug might have decomposed to below testable levels.

The Elavil issue seemed at a standoff, until Tamayo brought in the same pharmacist who had already testified for Aragon about refilling Billie Joe's prescription back in February 1987. An elderly gent who walked with a cane, the pharmacist struggled to the stand for a second time. He *confirmed* that Billie Joe McGinnis had filled prescriptions for Elavil numerous times in 1986 and once in 1987.

Aragon felt as if he were losing the thread of Tamayo's case. The pharmacist clearly undercut the theory that Billie Joe refilled the Elavil prescription as part of the conspiracy to kill Deana. But why, after spending so much energy to impeach the People's lab reports, would Tamayo want to *reaffirm* that a regular supply of Elavil was always on hand at the McGinnis house?

Aragon wasn't left with much time to mull that question over. Tamayo quickly began unveiling his quartet of high-priced expert witnesses. Under a long-standing U.S. Supreme Court rule, an expert scientific opinion must be "generally accepted" within the scientific community to be admissible in a trial. Keeney, the son of two respected physicians, felt burned that, while many of the hard facts he had assembled never would be heard by the jury, plenty of dubious and even misleading theories easily made the cut.

Dr. Gail Waldron, a respected psychiatrist, lead the charge. She offered the jury what the defense termed a "psychiatric autopsy" of Deana. Aragon objected that Waldron had never interviewed Deana's relatives or her acquaintances, let alone Deana herself. But Judge Revak disagreed. Dr. Waldron, he ruled, could give a limited diagnosis based on the voluminous materials provided to the defense during discovery.

"I'd call her a troubled young woman who was glad to be going on an outing," Waldron said. "She was someone without any conscious intention that we can find to commit suicide, but nevertheless someone with a history of carelessness, recklessness, self-sabotaging behavior, endangering herself. I know that she wore a smiley face and that probably this court's heard an awful lot about it. But I think it's fair to say that can't be taken at face value. In her case, it was a compensatory attempt or effort to ward off troubled feelings, depressed feelings."

It seemed that Tamayo had at last found a way to introduce the notion of suicide—until Waldron thoroughly obliterated the idea.

"I found no clear evidence of intention to commit suicide," Waldron remarked. "Nor did I find any background material that would suggest a kind of gross un-coordination—clumsiness. There's also no good evidence that at the time of death she was using nonprescription medication or was intoxicated by same. . . . Methamphetamine and marijuana hang around; cocaine hangs around in the blood and would have been picked up in a quantitative analysis of this woman's blood after death. That wasn't there."

Aragon silently rejoiced, keeping a poker face. Tamayo might have painted Deana as a secretly depressed girl, one with a prolific sex life and illicit drug habits, but Waldron had just informed the jury that Deana didn't kill herself, she wasn't clumsy, and she wasn't high or drunk when she fell. He and Anna Long exchanged furtive smiles just before Aragon rose to announce he had no questions for Dr. Waldron.

Dr. Elizabeth Loftus was young, dynamic, and an eminently practiced witness. Her horn-rimmed glasses and unruly, professorial haircut made her all the more engaging. Aragon sensed the jurors drinking in the lessons of this nationally recognized expert in human memory. In his memo to Aragon, Keeney had warned that no cross-examination might be the best approach. Loftus was an eminently practiced courtroom performer.

"I think it's a matter of common sense," she said, "that the longer the interval between the event and its recall, the less accurate memory is going to be. We all know that from personal experience. We can even plot a 'forgetting curve' where we plot how good a memory is as a function of how much time has passed. What's not a matter of common sense, however, is that as the memory is fading, as more and more time is passing, that memory is becoming more and more vulnerable to postevent information. You're going to ask me what postevent information is." She smiled coyly at Tamayo.

"I was just about to ask," Tamayo said right on cue.

Loftus continued. "Postevent information refers, just as the name suggests, to new information that a witness gets after this event is completely over. The new information could come in the form of overhearing what another witness says; it could come in the form of seeing media coverage; it could come in the form of being asked suggestive and leading questions. It has the potential for altering or contaminating or distorting a witness's recollection, and that contaminating process or distorting process is greater when more time has passed.

"We've done experiments that show that we can get people to say they saw barns that didn't exist, tape recorders that weren't there, that people were more violent or more belligerent in an altercation than they actually were, simply by exposing them to postevent information."

Loftus went on in her academic vein for forty-five minutes. The object of her theorizing was obvious to Aragon. Five years had passed since Deana's death. A number of witnesses had come forward to put words in Virginia's mouth, but many of those highly damning statements weren't recorded or written down. Mac and Art McCain, Martha Grant, Deborah Cross, Brian Lyke, each testified from pure recall and each had been interviewed countless times. Tamayo had elicited from many witnesses that they had talked about the case "over and over" or read about it in newspapers. Aragon didn't like it, but the possibility of postevent information infecting their testimony could not be dismissed out of hand.

▼

After the jury left for the day, Revak asked Tamayo when he expected to complete his case.

"I think I'll be about another week," he said. "We've got Tim Simpson and Dr. McGrath and we're through."

"How about your client? Is she going to testify?" Revak asked cautiously. Aragon's ears perked.

"We're still discussing it, Judge."

"That's all right," Revak said. "You don't have to tell me now."

When Aragon got back to his office, he still didn't know whether Virginia would testify, but he did discover one development in the defense case. A copy of a fax sent that morning from the San Diego Public Defender's Office to Louisville lay on his desk: Steve Keeney was officially off Tamayo's witness list.

That meant the case was down to two more experts and Virginia. The "Keeney defense" was out. So was the "B.J. did it" defense. Dr. Waldron had nixed suicide. Aragon guessed Tamayo had weighed in for accident.

But at the same time, he realized that Tamayo no longer needed a positive theory of his own. Mac McCain's credibility had been severely undermined. Deana's engagement to James Coates could appear entirely in character, if the jury had believed even half of Donnie Moore's testimony. There was the stake at the cliff edge and the A-frame house overlooking the scene of the crime. Dr. Hoops hadn't noticed anything unusual about the condition of Deana's fingernails. Dave Dungan hadn't amended his report to include the fact that the McGinnises said they didn't know about any insurance on Deana.

With Loftus now casting doubt on every phrase not transcribed from a tape recording, Aragon felt the case had slipped out of his control.

The next day, Tim Simpson, a geotechnical and environmental engineer, took the stand to begin an orchestrated assault on the notion that murder by pushing was even possible. A nattily dressed young man, Simpson reveled in describing the expensive gadgetry he had brought to bear on the question.

Using aerial photography, computer-aided design, and an analytic stereo plotter, Simpson had assembled an immensely detailed map of the Seal Beach overlook, one that outlined many of the outcroppings and indentations too small to appear on the prosecutor's map.

He and a team of rock climbers also had gone to the turnout to perform "coefficient of friction" tests at various points at the cliff edge. Using a pocket penetrometer, he had measured the variability of soil conditions in the precise area where Deana had fallen.

Simpson determined that just below the top of the turnout the steepness of slope and crumbly soil with its extremely low coefficient of friction made for treacherous footing. For Deana to try to negotiate even a few steps in high heels there, he explained, would be foolhardy. Once she tripped, her body would continue sliding.

It all seemed beside the point until Tamayo began a line of questioning that made Aragon's hands turn cold.

"One of the calculations I asked you to complete for us is the amount of force that would be necessary to propel a certain weight fifteen feet down a cliff. I asked you to assume that we had a body about one hundred and thirty pounds and a height of that individual about five eight to six feet. Given those facts, were you able to make calculations as to just how much force would be needed to propel that body that distance?"

The fresh-faced expert pulled out a folder and read from his notes: "There are certain approximations we have to make. Namely, the duration of the push, which is a factor. If we make some assumptions about what the duration of the push was, and what the center of mass of the person being pushed is, I come up with a likely amount of about three hundred foot-pounds."

Even pushing together, it was obvious that B.J. and Virginia couldn't muster that kind of strength. If Simpson was right, his calculation amounted to objective proof that Deana could not have been pushed and have landed fifteen feet below the edge—just where Deputy John Burke recalled seeing the first sign of disturbed soil and brush. It simply wasn't physically possible. On the other hand, the notion of an accident made perfect sense.

Aragon knew he had to take a few blind stabs at Simpson. To let his testimony go unchallenged would be to admit defeat on the spot.

"You testified that there are places on the cliff face with a coefficient of friction near zero, is that right?" he began.

"Yes, there are a number of places just below the edge."

"Given your analysis of the site and the composition of the soil, would you expect to see any soil disruption if the point of impact was at a coefficient of friction of zero?"

"It may leave a depression, but that would fill in very quickly with these granular soils," Simpson explained. "They naturally fall back to their, what's called 'angle of repose.' It's like digging a hole in loose beach sand. It may leave some indentation, but it wouldn't be very significant."

That effectively disposed of one tenet of Simpson's "death push" calculation. Deana's body could have landed five feet below the edge and left only an insignificant mark. Aragon pressed ahead, feeling considerably relieved.

"Mr. Simpson, what did you assume to be the duration of the push?"

"Point fifteen seconds," he answered.

"Point fifteen seconds?" Aragon asked with genuine surprise. *"One-sixth* of a second?"

"Yes."

To Aragon, that sounded more like the speed of a pneumatic drill than of a human arm.

"What if the push had taken one second, can you tell us whether it would take greater or lesser force if the push was over a second?"

"I probably could, but I would be afraid to. I would like to run through the numbers."

After a few more peripheral questions, Judge Revak called a recess. Simpson remained on the stand, completing the calculation.

When court resumed, Aragon returned to the question he had left hanging. "I asked you before if the push was one second in duration, what mass would be required to arrive at a point fifteen feet below the edge. Have you had an opportunity to calculate that?"

"Yes." Simpson looked up, reading off his work sheet. "Using the equation that I used to model my previous calculation, if the time duration is one second, I come up with forty-seven pounds required."

"Forty-seven pounds?" Aragon repeated.

"Intuitively, I don't think so," Simpson answered, his young face starting to crease. "I would question a result of forty-seven pounds."

"But that's a figure you arrived at using your calculations?" Aragon pressed the point home.

"Yes."

"So, sometimes calculations don't really tell us much in practical effect."

"That's correct," Simpson answered weakly.

▼

Dr. James J. McGrath, a rugged-looking man in his sixties with a walrus mustache, was Tamayo's last expert. He spoke with a pedantic manner and a dangerous twinkle in his eye, describing himself as a "human factors engineer," a science he claimed dated back to the advent of industrial psychology.

McGrath's credentials were impressive: summa cum laude from the University of Southern California, with a Ph.D. in psychology; senior scientist with the Navy Personnel Research Center; lecturer at the American Psychological Association, Royal Geographic Society in London, Institute of Perception in the Netherlands, Luftwaffe Institute in Munich, NATO Science Advisory Council in Paris, and the National Academy of Sciences in Washington, D.C.; recipient of the navy's Distinguished Civilian Award, among dozens of other awards and affiliations. But to lawyers in the tort trade, McGrath belonged to a notorious class: the group of professional witnesses known as "slip-and-fall experts."

Aragon listened intently to the opening refrains of McGrath's testimony and wondered what, if anything, he had to do with a murder case. Deana hadn't slipped in a supermarket aisle on some fresh floor wax. The question here was "accident or murder." And, as far as he could learn from the defense, McGrath hadn't so much as submitted a report.

Once again, Aragon objected and the attorneys whispered their arguments at sidebar.

In hushed tones, Aragon argued that he still hadn't the foggiest idea what McGrath intended to say because the defense hadn't turned over any reports, much less the raw data on which McGrath based his opinions—all required under Proposition 115's reciprocal-discovery rule.

Judge Revak decided Aragon should have a chance to examine the witness on the record, but out of the jury's hearing, a procedure known as a "402 hearing." He cleared the courtroom, and kept McGrath on the stand.

Aragon began by asking McGrath what opinions he intended to render. These turned out to include a list of the possible ways to fall from the edge, how the coefficient of friction affected footing and the likelihood of an accidental fall, and an analysis of whether a scream could be heard at the cliff site.

"I told my daughter to take a station where she could observe the people who stopped at the site, stay out of the way, and record what everybody did," McGrath explained. "And also to take thirty-five-millimeter shots and video shots of those people."

McGrath also performed coefficient of friction tests by dragging a fifteen-pound bag of buckshot along the ground at various points.

"Did you give any of your notes to the defense?" Aragon asked, glancing toward the judge.

"Yes, I've given them notes."

"On an ongoing basis?"

"I believe so, during our meetings."

Tamayo twisted in his seat. Failing to give Aragon McGrath's reports clearly violated Judge Revak's reciprocal-discovery order.

Aragon followed the new lead: "And have you been interviewed by the defense in anticipation of your examination today?"

"Yes. We have had several meetings. In one meeting last year, there were investigators present, I believe. I'm not sure who all the parties were. In other meetings, Mr. Simpson was present."

"Could I see the notes, sir?" Aragon asked.

Tamayo stood up and objected. "The entire line of questioning is irrelevant to the purpose of four-oh-two."

Aragon angrily riposted. "It now appears that the defense is in violation of the discovery order that this court made very clear. And I can tell the court that the People have received nothing besides a resume from this witness as I speak today."

Judge Revak's expression narrowed to a single edge aimed at Tamayo and Humphrey.

The two defenders alternately argued that McGrath's notes were never reduced to "reports" and thus did not qualify under the discovery order. The photos and the videotape, on the other hand, were made by McGrath's daughter, a witness they never intended to call.

Revak was not appeased.

"Here's the problem," he said. "Dr. McGrath is an expert witness. Not only is he an expert witness but he is in a very, very technical area, esoteric in some respects. I don't think Mr. Aragon had a clue that Dr. McGrath was going to talk about his daughter taking photographs of the scene, or the numbers of people, so that he could have presented an argument to exclude this evidence, or at least to prepare for cross-examination.

"Now here is the district attorney expected to cross-examine an expert witness and he has absolutely nothing. It seems to me there is a game out there. Nobody writes a report; therefore, there's nothing to turn over to the prosecution.

"For every witness the district attorney had put on, you have had thousands and thousands of pages and you have had them for months and years. And you guys knew you were going to put Dr. McGrath on the stand. You knew it! It's that simple as far as I'm concerned. I think you violated my order. I cannot tolerate this."

Revak was genuinely appalled, and the fire-and-brimstone prosecutor emerged. Tamayo and Humphrey waited to see where the sword would fall.

Revak concluded on a benign note of finality. "I'm going to let him testify, but I'll let the DA take what time he needs over the weekend to prepare."

Juliana Humphrey turned after Revak finished his admonishment and mugged to some public defender colleagues in the gallery. She acted as if this censure was no big deal. Taking a few hits in court meant earning your stripes as lawyer. And laws, apparently, were made to be broken.

Aragon, however, left Department 22 feeling ambushed. He had played by the rules from the first day of the preliminary hearing. He had watched Tamayo interview and cross-examine all of his key witnesses well before trial. Now here was the lawyer playing fast and loose with the trial itself, and there was nothing Aragon or Revak could do about it. Deana's sex life and her supposed drug habits, the memory expert, the slip-and-fall experts, even a psychiatric examination of a dead person, all had become part of the trial. And all he had to offer the jury was a purely circumstantial case.

The following day, Dr. McGrath lectured to the jury from a poster that read, "The Seven Possible Ways to Fall: Slip, Trip, Misstep, Heel Trap, Climb Down, Jump, Push." Deana's high heels, in his opinion, posed a very real danger of a heel trap in the loose soil—especially given the low coefficient of friction near the edge, where she had stood in Photo 11. He likened the "slipperiness" of the loose soil to "wet tile."

Tamayo next had McGrath address the issue of Deana's silent fall. McGrath began by giving a précis of his relevant background.

"I've done psychophysical experiments on the ability of the human to detect differences in sounds. I've done studies in auditory detection where I was mostly interested in measuring human alertness. I have also done studies of sonar operations that involve the human ability to analyze sounds."

Given the factors at the cliff site—the wind, the ocean, and the barking of the seals—McGrath concluded that a person standing on the surface might not hear the sound of a body tumbling down the cliffside. "It's problematic as to whether it would even be detectable," he opined.

Tamayo asked, based on McGrath's studies, whether a person might scream during an accidental cliff fall. McGrath said he had done studies for the U.S. Naval War College on human performance under stress, which apparently dealt with the question.

"In terms of crying out," he said, "it's hard to predict. Every time we see somebody fall in the movies off a roof or off a cliff or from a height, they always scream all the way down. And so we have a stereotype of people screaming when they fall. In my experience, they hardly ever do. There are several reasons for that. First of all, the time period is very short. And a person has to be at the inhale stage of the respiration cycle in order to scream to begin with—say a one-second interval. Secondly, the response time isn't that fast. And third, behavioral freeze—blocking of a response when a person is in an extremely high state of arousal. I don't think many people have been trained to fall off cliffs, so that would be a case where I would anticipate a high probability of behavioral freeze. . . ."

It was a forest of unlikely technical explanations and broad generalizations. Still, McGrath was not the sort to be lead into equivocating. Aragon decided, therefore, to devote his cross-examination primarily to McGrath himself.

McGrath earned more than 60 percent of his living from preparing cases for litigation. He earned $180 per hour for in-court testimony, and the total of his work cost the defense in excess of $9,000. The man was the quintessential gunslinger.

Moving on to McGrath's immense resume, Aragon asked, "You've provided a summary of some of the articles that you have written?"

"There's a short selected list in my resume. . . ."

"Some of the titles include: 'Cruise System Design,' 'Body Temperature and Temporal Acuity,' 'Cold Weather Operations,' 'Remedial Reading Methodology,' 'Electronics Maintenance, Training System Proceedings Maintenance, Training and Performance Aids,' 'Driver Expectancy and Performance in Locating Automotive Controls,' 'Aeronautical Maps and Displays,' 'Relationships Between Chronological Age, Intelligence, and Rate of Subjective Time.' Are these correct?"

"Yes."

"May I assume that one would have to be, if not an expert, at least very well informed on these topics before one could write this type of article?"

"That's true."

"Would you consider yourself an expert in the areas that I've just read to you?"

"I certainly would, in the sense that I know more about the subjects than the man in the street does."

Aragon left off, letting the comment speak for itself: Dr. McGrath considered himself an expert in practically everything. As far as human-factors jargon went, Aragon assumed that either the jury believed Deana screamed when she fell or they didn't. The respiration cycle wouldn't be the pivotal issue.

Tamayo and Humphrey consulted in whispers after McGrath left the courtroom. The moment for Virginia to testify had arrived. Aragon's stack of eight hundred questions sat under the table in his attaché case; the questions represented two years of planning.

Tamayo rose and looked down at Virginia.

"Your Honor, the defense rests."

CHAPTER 30

THE DARK, DARK SOUL

▼

As he prepared his summation speech over the weekend, Aragon felt unsure how to read the jury.

Many of the old pros around the DA's Office prided themselves on being able to read a panel. But in eight years of trying cases, Aragon had seen jurors smile and bob their heads at every point he made and then return Not Guilty verdicts. Other folks who sat with their arms crossed voted Guilty in half an hour. The only thing you could know for sure, Aragon believed, is that you can't ever *know.*

The trial had taken an odd turn. Virginia McGinnis got lost in the shuffle of seventy-five witnesses, forensic experts, and a maze of exhibits stacked against every available surface. Instead, the lawyers had drawn one another into a turf war over Deana Wild's soul. Was she a nice girl from Kentucky, short on common sense but filled with goodwill? If so, the defense contended, how could she have fallen in with the likes of Donnie Dale Moore, Bones Sherman, and James Coates? But did her supposed promiscuity and drug use mean she really harbored the self-destructive urges Dr. Waldron detected in her "psychiatric autopsy"? And did all that mean she copped some

Elavil from B.J.'s medicine chest and accidentally stumbled off the cliff?

Aragon thought the arguments built one upon the next in an absurdly involuted pattern, like a dog chasing its tail. None of the supposed revelations about the girl's sex life or drug habits or inner self-hatred spoke to the question of murder or of Virginia's state of mind. None of Tamayo's experts answered why Virginia bought the life-insurance policy, or how Elavil had found its way from Billie Joe's prescription bottle into Deana's system. Tamayo never even offered an explanation. But he had offered the jury a way to believe Virginia was not guilty, if they chose.

Aragon arrived in the courtroom looking pale. By 2:00 A.M. the night before, he had rewritten his fifty-page summation speech so many times he lost all perspective. He kept repeating to himself that it was just another murder. But after he crawled into bed, he admitted to his expectant wife, Julie, that, other than their having a healthy baby, he wanted to win this case more than anything in the world. It wasn't only Deana's murder that fueled his ardor. It was the image of Cynthia Elaine Coates—an innocent three-year-old—dangling from a loop of baling twine in a cold barn. He held that image in his mind as he delivered his closing argument.

"We have been in trial now for two and a half months," he began. "Multiplied by the fifteen of you, that represents about three years collectively that you've dedicated in the search for the truth in this case. . . .

"You know that this case matters. It matters because Deana Hubbard matters. . . . Deana Hubbard had a right to live her life. As you search for the truth about Deana's death, you celebrate life, you celebrate justice. . . ." Aragon paused, looked across the faces of people he had come to know, even if only through their silent expressions and reactions.

"Deana hungered for acceptance. She hungered for attention," Aragon went on. "And if that meant associating with people that others might shy away from, so be it. It didn't matter to her that James Coates had spent most of his adult life in prison. That didn't matter because he accepted her.

"Why is it relevant who Deana is? It's very important, ladies and gentlemen, because by understanding Deana, you understand so very much about this case and why she was murdered. Deana, as you look at her, as you evaluate her, sadly presents the portrait profile of a victim. When you understand that she was the—if I may—ideal victim, then perhaps you understand why she was so irresistible to Virginia and Billie Joe McGinnis.

"Now we weren't there, but can you imagine what the conversation might have been like between Mr. McGinnis and the defendant: Well, if we kill Deana and make it look like an accident, who's going to care? Who's going to be there to ask the questions? And how about this: What if we take her outside of Chula Vista as far as we reasonably can go where nobody knows us, nobody knows her. Who's going to ask questions? Who is she, anyway? She's a twenty-year-old from Kentucky. Her mother is a single parent living on a teacher's income in Louisville. Is she going to be asking questions?

"This was pure and simple a case of risk analysis. They added it up and decided they could get away with it. The formula for success was: obscure victim; remote, faraway death site; and an amount of insurance that wouldn't raise too many questions. . . ."

Aragon then turned to the insurance policy, what he called "the smoking gun."

"It can't be explained away by coefficient of friction tests," he said. "It can't be explained away by psychiatric autopsies. It stands as a stunning monument to their audacity, to their greed. Here they paid for the policy on April first and they murdered her April the second.

"What did the defendant say? She told Diana Rael, Bobbie Roberts, and Detective Smythe: 'Well, B.J. went to State Farm to get some life insurance and after he filled out his application, Deana said, "Well, what about me? What am I, chopped liver?" ' . . . This is a whim apparently. And, sure, they are on a fixed income, but if Deana wants it, well, we are going to get it for her. Does that make sense? If you are going to buy insurance"—Aragon drew the words out—"you buy *medical* insurance. . . .

Aragon broke off briefly to dim the courtroom lights and turn on a slide projector.

"Now we come to the fatal trip itself."

One by one, Virginia's snapshots appeared on the wall. Aragon narrated the trip up the coast, then described how Deana became drowsier as the Elavil came over her. Finally, they arrived at Seal Beach and took Photo 11.

"Photograph eleven is an amazing photograph if you look at it carefully," Aragon said, pointing out details on the projected image. "Now look at Mr. McGinnis's feet and legs. He appears to be in stride. He is looking at this highway. He is about seven or eight feet from the cliff, but he is not looking there. He's looking at this highway. . . .

"Where is Deana looking? She is looking where any reasonable person would be looking. She is looking at the edge of the turnout. Isn't it interesting that Mr. McGinnis is in stride, a hand on Deana Hubbard Wild. He appears to be walking into her. Does that make any sense? Or could this, ladies and gentlemen, be the beginning of the end for Deana Hubbard Wild? The coast, literally, is clear."

With the lights back on, Aragon used the People's topographical map to detail where Virginia stood when she snapped each of the last four photographs.

"When you calculate the number of feet that Virginia McGinnis had to move, let's say she is doing this rather quickly . . . let's say she moves from position eleven, she goes to position twelve, she takes a photograph, she then moves to position thirteen, she takes a photograph, she moves to position fourteen, takes a photograph, position fifteen, takes a photograph. Even if she is doing it in split-second time, that's four or five seconds. It's probably longer. This is the point: Remember, Photograph eleven, right after that's taken, the defendant says, 'It got cold. We went to the car.' . . ."

"The truth is that these photographs, twelve, thirteen, fourteen, and fifteen, were taken in large measure to make sure that the coast was clear and to finish the roll."

Then Aragon turned to the question of Deana's "silent fall."

"You were at Seal Beach two days. Did you hear anything? Did you see anything? The only reason that the defendant and Mr. McGinnis didn't hear anything is if this was in fact murder. Because if it's an accident, there was plenty to be heard. The only way the defendant didn't hear anything is that she chose not to hear anything. As calculating and cold-blooded as she is, she could not bear to her the scream of this young lady as she fell to her death, fighting for her life, scratching and clawing. She chose not to hear that because even for Virginia McGinnis, the person who masterminded this murder plot, she couldn't stomach it. . . ."

Aragon then held up two autopsy photographs. Dr. Hoops the pathologist, he knew, hadn't been able to recall anything unusual about Deana's hands, but that did not prevent him from showing them to the jury.

"These are Deana's hands," he said. "Look at her fingernails. Are these the hands of a person who went silently to her death?"

During the lunch recess, Aragon thought back over the remainder of his closing. He felt good about it. "Virginia provided information only on a need-to-know basis," he had said. Then he hit upon all the lies Virginia had passed off on Bobbie Roberts, the McCains, Don Smythe, Diana Rael. It was a long list: She never heard of life insurance on Deana; she could see Deana's body down among the seals; the police gave her and B.J. the third degree; she didn't know Deana was married; she didn't own a dog at the time they drove to Seal Beach; the coroner wouldn't give her Bobbie Roberts's number. Aragon hoped the jury would find the list impressively long.

"Does an innocent person lie? Does an innocent person have a motive to lie? What does an innocent person have to hide?" He had asked the jury that series of questions three times. But still worry nagged him. At bottom, his case came down to accident or murder. He never even mentioned the stake at the cliff edge, right where Deana had been standing in Photo eleven. Had he really eliminated slip-and-fall as a reasonable alternative? He bore the burden of *proving* Deana had been murdered, not just responding to insinuations from the defense.

Albert Tamayo's four-hour summation played directly to Aragon's worst fears:

"You can't rule out accident," he began. "You simply cannot rule out accident in this case. And unless and until you are able to completely and absolutely rule out accident as a reasonable alternative, conclusion, or explanation in this case, you must come back with a verdict of Not Guilty. . . ."

After naming his theme, Tamayo turned to a peroration on the prosecution's weaknesses.

"Now, you heard a lot of evidence over the last eight weeks and there are two facts that rise above the level of suspicion and go into the area of proof. The first fact is this: that the insurance policy was paid for the day before the fall on April 2, 1987. And fact two is that the signature of Alice Kissane was made by Virginia McGinnis. Everything else from the prosecution's case does not go beyond that suspicion into the area of proof. . . .

"What we have sought to do in bringing forward the evidence that we did was to bring a more complete picture, a balanced picture, something that wasn't slanted. The prosecution's, in this case, was based on selective presentation. They have brought forward certain facts, and, even though they knew about other facts, they decided they wouldn't present them to you.

"For example, when they talked about Deana Hubbard and her personality, what was brought forward to you? They paraded in all those witnesses from Kentucky and Kentucky alone, people who knew Deana before she left for California. By doing that, they give you a very slanted, stilted picture of Deana. It wasn't complete and it wasn't realistic.

"Additionally, when we talk about the drug screen test, the prosecution was well aware of all the tests, including the one by Dr. Giorgi where they found absolutely nothing. But he chose to give you only two drug tests in this case. . . .

"As the judge indicated, we are advocates. Mr. Aragon is going to bring only those facts that tend to prove that in fact Virginia McGinnis committed a murder, but, by doing so, he did not provide to you the truth, because the truth encompasses all of the facts. . . ."

Aragon thought he sensed the jury's mood shifting. A few members of the panel looked at him, then looked downward the moment he tried to make eye contact. Tamayo moved forward smoothly, with direction.

"The prosecution's case was also based on what I term reaching or stretching or an extension. For example, in order to prove that Virginia really wanted to and did in fact drug Deana, you should believe that because she had this"—Tamayo held up the book Officer Lutzi seized from Virginia's home—"this drug book. This is an example of reaching and stretching, wanting you to draw an inference that Virginia McGinnis did in fact want to drug Deana simply because she had a drug book in her library. . . .

"There were other examples that we will go into later on. But the idea here is that they want you to draw inferences from a set of facts, and it's a tremendous leap from point 'A' to point 'B' and they failed to bring in any points from in between. . . .

"When I heard Mr. Aragon this morning, it appeared that the entire case by the prosecution, aside from those two facts I mentioned, hinges upon Virginia McGinnis's statements. One, she is inconsistent; two, because she is inconsistent, she must have lied; and three, because she lied, she must be guilty. That is a summary of what we have here. But it's a logic that doesn't make any sense, and it's a logic that asks you to take a leap. . . .

"In this trial, we are going to ask you to do something that's unpopular and something that's unnatural. We are going to ask you to follow the law, and the law is to presume my client Virginia McGinnis innocent until and unless the prosecution can prove that she is not. And with respect to accident, understand that we don't even need to raise the inference or the possibility. Rather, the prosecution must prove murder beyond a reasonable doubt to the complete exclusion of accident. . . .

"Once you have that reasonable doubt, you stop right there and you go no further. The biggest decisions in your life are not on proof beyond a reasonable doubt. The only time you are going to apply that standard is in a criminal case such as this. . . ."

Tamayo then went deep into a discussion of circumstantial evidence. After citing sections of the penal code, he built to a single point: "This case boils down to this: A finding of guilt as to any crime may not be based on circumstantial evidence unless two things happen." He held up a printed poster of the penal code and read: " 'One, the circumstances are consistent with the theory that the defendant is guilty of the crime; and two, it cannot be reconciled with any other rational conclusion.' "

He put down the sign and went on: "You must be able to sit down and say to yourself, There is absolutely no way; accident is completely devoid of logic; it is absolutely unreasonable given the facts of this case. . . . This is the law."

Aragon always hated this part of defense closings. After a good defense lawyer finished on the subject of doubt and circumstantial evidence, you wondered whether you had a reasonable doubt about your own name.

When Tamayo returned to the evidence, he began by damning the prosecution with faint praise. The Kentucky contingent came off as remarkably consistent, but, he added, "it appeared that much of their testimony was, perhaps, rehearsed. . . . For example, they came into court and they basically told you the same things, almost as if it was a litany or a rosary, or something like that. But they parroted the same words."

Regarding Deana's learning disability, Tamayo concluded that "the bottom line with respect to all of this intelligence talk was that Deana was capable of functioning as a person, as a citizen, as anyone else in this community. This idea that she was an idiot, the idea that she could not function, this idea that she was completely vulnerable to other individuals was highly overinflated, and you should view the testimony with extreme caution.

"Now you may say, Well, look, we have all these convicts coming in and all these people who have chronic drug use in their backgrounds and how can we believe them? Well, the answer is that if there was just one, you might have a problem with their credibility. But when you have a number of individuals who testify to the same thing consistently, you start obtaining the credibility that you need. . . .

"Now the witnesses from Kentucky were all paraded in for one significant reason. They want you to believe that Deana never used drugs, not even aspirin. . . . But that's not realistic. Let's get real here. Deana was a regular kid. She had a personality, she wasn't devoid of character and she experimented with drugs. Nothing big, nothing earth-shattering. Some of your kids may have done it in the past. . . . And when Deana got to the McGinnises', prescription drugs were clearly available there and we know that. So logic would dictate that no drugs were ever induced into Deana. . . .

"One, we know her history of experimentation. . . . Second, we know there was an availability of the drug Elavil. And three, we know about her personality. We know about her self-destructive nature. . . .

"But the prosecution is now saying, Wait a minute. Time out. We found this drug book. Now it all makes sense. Virginia tried to drug Deana because we know she had this drug book. This is an example of stretching. . . ."

Holding the book entitled *Drugs* over his head, Tamayo asked what the DA was really doing here. So Virginia had this book in her home? Was that proof beyond a reasonable doubt?

Witness by witness, Tamayo went through the prosecution's case. Aragon kept his eyes on the jurors, although he sensed Virginia's cool presence behind him. He wanted to look around and watch her taking in the words of her defender, but he felt that it was more important to focus on the panel.

"Mac McCain told you that he was suspicious, that he thought Deana was going to be killed. Well, we know eventually at the end of March the policy comes back from State Farm and now he becomes real heroic." Tamayo's voice became sarcastic.

"He has been in the insurance business for the last thirty years. This is his time when he could at least exercise some discretion. . . . But what does he do? He goes and gives the policy to the McGinnises and takes their check. Thank you very much. It's business as usual. I have a deep-seated feeling that Deana was going to be killed, but all I could do is take their money and issue the policy and send them on their way.

"Is all this credible? In order for you to believe that it is credible, you are going to have to find that Mr. McCain is the coldest businessman you've ever met. I don't think he was. But I do think he was lying when he told you that he was so suspicious that the girl was going to be killed."

The following day, toward the end of his closing, Tamayo at last turned to the argument the jury had been waiting for.

"Why would you commit an act, why would you push someone off a cliff, just one day after you take and pay for the life-insurance policy? Why would anyone with this sophistication do it just one day later? Why not one month, six months, twelve months later? Why just one day?

"The prosecution has indicated that it's because of greed. I don't think that fully answers the question. Greed is responsible for hatching this sort of scheme. It doesn't explain why it's done one day later.

"Why would you tell a story, a contrived story about Mexico and the visa, therefore drawing further suspicion toward yourself? I think the answer here is because it never did happen. This is just the result of the McCains talking about this over and over and over and making something out of nothing.

"Why would you purchase life insurance from the same company, from the same agency, where you just had four claims within the last year and they just paid out close to fourteen thousand? Wouldn't you draw attention to yourself?

"The prosecution indicated this was, and I quote, 'Risk analysis all the way.' Well if you are doing risk analysis, you have to weigh the chance and the potential of being caught, prosecuted, and convicted for a murder . . . and all for what? Thirty-five thousand dollars. . . . The prosecution says you should go to a faraway location and do this. Why not do this in Mexico? Why Monterey?

"And why try to make a fall look like an accident when you were just told in no uncertain terms that the insurance policy did not, did not cover accidental death? When Virginia left, she asked, 'Does this cover accidental death?' And the next response was 'No.' . . . When Virginia left, she had the expectation that if there was an accidental death, there would be no coverage. . . .

"Why would you take photos of the scene? Why would you document your crime for all the world, for the jury, for the court, for the prosecutors, for law enforcement?

"What you have in this case is a suspicion. And that suspicion may remain with you. But that suspicion is not proof. Coincidence is not proof. Probability is not proof. And likelihood is not proof. You must vote Not Guilty in this case because you cannot totally and absolutely rule out accident."

Aragon came back before the jury for a brief rebuttal. Before he had even walked all the way to the jury stand, he lashed out at Tamayo's insinuation that witnesses were coached. "That's not the way things work here," he said definitively.

"In summation I talked about the conspiracy that the defense is alleging in this case, the conspiracy of the prosecution witnesses, all forty of them, to slant their statements, make up statements, remember things that didn't happen. Well, at the time I argued that to be outrageous, but now I see that I have been included in the conspiracy. . . . You took the measure of the witnesses; you will decide if they are lying. You will decide if the witnesses have been coached by the prosecution. Thankfully, that is your task, not Mr. Tamayo's.

"There are a number of things that the defendant did in spite of her best efforts and intentions to pull this off. Don't reward her for her sloppiness. Don't say, Well, you know, you were so foolish, we can't convict you.' . . .

"Why was this area selected for a murder? It's not a dark alley. There are people there, potentially. They can see you. . . . And let's say you are about to begin your murderous deed and then you see a car coming. You step back and you then go into the tourist mode because being there is perfectly normal. It's a beautiful disguise because it's invisible when you don't need it and it's visible when you do.

"And why was Virginia in such a hurry to kill Deana Hubbard

Wild? That was a legitimate question I had. . . . But Deana was free to change the beneficiaries at any point. Do you think that Virginia might have been concerned about that and said, 'The clock is ticking'?"

Aragon left the jury with a final admonition.

"It's a tough decision. Finding somebody guilty of this horrible offense is tough. When we really believe that one of our fellow travelers on this earth could do such a horrible thing, it diminishes us a bit because we are of the same fabric, and we bridle at that. It's never easy to do this. It's to indict that dark, dark part of our soul that you acknowledge the frailty of the human spirit. But you can't ignore the evidence. It cries out so clearly to you. We ask that you convict her of everything."

CHAPTER 31

A VALID CLAIM

▼

One day after Judge Revak finished instructing the jury, foreman Ron Fox sent back a handwritten question to the court: "If someone forges a signature on an otherwise valid insurance claim form, is that insurance fraud?"

Anna Long's heart sank when she heard the query. *A valid claim.* Long had been told that jurors' questions often didn't signal the final verdict, but this question bade especially ill.

The four counts—murder, conspiracy, insurance fraud, and forgery—were presented to the jury in just that order. She imagined that the question meant either they had already decided the insurance claim was valid and therefore Deana died by accident or they wanted the question answered for hypothetical purposes.

But why would a jury waste its time with a *hypothetical* question? The only possible explanation was that they went about deciding the charges in *reverse* order. And that seemed a pretty long shot.

In all likelihood, the jury proceeded in the order the charges appeared on the indictment. That meant they had already acquitted

Virginia of murder and conspiracy. In one day. Now they were simply down to wrangling over insurance fraud.

▲

▼

Six P.M. Louisville time. The jury had been out since Wednesday afternoon. Over the weekend, Keeney mailed letters to Ed Miller and Luis Aragon, thanking them for their devotion and courage in taking on this complex, vastly expensive case—regardless of the outcome. Then the phone rang.

"Steve, we've got a verdict," Aragon said, his voice shaking.

"W-e-ll?" Keeney asked, drawing out the word. He prided himself on his nerve, but five years' work was about to be weighed in the balance and he could feel his pulse accelerate.

"I don't know yet," Aragon said. "I just got the call. I'm on my way over to Department twenty-two."

"I'm calling Bobbie over to our place and breaking out the champagne," Keeney said, forcing a cavalier mood. "Call us when you get the word"—he paused, then finished—"so we can start celebrating."

Aragon didn't like the reference to champagne. During jury deliberations, he tended to become superstitious. The universe felt as if it were breathing gently all around, every nuance tied in subtly and inscrutably to the whole. He didn't want to disturb the invisible balance.

On his walk between the DA's office and the courthouse, across the broad, busy San Diego thoroughfare, one event circled through Aragon's thoughts: the jury question. *A valid claim.* The thought made Aragon's palms sweat. He met Anna Long outside Department 22 and they went in together, afraid even to think.

Deputy Marshal Bruce Pennings went behind the judge's bench to escort Virginia in. She waited quietly on a wooden chair in a bleak, tiled hallway, wearing the same crimson and blue striped vest she had worn at the cliff site.

Bruce liked Virginia. In his twenty years in Department 22, he had never dealt with as cooperative a defendant. And guilty or not, she was still a human being.

"Ready?" Bruce asked, smiling down at her, trying to ease the tension.

"I've decided what I'm going to do," Virginia said. "While the jury reads their verdict, I'm going to stare straight ahead at that gold seal of the state of California over the judge's head."

"That sounds like a good idea," he agreed. "Let's go."

Tamayo and Humphrey greeted their client with nervously confident smiles. They, too, had been thinking over the jury's question and it looked as if they had successfully planted the seeds of reasonable doubt. Billie Joe's counsel Gary Edwards had sat in on parts of the trial and he believed Virginia would be walking out the courtroom door that afternoon. Even members of the press were betting on acquittal—yet they added they were sure she was guilty.

Revak ordered the jury in. They had been as tight a group throughout the two months of trial as anyone in Department 22 could recall. They had joked during breaks and passed bags of Hershey's Kisses. No one doubted that they would reach a verdict.

Jury foreman Ron Fox handed a slip of paper to Bruce, who took it to the clerk.

"Will the defendant please rise," Judge Revak asked.

He watched the lawyers' faces as his clerk read from the slip.

"Count one," the clerk said. "Murder in the First Degree. Guilty."

Aragon immediately dropped his head in his hands. Anna Long started to cry. Tamayo and Humphrey blanched. Virginia kept her eyes focused on the Great Seal of the State of California, exactly as she had promised.

The jurors all noticed Virginia's nonreaction. It was hardly a surprise. After two months of observing her from across the courtroom, they felt they had some sense of her character and, accordingly, gave her a nickname: the "Ice Lady."

"Count two, conspiracy. Guilty.

"Count three, insurance fraud. Guilty.

"Count four, forgery. Guilty.

"Special circumstances, murder for financial gain. Guilty."

Bobbie showed up at Steve Keeney's house an hour after the final word was in. She walked in the door and saw a fire flickering in the hearth, Wynn sitting on a sofa and crying, Keeney uncorking a bottle.

"Come on in, Bobbie!" he called from across the living room. "Say, what's that you've got there?" Keeney pointed to a bright bundle Bobbie clutched in the crook of her arm.

"This? It's an old dress of Deana's," Bobbie said tearfully. "And I brought some pictures of her. I thought we could all look at them."

"Well, first have a glass of champagne," Wynn joined in. "You deserve it."

"Steve," Bobbie said. "After you called, I got down on my knees and prayed for Virginia's soul. But I was glad it would be saved in prison."

CHAPTER 32

LADY V

▼

Stonybrook Estates occupies a small pocket in one of the inner arcs of Louisville suburbia, a swath of green dotted with homes. The community looks something like a 1950s vision of the American dream sprung into spotless, almost unreal three-dimensionality. The manicured shrubbery—chinaberry and Japanese maple trees, bushes of yew, rhododendron, and azalea, stretches of Bermuda grass—seems to retain a year-round, freshly raked perfection. The large-windowed redbrick or white clapboard homes with tall, slatted shutters, brick chimneys, and two-car garages tucked discreetly away underground sit on rolling lots with plenty of elbowroom. If you ask the residents, they will tell you their community is America's best-kept secret.

Outside, Keeney's home looks nearly indistinguishable from its neighbors. His white Jaguar sits parked beside a black Alpha-Romeo, Wynn's present on their first anniversary. Their three kids play ball below the porch; azaleas grow in the front yard. Christian was ten; Wynn's kids were just entering adolescence.

Once a week, Steve brings Wynn bundles of fresh flowers for the house. He operates his law practice out of a living room dubbed "the library," partly in self-defense against growing children bringing home science projects and basketballs.

He continued to practice business law—that was what he knew best and what he loved. But it occupied a different role in his life. Between telephone conferences, he answered homework questions or tended to bouts of the flu.

And the subject of death still hung in the air—an odd mood in the home of a healthy couple with three energetic children. A few weeks after the trial ended, Scott Lawrence had sent Keeney a care package. One part was a rock from Seal Beach, something Scott had kept as a memento after rappeling down the cliff. Along with the rock, Scott included pictures of James and Ronnie Coates.

"You might want to put the photos on the refrigerator," Scott suggested. "Ronnie skipped parole and Jimmy's due out soon. You should get to know their faces in case they decide to pay you a visit."

Keeney decided not to worry his wife and kids with a pair of mug shots, so he pasted their faces to his library wall. That same day, he loaded his .45 pistol and put it in his top desk drawer—in case the Coates boys came crashing through the glass doors from the yard.

Every week or so, Keeney stayed up after Wynn and the children were asleep and continued reading psychiatric texts and studies on criminology in order to finish his profile of Virginia. The woman's evil defied anything he had ever imagined would become a part of his life. And yet, though he tried to rid himself of the memories, she remained with him.

He thought of the chaotic scene at Bostwick Road—mother out at night, father married to his beer cases, shooting at trees and bailing out of moving cars. It must have been terrifying to a little girl. Had Virginia's instincts for survival led her to create a more satisfying internal world, albeit one that was purely artificial?

At the hands of her brother, father, and school-bus driver, she simultaneously must have begun to equate violent, foreign touching with love and attention. In her self-created reality, she converted these misdeeds into some misshapen form of love. And like most abused children, she probably began to believe that she deserved her mistreatment. Virginia began to hate herself.

Her continuous proximity to fires, shoplifting, and physical abuse also keyed in to a word Dr. Tanay had used: *underaroused*. She needed the excitement of rule breaking, Keeney suspected. The more brazen, the better the chance of getting caught, the more exciting. And she succeeded at her crimes, which led her to repeat them and take ever deeper risks.

By the time Virginia found Dick Coates, she had probably lost the capacity for healthy human contact. Coates was no more than a base of operations. From his home, she went out to sate her appetite for arousal: stealing food from Fran Newhart's store, clothes from town, and Mrs. Pierson's silverware; carrying on illicit affairs. And she re-created the same unhappy, abusive life she had fled from at Bostwick Road.

Her precocious, trouble-making boys surely added a new set of strains. And so, over the years, her emotions receded further as she shored up the self-image of Virginia the Princess. At last, Dick Coates couldn't take it any longer.

Virginia fled to California. She might have made a break there with her ugly past. But suddenly she found herself knocked up with Cynthia Elaine. Bud Rearden came along and offered some respectability, but his sudden illness—just beginning at the time of Cynthia Elaine's death—and her two sons' burgeoning criminality led to a further retreat from reality. That moment marked the triggering point, Keeney figured.

Had a little "discipline" with Cynthia Elaine gotten out of hand? Or did Virginia vent her pent-up anger and self-loathing in one wild, uncontrolled burst? Or did she slip the child some of Bud's medicine?

However it happened, if she crossed that line and reduced Cynthia Elaine to an encumbrance to be disposed of, killing might have become one more way to find arousal.

More fires broke out around her. Then her husband died—right on cue. Soon after, she offered to buy Debbie Abell's baby. And once more she left town before anyone put the pieces together.

Keeney imagined Mary Agnes receiving her fatal insulin shot from her daughter, and Bud in his sick room. They must have known by then—yet they lay inert and helpless, waiting to receive their final dose. Like everyone else they sensed the evil in Virginia's soul, but it was too late. They followed her lead and kept quiet, cowed by mama and her two felonious boys.

Keeney recalled Virginia's front door in 1989 with the newspapers piling up, and the icy look everyone read in her eyes. Hers was a life without community or love or ties to anything other than a great looming self, beyond which there was nothing, no point of connection. Only a world filled with things to take and destroy.

Among the fragments of Virginia's life, Keeney found one more thread of consistency: *poisoning.*

Debbie Williams once tasted Virginia's "medicine" after asking too many questions about Cynthia Elaine. Virginia's mother's dogs died from poisoning. She kept B.J. in a complacent stupor, perhaps toying with when to administer a final dose. Bud died while under her ministrations, as had Mary Agnes Hoffmann. Deana had been drugged with Elavil.

Being deprived of food as a child—if those stories were to be believed—might have translated itself into a need to "feed" others with the same medicine; a complex combination of inflicting pain while expressing the maternal nurturing she never received. Her main disguise, after all, was as a nurse. Her father, too, had passed off his milk—the very emblem of motherhood—as something it wasn't. And as Virginia grew old, she became fat, then obese, turning the pattern of unhealthy feeding in on herself. At least, Keeney thought, it was a possible explanation.

Whatever the true cause of Virginia's evil, he thanked God that the jury had understood.

One by one, new facts trickled in from R. D. Jones, or Chuck Warner. An investigator found the Coroner's Register for Virginia's father, Christie Hoffmann. In a few terse sentences, it described how someone turned off his respirator just hours before he expired. The coroner, apparently, didn't find that fact unusual enough to justify an autopsy.

While tracing Virginia's assets, Keeney had stumbled across the name of a Louisville jeweler, John W. Moore. Moore's widow ferreted through her old records.

"I always said this woman had it made," Moore said. "Said she was a private-duty nurse—lived with elderly people, people who needed close attention. She said she lost a patient and she'd been contacted by people in California to come and take care of someone. What a racket—private-duty nurse!" she snorted. "And here she was getting all these jewels and diamonds and other things."

Mrs. Moore dug up a series of appraisals starting in November of 1974 and ending in May of 1975, all conducted at the request of Virginia Rearden. The sheets listed a white gold and diamond ring set with twelve diamonds and valued at $4,500; a gold and diamond pendant valued at $1,950; a gold, diamond, and emerald pin valued at $1,450; and a whopping gold and diamond solitaire, valued at $6,880! All told, $14,780 in jewelry, probably fifty thousand in 1992 dollars—about the same value as the house Virginia had been living in back in Fairdale. Her neighbor on Jefferson Hill Road had Virginia pegged. Virginia's expensive trinkets were like "thousand-dollar wheels on a fifty-dollar car!"

The little girl who flashed paste rings in her Ithaca schoolroom had grown up. She had transformed herself into Virginia the hot house-wife who decked herself out with jewels and played the role of the deadly nurse. Keeney remembered a photo found among Deana's possessions. It was a Polaroid of Virginia wearing an evening gown and sporting her jewels. On the front, she had written, "Me at a party. November 1979." And on the back of B.J.'s "riverboat gam-bler" photo were the words "To Deana, from Billie Joe and Lady V." Lady V: The name perfectly mirrored the joyless, haughty expres-sion on Virginia's face. It was an inscrutable title, at once pretentious and whorish.

Yet, outwardly, she still appeared so *normal,* the lady next door who efficiently did away with her houseguest and who had left a wake of fires and strange deaths. In the hours she drove with Deana up to Big Sur, making small talk, smiling like a loving friend, she had countless opportunities to turn around. Instead, she was intent on betrayal.

Keeney knew this wasn't the abstract evil he had studied in semi-nary. This evil had a human face and a human heart. It lived next door, smiled as it passed you on the street, and called you neighbor. This evil was woven into the fabric of the human soul. Aragon is right, Keeney thought, we are all "of the same fabric." The walls of his terrarium world seemed fragile.

Every now and then, Keeney read about his still-smouldering ex-law firm, renamed Alagia, Day.

Charlie Barnett was eventually acquitted of all charges. But, just two weeks after Virginia's conviction, the Louisville papers ran a headline: LAW FIRM IS TARGET OF FEDERAL PROBE. It was early one morn-ing, well before the kids were up. Keeney eagerly read through the details. The article ended, "Alagia, Day, which was once one of the largest firms based in Kentucky, with over 100 lawyers in eight cities, has been wracked in recent years by defections and layoffs. . . ."

The feds were nosing around B & A's old accounts. The article rehashed Stan Chauvin's losing fifty-five thousand dollars at the ABA conference and speculated about a connection between the incidents. "These just aren't the sort of folks I'd pick as my law partners today." Keeney smiled to himself.

Even Sarah West, his former secretary from B & A, had called looking for some part-time work—the old outfit had shrunk down to forty-five attorneys and she figured it was time to leave. Keeney said he could use some help since tax time was right around the corner.

Then the thump of feet running to the bathroom upstairs interrupted the morning quiet. Another school day beginning; time to put away the paper and help Wynn get things off to a sane start.

Almost immediately after the trial, Aragon and Anna Long began disassembling the "war room," the little office where charts, photos, posters, and newspaper clippings had crowded the walls for three years as the case limped forward to trial. One handwritten poster listed two columns of inconsistent statements given by Virginia to the police. Another wall was devoted to topographical maps and aerial photographs. Scraps of paper hung everywhere from yellowed pieces of Scotch tape: "Tsunami in yard for days"; "B.J. never tried to get his own insurance"; "Deana afraid of heights."

On March 30, 1992, Virginia Rearden returned to Department 22 for sentencing. Judge Revak offered her attorneys the chance to extend the date if they wanted to file motions. Tamayo declined, opting in favor of an immediate appeal. Juliana Humphrey added, "Virginia wants to get it over with."

Luis Aragon stood at counsel table, hands clasped easily before him.

Virginia was standing, too.

Bobbie Roberts sat with a small circle of relatives in the rear of the courtroom gallery. They had come all the way from Louisville and Lexington to see the sword of justice fall and to make concrete the kind of information that usually fills a few lines in a newspaper column. Six of the twelve jurors had showed up, too.

Bobbie Roberts made a statement, as permitted by another of Proposition 115's new provisions regarding victim impact. She spoke for fully half an hour.

Judge Revak then turned to the defense table. Albert Tamayo and Juliana Humphrey declined comment but added that their client wished to say a few words. The television cameras and reporters' microphones all swung toward Virginia. These would be her first and possibly her last statements ever about the case.

Virginia stood. Then she turned to face Bobbie Roberts, standing behind her in the audience. In a vicious tone, she spat out: "Bobbie, I don't have a guilty conscience about what happened. Can you say as much?"

In most cases, judges try to fit the punishment to the criminal, not the crime. But here the statute left Revak no real options. Murder in the first degree with special circumstances is punishable by one of two sentences under California law: life without possibility of parole, or death. The crime itself has no statute of limitations, and by virtue of some odd parallelism, perhaps also a vestige of *lex talonis,* the punishment lasts forever.

Under Revak's sentence, Virginia would die of old age in prison.

April 2, 1992, fell on a Thursday. The Second Presbyterian Church steeple in Saint Matthews stood white against an uncertain evening sky. An ambling crowd carrying raincoats spilled over church steps lighted by street lamps.

Deana's memorial service lasted an hour. Bobbie Roberts spoke, as did Steven Keeney, the pastor, and a few friends. Then the lines of a Bach invention played on the organ twined down among the listeners in the pews.

After the service, Keeney spotted a familiar figure ambling out the side exit. There was no mistaking the silver hair, dusty gray mustache, and professional eyes of a twenty-five-year veteran cop.

"R.D.!" Keeney called, extending a smile and a handshake as they met outside under the open night sky. "I didn't expect to see you here. How goes it?"

"Going fine, buddy. Just fine." They paused, wondering where to take the conversation. "I just thought I'd come to pay my respects.

How's Bobbie taking it all?" R.D. asked quietly. "I didn't get a chance to speak with her."

"She's good. Back teaching at Mann High School. Janie's ready for college." Keeney hesitated, then asked, "Did you speak to the Rearden boys?"

"I called them right after the verdict. Kinda hard to tell how they felt about it. Good, I think."

"You still looking into Cynthia Elaine?" Keeney kept his voice low.

"Well, yes and no." R.D. smiled. "Case is still open, but there's not an awful lot to go on. We exhumed the body. George Nichols is still working on it."

"I've got one piece of news. Word has it Virginia says Cynthia Elaine's death *is* a homicide, only Virginia insists she didn't do it. At least that's what her defense team says."

"Oh, brother," R.D. sighed.

They looked at one another, a silent acknowledgment of how far they had come since they first met in the basement of the Hall of Justice. But Keeney's thoughts quickly returned to Wynn and the children waiting at home.

"Thanks again," Keeney said.

"Anytime." R.D. shook his hand and headed off.

Keeney glanced up at the shifting clouds that scudded above the steeple. They presaged another Louisville spring of tumultuous rains and perfumed evenings. He turned to leave, blending into the press of friends, relatives, and acquaintances who had all paused briefly to celebrate a life and a death.

EPILOGUE

▼

In early summer of 1992, George Nichols, the Chief Medical Examiner for the Commonwealth of Kentucky, drafted a report. Subject: Cynthia Elaine Coates. Her body had been exhumed and examined by Nichols, bone by bone (little else remained). Nichols enlarged and studied the handful of photographs taken at the hospital when Cynthia was pronounced DOA back in 1972, along with photos of the barn and shed where Virginia claimed the child had been accidentally hanged. He had also read a memorandum from Detective Jack Haeussinger regarding Virginia McGinnis's trial and conviction in San Diego.

Chief ME Nichols's report closed with the conclusion that the likely manner of death is *"not* ligature strangulation by accidental or any other means." He ruled that "the manner of death is homicide."

Sergeant R.D. Jones and the Kentucky Commonwealth's attorney, Ernie Jasmine, both received copies of Nichols's report. It wasn't long before they both put in calls about the homicide to an old friend, Steven Keeney.